The Bible Speaks Today

Series Editors: J. A. Motyer (OT)
John R. W. Stott (NT)

The Message of Deuteronomy

Not by bread alone

Titles in this series

The Message of Genesis 1—11
The Dawn of Creation
David Atkinson

The Message of Genesis 12—50
From Abraham to Joseph
Joyce G. Baldwin

The Message of Deuteronomy
Not by Bread Alone
Raymond Brown

The Message of Judges
Grace Abounding
Michael Wilcock

The Message of Ruth
The Wings of Refuge
David Atkinson

The Message of Chronicles
One Church, One Faith, One Lord
Michael Wilcock

The Message of Job
Suffering and Grace
David Atkinson

The Message of Ecclesiastes
A Time to Mourn,
and a Time to Dance
Derek Kidner

The Message of Jeremiah
Against Wind and Tide
Derek Kidner

The Message of Daniel
The Lord Is King
Ronald S. Wallace

The Message of Hosea
Love to the Loveless
Derek Kidner

The Message of Amos
The Day of the Lion
J. A. Motyer

**The Message of the
Sermon on the Mount
(Matthew 5—7)**
Christian Counter-Culture
John R. W. Stott

The Message of Mark
The Mystery of Faith
Donald English

The Message of Luke
The Saviour of the World
Michael Wilcock

The Message of John
Here Is Your King!
Bruce Milne

The Message of Acts
To the Ends of the Earth
John R. W. Stott

The Message of 1 Corinthians
Life in the Local Church
David Prior

The Message of 2 Corinthians
Power in Weakness
Paul Barnett

The Message of Galatians
Only One Way
John R. W. Stott

The Message of Ephesians
God's New Society
John R. W. Stott

The Message of Philippians
Jesus Our Joy
J. A. Motyer

**The Message of Colossians
and Philemon**
Fullness and Freedom
R. C. Lucas

The Message of Thessalonians
Preparing for the Coming King
John R. W. Stott

The Message of 2 Timothy
Guard the Gospel
John R. W. Stott

The Message of Hebrews
Christ Above All
Raymond Brown

The Message of James
The Tests of Faith
J. A. Motyer

The Message of 1 Peter
The Way of the Cross
Edmund P. Clowney

The Message of John's Letters
Living in the Love of God
David Jackman

The Message of Revelation
I Saw Heaven Opened
Michael Wilcock

The Message of Deuteronomy

Not by bread alone

Raymond Brown

Inter-Varsity Press
Leicester, England
Downers Grove, Illinois, U.S.A.

InterVarsity Press
P.O. Box 1400, Downers Grove, IL 60515, USA
38 De Montfort Street, Leicester LE1 7GP, England

InterVarsity Press®, USA, is the book-publishing division of InterVarsity Christian Fellowship®, a
student movement active on campus at hundreds of universities, colleges and schools of nursing in the
United States of America, and a member movement of the International Fellowship of Evangelical
Students. For information about local and regional activities, write Public Relations Dept., InterVarsity
Christian Fellowship, 6400 Schroeder Rd., P.O. Box 7895, Madison, WI 53707-7895.

Inter-Varsity Press, England, is the book-publishing division of the Universities and Colleges Christian
Fellowship (formerly the Inter-Varsity Fellowship), a student movement linking Christian Unions in
universities and colleges throughout the United Kingdom and the Republic of Ireland, and a member
movement of the International Fellowship of Evangelical Students. For information about local and
national activities write to UCCF, 38 De Montfort Street, Leicester LE1 7GP.

USA ISBN 0-8308-1234-2

UK ISBN 0-85110-979-9

Photoset by Parker Typesetting Service, Leicester, England
Printed in the United States of America ∞

Library of Congress Cataloging-in-Publication Data

Brown, Raymond, 1928-
    The message of Deuteronomy: not by bread alone/Raymond Brown.
        p.   cm.—(The Bible speaks today)
    Includes bibliographical references.
    ISBN 0-8308-1234-2 (USA)
        1. Bible. O.T. Deuteronomy—Commentaries.   I. Title.
    II. Series.
    BS1275.3.B766   1993
    222'.1507—dc20   93-27974
                                                                CIP

British Library Cataloguing in Publication Data

A catalogue record for this book is available from the British Library.

17	16	15	14	13	12	11	10	9	8	7	6	5	4	3	2	1
07	06	05	04	03	02	01	00	99	98	97	96	95	94	93		

General preface

The Bible Speaks Today describes a series of both Old Testament and New Testament expositions, which are characterized by a threefold ideal: to expound the biblical text with accuracy, to relate it to contemporary life, and to be readable.

These books are, therefore, not 'commentaries', for the commentary seeks rather to elucidate the text than to apply it, and tends to be a work rather of reference than of literature. Nor, on the other hand, do they contain the kind of 'sermons' which attempt to be contemporary and readable without taking Scripture seriously enough.

The contributors to this series are all united in their convictions that God still speaks through what he has spoken, and that nothing is more necessary for the life, health and growth of Christians than that they should hear what the Spirit is saying to them through his ancient – yet ever modern – Word.

J. A. Motyer
J. R. W. Stott
Series Editors

Contents

General preface   5
Author's preface   9
Bibliography   11

Introduction   13

A. Introducing the covenant (1:1 – 4:43)

1. The leader and his partners (1:1–18)   29
2. Afraid of the future? (1:19–46)   38
3. Time to begin again (2:1 – 3:11)   45
4. Present blessings encourage future service (3:12–29) 54
5. Seeing him who is invisible (4:1–43)   61

B. Expounding the covenant (4:44 – 11:32)

6. Proclaimed in a loud voice (4:44 – 5:22)   75
7. Truth to tell (5:23 – 6:25)   94
8. God's people in a new land (7:1–26)   103
9. God's word for a time of change (8:1–20)   118
10. When rebels are forgiven (9:1–29)   125
11. Love matters most (10:1 – 11:32)   134

C. Applying the covenant (12:1 – 26:19)

12. Honouring God (12:1 – 14:29)   143
13. Festivals of praise (15:1 – 16:17)   164
14. Responsible leadership (16:18 – 18:22)   175
15. When things go wrong (19:1–21)   190
16. Soldiers with a difference (20:1–20)   196
17. Families in need (21:1–23)   203
18. Loving the neighbours (22:1 – 23:16)   212
19. More about the neighbours (23:17–25)   223
20. Basic rights (24:1 – 25:4)   227

21. Community care (25:5–19)   242
22. What happens when we worship (26:1–19)   252

D. Confirming the covenant (27:1 – 30:20)

23. Carefully follow all his commands (27:1 – 29:1)   263
24. Choose life (29:2 – 30:20)   273

E. Sharing the covenant (31:1 – 34:12)

25. Israel's leaders and their message (31:1–29)   283
26. Learning by singing (32:1–47)   291
27. Parting words (33:1–29)   308
28. None like him (32:48–52; 34:1–12)   322

Author's preface

Moses' preaching to the Hebrew pilgrims at the end of their tortuous journey well over three thousand years ago is in danger of being either dismissed or marginalized as irrelevant data in the complexities of contemporary society. Yet, as a vital part of inspired Scripture, the message of Deuteronomy continues to make its authoritative appeal to modern readers, addressing people with similar needs in an albeit dissimilar context. This important biblical book enriches our understanding of God as sovereign, compassionate and generous, it highlights our constant need of his promised resources, it widens the horizons of our ethical and social responsibility, and points us beyond its own clear message to the Christ who loved, practised and shared its teaching.

The concern for relevant application is one of the most demanding aspects of the expositor's task. Earlier this century Karl Barth commented on the skill of the Reformers both in interpreting and applying the biblical message:

> How energetically Calvin, having first established what stands in the text, sets himself to re-think the whole material and to wrestle with it, till the walls which separate the sixteenth century from the first become transparent! Paul speaks and the man of the sixteenth century hears ... a distinction between yesterday and today becomes impossible.[1]

I do not suggest that I have always succeeded in that exacting yet essential exercise but I have certainly made it my constant aim.

In the course of my work on the biblical text I have drawn gratefully on the work of several commentators and writers and have tried to acknowledge my debts in the bibliography and footnotes. I have also been helped to sharpen my own thinking by expounding Deuteronomy to a stimulating Tuesday evening Bible Study meeting in Eastbourne. I have specially appreciated those occasions when I was able to share its message at the Southsea,

---

[1] Karl Barth, *The Epistle to the Romans*, trans. by Edwyn C. Hoskyns (Oxford, 1968), preface to the Second Edition, p. 7.

Derwent (Cliff College) and Portstewart Conventions, at the Baptist Ministers' and Missionaries' Wives' Conference at High Leigh, and within the warm-hearted fellowship of the Irish Baptist Ministers' Conference at Portrush. I treasure particularly happy memories of a privileged visit to the SEAC Conference at Swanwick when over three hundred senior Anglican clergy and wives gave a generous welcome to the solitary Baptist in their midst as I attempted an exposition of the book's opening and closing sections.

I am grateful to the Old Testament Editor of this series, Alec Motyer, for his invitation to write this book and for many helpful suggestions in the later stages of my work. Its final touches have been added as I stand on the threshold of retirement from the pastoral ministry at Victoria Baptist Church, Eastbourne. I am indebted to many friends in that congregation for their prayerful support during the past six years, and want in particular to express my gratitude to my kind and dedicated secretary, Brenda Dant, and to my colleagues on the church's ministerial team, Roy Lanning, Val Tattersall and Paul Wilson, for their friendship and help during my time among them. Without the love, encouragement and partnership of my wife, Christine, this book would never have been started, let alone finished. My warm thanks, finally, to Colin Duriez and the editorial team at IVP for all their gifted, practical assistance.

Raymond Brown

Bibliography

Commentaries
Cousins, Peter E., 'Deuteronomy' in *The International Bible Commentary* (Marshall Pickering, 1986).
Craigie, Peter C., *The Book of Deuteronomy* (*The New International Commentary on the Old Testament*, Eerdmans, 1976).
Harrison, R. K., and Manley, G. T., 'Deuteronomy' in *The New Bible Commentary Revised* (IVP, 1970).
Kline, Meredith G., 'Deuteronomy' in *The Wycliffe Bible Commentary* (Oliphants, 1963).
Mayes, A. D. H., *Deuteronomy* (*The New Century Bible*, Oliphants, 1979).
Payne, David F., *Deuteronomy* (*The Daily Study Bible* – Old Testament, St Andrew Press, 1985).
Phillips, Anthony, *Deuteronomy* (*The Cambridge Bible Commentary*, CUP, 1973).
Robinson, H. Wheeler, *Deuteronomy and Joshua* (*The Century Bible*, 1907).
Thompson, J. A., *Deuteronomy: An Introduction and Commentary* (*Tyndale Old Testament Commentaries*, IVP, 1974).
von Rad, Gerhard, *Deuteronomy* (*The Old Testament Library*, SCM, 1966).
Wright, G. E., 'Deuteronomy' in *The Interpreter's Bible*, Vol. 2, (Abingdon Press, 1953).

Other works
Blanch, Stuart, *The Ten Commandments* (Hodder and Stoughton, 1981).
Clements, R. E., *Deuteronomy: Old Testament Guides* (Sheffield Academic Press, 1989).
Clements, R. E., *God's Chosen People: A Theological Interpretation of the Book of Deuteronomy* (SCM, 1968).
Davidman, Joy, *Smoke on the Mountain: An Interpretation of the Ten Commandments in Terms of Today* (Hodder and Stoughton, 1966).

Eddison, John, *God's Frontiers* (Scripture Union, 1972).

Field, David, *God's Good Life: The Ten Commandments at the End of the Twentieth Century* (IVP, 1992).

Kidner, Derek, *Hard Sayings: The Challenge of Old Testament Morals* (Tyndale Press, 1972).

Kline, Meredith G., *The Structure of Biblical Authority* (Eerdmans, 1972).

McConville, J. G., *Law and Theology in Deuteronomy* (Journal for the Study of the Old Testament Supplement Series 33, 1984).

Nicholson, E. W., *Deuteronomy and Tradition* (Blackwell, 1967).

Phillips, Anthony, *Ancient Israel's Criminal Law: A New Approach to the Decalogue* (Darton, Longman and Todd, 1961).

Shields, Norman, *Pattern for Life* (Evangelical Press, 1983).

Weinfeld, M., *Deuteronomy and the Deuteronomic School* (Clarendon Press, 1972).

Wenham, John W., *The Enigma of Evil: Can we believe in the Goodness of God?* (IVP, 1985).

Wright, Christopher J. H., *Living as the People of God: The Relevance of Old Testament Ethics* (IVP, 1983).

Wright, Christopher J. H., *God's People in God's Land: Family, Land and Property in the Old Testament* (Paternoster/ Eerdmans, 1990).

Chief abbreviations

NBD *The New Bible Dictionary* (IVP, 2nd edition 1982).

NEB *The New English Bible* (NT 1961, 2nd edition 1970; OT 1970).

NIV *The New International Version* of the Bible (Hodder and Stoughton; NT 1973; OT 1979).

RSV *The Revised Standard Version* of the Bible (NT 1946, 2nd edition 1971; OT 1952).

Introduction

1. The importance of the book

No Old Testament book has exerted a greater influence on the formation and development of both Jewish and Christian thought and practice than Deuteronomy. Its doctrine is foundational within the Old Testament itself. The prophets recall its teaching and challenge their contemporaries with Deuteronomy's clear and unequivocal demands.[1] Kings were reminded of its high ideals[2] and leading officials rehearsed its truths in times of national crisis.[3] The psalmists wove its message into their great songs of exaltation, adoration, confession and intercession. Israel's wisdom teachers, those 'middlemen' who framed their instruction in short, pithy sayings, applied its themes to the practical issues of human behaviour and everyday social conduct.

The book is also of outstanding importance in the development of Christian life and thought. The Lord Jesus treasured its distinctive message, making use of it both privately and publicly. He memorized passages from it and quoted them during his days of severe testing in the wilderness of Judea[4] and its leading ideas figured prominently in his public ministry.[5]

The early church was equally persuaded about the centrality of its teaching.[6] It is among the four main Old Testament books (Genesis, Deuteronomy, Psalms and Isaiah) most frequently referred to by New Testament writers. Its quotations are found in 17 of the New Testament's 27 books and over 80 references from its pages are

---

[1] Elijah, 7:5 (1 Ki. 16:31 – 17:1; 18:19, 21); Amos, 14:28 (Am. 4:4); 25:13–16 (Am. 8:5); Hosea, 19:14 (Ho. 5:10); Micah, 25:13–16 (Mi. 6:10–11).
[2] 17:18; 2 Ki. 22:8–13.   [3] Ne. 8:1 – 9:38.   [4] 6:13, 16; 8:3; Mt. 4:1–11.
[5] For example, 5:16 (Mt. 15:4); 5:11 and 23:22 (Mt. 5:33); 5:16–20 and 24:14 (Mt. 19:18–19a); 6:4 (Mk. 12:29); 6:5 (Mt. 22:27; Lk. 10:27); 19:15 (Mt. 18:16); 19:21 (Mt. 5:38); 24:1 (Mt. 5:31); 24:1, 3 (Mt. 19:7; Mk. 10:4); 25:5–6 (Mt. 22:24).
[6] Paul uses 30:12–14 (Rom. 10:6–8); 32:21 (Rom. 10:19); 32:35 (Rom. 12:19); 25:4 (1 Cor. 9:9); 32:16, 21 (1 Cor. 10:22); 27:26 (Gal. 3:10); and 21:23 (Gal. 3:13).

found within the whole New Testament literature.

The book is important for us, as well as for Jesus and his earliest followers. When Stephen preached before the Sanhedrin he told his hostile audience that God communicated to Moses a message he was 'to pass on to *us*',[7] not, surely, a reference to the Hebrew nation alone but to that believing community to which Stephen belonged, the new Israel of God[8] comprised of Jews and Gentiles who had trusted Christ. Moses communicated 'living words', not detached truths from a remote and antiquated past. As we study the message of this important biblical book we must listen carefully as Moses addresses *us*. It is not a word about 'there and then' in far-off Israel but is for the 'here and now' in contemporary society. Moreover, Paul tells us that 'all Scripture is God-breathed and is useful for teaching, rebuking, correcting and training in righteousness'.[9] So, according to the apostle, the whole Bible is uniformly authoritative and uniquely relevant, which means that Deuteronomy has signifi- cant things to say to us in our present life, just as it had for Paul's contemporaries in the emergent, vigorous Christianity of the first century. What Moses says he is saying now.

2. The context of the book

The long years of Israel's wilderness travels were almost at an end. Moses has reached the plains of Moab, and knows that he cannot accompany the desert pilgrims into Canaan. The words preserved in this book represent his final opportunity to preach God's word before the people move on to their new land. He has vital teaching to share, and though the word 'law' is embedded in its title, Deu- teronomy is not strictly a law book. It is a collection of well- constructed, brilliantly illustrated sermons, based on the message given initially by God to Moses soon after he left Egypt. That revelation at Sinai (or Horeb as it is sometimes called) contained basic truths, facts and rules which were essential for the religious, moral and social well-being of the pilgrim people. Now they are about to enter new territory; their lifestyle must change from that of desert nomads to permanent citizens who will be making their home in a different and vulnerable environment. In Moses they have the authoritative message of a faithful preacher, the encouraging support of a compassionate pastor, and the inspiring example of a committed believer. All three elements of preaching, pastoral care and spirituality are found in this important book.

Deuteronomy owes its title to the saying in 17:18 that Israel's future kings are to write out a 'copy' or duplicate of God's law. The

---

[7] Acts 7:38.   [8] 1 Pet. 2:9; Gal. 6:16.   [9] 2 Tim. 3:16.

Greek translation of the Old Testament (the Septuagint) called it Deuteronomy which means 'second law'. It is not another law, different from that conveyed to Moses at Sinai, rather a faithful repetition and more detailed amplification of God's word addressed to his servant at Sinai, applied to life in a different context prior to the entry into Canaan, and relevant to us in present-day life.

3. The structure of the book

One of the most interesting aspects of Old Testament study over the past few decades has been that of comparing key passages in the Old Testament with the literary structure of political treaties or covenants in the ancient Near East. These agreements were frequently made between two kings, when a stronger ruler (the suzerain) agreed to provide military protection and economic resources to a threatened one (the vassal) in return for the promise of submissive loyalty. These covenants generally follow a predictable literary pattern and are of special interest when compared with the structure of Deuteronomy. Treaties of this kind go back to the third millennium BC, well before the time of Moses, and, as a well-educated courtier in Egypt,[10] he is likely to have been thoroughly familiar with these important political transactions and the literary form in which their terms were presented.

G. E. Mendenhall identified the remarkable similarities between the Hittite suzerainty agreements of the second millennium BC and the covenant which God made with Israel at Sinai,[11] and M. G. Kline later noted the striking parallels between these Hittite covenants and the literary structure of Deuteronomy. The Hittite treaty usually began with a brief preamble (1:1–5) and a historical introduction (1:6 – 3:29) which traced the nature of the relationships between the two parties, normally emphasizing the suzerain's generosity. Such a prologue was normally followed by the basic stipulations (4:1–40; 5:1 – 11:32) of the covenant, and to this was added a more detailed application of their demands (12:1 – 26:19). At this point the agreement often required that a copy of the document be placed in the temple of the god, and that its terms be read publicly at agreed intervals (27:1–26; 31:9–13). This was always followed by 'blessings' (28:1–14) which were guaranteed if the treaty's terms were obeyed, and 'curses' (28:15–68) if they were ignored. These agreements often closed with some kind of recapitulation (29:1 – 30:20) and witnesses were summoned, a feature not absent from the concluding section of Deuteronomy (30:19, 28).

More detailed study has frequently followed Mendenhall's thesis

---

[10] Acts 7:22.   [11] Ex. 19:3–8; 20:1–17.

and the dates of different types of treaty have played some part in the on-going discussion about the date of the book. The language, provisions and form of these treaties have greatly influenced our thinking about the nature of Deuteronomy as an interpretation of the covenant, presented not simply in a similar literary form but as a persuasive homiletical device. In the exposition of its teaching the covenant form has not been followed slavishly; indeed, it has been transformed theologically. It has been used to emphasize God's unique commitment to Israel, which is not an agreement between equals, and to show that his grace far transcends what would be expected of any human treaty. It is also used to underline the need for Israel's regular renewal of their covenant obedience.

Peter Craigie[12] made the suggestion that a different kind of treaty may be behind the structure of Deuteronomy. A careful examination of its language led him to propose that the book may owe something to Egyptian labour contracts. Moses spent the early decades of his life in an Egyptian palace, and he would certainly have been conversant with employment agreements of this nature. The disadvantaged Israelites had worked as slaves under a detrimental labour contract in Egypt, but they had been miraculously delivered by a greater and better Master who had made a generous, compassionate agreement with them. He had committed himself fully to them as their Protector and Provider, but naturally expected them to keep their part of the covenant, by recognizing his total authority over every part of their lives.

4. The date of the book

The question of the date of Deuteronomy cannot be divorced from its authorship. The vast majority of the book claims to contain the words of Moses as preacher (1:1–5; 4:1, 44–46; 5:1; 29:1–2) and writer (31:9, 24–26) in the closing period of his life, though these ascriptions have been widely challenged since the early nineteenth century. Those who wish to study the question of its origin in detail will need to consult Old Testament introductions and major commentaries. It is scarcely possible or appropriate here to examine with any degree of comprehensiveness the wide variety of suggestions which have been made about its source. Some brief reference, however, to some main views may be helpful if only to provide the context for the position assumed throughout this present interpretation that, whatever the nature of later editorial work, the book is composed of authentic teaching by Moses, devoutly treasured by generations of Israelite people throughout

---

[12] Peter C. Craigie, *The Book of Deuteronomy*, pp. 79–83.

their eventful and significant history.

Some scholars have contended that the book is an attempt to present the leading ideas of, say, Josiah's Reformation[13] in a literary form, using Moses' influential name to authenticate its key truths. Nowadays it is more frequently argued that it is the product of a 'Deuteronomic movement' which developed during the late eighth century and the seventh century BC and came to a climax in Josiah's Reformation.

Theories which suggest a late-monarchy date for its composition, however, are not without their difficulties. One of the main aims of the Reformation under Josiah was to centralize worship at the Jerusalem sanctuary, but Jerusalem is never mentioned in Deuteronomy although the city's name pre-dates Moses and is mentioned as early as the Ebla Texts from the twenty-fourth century BC. A document specially composed to promote centralized worship would surely need to be specific about where that worship should take place. It is possible that Deuteronomy is generally more concerned about authorized (as opposed to Baalism, 12:31) than centralized worship, for the book presumes the existence of several altars (16:21). It also provides us with considerable detail about a worship-centre at Shechem, about thirty miles north of Jerusalem, and commands the erection of an altar at the mountains of Ebal and Gerizim (27:1–13), historical detail which would hardly have encouraged the Josianic emphasis on a centralized cult in Jerusalem.

If the book was purposely written as a plan of campaign for Josiah's Reformation, moreover, it is strange that an issue as important as its clear provision for 'country' priests and Levites (18:6–8) could be so blatantly disobeyed by Josiah's religious leaders.[14] One would also have thought that the 'high places', so troublesome at the beginning of Josiah's reign, would at least have been mentioned by their technical name (Hebrew, *bamoth*) but it never appears in Deuteronomy. The book itself hardly reads like a preconceived programme of religious reformation and, if it is a product of Josiah's (or Hezekiah's) time, Deuteronomy's repetitive *'all* Israel' (1:2, *et passim*) is puzzling when, by that time, only the southern kingdom survived.

Some hold that the book belongs to a much earlier time, dating it in the period of the Judges or during the administration of Samuel, and even composed from surviving, though limited, oral or written material from the early conquest period.

Gerhard von Rad suggested that the book arose among Judah's 'country Levites' (18:6–8).[15] Others prefer the view that it

---

[13] 2 Ki. 22 – 23.   [14] 2 Ki. 23:9.
[15] Note, for example, 10:8–9; 12:12, 18–19; 26:12–15; 27:14; 31:24–29; 33:8–11.

originated in northern kingdom prophetic circles whose adherents were compelled to move south when the Assyrians defeated that kingdom in 722 BC. When the Assyrian armies went on to invade the southern kingdom, these devout Israelites were concerned about such issues as the national and religious unity of Judah, and its necessary military strength, and composed the present book soon after 701 BC, emphasizing these important themes.

Some have maintained that the book was composed much later and belongs to Israel's post-exilic period, representing an idealistic portrait of restored Judaism as seen through the eyes of its religious leaders somewhere between 520 and 400 BC.

Many contemporary Old Testament scholars now prefer to study the variety and development of strands of oral (as opposed to written) communication which led to the compilation of the book. They regard Deuteronomy as 'the final product and expression of a long history involving the transmission and constant adaptation of the old traditions of early Israel'. Many of them suggest that, having its source in the early conquest period, this 'stream of tradition' was cherished by the northern tribes and (following their destruction) was developed in the remaining southern kingdom of Judah 'in an attempt to revive the nation and ensure its future' as the covenant people of God.[16]

Despite the wide range of these divergent views, this exposition of Deuteronomy's message presupposes the reliability of the biblical claim concerning its Mosaic origin, though it naturally recognizes that considerable editorial work may have taken place after these sermons were first preached by Moses prior to the invasion of Canaan. The concluding Song and Blessing, for example, and the account of Moses' death, all found in the closing chapters, are likely to have been added to the earlier material,[17] and, under the reverent supervision of later editors, there may have been further careful work on the narrative which, whilst preserving its original message, presented the account in a more readable form for contemporaries.

The text of the book itself plainly records that it contains the literary work of Moses (31:9, 24–26) and Jesus clearly accepted that statement as fact[18] as did a number of New Testament preachers and writers.[19] We have already seen that written records of political and religious transactions were extant long before the Mosaic period, so there is no firm reason why this book should not be the literary work of Israel's well-educated religious leader at that time. Some references in the present text of Deuteronomy also raise historical

[16] E. W. Nicholson, *Deuteronomy and Tradition*, p. 121.
[17] Possibly by Joshua, or Eleazar, 10:6; Nu. 27:18–23.
[18] Mk. 7:10; 10:3–5; Jn. 7:19.
[19] Acts 3:22; 13:39; 28:23; Rom. 10:5, 19; 1 Cor. 9:9; 2 Cor. 3:15; Heb. 10:28.

difficulties which militate against the later dates which have been mentioned. For example, the 'Amalekite' judgment (25:17–19) would be an anachronistic item to include if it was a later composition, for by the period of the monarchy the Amalekites had long ceased to exist. If, however, the book belonged to the time of the conquest, then the injunction was particularly significant. Moreover, the regulations about the *introduction* of kingship (17:14–20) would read strangely when the nation had been ruled by a monarchy for about 400 years. Certain geographical details in the book (*e.g.* 2:8, 13, 26; 3:29) also support the traditional date of writing, and the personal reminiscences of Moses (1:9–18; 9:22, 25–29; 10:1–6; 24:9) have more than a 'ring of truth' about them; it is hard to believe that they are little other than an anonymous writer's pious fabrications about a great leader.

5. The relevance of the book

The casual reader, however, unacquainted with the treasures of this important biblical book, may well ask how its message from the distant world of antiquity can possibly be applicable to contemporary life. How can the extended migration and ultimate settlement of a large tribe from one part of the ancient world to another in the second millennium BC, be remotely significant in the closing years of the second millennium AD, with its increasingly technological, highly sophisticated, largely urban, society. However incredible it may sound, the message of this book is arrestingly relevant in this admittedly different world because it deals with timeless truths as well as contemporary issues.

a. Timeless truths

It is not relevant merely because it happens to raise moral and social issues which are markedly applicable to modern society. It is of crucial importance because it also expounds some key biblical themes which are *always* relevant to the life of God's people and to the world in which their witness is set. Late twentieth-century society needs Deuteronomy's doctrine of God, Revelation and Grace.

God

Our generation needs this book's balanced doctrine of God. In his unique triune being, God is so great that our limited spiritual and intellectual capacities cannot fully comprehend him in every aspect of his nature. The doctrine of the Trinity has certainly helped to preserve a balanced doctrine of God, but in different centuries the

Christian mind has tended to concentrate on one person of the Trinity rather than the others, even to the partial exclusion of the others.

In the early Christian centuries, for example, most believers concentrated their attention on the person of Christ, and that was natural enough. In many respects, they shared the same understanding of God as their Jewish neighbours. There was little need for them to defend the doctrine of God's uniqueness, holiness, power and mercy, the God who had manifested himself in creation, in history and through the pages of the Hebrew Scriptures. What was particularly distinctive about Christian teaching was its insistence that this God had perfectly revealed himself in his Son, Jesus, and it rightly focused on the deity of Christ. Many of the controversies which seriously divided Christians in the first five centuries were on the person of Christ, especially on the delicate relationship between his humanity and divinity. When most (but not all) of these controversies were resolved, the doctrines of a transcendent God and a conquering Christ came to dominate the thinking of medieval Christians, particularly the aspects of God's holiness and Christ's role as King and Judge.

In the Middle Ages, the portraiture of God and Christ was frequently awesome and overwhelming, causing believers to envisage them as distant and remote. It is easy to see how, in such an environment, Christians came to be attracted to the idea of mediators, so that increasing attention was devoted to intercessory figures – the virgin Mary, saints and angels. That was largely due to their limited or defective doctrine of God. Believers forgot that he is loving as well as holy, and that Jesus is the only Mediator, our Saviour in this world as well as Judge in the next.

With the sixteenth-century Reformation, and the acute awareness of human guilt, interest came to be concentrated on Christ's mediatorial work on the cross, his redemptive death, saving sacrifice and substitutionary atonement. The great Reformation writers forcefully drew attention to the salvation that is ours in Christ, to the complete forgiveness we may enjoy in this life as well as the severe judgment we must avoid in the next.

It would be foolish and untrue to suggest that during this entire period the doctrine of the Holy Spirit was totally neglected, but there were certainly times when his person and work were not given the attention they deserved. Significant interest in the Spirit's ministry gained fresh impetus at the Reformation and was given further emphasis in the teaching of the Puritans and the hymns of the Wesleys as well as by later preachers and writers. Within the past few decades, that necessary interest has come into greater prominence all over the world by the Renewal or Charismatic movement, and many rich and lasting things have derived from it.

There is always a danger, however, that (albeit unintentionally) by asserting one doctrine we minimize another. God's thoughts are higher than our thoughts[20] and it is not always easy to give equal emphasis to every aspect of truth or be as balanced as Scripture is in our thinking about God. The history of Christian thought seems to suggest that when one particular truth is given special prominence, complementary truths can be seriously neglected.

These are days when we urgently need to recover a majestic doctrine of God. There is a serious danger that even our acts of worship can become dominantly subjective, their value judged by their effect on our feelings and not on how they feed our minds. In these contexts, some of the superlative aspects of our faith, the greatness, holiness and glory of God, can be marginalized or trivialized. Contemporary evangelical theologians, notably James Packer, Thomas Smail and Sinclair Ferguson, have reminded us of the importance of 'knowing God' and of the renewed attention all Christians should give to 'the forgotten Father'.[21] The entire range of Scripture is instructive for all believers[22] and every book in the Bible helps to provide us with balanced, not distorted teaching. God's name is found almost two hundred times in Deuteronomy, and its teaching serves to remind us of the theological importance and spiritual enrichment of a full-orbed doctrine of God. Its theocentric message can strengthen the confidence and inspire the commitment of Christian believers in the late twentieth century, enabling them to have a majestic vision of God and deeper faith in all that he is and does for his people.

Revelation

Our contemporaries would also be enriched by this book's doctrine of Revelation. In Old Testament times (as in New) God was pleased to reveal his nature and unfold his will to his people verbally, and this concept of God's unique, authoritative and effective word is one of Deuteronomy's central themes. From its introductory sentence ('These are the words ...' 1:1) to its dramatic conclusion ('Then the Lord said to me ... 34:4) this book reminds us that men and women are not left to grope in dark and bewildering uncertainty about the character and attributes of God, or to be constantly puzzled about his mind on issues of spirituality, worship, ethics and society. The God who has spoken to his people so eloquently

---

[20] Is. 55:9.

[21] J. I. Packer, *Knowing God* (Hodder and Stoughton, 1973), Thomas Smail, *The Forgotten Father* (Hodder and Stoughton, 1980), and Sinclair B. Ferguson, *A Heart for God* (Banner of Truth Trust, 1987).

[22] 2 Tim. 3:16.

through the pages of Deuteronomy has, with equal effectiveness, communicated his truth throughout the rest of the Bible. This book's message about the supremacy and vitality of God's word is a persuasive reminder of the equal and inestimable value of all Scripture. Throughout the centuries Deuteronomy has reminded its readers of the character, authority and importance of God's word.

The multiform character of God's revealed word is frequently illustrated in the inspired message entrusted to Moses. In the book's opening three chapters, for example, God's word is presented as practical instruction (1:6, 21), sensitive comfort (1:29), inspiring promise (1:30; 3:22), timely reminder (1:31; 2:7), necessary rebuke (1:32–33), serious warning (1:34–46), merciful reassurance (2:2–3), explicit command (2:4–6, 9–13, 16–19) and sustaining encouragement (2:24–25; 3:2–3).

God speaks clearly to his people about the authority of his message. In a variety of different contexts Deuteronomy reiterates the claim that what the Lord spoke Moses said; there is a deliberate focus on exactness of expression. Here are words transmitted by Moses but spoken by God, verbally inspired and completely trustworthy: 'Moses proclaimed to the Israelites all that the Lord had commanded him' (1:3; cf. 4:5; 10:1–5). Such crucial words are not to be ignored, dismissed, manipulated or minimized by people who are meant to 'hear ... teach ... follow ... and keep' them (4:1–2). Its truth is unique, and men and women are not free to add to it or subtract from it (4:2). Deuteronomy's insistence on the inviolability of this word is important for our appreciation of the value of all Scripture. What God says here about his imperishable truth is descriptive of all he says elsewhere within the pages of both Old and New Testaments. God does not speak authoritatively in one place and tentatively or indifferently in another.

This book underlines the importance of God's word by describing how it is to be made known through a wide variety of different methods of communication. It is a fascinating example of the creativity of a God who is not uniform, stereotyped or dull in his plans for transmitting his message to his people.

The format of the book reminds us that the word was arrestingly conveyed through Moses by means of impassioned preaching; in this collection of 'preached' laws and applied truths we are listening to Moses as he delivers a series of sermons, not as he coldly rehearses a set of rules. This responsibility to pass the message on, however, is not left solely to the gifted preacher addressing a large public audience, as in Deuteronomy. The word must also be faithfully shared within the smaller unit through family education (4:9–10; 6:6–7, 20–25; 11:19). Additionally, it is to be preserved and promulgated by means of written instruction; it must be set down in writing and deposited in the ark (4:13; 10:1–5; 31:9). More publicly, the law is to be placarded before the people in a clear and legible script which anybody can understand (27:1–4, 8). That same truth will also be vocalized within corporate worship through liturgical response, as when the Israelite people brought their offerings of first-fruits (26:3, 5–10). The sacrifices described in Leviticus were not accompanied by verbal testimony. When we read about such offerings we clearly envisage what could be seen but the worship seems strangely silent, yet here at Deuteronomy's harvest-thanksgiving the adoration becomes eloquent as individual Israelites publicly witness to the sovereign goodness of God. The worshipper recalls the word of a God who is consistent in nature (unlike the capricious Baals), active in history and generous in providence.

This book also recognizes that God's word can be communicated through personal and corporate experience. People reflect on what has happened to them in life and on what they can learn from these events (29:24 – 30:10). The word is also communicated in Deuteronomy through geographical illustration – the two mountains, Gerizim and Ebal, one for blessing and the other for the curse (27:11–13), are visible reminders of the importance of making the right response to God's decisive message. In this book's closing chapters, the truth is publicly conveyed by the reading of the word (31:10–11), imaginatively presented through the lines of a memorable song (31:19, 21–22, 30; 32:1–47), and by the more personalized means of specific pastoral encouragement and tribal exhortation (33:1–29). Nobody reading this book can doubt the importance of God's revelation in Scripture.

Grace

Another 'timeless truth' which directly addresses our contemporaries in this book is its doctrine of Grace. Its repeated insistence on obedience to God's commands might initially suggest that here we are at the centre of legalized religion – if we do certain prescribed things then God may choose to reward us with his favour. That, however, is not the message of Deuteronomy. The book opens with a historical introduction which deliberately heightens our understanding of the electing, saving acts of a compassionate God. It reminds us that he takes the initiative in coming to us in totally undeserved grace and mercy. Our obedience is responsive. The loving and serving begins with him, not with us.

Moses knows that his fellow-travellers will soon be on Canaanite soil, immediately confronted with religious teaching about Baal, an agricultural deity who gives rewards to those who will do what he requires. Ideas of that kind were characteristic of religious thinking in the ancient Near Eastern world. Many believed that the gods could be coerced and cajoled into making appropriate beneficial gifts if they were fed on a correct diet by offering them appropriate sacrifices. It was essentially man-centred and works-orientated so, from the start, the Israelites were told that God has acted savingly for them long before they were able to do anything whatever for him. He owns the land they are about to possess, and they have done nothing whatever to deserve his gift. The produce of that land which they may offer at their first-fruits festival are tokens of his bountiful generosity. Do they imagine that he will be influenced in their favour if they offer a gift to him of something he has already given to them? He is more interested in how they live (as holy people) than in what they give.

This book frequently illustrates God's grace in the election of his people. They are what they are because he has done something unique for them, not because they have done something special for him. The Lord reminds his people that they have been chosen by him not, as they vainly imagined, on the basis of their superior numbers (7:7), power (8:17) or morality (9:4), but simply because he loved them and wanted to use them.

Throughout Jewish and Christian history, the doctrine of God's undeserved grace has always been in danger of subtle distortion. Evangelical Christians are not free from the temptation to exalt works at the expense of grace. It is possible to construct theologies and patterns of spirituality which portray faith as a 'work', in terms almost of quantitative substance which needs to be drastically increased if God is to be persuaded to act on our behalf. The thinking goes something like this: Our friends or family might be converted if we only believed a bit more enthusiastically. It is suggested that God surely wants us to have better material resources than we at present enjoy, and great faith in a bountiful God would ensure our prosperity. Physical healing may not be taking place, it is argued, because our faith is limited and if we only increased its quantity and improved its quality, the illness would disappear and we would be as healthy as he wants us always to be. The idea of a God who desperately wants to convert, prosper or heal, but is sadly inhibited from doing so because of something defective in us, is totally unbiblical, however; it is not the size of our faith which achieves anything, but the incomparable power of the God in whom we place our trust.

Within a few decades of the church's birth, misleading ideas about works began seriously to distort the Christian message of salvation by God's grace. Paul wrote his letter to the Galatians because some Jewish Christian teachers insisted that salvation could only be assured by means of essential works in addition to grace, but not by grace alone. Believing in Jesus was obviously necessary, they said, but to be a genuine Christian one must also obey the Mosaic law by being circumcised. Despite strenuous opposition by the apostle Paul and others, the concept of 'salvation by works' soon became deeply embedded in Christian life and thought. One of the sad aspects of human sinfulness is that people still want to earn rather than receive their salvation.

When we come to the teaching of the early Church Fathers, we see that the erroneous teaching Paul opposed was subtly transmitted in a different form in the following century as 'works' began to replace 'grace' as a central theme in Christian teaching: 'Fasting is better than prayer, but the giving of alms is better than both … Almsgiving lightens sins.'[23] Claims of this kind were made not by people determined to perpetrate false teaching but by godly writers with an inadequate portrait of God and a defective doctrine of grace. They maintained that men and women could scarcely be saved simply by relying on what Christ did for us on the cross; it must surely be necessary, they said, to contribute something by our own effort.

Any appreciation of the biblical teaching about God must begin with what he gives to us rather than with what we do for him, and Deuteronomy's corrective teaching exalts the supremacy and sufficiency of God's unmerited grace. In the modern world, the failure to grasp that basic truth lies at the heart of a good deal of unconscious Christ-rejection. Our contemporaries vainly imagine that their commendable honesty, kindness, neighbourliness and community service will, somehow, win the approval of God. This book reminds us, however, that his first claim is not on our service but on our love for him (6:5), and that can only be in response to his love for us. Love is more important than all our 'works'. God's mercy cannot be bought. We accept it with outstretched hands as undeserving beggars, not as meritorious achievers.

b. Contemporary issues

In addition to its exposition of these constantly relevant doctrines, this book also deals with a wide range of social and ethical themes of crucial importance in today's world. Alongside its timeless teaching about personal spirituality, corporate worship and general ethics, we are also confronted with practical instruction of contemporary significance on subjects such as the principles of management and effective leadership (1:9–18), the importance of community responsibility (3:12–22), the need for imaginative witness to our unbelieving neighbours (4:5–8), the educative responsibility of

---

[23] 2 Clement 16:4; see Thomas F. Torrance, The Doctrine of Grace in the Apostolic Fathers (Edinburgh, 1948).

parents (4:9–10), the perils of secularist materialism (6:10–15), and how to cope creatively with change in a highly mobile society (8:1–20).

Deuteronomy addresses the moral challenge of poverty and homelessness. It suggests an appropriate response to the emergent new religions, as well as the militant tendency of some of the old ones. The book contributes helpfully to contemporary discussion about the dangers of debt, alcoholism and drug abuse. It emphasizes the necessity of compassionate but uncompromising biblical teaching on matters such as honesty in business, the management of money, community welfare, social hygiene, marital fidelity and sexual ethics. Here is a book which has something to say to the present ecology and conservation debate, and which comments on responsibility for the deprived millions in our world, the care of the elderly, human rights, sexual equality, child abuse, injustice, safety in the home, urbanization and animal rights. Deuteronomy also issues serious warnings regarding moral indifference, social misconduct, and the perilous nature of Spiritism and the dangers of involvement in occult activity of any kind.

This does not mean to say that every detail of this book's teaching can be automatically transferred to the modern world or rigidly applied to the complex contemporary issues we have mentioned. Its specific regulations are addressed to a different culture, but that does not make it irrelevant. The teaching of Deuteronomy must be neither woodenly copied nor summarily dismissed. The book provides us with an invaluable pattern of personal and corporate spirituality and we need to study its underlying principles in order to apply them to life in our very different world. Christopher Wright makes the helpful suggestion that we ought to regard Old Testament ethical teaching as an illuminating paradigm.[24] A paradigm is something 'used as a model or example for other cases where a basic principle remains unchanged, though details may differ'. It is commonly used in explaining grammatical construction where, for example, the paradigm may be a verb-pattern demonstrating how the endings or suffixes will appear for verbs of a similar type. We do not slavishly copy the exact paradigm, or we would only have one verb, but we apply it, recognizing that, although there may be occasional adjustments, all verbs of this type will generally conform to the model of the paradigm before us.

Wright believes that 'paradigm' is a 'useful category for ethically understanding and applying the Old Testament', and offers the helpful comparison of the incarnation and ministry of Christ. Jesus calls us to 'follow' him but we are not meant to take that literally so

[24] Christopher J. H. Wright, *Living as the People of God*, pp. 40–45.

that we all 'practise carpentry, wear seamless clothing, pursue an itinerant and homeless lifestyle, worship in synagogue or temple, eat with tax-collectors and prostitutes, or teach by parables'. But neither are we to dismiss the example of Christ described in the gospels as 'ethically irrelevant, choosing to pay attention only to his teaching. For it was in part the quality of Jesus' *life* which authenticated his teaching.' So, we 'move from what we know Jesus *did* do to what we might reasonably presume he *would* do in our changed situation. The overall shape and character of his life . . . becomes our pattern or paradigm, by which we test the "Christ-likeness" of the same components of our own lives.'

With this model in mind, we venture the conviction that the message of Deuteronomy is as applicable to the contemporary scene as when it was first given by Moses on the plains of Moab and the principles underlying this profound teaching are as relevant as ever. Tyndale regarded it as 'a book worthy to be read in, day and night, and never to be out of hands: for it is the most excellent of all the books of Moses. It is . . . a preaching of faith and love . . . love to God out of faith, and the love of a man's neighbour out of the love of God.'[25] With the Reformer's encouragement that this book can deepen our faith and stimulate our love, we turn now to its influential message.

[25] William Tyndale, 'Prologue to the Book of Deuteronomy' in *Doctrinal Treatises and Introductions to Different Portions of the Holy Scriptures*, Parker Society edition of Tyndale's Works, I (Cambridge, 1848), p. 441.

A. Introducing the covenant (1:1 – 4:43)

Deuteronomy 1:1–18
1. The leader and his partners

The good leader is an inestimable gift to any country or community. Twentieth-century world history has been marred by the repeated sadness of tragic leadership. Appalling poverty under the Russian Czars was replaced in 1917 by revolutionary policies which eventually led to fresh tyrannies. Statues of an arrogant Stalin have tumbled in his country's streets. The 1930s witnessed the incredible wickedness of Hitler in Germany and Mussolini in Italy. Inevitably, their actions brought incalculable distress to millions of people well beyond their borders, whilst in successive decades other nations have witnessed increasing grief through the activities of fanatical dictators, prejudiced ayatollahs and heartless aggressors. One is astonished how thinking people could have followed so blindly, with indiscriminating allegiance, the leadership of men so obviously malevolent and destructive. The phenomenon is not peculiar to this century. In Old Testament times, Israel also suffered periodically under the damaging leadership of unworthy men. Moses was a glorious exception. The nation's emergence from slavery and their settlement in a new country owed much to his divinely inspired gifts and qualities.

Most successful community enterprises depend heavily on gifted leadership. Although the Old Testament relates the story of the whole people of God, for the most part its narratives focus our attention on Israel's leaders. As Deuteronomy begins, we are told that Moses' message was for *all* Israel (1) but initially the spotlight is on the leader of these desert pilgrims. God speaks to them through the compelling words of a brilliant communicator.

The introductory paragraphs of the book outline some important biblical principles about those qualities of leadership which will always enrich the life of the people of God. They are as relevant today as when they were first given over three thousand years ago. These verses make it clear that those who lead in God's work must be loyal to God's word, honest concerning their personal inadequacy, confident of God's unchanging faithfulness, prepared for sacrifice, and willing to share responsibility with others. The opening verses of the book portray Moses as a vivid example of submissive, realistic, confident, sacrificial, shared and vulnerable leadership.

1. Submissive leadership

Deuteronomy is an extended sermon or a series of addresses. From time to time, however, we are given not simply the content of the message but a glimpse of the communicator. The book's opening chapters offer some graphic portraits of Moses. He is presented as an impartial judge (1:17), a victorious conqueror (2:32–33; 3:1–3), an able administrator (3:12–17) utilizing the initial advantages of victory, a wise strategist (3:18–22) planning carefully for the future, a disappointed petitioner (3:23–27) coping with a different answer to prayer from the one he desperately wanted, an encouraging colleague (3:28; 31:7–8) and a fervent intercessor (9:25–29).

In the opening paragraph, however, Moses is introduced in his most significant role. He is primarily a preacher, a faithful communicator of God's word. The true leader must be totally subservient to God's revealed word. There are several truths here which are relevant for those who are called to share God's word in our own generation.

The first words of the book emphasize the priority of the message: *These are the words which Moses spoke* (1). His preaching was paramount. In the contemporary world, however, preaching is in the doldrums. The television screen has replaced the pulpit as a symbol of communication. The majority of people in modern society pay little attention to preachers. But, however dismissive many of our contemporaries choose to be about preaching, it is still God's declared priority as a means of communication.

Clearly, God has many ways of conveying his message. Throughout Jewish and Christian history good literature has played an extremely important part in the communication of God's truth. In our own times, the carefully guided discussion group has also been effectively employed. Personal conversations concerning eternal issues have also been of inestimable worth in the life of millions of people. From the Middle Ages onwards, religious drama has opened the minds of thousands who might otherwise have thought little about the great issues of life and death. Nothing, however, replaces or will ever supplant preaching as a divinely appointed means of effective communication. To read Deuteronomy is to realize that one is part of a congregation listening to the words of a man burdened with a message which is not of his own choosing.

Moreover, the opening sentences of the book are an intentionally stark reminder of the necessity of the message. God's word is a vital ingredient in life because by nature men and women are stubborn and wilful. God has to speak to them again and again about the things they have heard repeatedly in former days. There is surely an intended contrast in the opening words between *eleven days* (2), the relatively brief time it took for the first part of the journey, and the forty years (3) it did take. In other words, it might all have been accomplished in a few weeks. The additional, agonizing years, with all their extended pain, continuing hardship and unnecessary discomfort, were entirely due to the disobedience and rebellion of the people.

These verses also describe the source of the message. Moses stands before the people in the plains of Moab with a word which comes from beyond himself. Moses shared with the people of Israel *all that the LORD had commanded him concerning them* (3). The preacher is a communicator not an innovator. It is not his message but God's. At later stages in the narrative this same point is reiterated with unmistakable clarity. Human beings must not tamper with the message: 'Do not add to what I command you and do not subtract from it' (4:2; 12:32). The word he was to pass on to the people was not of his own devising. On many occasions, Moses' primary role had been that of the attentive listener. God had spoken clearly to him at the very time when his idolatrous contemporaries had deliberately closed their ears to the divine voice (9:11-12). The preacher must hear before he can speak, and then he must tell it as it is.

The word is not ours to amend, correct, modify or strive to improve. It is God's word and we are no more entitled to change it than a musician is free to ignore the declared wishes of the composer whose work he is paid to interpret. Julian Lloyd Webber says that his fellow cellist Rostropovich 'has always put the wishes of the composer first – unlike some performers, who seem more concerned with projecting themselves than the music'.[1] Those who have given themselves to the exposition of Christian truth covet the same integrity, dedication and commitment.

This introductory section about Moses' preaching also describes the communication of the message. *Moses began to expound this law.* That word *expound* is an interesting one. It tells us something extremely important about the preacher's role. The word means 'to make something absolutely clear and plain'. It is found later in Deuteronomy in a context which illuminates its meaning here. As Moses' preaching to the congregation was drawing to its close, he gave instructions about what the people were to do when they

---

[1] Julian Lloyd Webber, *Travels with my Cello* (Pavilion Books, 1984), p. 110.

crossed the river Jordan and entered the promised land. On that unforgettable day they were to 'set up some large stones and coat them with plaster' and were to 'write on them all the words of this law'. They were to 'write very clearly all the words of this law' (27:2–3, 8) so that everybody could read it. That term 'very clearly' is the same as the one here which describes the preaching of Moses when he set himself to *expound* (5) God's word to his contemporaries. The dedicated communicator will do all within his power to ensure that the key truths are clearly evident. By this means the people will appreciate its importance, discern its relevance and apply its teaching to their everyday lives.

The book's opening description of Moses as a communicator of God's word also says something about the content of the message. Moses is here concerned about the word and the works of God, what God has said (3) and what he has done (4). The Lord has revealed his nature by his truth and his acts. This congregation assembled in the plains of Moab heard *all that the LORD had commanded* Moses *concerning them*, but it was all in the context of a totally undeserved and divinely achieved conquest of their enemies (*after he had defeated*, 4). The alien territory of the Amorites and the hostile kingdom of Bashan lay directly across the path of their entrance to the land which had been promised to them. At that strategic time in their history God had been pleased to reveal himself by his deeds as well as by his words. The word was declared to the people in the wake of a remarkable and humanly impossible victory. It is surely intended as a forceful reminder to the Israelites of the great exodus event. God defeated the Egyptians and then gave them his word at Horeb. Now he had overcome fresh opponents and proved to them beyond all doubt that his achievements were not distant tales, locked away in a remote past. He was still with them, in power as well as in word. He had promised to give them the land (8) and had no intention of breaking his word, though his people had repeatedly broken theirs. What he had said he would certainly do.

Finally, in their introductory detail about preaching, these verses define the aim of the message. The word is not only confirmed by the acts of God; it demands the response of those who hear. Good biblical communication always leads to a verdict. It is forcefully and relevantly applied to the present condition of those who hear it. Moses' preaching was designed to lead the people to the place of obedient response. God's word to the people way back at Mount Horeb is repeated at the beginning of Deuteronomy. Moses recalled that, in those days, *The LORD our God said to us . . . Go in and take possession* (6–8).

Just as the Hebrew people, at the exodus and at Sinai, had heard that word, so it was to come to them again with persuasive appeal at Kadesh Barnea: *Go up and take possession of it as the Lord, the God of your fathers, told you* (21). As we shall see, the Israelites did not always respond to God's word as they had been commanded. The effective communicator strives to create in the mind of the hearer the desire to do what God has said and so encourage an eager response. This emphasis, so clear in Moses' understanding of the preacher's role, is given rich expression in Deuteronomy. When the sermon he preached moved towards its majestic conclusion, the congregation was confronted with a choice which determined their destiny. Moses calls to the people: 'See, I set before you today, life and prosperity, death and destruction . . . blessings and curses. Now choose life . . . listen to his voice, and hold fast to him' (30:15, 19–20). The distinctive thing about the Lord's people is their possession of and submission to his word.[2]

2. Realistic leadership

Important as the message undoubtedly is, however, Moses knows that he is not simply a speaker. He is a pastor as well as a preacher, and the prospect of leading such a vast company of intractable people is daunting. He frankly confesses his deep sense of inadequacy: *You are too heavy a burden for me to carry alone* (9). Above all else, the effective spiritual leader is a genuine realist. He has no cause to parade his personal capabilities. Utterly dependent upon the God who has called him, he openly acknowledges his inability to meet the necessary demands. It is at this very point that the reader is confronted with the stark difference between natural and spiritual leadership. As the world views it, the self-confidence and self-assertion of the leader is a vital factor in successful management. The biblical concept of leadership begins not with natural ability but with personal inadequacy. That is not self-deprecating pessimism; it is essential biblical realism. But the message of Scripture is superbly balanced. There is radiant optimism here as well as necessary realism. Although the leader is not remotely self-confident, he does not depend on the meagre resources of his own ability nor grovel in his evident weakness. He is unfailingly supported by his strong confidence in God. Undergirded with the promise of God's declared sufficiency he is enabled to cope creatively with every possible difficulty.

[2] Jn. 14:23–24.

3. Confident leadership

Moses' confidence is not in himself, therefore, but in the unlimited power of God to see him through. His confidence is in God's nature, word and deeds.

It is God's nature to help his people and he will be true to himself. The human leader is certainly not able to bear the congregation's many burdens (9) but God has promised to bear them like a loving father (1:31; 33:12) and 'carry' his people like a mother eagle, supporting her young on outstretched wings as she teaches them to fly (32:11). If God failed his people it would contradict his essential character.

Moreover, in helping his people, God is being true to his promise. The reference to the Lord God as the one who has multiplied his people *as the stars in the sky* (10) is a deliberate echo of the promise given to *Abraham, Isaac and Jacob* (8). He gave them the assurance that he would not only give them the land but also the people to fill it. It is all *as he has promised* (11) and he will not break his word.

Their confidence is in his works as well as in his word. He is the God of their fathers (11), the God who from patriarchal times onwards has recognized their weakness, pardoned their sins, heard their prayers, vanquished their enemies and provided their needs. The God who had delivered them in the past will not fail them now. When God's people are fearful they must remember who he is, what he has promised and what he has done.

4. Sacrificial leadership

Moses knew that his work was nothing if not exacting. He was incapable of carrying such heavy *problems* and *burdens* on his own. After all, it was not as if they were a united, compliant and spiritually responsive community. Far from it. Within days of leaving Egypt they were grumbling and complaining, wishing they had remained in slavery.[3] Later, their life in the desert had been marked by continual *disputes* (12) rather than supportive harmony. The fact that the Israelite community was quarrelsome and divisive was a constant drain on the physical stamina and emotional resources of Moses. But all those who are called to responsible leadership have to recognize from the start that the work is not easy. It will make immense demands upon us as it did upon him, and nobody can hope to escape the cost.

[3] Ex. 14:10–12; 16:3; 17:3.

5. Shared leadership

The chosen leader knew that he could succeed only if the work was properly delegated. It had to be a shared responsibility if it was to be a successful enterprise. In these verses (13–15) three leadership issues are selected for special mention.

First, Moses identified the necessary qualities. Those who were to share with God's servant the demanding responsibility of leading these provocative people had to be *wise, understanding and respected men* (13). The task of meeting the pastoral needs of such a diverse congregation was not to be entrusted to anybody who might consider himself suitable for the work. Wisdom (God's promised gift) and understanding (a perceptive and sympathetic sensitivity to the needs of others) were the twin qualities necessary for service. The gifts which only come from heaven[4] are given for work which must be done on earth. Nobody has enough natural resources for God's work. That is why he has told us to ask for everything we need. Moreover, such gifts must be evident to and evaluated by the community; only *respected* people will be chosen for such responsible and influential work. Biblical teaching hardly encourages self-appointed leaders.

Notice, secondly, that Moses utilized the various gifts. God has given different abilities to us all. We are not all equipped to undertake any or every aspect of his work. It seems that in Moses' time some were gifted as military commanders, whilst others were to be used as tribal leaders (15) and legal advisors (16). God is still pleased to provide us with different skills for ministry in the contemporary world. Paul rejoiced that, in the first-century churches, the various gifts complemented each other.[5] It is better to discern, cultivate and use our own gift rather than covet or decry somebody else's.

Thirdly, Moses valued the smaller unit. He knew that it was quite impossible for him personally to undertake the spiritual and moral welfare of such a huge crowd. If pastoral care was to be exercised in an effective manner, the people must be divided into manageable groups. John Wesley knew that the spiritual life of the early Methodist people would be heightened beyond measure if they could be organized into small units where the faith of young converts could be fed and strengthened. Their imaginative structure of bands, classes and societies proved to be an inestimable blessing in the eighteenth century and later. The smaller unit provided them with regular opportunities for the sharing of personal experience and for that mutual care and encouragement which is always

[4] Jas. 1:5; 1 Ki. 3:9, 12.   [5] Rom. 12:4–8; 1 Cor. 12:4–11.

35

necessary within any company of Christian people. In our own day, many hundreds of churches have discovered the immense value of house-groups. They are simply giving twentieth-century expression to an important biblical principle implemented by Moses long before anyone talked about 'group dynamics' and the like.

6. Vulnerable leadership

Moses recognized the greatest dangers. He makes special mention of three perils to which spiritual leaders are particularly exposed: favouritism, fear and loneliness (16–17).

Within the oversight of these smaller units, some leaders would have the responsibility of passing a judgment on some legal matter or other. For example, any two people in a group might have a serious difference of opinion on a particular issue, possibly involving the allocation of land or the distribution of property. The leader had to serve as local magistrate and decide on a just and righteous settlement. In such matters, anyone acting as a judge was naturally exposed to the danger of bribery and, without careful legislation, corrupt legal practice might easily follow. A rich man might offer to pay a greedy judge in advance for a decision to be pronounced in his favour. That would be at the high price, however, of deliberate disobedience of the last three commandments: theft, false-witness and covetousness were clearly prohibited by a generous, righteous and holy God. Favouritism was forbidden. The rich and the poor must be treated exactly alike. The leader must *not show partiality in judging* whether the troubles affect domestic (*between your brothers*), ethnic (*or between one of them and an alien*) or social (*small and great alike*) differences. There is no room for favouritism. The exclusively privileged minority is contrary to the teaching of Scripture. God loves all men and women whatever their class, colour or creed and the cry of the oppressed is ever in his ears.[6]

In addition, however, to the danger of pleasing others (by doing what they want rather than what God demands), there is also the peril of dreading others. The group leader is clearly told that he must *not be afraid of the face of man* (17). In God's work in the modern world, fear is probably a greater danger than favouritism. A man or woman in any position of leadership might be afraid of acting in a particular way because of what others might think, say, or do. The 'fear of man' is a cruel and crippling enemy and the Bible frequently warns its readers against it.[7] Believers who honour God have no need to fear anybody else.

[6] Jas. 5:5.   [7] Pss. 56:4, 11; 118:6; Heb. 13:6.

Loneliness is the leaders' third danger. Those who shared with Moses the heavy responsibility of leadership knew that, if they were genuinely unable to solve any of the moral, spiritual and legal complexities which were brought before them, they had direct access to Moses himself (17). They had the divinely imparted rules to guide them (18) but they were not left without the personal support and pastoral skill of their gifted leader. However carefully and necessarily leadership responsibilities are delegated, every leader should have someone he or she can talk to when the problems seem too great to solve and the pressures too intense to bear. Those who constantly bear the burdens of others, need to know how and where they can share their own.

Deuteronomy 1:19–46
2. Afraid of the future?

We have noticed already that God reveals himself to his people by his word and by his deeds. In this section Moses reminds the congregation gathered in the Moabite plains of the acts of God in their history – the gift he offered, the fears they expressed, the rebellion they displayed and the opportunity they lost.

1. A secure future (1:19–25)

After the hundred mile journey through the *vast and dreadful desert* the people arrived at Kadesh Barnea. They were naturally weary but the worst days were over and, in God's goodness, they were on the threshold of victory. Before they could enter the promised land, however, it was necessary to pass through dangerous Amorite territory and they were naturally fearful. They were not trained for war. Physically exhausted after their long journey, many in the camp were terrified at the prospect of fierce battle and ultimate defeat.

Their fear was natural enough but it is how we handle fear that matters. In those moments the tired travellers were presented with a spiritual crisis as well as a physical challenge. The scene is firmly set in Hebrew history but also it vividly portrays the experience of millions of believing people across the centuries. Like every other Old Testament event, this particular story has been 'written for our instruction' so that both by inward steadfastness and the external encouragement of Scripture 'we might have hope'.[1] The narrative throbs with life because it is still relevant in the experience of anyone who is frightened about the future.

In time of fear we must, first, accept God's gift (20–21). The future is not something to dread. It is God's gift to us.[2] It is his future and not simply ours, as if we faced it all alone or without the

---

[1] Rom. 15:4.   [2] Je. 29:11; 31:17; Rev. 1:4, 17.

assurance of his providential care. He knows all about it and, in his sovereignty, can use every aspect of it for our blessing, the enrichment of others, and the glory of his name. When we look into a dark and uncertain future we too must hear the words which were addressed to these despondent Hebrew pilgrims: *See, the LORD your God has given you the land* (21). In his sovereignty God knows everything about our future. It is his gift before it is our threat.

Then again, when our hearts fail us for fear, we must hear God's word (21). The Israelite travellers were given clear instructions to do what God had said and enter that potentially hostile Amorite territory *as the LORD, the God of your fathers, told you* (21). The word of God, the Bible, is our strong support in times of bewilderment or fear. In those unique pages he has given us rich promises about his sufficient help, clear guidance as to how we should behave, pictorial descriptions of his unique deliverances and immense encouragement from the lives of others.

Further, we need to recall God's faithfulness. The Lord is deliberately described here as *the God of your fathers*. He is the dependable Lord who made firm and reliable promises to Abraham, Isaac and Jacob (1:8) that their seed would possess his land.[3] Those two closely related promises of a seed and a land are frequently repeated in the message of Moses (1:35; 6:10, 18, 23; 7:13; 8:1; 9:5; 10:11). When the Lord first made those promises it was hard to envisage their fulfilment, but the patriarchs held on in faith to the reliability and certain performance of what God had promised on oath to give to them.[4]

In time of difficulty, we peer anxiously into the uncertain future but this divine title, *the God of your fathers*, invites us not in the first instance to look ahead but to look back and remember how good and generous the Lord has been in the past. He is the God of the Bible, the God who strengthened Jesus his own Son through his darkest hours, the God of Christian history and the God of our own earlier believing experience. He has not failed across the centuries and do we seriously think that he intends to start with us?

Moreover, we must remember God's mercy. The Lord was not a remote and detached God, totally aloof from their present difficulties. He anticipated their emotional reactions and, knowing their fear, sent his servant Moses to exhort them lovingly: *Do not be afraid; do not be discouraged* (21). He does not expect us to undertake tasks which are utterly beyond us nor does he coldly demand that we embark on ventures without the necessary help.

---

[3] Gn. 12:1–7; 13:14–17; 15:18; 22:15–18.   [4] Heb. 6:13–17; 11:8–12.

He understands our natural fears and hesitancy and, in his loving mercy, accommodates himself to these frail and perfectly understandable reactions.

Because Moses knew how terrified the people were, he responded to their suggestion that they be allowed to send a small advance party on ahead.[5] These spies were to explore the land and report on the best route to enter it. The twelve men went off and returned with exciting news. They had something to tell and something to show. They told of a *good land* (25) which God had certainly given to them and, in case people found it difficult to accept their word, their hands were laden with the luscious fruit which was growing there, present tokens of future help. Surely there was nothing now to hold them back.

2. A poor memory (1:26–33)

Instead of responding to God's clear command (21) they stubbornly disobeyed it: *But you were unwilling to go up* (26). It is a picture of men and women at their worst, a story of stark rebellion (26), ungrateful murmuring, total misunderstanding (27), needless fear, widespread panic (28) and blatant unbelief (32). And the revolt was all due to one fundamental sin, as prevalent now as then – forgetfulness. If only they had stilled their disturbed hearts, quietly listened to the word of Moses and recalled what God has been to them, said to them and done for them. A poor memory has robbed many a Christian of potential blessing.

Notice first, that they were deaf to what God said. They insisted that God hated them (27) but in fact he could not have loved them more (4:37). They feared they would fall into Amorite hands whereas he had plainly told them that the enemy would fall into theirs! They maintained that these grim experiences would end in death whereas God was determined to give them life. They anticipated an overwhelming defeat when God had promised an assured victory. Instead of attending to the reliable word of God they listened to the distorted opinions of men.

Jaundiced pessimism always distorts the truth. The spies came back with grapes[6] but the murmurers talked about giants, *the Anakites* (28). The spies assured them that it was *a good land* but the fearful said it would be their grave. The spies had fixed their eyes on God, the generous giver (25), but the pessimists kept their eyes on men. They had nothing to talk about but the Amorite's physical superiority (*stronger and taller than we are*), architectural advantages

[5] The spy-project was both human request (22–23) and divine command (Nu. 13:1–3). Moses doubtless sought the Lord's mind on such an important issue.
[6] Nu. 13:23.

(*the cities are large*), and military prowess (*and walls up to the sky*).

Additionally, the people were blind to who God is. Moses was patient and pleaded with the terror-stricken multitude not to *be afraid of them* (29). He presented them with three vivid word-pictures of the God who had spoken to them so clearly about their promised possession. He is a victorious soldier, caring father and dependable guide.

Had they forgotten that God is a victorious soldier (29)? They will not be taking the first steps on to Amorite soil. God goes before them and has promised to encounter the enemy long before they get anywhere near the battle-lines. He *will fight for you*, says Moses, *as he did for you in Egypt, before your very eyes* (30). They had seen for themselves how he had conquered their enemies at the beginning of the journey.[7] Did they seriously think that he had brought them all that way to let them down at the end?

What God accomplished in Egypt is followed by what he achieved in the wilderness. They have also forgotten that God is a caring father (31). How could they possibly have made their way in such vast numbers across that dry and inhospitable desert-waste if, day after day, they had not been carried along by a God who bore them up on his shoulders just as a proud father carries his dearly loved son?

They had failed to remember another truth which they ought to have learnt from those days and nights in the desert: God is a dependable guide (32). How could they forget so easily and quickly the fact that he had been their advance-guard in days gone by? What he had done so brilliantly in the Sinai peninsula he was perfectly able to continue on the Amorite borders. Every day the steadily moving pillar of cloud had marked out the safest way to the best camp-site. As the afternoon wore on, the cloud which had sheltered them from the blazing sun was replaced by a pillar of fire to light up the camp. It warmed the cold night air so that they could go to sleep in comfort, and it also served as a protection against marauders so that they could sleep in peace. What more could he have done to show them how much he loved and valued them? He had chosen their leaders, conquered their enemies, guided their steps, sent their food, provided their drink and assured their future.

In spite of this, you did not trust in the Lord your God. The word of Moses is spoken by a crushed and astonished leader. Leadership is painfully difficult when people who ought to be grateful forget God's former mercies, ignore his present word and reject his future blessings.

[7] Ex. 15:3.

3. A lost opportunity (1:34–46)

There are key moments in life when we are confronted with crucial opportunities. It is tragic if we miss them through preoccupation with lesser things. Shakespeare captured the theme perfectly when he put these words into the mouth of Brutus:

> There is a tide in the affairs of men
> Which, taken at the flood, leads on to fortune;
> Omitted, all the voyage of their life
> Is bound in shallows and in miseries.[8]

Life frequently confronts us with stark alternatives. We must choose. God does not treat us as mechanically operated robots. Human freedom is a choice gift but it is also a serious responsibility. The wrong decision may rob us in minutes of what we might have enjoyed for years. By means of these earlier word-pictures, Moses had described God's love. But that is not the whole of the story. Genuine love has to expose itself to the risk of rejection and, in this case, rejected it was. When the Lord heard their words *he was angry* (34). The statement reminds us of an important biblical truth we ignore at our peril. We must consider God's wrath[9] as well as his love, his holiness as well as his mercy.

God announced the punishment (34–35). The opening chapter of Deuteronomy not only demonstrates God's love but it explains God's wrath. We do no justice to the biblical portraiture of God if we regard him as some persistently generous donor who gives but never demands, who constantly pleads but is scarcely interested in how we respond. We have already seen that God is portrayed in this book as a father (31), but if he is a father then he needs to be honoured[10] and obeyed and not simply regarded as a benevolent source of unfailing supply. The good father does not only love, feed and protect his children. When it is necessary, he disciplines them as well (8:5).[11] Emil Brunner has put it like this: 'The wrath of God is the contrary wind of the divine will; he soon discovers who runs against it.' God had prepared the promised land for a believing community not an *evil generation* (35). The disobedient rebels would not even see the land, let alone enter it.

Some escaped the punishment (36). The children would not be allowed to suffer because of the disobedience of their parents. In their fear, the depressed murmurers said that the hostile territory of the Amorites would swallow up thousands of innocent Hebrew children. In fact, years later, those very children would pitch their tents on the ground where their fearful parents imagined they

---

[8] Shakespeare, *Julius Caesar*, IV, iii.   [9] Jn. 3:36; Rom. 1:18.   [10] Mal. 1:6.
[11] *Cf.* Heb. 12:5–10.

would dig their graves (39). Many of the things we worry about never happen. Spurgeon said that anxiety does nothing to rob tomorrow of its problems; it only robs today of its strength. Anxiety is both a waste of emotional energy and a sad expression of spiritual forgetfulness. It envisages circumstances which may never occur and ignores truths which never change. They said their children would *become a prey* (39, RSV) whereas the Lord had planned that they would become a testimony, victorious conquerors rather than helpless victims.

In addition to the younger generation, two adults were also exempt from the punishment of not entering the land, Caleb and Joshua (37–38). Caleb, one of the spiritually confident spies,[12] was the devoted servant who *followed the LORD wholeheartedly* (36). Joshua was the chosen leader destined to take over the responsibilities which Moses had carried for so many years (34:9). Caleb was allowed to enter because of what he had been before God. Joshua was chosen because of what God wanted to do through him. There can scarcely be anything of greater importance in life than those two issues – what God wants to do in us and with us.

Moses bore the punishment. Moses explains to the people that the Lord was angry, literally *because of you* (37); *they* were to blame. Yet, at the close of the book Moses is told that he will not enter the land because *he* had struck the rock (32:51).[13] There is no contradiction here, however. The rock incident would never have happened if the people had entered the land when God told them to, and even that later event at Meribah Kadesh was provoked by Israelite rebellion and discontent.[14] The most destructive thing about sin is the way that it constantly reproduces itself; one transgression quickly incites another. The repeated story of Moses' rejection emphasizes the seriousness of Israel's sin (3:25–27). When the people knew that, because of their folly, even Moses had been excluded, they knew beyond all doubt how deeply they had grieved God.

The Hebrew community was not only fearful but perverse and presumptuous. God plainly told them that because of their sin they would not enter the land: *But as for you, turn round* (40). When the Lord told them to go (21) they refused (26). Now he tells them not to go (35), they insist on going (41). When it was promised territory they would not enter it. Now it is forbidden territory, they will not stay away. We may think it unbelievably perverse but it is entirely typical of human sinfulness. P. T. Forsyth, a perceptive theologian of an earlier generation, put it memorably when he said that we are not straying children, innocent 'babes in the wood', lost

[12] Nu. 13:30; Jos. 14:9–14.   [13] *Cf.* Nu. 20:11–12.   [14] Nu. 20:2–5.

43

and longing for home: 'We are mutinous ... rebels taken with weapons in our hands.'[15]

Their presumption is even more serious than their perversity. Off they went, an ill-prepared crowd of cocksure warriors arrogantly presuming that, because they had used some appropriate religious phrases (41), the Lord would give them the victory. God is not likely to be impressed by what we say if we have stubbornly refused to hear what he says. When Moses refers to their *arrogance* (43), the word he uses describes an action characterized by gross insolence. Those who sin blatantly against a holy God, fully aware of the divine warning, cannot hope to get away with it. The Amorite soldiers need not have terrified them if, initially, they had done what God had commanded. Now the enemy swept down on them and they fled, like a man pursued by angry bees whose nest has been disturbed (44). The memory of those bitter stings was to last for *many days* (46), thirty-eight years to be exact. The apostle Paul once said of a similar Old Testament rebellion-narrative: 'Now these things occurred as examples to keep *us* from setting *our* hearts on evil things as they did ... So, if you think you are standing firm, be careful that you don't fall!'[16] The Father's best gifts are not distributed to people who simply have the right phraseology.[17] They are reserved for responsive and dependent children. God is far more impressed by how we listen than by what we say.

[15] P. T. Forsyth, *Positive Preaching and the Modern Mind* (Independent Press, 1949), pp. 233, 238.
[16] 1 Cor. 10:6, 12.   [17] Mt. 7:21.

Deuteronomy 2:1 – 3:11
3. Time to begin again

The beaten and dejected rebels were driven back into the bleak wilderness. A grim collection of closely related sins – forgetfulness, disobedience, perversity and presumption – had robbed them of better things. It all might have been so different. Because they had ignored the word of God, the rumours dwarfed the realities. Imaginary dangers became more persuasive than dependable promises; the cowards outnumbered the heroes. During the years that followed many hundreds of those sad unbelievers were carried to their graves. Every funeral was a renewed testimony to the seriousness of sin.[1] Yet their bitter defeat by the Amorites became a fading memory. Gradually, a new day began to dawn. It was time to begin again.

The extended narrative in this section of the book recalls a group of historical events through which God's plans for his people began to unfold, but they also serve a higher purpose. They help us to see that although the Lord may have to discipline his people, he does not abandon them. As we read the details of this graphic story a number of great theological themes begin to emerge. On the surface it all seems to be about homeless nomads, tribal squabbles, occasional giants, fortified cities and even iron bedsteads! Although this is the factual material out of which the history is written, the purpose of the narrative is far deeper and conveys truths of continuing significance. The day-to-day life of these once-dejected Hebrew pilgrims stands as a continuing reminder of God's unchanging nature. These stories illustrate the message that God is merciful, generous, just, strong and sovereign.

1. God is merciful

You have made your way around this hill country long enough (3).

---

[1] Ps. 95:10–11; Heb. 3:15–19.

He will not accuse his people continually. However irksome the correction, it is not nearly as severe as we deserve, for, as the psalmist observed, God 'does not treat us as our sins deserve or repay us according to our iniquities'.[2] Discipline is not meant to last for ever. The correction was necessary not simply that these offenders may learn how to live good and happy lives but so that, in coming days, their children would not minimize the seriousness of sin.

It is likely that even those wilderness years may not have been entirely wasted. Centuries later, some of the prophets were persuaded that those decades in the desert had become a time of special devotion. Their reference to that period when, as a nomadic people, Israel was 'holiness unto the Lord' can hardly be limited to the eleven-day journey which followed the exodus. The prophet Jeremiah, like Hosea before him, believed that in those homeless years they renewed their love for God and, as a chosen bride followed him, eager to pursue his perfect will through difficult circumstances, even 'through a land not sown'.[3] However painful the discipline, little is lost if we can learn something from it which makes us better people in the future.

Happily, the days of refining judgment were drawing to a close. Why should the younger generation continue as refugees because their parents had grieved God? The thirty-eight years in the desert remind us, as they certainly convinced them, that we must not trifle with sin. It is the greatest of all mistakes to turn a deaf ear to the voice of God. God disciplined them because he is righteous, but if the correction had continued he would not have been merciful.

This is not a tale confined to the distant past. It addresses us still, and with persuasive appeal. There are times in most of our lives when we grieve God and, for a sensitive man or woman, the sense of guilt can be intense. It is possible, however, that, in the sad aftermath of our transgression, we walk in the dark shadows of remorse far too long. Tennyson was right to observe that sinful men and women may rise ' . . . on stepping-stones/Of their dead selves to higher things'.[4]

Peter knew what it was to fail, but, by a charcoal fire in the early morning, an opportunity came to renew his loyalty and his love. A few decades later, John reminded his readers that the contrite confession of our sins guarantees their immediate cleansing. The author of Hebrews urges us to lay aside the grim mistakes and hindering 'weights' of former days so that, once more, we can join our fellow-athletes in the race.[5] As we run we must be willing to forget

[2] Ps. 103:10.   [3] Je. 2:2–3; Ho. 2:14–15; 11:1.
[4] Alfred, Lord Tennyson, *In Memoriam*, 1.
[5] Jn. 21:15–17; 1 Jn. 1:9; Heb. 12:1, rsv.

the past, looking no longer to our sins but to the one who has pardoned them.

2. God is generous

The people had been disobedient but, despite their appalling wickedness, God had been good to them. Looking back over all the years which had followed their release from Egyptian slavery, Moses reminded the people that it was the Lord who had looked after them. *The LORD your God has blessed you in all the work of your hands. He has watched over your journey through this vast desert. These forty years the LORD your God has been with you, and you have not lacked anything* (7). Although they had grieved him, he had helped them with the practical details of their daily work, remained sensitive to their basic needs, assured them of his protective presence, and provided everything necessary for the maintenance of life.

The fact that they had sufficient money to pay for whatever food and drink they needed as they passed through Edom (6) and Heshbon (28) is proof enough of the Lord's generous provision during the wilderness period. Although the better future was with their children, even the rebels had cause to be thankful. God does not deal with us in the same way we treat him. If that were so, he would have forsaken us long ago.

3. God is just

It is typical of the divine kindness that, following the bitter memories of the past, this time there was to be a new route into the promised land. They were not now required to travel through the infamous hill-country of the Amorites but along the borders of Edom, Moab and Ammon. It was impossible for history to repeat itself with an Amorite victory. But, however comforting that thought may be, the march would still involve a journey across other people's lands. The news of an alternative route would not automatically rob them of their fears.

The new generation was far more attentive, however, to what God had to say than their fathers had been, so they listened with special care when the instruction came *not* to fight the occupants of Edom (5), Moab (9) and Ammon (19). They could scarcely hope to conquer Canaan and some of its surrounding territories without conflict, but the time for battles was not yet. They must not engage in any kind of military skirmish with any of those three nations because God had not given those particular lands to the people of Israel. He was not only generous to the Hebrew people but to other

47

nations as well. They too deserved a home of their own.

The Israelites were not his sole interest, nor was the Lord their exclusive possession. He chose them because he wanted to use them, and they were not to imagine that God's favour entitled them to do or have anything they wanted. The Edomites, Moabites and Ammonites did not have any time for the God of the Hebrews but he certainly had time for them. His interests were world-wide and not narrowly confined to Israel's affairs. As their great ancestor, Abraham, confessed many years before, God was the 'Judge of *all* the earth' and for that reason was determined to 'do right'.[6]

The Lord had wider interests than Israel and still has. He had allocated certain areas of land to the people of Edom, Moab and Ammon and it was not for these desert-pilgrims to think that they could possess it. Their allotted territory lay some way beyond and they must not imagine that they can demand it now.

4. God is strong

The orders not to attack the first three nations they encountered are followed by the assurance that, further along the route, the lands occupied by the kings of Heshbon (2:26–37) and Bashan (3:1–11) would certainly be conquered by the Israelite travellers. In the past, God had dispossessed earlier nations in order to provide for new ones – a point made with obvious insistence in these verses (2:10–12, 20–23) – and he was about to do the same for Israel. Yet they must listen for his instructions; yesterday's orders would not do for today's battles. Some territory was clearly given (2:24, 31; 3:2) and some strictly forbidden (2:5, 9, 19, 37).

Conquests had to be made but, days before the Hebrews commenced their march toward Heshbon, God began to invade the mind of its pagan king. Worry became God's weapon. He simply filled Sihon's heart with fear, and the terror became infectious. Before long, the *terror and fear* of them reached every neighbouring encampment and the surrounding tribes began to tremble and *be in anguish* because of them (25). Decades earlier it was the Israelites who were afraid; now it was their enemies who were terrified. That is exactly how God could have managed it four decades earlier if the fathers of the present warriors had only done what they were told.

In our minds, we put ridiculous limits on the power of God. He overcame immense obstacles for these homeless refugees and has promised to deal effectively with our problems too. The king of Bashan was a 'superman' if ever there was one. His immense physique was the talk of all the surrounding region. His iron

[6] Gn. 18:25.

bedstead (3:11)[7] was huge, a museum piece in an Ammonite town. But he was not too big for God. Giants are scarcely a problem if they are in their coffins.

5. God is sovereign

There is a further important detail in the narrative which we are surely meant to notice. When they came to the frontier of Sihon's kingdom, the Israelites were told that they had now reached the territory which God had planned to give them (2:24). Initially, however, they were not to engage in a direct military confrontation. As on earlier occasions, they were to ask if they might purchase food and drink on their way to lands beyond, and be given the same hospitality as they had received from other nations (26–29). The messengers, however, were given a hostile reception by the king and this happened, says Moses, because God had hardened his heart (30). God was working out his sovereign purposes just as he did before they left Egypt.[8] In those days Pharaoh stubbornly and persistently refused to let them go, but did that mean that a godless ruler could frustrate the will of the eternal God? Surely not. In order to appreciate the assertions that God made these rulers obdurate, we must understand the Bible's lofty conception of God. It did not mean for a moment that the king of Heshbon had no mind of his own, but it did mean that, whatever the nature of Sihon's freedom, God was in control of human history, shaping the destiny of his people and would not be thwarted by the mercurial decisions of men. An example of God's sovereignty near the end of their journey similar to those at the beginning would be a continuing guarantee of their safety and security. It was not in the power of human kings to do anything to them which could frustrate God's plans.

Whilst we are thinking about God's sovereignty, it is important to look at what is, for many people, a serious difficulty about these verses. Did God really intend the wholesale slaughter of hundreds of men, women and innocent children in Heshbon and Bashan (2:34; 3:6)? This difficult topic will emerge again later in the book in passages which contain further instruction about the occupation of enemy territory (7:2; 33:27). Thoughtful and sensitive people are often pained, embarrassed or puzzled by this aspect of the conquest story. We recognize that it is a difficult theme, but it is one which the Scripture not only describes but interprets. One thing is clear: we have already observed from this section that God is just, righteous, merciful and good. It is not his nature to contradict himself

---

[7] or 'coffin' or 'sarcophagus' which may be intended here.   [8] Ex. 7:13.

and we have also seen that he is certainly not indifferent to the needs of other nations, even those who have grieved him sorely. How then are we to explain the insistent command that the occupants of the land be removed?

First, we must remember that these passages describe *a specific occasion*. In no other place in Scripture does God command a 'holy war' of this nature and these verses cannot be used as authority for modern warfare or compulsory land-occupation, either for this admittedly unique nation, Israel, or for anybody else. That which God wanted to happen was for that particular time, once and for all, in the nation's early history, and it does not provide *carte blanche* authority for the future. Israel's God was not a war-lover like Baal. King David's military activities disqualified him as a potential builder of God's temple.[9] The psalmist rebukes those nations which delighted in war,[10] and aggressors like the tormenting Assyrians are forcefully condemned.[11]

Then, we must note that the occupation of the land was *a divine right*. From Abraham's time, at least, it had clearly been God's intention to settle his people in that territory[12] and, as the entire world belonged to him, he was entitled to give any part of it to whichever nation he wished. He was not only the world's Creator[13] but also its Owner[14] and Administrator. The land could hardly be occupied without dispossessing the Canaanites and God knew that, although severe, such an action was best.

In Scripture, however, the occupation was regarded as *a judicial process*. Abraham described the Lord God as 'Judge of all the earth'.[15] The Hebrews were to be the agents of God's judgment on Canaan which came under the same condemnation and punishment as was earlier pronounced upon Sodom and Gomorrah for their appalling sexual perversion. The Canaanites were a grossly immoral people, openly practising, in the name of religion, ritual prostitution and child sacrifice.[16] God gave them time to turn from such idolatrous and inhumane practices but told Abraham that, in his day, 'the sin of the Amorites' had 'not yet reached its full measure'.[17] These Canaanite sins were so offensive and 'detestable' to God that he says that the land needs to be rid of them and 'vomit' out its degrading and pernicious inhabitants.[18] The Israelite invaders were therefore the agents of God's threatened judgment.

[9] 1 Ch. 28:3.   [10] Ps. 68:30.   [11] Is. 10:12–16.   [12] Gn. 12:1, 7; 13:14–17.
[13] Gn. 14:19.   [14] Pss. 24:1; 89:11.   [15] Gn. 18:25.
[16] Although this depraved religion is described both within the Old Testament (12:31; 18:10–11; Lv. 18:21; 2 Ki. 16:3; 17:17; 21:6; Je. 7:30–31; 19:5; 32:32) and outside it (*NBD*, p. 836) the need for its extermination does not rest finally on our assessment of such evidence but on our faith that the Judge of all the earth does right.
[17] Gn. 15:16.   [18] Lv. 18:24–27.

God also makes it clear that the command to remove the Canaanites conveyed *an explicit warning*. If the Hebrew people ever become guilty of similar practices when they occupy the land, they too will be removed.[19] The Hebrews are a uniquely chosen people but not protected favourites whose sins are overlooked or condoned. God is just, holy and righteous, and if, in their disobedience they come to adopt pornographic and idolatrous worship of this or any other kind, they will be severely judged and sent into exile.

Again, the command to possess the land in that radical way, was *a theological necessity*. The Lord knew that if the Israelites had lived alongside their Canaanite neighbours, their worship of the only true God would soon be compromised and corrupted by idolatrous religious practices. The purity of their God-given faith would soon be defiled by syncretism; essential aspects of their unique message would gradually become mixed with items from Baalism. Canaanite statues, however, could not possibly exist alongside a law of God which expressly forbade the worship of images (5:8–9).[20] The sexual practices which took place at these pagan hilltop sanctuaries were totally inconsistent with a covenant that condemned adultery (5:18; 23:18).[21] The Israelite nation was destined in God's purposes to be the unique instrument whereby the divine revelation was to be faithfully conveyed to the rest of the world. Nothing must be permitted which, at the very beginning, could dilute or distort that distinctive message.

We ought also to notice that, harsh as this provision appears, it was *a protective measure*. Truth to tell, the Israelites did not obey the command completely and the remnant of Canaanite residents who remained caused perpetual trouble to generations of God's people.[22] It can certainly be argued that if they had obeyed the admittedly severe command, it could have prevented more extensive loss of life for both Israelites and others at later stages in their history. Life in a fallen world does not always allow us to choose simply between 'good' and 'bad'; the choice is sometimes between an initially painful course of action but with good effects, and an effete delay resulting in devastating consequences. A wise God urged his people to take the former course, but they did not respond with total obedience.

This topic also raises *a hermeneutical issue*. The subject of correct biblical interpretation (hermeneutics) is extremely important. We must always ask precisely what a particular biblical passage is teaching us, and its message must be set alongside other aspects of biblical teaching. Plainly, the Lord had to reveal his will to the Israelite people in intelligible stages and within the thought-patterns and

[19] Lv. 18:28; Jos. 23:15–16. [20] *Cf.* Jdg. 2:13; 10:6. [21] *Cf.* Je. 13:27.
[22] Jos. 23:12–13; Jdg. 1:27–36; 3:1–6; Ezr. 9:1–2; Ne. 13:23–27.

culture of their day. What is forcefully conveyed at one period may well illustrate an important aspect of God's nature which is later supplemented by teaching or narrative which illustrates another complementary aspect. The command about the Canaanites certainly expressed God's holiness, wrath and judgment. Deuteronomy equally emphasizes God's love, patience and mercy. We need the whole of Scripture if we are to discern a balanced and reliable portrait of God's nature. As with this Canaanite issue, the Lord sometimes provides an example of what sin actually deserves in order that we may for ever be warned off it, but after that he allows his merciful forbearance to reign. In the New Testament, the Ananias and Sapphira story illustrates the same principle;[23] not every deceiver died as they did, but the warning is given to illustrate the seriousness of sinning against God by deliberate hypocrisy.

The seemingly harsh instructions about the Canaanites have to be balanced, for example, by the narrative about the Gibeonites. The story in Joshua 9 describes the ingenious yet dishonest ploy used by one Canaanite group to protect themselves from extermination. Disguising themselves as exhausted travellers from another country, the Gibeonites extracted a promise from the guileless Israelites that they would not be killed. Genuinely believing that these dishevelled people were not Canaanites, the Hebrews gave their word that they would not be harmed. When their true identity was revealed, the invaders realized that they had been deceived. They had made their promise, however, and under no circumstances must that covenant-oath be broken. They worshipped a God of truth as well as holiness. Caught in a moral dilemma they honoured their word and spared the Gibeonites, employing them as servants. The story illustrates the point that even an injunction like that to remove the spiritually dangerous Canaanites must be balanced by other facets of equally vital truth, in this case the necessity of dependable words. Similarly, the exemption of Rahab and her household illustrates the complementary truth of God's generous mercy to her, despite the extermination decree, as earlier to Noah and to Lot and their families in similar circumstances. The biblical message must be studied as a whole and not in isolated fragments, however important and instructive they may be.

It is necessary, therefore, to recognize that this command to remove the Canaanites is an important story which presents one aspect of an unfolding revelation. The teaching of Jesus makes it abundantly clear that enemies are to be loved not slain.[24] The Canaanite command was a unique injunction, a moral necessity and a spiritual safeguard. It was never intended as an invasion-pattern

<hr />

[23] Acts 5:1–11.   [24] Mt. 5:44–45.

for others to follow either in Israel or anywhere else.

Finally, the divine command regarding the Canaanites enshrines *a vital spiritual principle*. It reminds us that the element of conflict can never be eliminated from our spirituality. In the New Testament the Christian life is portrayed as warfare, struggle or contest, as the strenuous activity of a soldier, an athlete, a boxer or wrestler competing at the games.[25] Jesus did not minimize the cost of discipleship; he said that following him would never be easy.[26] On entering the land which God had given them, the Israelites' greatest danger was gradually to become accommodated to a morally and spiritually damaging culture. That is our problem too. Paul urged his friends at Rome, 'Don't let the world around you squeeze you into its own mould, but let God re-mould your minds from within.'[27]

On two occasions in the history of the Israelite people they were summoned by God to leave the alien country where, unhappily, they were living and travel to the land which God had given them. First, they left Egypt with the divine command that they live no longer as slaves but as God's different, holy people.[28] Some centuries later they were again in captivity, this time in Babylon and, once again, the Lord told them to come away, 'Depart, depart, go out from there! Touch no unclean thing! Come out from it and be pure.'[29] The apostles Peter and Paul use both these Old Testament events and sayings to depict the Christian call to leave the old life and enjoy the new.[30] In the contemporary world, the Lord calls us to a radically different lifestyle. Believers who gladly respond to that call to total commitment do so because the Lord has guaranteed the strength it demands.

[25] 2 Tim. 2:3–5; 1 Cor. 9:24–27; Col. 4:12; Eph. 6:10–17.   [26] Mk. 8:34–38.

[27] J. B. Phillips' paraphrase of Romans 12:2 in *The New Testament in Modern English* (Collins, 1958).

[28] Lv. 11:45.   [29] Is. 52:11.   [30] 1 Pet. 1:14–19; 2 Cor. 6:17.

Deuteronomy 3:12–29
4. Present blessings encourage future service

The narrative in this section describes the events which followed the conquest of the two kingdoms, Heshbon and Bashan. From a historical point of view, the passage vividly reminds the Hebrew people of blessings in the past, but it also conveys a number of basic lessons for believers in every century. It emphasizes the necessity of love, worship and submission.

1. Love the Lord's people (3:12–22)

We need to notice, first of all, God's concern for the *whole* community. Once the Israelites had taken possession of their newly conquered territory, it was important for Moses to tackle the strategic question of land-allocation. The stories of their ancestors, told and treasured for generations, made it abundantly clear that, unless these issues were decisively settled, there could be bitter divisions and severed relationships.[1] The first thing, therefore, was to determine where the various Israelite tribes would live and, as some of the territory they needed was already in their possession, it was best to start the allocation there and then, east of the river Jordan.

Although the matter concerned the rights of particular tribes, it was the whole community which was uppermost in God's thinking. They had stayed closely together during their long wilderness journey and this was no time for breaking up. Some (Reuben, Gad and half of Manasseh) were given the land which had previously belonged to Heshbon and Og.[2] Yet, those two and a half tribes whose new land was already secure were still required to send their troops into Canaan in order to share in a victory which would benefit the entire nation. There was no 'every-man-for-himself' attitude here. The tribes must consider what was good for

[1] Gn. 13:7.   [2] Nu. 32:1–5; Jos. 22:1–3.

all and not simply what was best for themselves.

This 'corporate solidarity' is one of the many impressive features about the life of the Lord's people. They felt themselves inextricably bound together. Each belonged to the whole. Their unified life both embodies and illustrates a key spiritual principle with important consequences for the church in today's world. In the New Testament the community of those who believe in Jesus are regarded as the new Israel.[3] When Peter wrote to the first-century churches he applied to the church the great Old Testament titles for the Hebrew nation, and reminded them that believers are like 'living stones' joined together in a spiritual temple.[4] The close and interdependent life of God's people in Old Testament times is a model for the church but, all too often, we are detached soloists rather than supportive partners.

Some individual Christians make the sad mistake of 'going it alone'. However pure their motives, it seems impossible for them ever to find a church which is good, pure, keen or large enough to meet their predetermined needs. The Lord Jesus valued the love and companionship of his disciples for three years, though they were far from perfect. No believer can afford to remain in spiritual isolation. We are meant for one another.

Living in self-imposed spiritual isolation can be a particular temptation for the Christian leader. It is possible to be so totally absorbed with our own work for God that, albeit unintentionally, we cut ourselves off from the fellowship of others. In the mid-seventeenth century, Richard Baxter urged his fellow-ministers: 'grow not strange to one another; do not say you have business of your own to do'.[5] Leaders need to meet with others, not simply for their own encouragement but for the stimulation which can come from different minds, the enlarging of our horizons through other people's vision and, at times, even for helpful correction.

Isolationism is not simply a problem for individuals, however; it can be the snare of churches, large or small. It surely cannot be right for a company of Christ's people to order their corporate life as though other churches did not exist. We need bigger maps. The prosperous suburban church can live in total ignorance of the difficulties faced by believers in the inner-cities. Small congregations in rural communities may be forgiven for feeling that larger churches in nearby towns have forgotten they exist. All our friends in missionary situations, at home or overseas, are in danger of serious neglect by those who live alongside them in the same global village. Christians should have the widest possible horizons.

[3] Gal. 6:16.   [4] 1 Pet. 2:4, 9–10.
[5] R. Baxter, *The Reformed Pastor*, Chapter 6, V.

Moreover, these verses make it clear that God was also concerned about the *weaker* members of the community. The 'men of valour' from the newly settled tribes were to go out to war so that the other tribes might also have a home, but their wives and children were not to travel with them. They must patiently await the return of fathers and sons until *the Lord gives rest* to their brethren (20). Children must not be anywhere near the scene of battle; they need the continuing care of devoted mothers. As we shall see, family life is given a prominent place in the teaching of this book.

These issues are important in our own society as well. At a time when there is a frightening escalation of family breakdown, believers ought by their example, prayers and personal effort to do everything within their power to preserve these divinely ordained units of love, care and security. The alarming rise in crimes associated with innocent children makes sick reading in newspapers the world over – serious neglect, mental cruelty, pederasty, sexual offences, physical abuse, the transmission of drugs to young people, to name but a few. With the serious decline of moral values, teenagers are seriously vulnerable in contemporary society. A survey recently commissioned by the BBC in preparation for a new Radio 4 series, *Best Behaviour*, revealed that one in twenty girls aged fifteen to seventeen thinks it reasonable in today's society for a man to expect sex on the first date. The detailed provision in Deuteronomy makes it clear that God is deeply concerned that children and young people should not be put at risk; neither should we.

In his compassion, the Lord also made provision for *animals* (19). Those Israelites who had acquired cattle and whose allocated territory lay in Canaan were to leave their cattle in the recently occupied lands so that they could be properly cared for by the women, children and any members of the community unable to go to war. God's concern for animals is another highly attractive feature of this book which we shall have occasion to notice in later chapters. God is the Maker and Sustainer of his world. He created the various members of the animal kingdom and saw that they were 'good'.[6] Animals and birds were companions of human beings because it was not good that they should be alone. Mankind was appointed as a steward in God's good world[7] and for that reason the Hebrew people were told to look after their cattle. God was concerned about ecology long before the term was invented.

Moses also gave expression to God's compassion for the *fearful*. There is even a word here for the men who are leaving home in order to secure the promised land. Even *able-bodied men* (18) need the occasional word of encouragement. They are reminded of two

[6] Gn. 1:25.   [7] Gn. 2:18–20.

recent conquests and two eternal truths. The soldiers are reassured by God's servant as he tells them that what the Lord *has done* is a pledge of what he *will . . . do* (21). Their recent victory over the two kings must surely encourage their belief that what he has accomplished in the past, he will repeat in the future. They are also given two truths to treasure in their minds as they leave home: what God has given and how God will work. He *has given* the land of Canaan to them (18) so they are entering God's property, and he *will* secure it for them by acting as their invincible warrior. *Do not be afraid of them; the LORD your God himself will fight for you* (22). Their eyes had *seen* (21) the earlier deliverance; their ears must hear the sustaining promise.

2. Exalt the Lord's name (3:23–24)

When *at that time* Moses saw the troops waiting to depart, his heart was full of thanksgiving for the greatness, uniqueness and achievements of God (24). In the recent conquests of Heshbon and Bashan he had *only begun to show* his majesty and might. The fathers of these warriors were paralysed with fear nearly forty years earlier because they magnified the strength of the enemy; their sons became victors because they exalted the greatness of God.

In this ascription of praise, Moses also testified to God's uniqueness. God is not only great; he is incomparable. Moses asks whether there is any other god *in heaven or on earth who can do* such *deeds and mighty works.* The soldiers were about to enter a land notorious for its idolatry but Moses knows that such gods are no gods at all, the vain figment of human imagination with no substance whatever in reality. To serve them is to worship the sick projection of man's impure and fickle mind.

Could these not-gods of Canaan or any other nation achieve such *mighty acts* as their God had performed over the centuries? This book has much to say about the vanity, danger and offensiveness of idolatry in the sight of God. Their powerlessness was to become a familiar theme with the Israelite people. God alone can meet their needs and he alone is worthy of their allegiance.

Moses began his prayer to God with worship; literally, he acknowledged God's worth, which is the derivation of the word. He had entered God's presence with something special to ask but, before he mentioned what he wanted, he had something special to give. Praise ought always to precede petition. It reminds us of what we already have and provides the necessary perspective for what we request.

3. Accept the Lord's will (3:25–29)

These verses bring the book's introductory section to a dramatic conclusion. The story began (1:1–8) with Moses in public; it ends here with Moses in private. It starts with a preacher in the presence of the people; it closes with a praying man in the presence of God. The following chapters record the substance of Moses' preaching to the people. Leaders, however, should not only share God's word; they must seek God's face. Without prayer, no Christian can hope to be effective in leadership. P. T. Forsyth reminded us that we must spend time with people in order to understand their problems, and spend time with God in order to solve them.

Moses often sought the Lord on behalf of the people (9:25–29)[8] but in this instance he prayed earnestly for himself. With the disappointing years of the wilderness experience behind him, he longed to see God's people safely installed in their new land. He was elderly and tired but nothing was too hard for God. The days ahead might well be difficult but, with God's help, even an old man might be given strength to enter the land. The Lord had clearly told him that, on account of the people's sins, he would not set foot in the promised land (1:37) but he felt he must ask again in case the privilege might yet be given. The answer was definite: *That is enough. Do not speak to me any more about this matter* (26). The narrative has some important things to say to us. Moses' disappointment might even be for our encouragement.

When we ask God for anything we must remember that we are not the only people concerned. Nobody can possibly live entirely to themselves. Our lives are intricately bound up with those of other people. Moses' request seems innocent and natural enough and, ostensibly, something which affected him only and nobody else. In point of fact, four issues were at stake: what was best for Moses, right for the people, good for Joshua and pleasing to God.

First, we ought to consider what was best for Moses. Doubtless, he believed that there was useful work still for him to do and, with all his experience, it would be good for him to see the people safely established in their new home. Even with the purest motives, however, the things we seek for ourselves are not necessarily wise and right. With our naturally limited vision, it is impossible for us to see the total picture; only God is capable of that. After all, what we want may not necessarily be best. Moses could not think of anything more wonderful than entering Canaan: God's plan was that he should enter heaven.

Next, we ought to ask what was right for the people. This request

---

[8] *Cf.* Ex. 32:11–14, 31–32; 33:7–11; Nu. 14:13–19.

was not simply a personal matter between Moses and God. The Lord may have responded to the prayer with such a definite 'No' because by Moses' exclusion he wanted to both warn and protect the people.

It was certainly a warning. On three occasions (1:37; 3:26; 4:21) Moses tells the people, *because of you, the LORD was angry with me.* By denying Moses access to the land, God was saying something to the people as well as to Moses. When we make requests in prayer we must remember that what we want may not always be best for others. Moses' exclusion was a perpetual reminder of God's holiness. It was saying that men and women must not trifle with sin.

Moreover, by the denial the Lord may have been protecting them. Moses was an immensely popular figure; when he died the people wept for a full month (34:8). By taking Moses to heaven before he entered Canaan, God may have deliberately prevented the veneration of his tomb with all its attendant dangers. Their intense admiration for him is eloquently conveyed by the eulogy which brings Deuteronomy to a close. There were great leaders, before and after, but 'none like him' (34:10–12). Ancestor worship was common enough in the ancient world and in the future it would have been all too easy for people to congregate at his grave for worship. There must have been some reason for the unique circumstances, also noted in the final chapter, that God buried Moses and that 'to this day no-one knows where his grave is' (34:6). As the years went by, the people gradually introduced many corrupt and forbidden elements into their worship. Possibly God wanted to ensure that the memory of Moses' life and work was recalled by his words rather than by his grave. When he had made such a unique contribution to Israel's history, a tomb in Canaan might soon become a national shrine, directing people's minds to the man rather than to the God who had used the man. The idolization of leaders is a sin not confined to the world of antiquity.

Additionally, when considering this prayer, we need to ask what was good for Joshua. On two occasions in the book when the refusal is mentioned, Joshua's responsibilities are given special prominence (1:38; 3:21–22, 28). Moses' work for the Lord was to lead the people across the desert; that was difficult enough. It was not his job, however, to settle the people in the land. God had chosen a different man for that task. One man's work had ended; another's was about to begin. Joshua's very different ministry was of equal importance to the Lord. People who have worked effectively for God do not always find it easy to hand their tasks on to others. The necessary break between the end of Moses' ministry and the beginning of Joshua's appears to be emphasized with stark clarity in Joshua 1:2: 'Moses my servant is dead. Now then ... get ready to cross the Jordan.'

Most important of all, in making any request, we must ask what is pleasing to God. Notice that as he begins his prayer, Moses is more concerned to exalt God than seek anything for himself. It is typical of great biblical praying.[9] Two key words are important in the prayer, *Sovereign* and *servant* (verse 24). God is pleased when we acknowledge his sovereignty and our servanthood. These important words in Moses' ascription of praise are the key to his submission and to ours. Throughout his entire life Moses had been God's willing slave. Therefore, the decision as to where and when that life should end was not the slave's concern; it was in the far safer hands of a wise, loving, sovereign Master who would not make any mistakes.

Finally, this narrative leaves us with an important guiding principle about prayer. It is better to seek for qualities rather than things. We long for material things but he has gifts money cannot buy. We yearn for improved health but, though God could heal, greater reliance on him would be better for us by far. Without our weakness, how could we be sure of our strength? We wish for a different job but in our present work there may be people alongside us only we can reach. We desire repeated success but occasional failure might prove a better teacher. Most ambitions need the refining fire. The ecclesiastical authorities in eighteenth-century England were bewildered when the saintly John Fletcher of Madeley, Wesley's 'designated successor', refused the bishopric of Rochester. Thinking he had set his sights on even greater preferment, they asked him whether there was anything more he wanted. Within seconds his priorities were crystal clear: 'I want more grace', he said.

[9] Ne. 9; Acts 4:24–28.

Deuteronomy 4:1–43
5. Seeing him who is invisible

To conclude the book's main historical introduction, this new chapter contains a substantial address given by Moses to the waiting people. It expounds a number of themes which will be given increasing prominence in Moses' preaching. Primarily, the leader's message is about the character and achievements of God. Before the people enter the land it is of the greatest possible importance that they understand who God is, what he has said and what he can do. They need to think deeply about the uniqueness of their God before they invade a land littered with other gods. If they are to survive the hazards and perils of the days ahead it can only be by seeing God. In Canaan they will see hundreds of idols but, if they wish to conquer and retain the land, they must look to the God who cannot be seen.

The failure of their fathers to occupy the land almost forty years earlier had been entirely due to defective vision. They had simply not known where to look. It scarcely ever occurred to them to look up. Looking ahead, they were more aware of giants than grapes. Looking around, they could see little but their own slender resources, totally dwarfed by the military strength and massive fortifications of the people whose hostile territories lay across their path. Looking within, their hearts failed them for fear. Looking back, they thought it might even have been better not to have left Egypt. Even when they did think about God, they had a pathetically distorted image of his nature. 'The Lord hates us,' they said, 'so he brought us out of Egypt ... to destroy us' (1:27). Nothing could have been further from the truth.

The portrait of God given to Moses to share with the people before they began their march into the land was that of a generous Giver (1–12), sovereign Lord (13–28), merciful Deliverer (29–34) and incomparable Lover (35–43).

1. The generous Giver (4:1–12)

Without the clear teaching of Scripture people imagine that, either by our religious observances or moral conduct, we must all make strenuous attempts to earn God's favour. It was to guard against the same danger of such man-centred religion that Moses began this particular address to the people by focusing on what God first gave to his people and not on what they give to him. His special relationship with them and favours towards them were not on the basis of what they had done. It was not because of their numerical strength (6:7) or moral goodness (9:4) that the Israelites had been marked out as God's special people, but because God loved them, chose them and wanted to use them. For this reason Moses began by concentrating on two of God's undeserved gifts to his children, the law and the land: *Hear now, O Israel, the decrees and laws I am about to teach you. Follow them so that you may live and may go in and take possession of the land that the LORD, the God of your fathers, is giving you* (1).

a. The word he gave

This section lays a firm foundation for later teaching in the book about God's revealed truth. Its verses emphasize that the word which God entrusted to Moses for us is one which has unique spiritual, intellectual, moral, universal, educational and social appeal.

Spiritually beneficial, the law was designed to impart life (1). It was not intended as a tedious list of unwelcome prohibitions. God knows that if men and women are to enjoy life, certain rules will always be necessary. Pressurized labour conditions with no opportunity for relaxation, child disobedience, family breakdown, murder, infidelity in marriage, theft, lying, legal malpractice and covetousness are not the usual ingredients for happy living in any society, and these are the main community prohibitions in the Ten Commandments. But the law as summarized in the Ten Commandments begins not with a list of prohibitions but with a declaration of God's uniqueness and saving achievement: 'I am the LORD your God, who brought you out of Egypt' (5:6). It begins not with what a person has to do or not do, but with what the Lord has done. His enslaved people in Egypt were under the sentence of death but he came to deliver them and release them from the cruel bondage to which they had been subjected in a foreign land. He gave them *life* and wanted them to continue to enjoy life, and it was for this reason that he provided this unique word to instruct them and us in the way of life.

Personally obligatory, this word is designed to inform, enlighten and stimulate the mind. Every part of it is of unique importance. It confronts its readers with serious responsibilities. Moses urges them and us to attend to its message (*Hear now*, 1), obey its injunctions (*Follow them*, 1), recognize its source (*the commands of the Lord*, 2), honour its authority (*Do not add to what I command you and do not subtract from it*, 2) and prove its value (*this will show your wisdom and understanding*, 6).

Throughout the centuries, some people have made the immense mistake of supplementing, mutilating, or ignoring the word of God. They sit in judgment on it instead of subjecting themselves to its judgment on them. This warning by Moses was certainly necessary; such addition and subtraction even took place within the Hebrew religious tradition. During Christ's ministry, the Pharisees added to the word of God hundreds of detailed prohibitions which were not contained in canonical Scripture. In the same period, the Sadducees subtracted from the word the things they found unacceptable – anything about the supernatural, the doctrine of the resurrection, angels and spirits.[1] The Pharisees were the first-century legalists, and the Sadducees the destructive rationalists of their day.

In early church history, certain teachers added to the biblical teaching about salvation, grace and sacraments, while, in later centuries, rationalist students of the Bible chose to remove from its teaching elements of the miraculous, or its claim to Christ's unique deity, virgin birth, atoning death, physical resurrection or promised return.

It would be a mistake, however, to suppose that the dangers of adding to the word and taking away from it are perils confined to the past. It is easier to castigate the sins of others than confess our own. We can make similar mistakes ourselves; because they are less public we must not imagine they are less serious. Believers add to God's word whenever they make compulsory rules about things on which Scripture is silent. There are forms of 'Christian' legalism which are not honouring to God. We also 'take away' from the word whenever we blatantly ignore or disobey what God is saying to us; we are saying in effect that, as far as we are concerned, Scripture might as well be non-existent. This word of Moses warns God's people about such dangers and clearly prohibits such addition, excision or manipulation. Moreover, Moses knew from the wilderness experience that some people totally ignore God's word and he draws attention to the disastrous effects of such behaviour by using an illustration (3) from the history of God's people.

Morally crucial, this word guards us from sin and protects us

---

[1] Acts 23:8.

from those harmful and destructive influences which would rob us of the happy life God intends us to enjoy. As an example of the serious consequences which follow the rejection of God's word, Moses reminds the people of *what the Lord did at Baal Peor* (3). At that time[2] some Israelite men had sexual relationships with Moabite women, participated in Baal-worship which encouraged such practices, and bowed down to pagan idols. A plague broke out in the camp and the offenders were executed. Moses deliberately contrasts those who died as an act of judgment and those who *held fast* to the Lord, and are *still alive this day* (4) to hear his address and heed its warning. It deliberately contrasts the way of life and the way of death, another key theme in the book (30:15–20).

Universally attractive, this word not only transforms our own lives but makes a profound impact on our unbelieving neighbours. Moses told his contemporaries that when people of other nations *hear about all these decrees* they will say, '*Surely this great nation is a wise and understanding people . . .*' *What other nation is so great as to have such righteous decrees and laws as this body of laws I am setting before you today?* (6, 8). In several important passages, the Old Testament anticipated the time when God's community would be a missionary people;[3] here Moses says that God's word will become his effective instrument in that missionary programme by making his name known to Israel's neighbours.[4] It would serve to attract unbelieving people to spiritual realities because of its authoritative, compelling and effective teaching. Moreover, unbelievers would recognize that God does not instruct his people from an infinite distance but draws close to them when they pray to him (7).

Educationally significant (9), the law was to play a creative part in the developing life of the Hebrew nation. The message was to be received by the individual (*Only be careful and watch yourselves closely*), treasured within families (*Teach them to your children*), and communicated to each successive generation (*and to their children after them*). As we shall see, the education of children as well as the preservation of home and family life are specially important aspects of the teaching in this book (10; 6:7, 20; 11:19; 31:13; 32:7).

Socially influential (10–12), the truth God gives in the law is to have a unifying and purifying effect within the life of the nation (*Assemble the people before me to hear my words*). It serves to

---

[2] Nu. 25:1–9.   [3] Is. 42:4, 12; 51:5; 66:19.

[4] Christopher J. H. Wright says: 'The law was not explicitly and consciously applied to the nations. But that does not mean it was irrelevant to them. Rather, the law was given to Israel to enable Israel to live as a model, as a light to the nations, such that, in the prophetic vision, the law would "go forth" to the nations, or they would "come up" to learn it' (*Tyndale Bulletin* 43.2, 1992), p. 227.

enrich corporate life for it recalls God's goodness in the past and reminds his people of their unpayable debt for his purposive revelation (*so that they may learn to revere me*, 10), majestic splendour (*the mountain ... blazed with fire to the very heavens, with black clouds and deep darkness*, 11), and uniqueness (*You ... saw no form; there was only a voice*, 12). One of the things which quickly destroys this sense of corporate solidarity is disobedience to the word, as at Baal Peor (3–4) when the Israelite people violated the Lord's teaching about idolatry (5:7–8) and adultery (5:18), and ignored his message concerning their exclusive loyalty to him (5:15–19).[5]

b. The land he provided

The hard years of their wearying existence as insecure refugees were almost over. The territory which lay ahead of them was God's property, for he owns everything (10:14).[6] It was also God's provision for his chosen people, and God's gift: it is *the land that the LORD, the God of your fathers, is giving you* (1, see also 21, 38, 40). The message of this book about the 'land' emphasizes that, in God's mind, there is no distinction between the sacred and the secular. All life belongs to God. He is not exclusively interested in the law; he is equally concerned about the land. God gave the word to them *at Horeb* (10) but he also gave them the land. The two were bound together: *I have taught you decrees and laws ... so that you may follow them in the land you are entering* (5).

God's gifts, however, are more than undeserved privileges; they are also accountable responsibilities. It was a good land (22) but it was possible to defile it.[7] It was a token of God's abundant generosity to them (8:7–9) but, overlooking that fact, they could fail to respect his gift and live ungratefully and selfishly in it (8:10–14). Moreover, although God entrusted it to them as a people, God was still its owner. They were answerable to him both for the way they treated it and their fellow Israelites who shared their stewardship of it. It did not belong to their kings, as their pagan neighbours believed about their lands, so Israel's rulers were not free to exploit their land-owning brothers, and claim land as royal property. A Baal-worshipper like Jezebel might well feel free to plunder a neighbour's property, but God's prophet made it clear that such conduct was totally unacceptable in Israel. That vineyard had been entrusted to Naboth by God, and a ruthless queen would be judged for violating the commandments about

[5] *Cf.* Ex. 19:5–6.   [6] *Cf.* 1 Ch. 29:11; Pss. 24:1; 89:11.   [7] Je. 2:7.

covetousness, bearing false witness, theft and murder.[8]

This teaching about the land is not merely an interesting geographical detail, mainly of interest to students of Israelite history. It has something extremely important to say to us, wherever we live in the world. The land was given by God on trust as the precise local sphere of Israel's future activity. They were not free to do exactly what they wanted with it. Just as definitely, God has given to each one of us areas of privileged opportunity where we are meant to spend our lives and where they can be lived to his glory – home, work, church, neighbourhood, nation. These 'spheres of operation' are God's gift to us but such priceless gifts can be grievously misused. Life is good and it is God's will that we should be happy in it. God is no kill-joy. Deuteronomy frequently makes its strongly positive assertion that experience under God's word in God's land should be thoroughly enjoyable. His people are urged to obey the word and 'possess' the land, 'that it may go well with you' and 'that you may prolong your days in the land which the LORD your God has given you' (4:40; 5:33; 6:2, 18, 24; 11:9; 12:28; 13:17–18). To enjoy the privileges, however, we have to live responsibly in obedience to God's word. Let us take some examples.

Our bodies are the Lord's choice gift to us but they can be thoughtlessly misused – some believers constantly disobey God's commandment to have a day of rest and recreation in each week, and push themselves far too hard. Others are so busy with other commitments, even with Christian service, that they have forgotten that home and family life is one of life's highest privileges. Almost exclusively preoccupied with other things, they will think little about home until a marriage is at risk or the children begin to lose their interest in a persistently absent parent. Work is an important sphere of potential witness but it is easily 'defiled'. We must testify to the reality of our faith by the quality of our work as well as by the faithfulness of our words. Sadly, there have been Christians at work whose commendable evangelism has been nullified by mediocre workmanship. Our local churches are further spheres of excellent opportunity but they too can be 'defiled' by apathy, or criticism, or a domineering attitude, or a selfish preoccupation with our own particular responsibilities, to the exclusion of almost everything else. It is possible to be an active Christian but a disappointing neighbour, to be so eager to attend the church's meetings that we neglect the lonely person across the road and so miss a natural opportunity for loving care, practical service and consistent witness. We can be so busy with local church activities that our

---

[8] 1 Ki. 21:1–28. For a perceptive discussion of 'the land' in Israel's theology, see Christopher J. H. Wright, *Living as the People of God*, pp. 46–62.

social and political opportunities are totally ignored. Life in the 'land' is God's priceless gift but it is also our privileged opportunity.

2. The sovereign Lord (4:13-28)

Moses goes on to remind the people of the Lord's initiative, uniqueness and warning.

a. His initiative (4:13-14)

He declared to you his covenant, the Ten Commandments ... and then wrote them on two stone tablets (13). These important words introduce us to one of this book's leading ideas. God is not simply a benevolent donor. He has generously given law and land to the Israelites because, as the sovereign Lord of the whole earth, he has chosen them as his special people. At Sinai he entered into a covenant or agreement with them because he wanted them to share a holy partnership with him.[9] We have already noticed the possible treaty-structure of Deuteronomy. This fourth chapter of the book makes imaginative use of some of the features characteristic of an ancient treaty. The stronger (suzerain) king took the initiative in declaring the terms of the covenant. In addressing the people, Moses emphasizes that the covenant made at Sinai was initiated by God.

The standard contents of a treaty can be clearly discerned in this address by Moses. First, there was the preamble in which the king was introduced (1). This was normally followed by a historical prologue which briefly surveyed the previous relationship between the two nations or parties (10-14, 20-21, 37-38). Then the treaty introduced some general principles (2) before moving to a number of specific regulations (5-9, 15-19, 23-24). It was then usual to deal with the treaty's sanctions – curses (25-28) for those who broke the treaty, and blessings (31-36) for those who honoured it. It was concluded by declaring the names of the witnesses (39-40), usually the gods who would guarantee the treaty.

We cannot be sure, of course, that this treaty-pattern determined either the content of this particular address by Moses or the compilation of Deuteronomy as a whole, but the similarities are striking and serve to emphasize some important aspects of our relationship with God. The usual plan was for a superior power to enter into an agreement with a weaker nation so that protection was offered by the stronger party on condition that the country with less resources honoured and obeyed the obligations of the covenant. This 'treaty address' by Moses is a stark reminder to his contemporaries that, in

[9] Ex. 34:27-28.

every spiritual encounter, the authority is with God. We are totally dependent on him.

b.   His uniqueness (4:15–24)

It was usual for these treaties to forbid the weaker or vassal country to enter into an alliance with any other nation. Deuteronomy makes it plain that God lovingly initiated the covenant-agreement by making his own distinctive treaty with his people. It had definite stipulations, tersely summarized in ten clear instructions which they were *commanded . . . to follow* (13). We recall that God's deliverance, and the covenant which followed it, was an act of unmerited grace and did not begin with what was required of them but with what had been done for them – but it certainly had conditions. God declared that he had delivered them from the *iron-smelting furnace* (20) of Egyptian slavery and they were now his vassal people. He rightly insisted that they acknowledge his uniqueness as the only true God by promising not to offer themselves to other gods – one of this book's most prominent themes. To become allied in this way to an alien power was to break the agreement (13; 5:7) and *become corrupt* (16, 25); it was to do *evil in the eyes of the LORD . . . provoking him to anger* (25). The warning of Moses, about breaking the covenant by worshipping other gods, was certainly necessary, and still is. Once the Israelite people were in the promised land, idols became a constant snare (16). Their prohibition, forcefully emphasized in this chapter, makes it clear that idols are totally inadequate, seriously misleading and strictly forbidden.

They are inadequate because God is far too majestic and transcendent to be crudely represented by a statue. To do so is to minimize his greatness and glory. It is a blatant insult to his matchless deity and a blasphemous attempt to reduce him to the narrow confines of the human imagination. It is for this reason that, when Moses recalls the events at Sinai, he repeats the fact that the Hebrew people *saw no form* (12, 15), and only heard *a voice*.

Moreover, idols are misleading; they feed the mind with wrong ideas about God. God is sovereign – he rules over the whole world and acts where and when he wishes. Idols create the impression that, precisely located in a particular place or restricted to a measurable area, God can be controlled or manipulated. God is immortal, living and active in the history not only of his own people but of all people; idols are lifeless, perishable objects, doomed to end in the dust. God is Creator, the Maker of the entire universe and everything within it. When people make representations of the things which God has generously made, they worship the creature rather than the Creator. God is love, eager to speak to his people and listen to their cry; idols are dumb and deaf (28). Moses has already made the point that surrounding nations will identify three outstanding things about Israel's God: unlike their silent, immobile, deaf idols, he talks to his people (*See, I have taught you*, 5), comes alongside them (*near . . . the way the LORD our God is near us*, 7) and hears their prayers (*whenever we pray to him*, 7).

The idols specially mentioned by Moses were common throughout the Near Eastern world. Countries such as Egypt, the one they had left, and Canaan, which they were about to enter, had innumerable images of humans, animals, birds, reptiles and fish (16–18). Many of the Israelite people remembered from their childhood the huge Egyptian winged-bird idols they had often seen in their captivity and many other statues of snakes, monkeys, crocodiles and bulls to which their slave-masters had offered their allegiance. There was another danger, more subtle than the manufacture of idols – the worship of the created world which God alone had made. Sun, moon and star-gods were common in most of their neighbours' religions and the worship of such deities is equally forbidden. It grossly misuses the gifts by forgetting the one who has given them.

The most serious thing here about idols, however, is that they are forbidden: *Be careful not to forget the covenant of the LORD your God that he made with you; do not make for yourselves an idol in the form of anything the LORD your God has forbidden you* (23). They have been delivered from the *iron-smelting furnace* (20) of Egypt but they will experience the *consuming fire* (24) of God's wrath if they deliberately disobey him by turning to other gods. He is *a jealous God* (24) and will brook no rivals. The Israelites were the *people of his inheritance* (20) which meant that they could not belong to anybody else.

Idols are still offensive to God. Luther said, 'If a man will not have God, he must have his idols.' Idols are God-substitutes. They are not necessarily made of wood, stone or precious metal. Idols of that material kind were certainly in Moses' mind when he spoke to the people, but they could scarcely have been uppermost in the mind of the apostle John when he closed his first letter with the dramatic warning: 'Dear children, keep yourselves from idols.'[10] Even in the first century, he may well have been thinking of less tangible forms of idolatry such as those prevalent in our own time. Peter C. Moore unmasks several late twentieth-century idolatries such as self-worship (narcissism) and the adoration of pleasure (hedonism), world-views which need to be exposed and skilfully 'disarmed' by the well-informed Christian apologist.[11] In today's society personal

[10] 1 Jn. 5:21.   [11] Peter C. Moore, *Disarming the Secular Gods* (IVP, 1989).

idolatry might easily take the form of an unhelpful relationship, a damaging habit, a controlling passion, a sinister attraction, a materialistic preoccupation, a dominant idea. In the life of nations, ideologies speedily assume idolatrous proportions. Utilizing that wider canvas, Bob Goudzwaard exposes sophisticated modern idolatries like prosperity, security, power and nationalism, believing that they lie at the root of the contemporary world's most serious problems.[12] Anything is idolatrous if it comes between us and God.

c. His warning (4:25–28)

Idolatry was the worst possible misuse of God's two gifts – the law and the land. It was condemned in the law and, if practised, it would cost the Hebrew people the land. God warned them that if they or their successors broke that part of the agreement they would forfeit the right to live happily in the country he had given them.[13] To honour the law is to enjoy God's love; to disregard the law is to experience his anger (25). To obey the law is to live (1, 4); to disobey is to die (26). To keep the law is to be a *great nation* (6, 7); to reject it is to become a scattered people: *only a few of you will survive* (27). To heed the law is to be rescued from an enslaving despot (*the LORD took you and brought you out*, 20); to defy the law is to be handed over to a vain and profitless tyranny (*There you will worship man-made gods of wood and stone, which cannot see or hear*, 28). Later generations of Hebrew people were to experience for themselves the painful truth of this warning. After their settlement in the land, and despite the warning of many prophets, the Israelites gave themselves up to idolatrous worship. They ignored the threat and paid the penalty.[14]

The end of Moses' own life was to be a testimony to succeeding generations of the seriousness of sin. The Lord was angry with him on account of the people (21) he had led, served and represented. Just as they would not enter Canaan, neither would he. He would *die* within sight of *that good land* (22) while they would not even see its borders. Moses exhorted their children not to ignore the warning, *Be careful not to forget . . . do not make for yourselves an idol* (23). Obedience in this matter to the word of their sovereign Lord is of the greatest possible importance. Their forefathers had not accepted the promise; their children were in danger of forgetting the covenant (23).

---

[12] Bob Goudzwaard, *Idols of our Time* (IVP, 1984).

[13] See Gn. 2 for the close relation between law and love; they enjoyed the garden while they kept its law.

[14] 2 Ki. 17:1–23.

3. The merciful Deliverer (4:29–34)

In expounding the truth of God's promised deliverance Moses turns, first, to the people's future sins (27–31), then to their former mercies (32–34).

First, he talks about God's goodness to them in the *later days* (30). God's threatened judgment in casting them out of the land will not be an act of vindictive punishment but an expression of refining love. He knows that, in their prosperity, they will quickly forget him (6:10–12; 8:11–14); only adversity will bring them to their senses. When they have everything, they ignore the God who has filled their hands with innumerable blessings. Only when they have nothing will they value what they have lost. Despite the warnings, they will forget God; yet, despite their sins, he will not forget them. Even when we forsake God, he does not fail us (31). He loves his people so much that he cannot bear them to be away from him. God is so determined to bring them back that he carefully explains the process by which the offenders may return.

Just as he brought them out of Egypt, so he will redeem them from their new *distress* (30), even *from there* (29), the place of estrangement, guilt and desolation: *But if from there you seek the LORD your God ... you will return to the LORD your God* (29–30). Here are the conditions of a renewed deliverance: earnest seeking (*with all your heart*, 29), genuine repentance (*return to the LORD*) and immediate obedience (*and obey him*, 30). When offenders become penitents they make fresh discoveries of divine mercy. They know of his generosity to others but they prove for themselves that he is merciful, close (*he will not abandon you*) and dependable (*or forget the covenant with your forefathers which he confirmed to them by oath*, 31).

Secondly, Moses speaks about God's goodness in the former days: *Ask now about the former days* (32). The people are invited to reach back in history (*long before your time*) and reach out in space (*from one end of the heavens to the other*), to see if anyone had heard of greater things than what God had done for his people. Surely, his earlier mercy encourages their present repentance. They are to recall God's mighty acts as Creator (*God created*, 32), Revealer (*the voice of God speaking*, 33) and Redeemer (*the things the LORD your God did for you in Egypt*, 34). He has made us. He now appeals to us. He will deliver us. Those who turn from their sins recall with gratitude that he has welcomed sinners before; moreover, he has changed them. *That outstretched arm* (34) continues to reach to all who acknowledge their need of forgiveness and reconciliation. The triple testimony of Scripture, history and experience is that those who *seek* (29) have always found.

71

4. The incomparable Lover (4:35–49)

God acts in mercy because he loves in truth. He does not overlook our iniquities. He sits in judgment on them, knowing that, unchecked, they will ruin us. Sin is ruthlessly destructive. It damages the sinner, adversely affects others, and always grieves God. He speaks against it knowing that he alone can deal effectively with it. Therefore, Moses here presents the people with a portrait of God which meets the need of both penitent and restored sinners: God is incomparable (35–36, 39) and God is love (37–38). God's love is vividly portrayed here as unique, vocal, visual, continual and relevant.

It is important first to establish that God's love is unique. The Lord who loved their fathers is the only God: *there is no other* (35, 39). The gods their neighbours ignorantly worship and the useless idols which even God's people come to serve are mere nothings. Ridiculous projections of human fancy, they are incapable of loving because they have no substance in reality. Once they enter the land, some of the Israelites were to break the covenant and give themselves over to Baal, the agricultural god of the Canaanite people. But Baal cannot possibly love them; he does not even exist.

Moreover, God's love is vocal. We are not left to guess at his nature and hope that we might be loved. He tells us about it: *From heaven he made you hear his voice . . . and you heard his words from out of the fire* (36). The word of love which God speaks to his people is both authentic and relevant; it has a heavenly origin and an earthly application. God speaks in a variety of different circumstances because he wants us to know how much he loves us.

There are times, however, when no matter how supportive, words are not enough. Therefore, God's love is visual. Quite naturally, the captive Hebrew slaves wanted to see God in action. They knew from the great patriarchal narratives that he could speak to his people and, through Moses, he had spoken to them. They longed, however, to see God at work in their own time, and they did. It was *because he loved* their forefathers that he brought them out of Egypt. In the exodus he manifested his presence (*his great fire*, 36; see also 33; 5:24, 26) and demonstrated his power: it was *by his Presence and his great strength* (37). How could they possibly doubt his love when he had done so much for them?

Again, God's love is continual. Some of those people who stood in the plains of Moab might be tempted to say, 'Yes, I am convinced that God proved his love for our parents but how can we be sure that he loves us?' Here Moses says that he acted redemptively in the past not only because he loved their fathers but because he *chose their descendants after them* (37, see also 5:3). The people who entered the land are loved as much as those who did not see it. God's love is not confined to any one particular generation. He loves the descendants as well as the forefathers; he loves us as much as he loved them.

Moses closes this address by reminding the people that God's love is relevant. It is not simply a doctrinal topic about revelation and redemption in the past. He brought them out of Egypt in order to give them a land which he had generously prepared: *to bring you into their land to give it to you for your inheritance, as it is today* (38). Note the repetitive *today, this day* (38, 39, 40). God's love was and is dramatically up to date.

It was so contemporary and relevant that it included the precise location of places of refuge for the two and a half tribes who had already been allocated their territory in the newly conquered lands (41–43). The other tribes were later to be given similar 'cities of refuge' (19:2–13) to which anyone who killed a person accidentally might go for protection until the case had been brought before an Israelite judge. Blood-feuds were common everyday practice throughout the ancient Near East and an 'innocent' offender would be in immediate danger from the angry relatives of a victim; legal provision of this kind could only have been thought out (in advance of any trouble) by a God who loves.

This first reference to these 'cities of refuge' is a reminder of God's loving provision for Israel's future lifestyle. He is passionately concerned about sociological as well as theological issues. A vast number of desert nomads were about to make their homes in a new and different social environment (3:4, 10, 12; 6:10; 9:1). Their portable tents were to be replaced by permanent homes, the spacious desert exchanged for crowded streets and markets, their temporary pilgrim existence pass to a more predictable pattern of life. The inevitable changes would expose human vulnerability, demanding not only social flexibility but spiritual resourcefulness. The new life would involve them directly in matters of trade, commerce, local industry, housing, and God made it clear that he would not leave them without firm guidelines regarding life in the city. The way ahead was crowded with rich opportunities but it would also confront them with perilous temptations.

Urbanization is an important theme in Deuteronomy. The phrase 'in your gates' occurs some 25 times in this book, and is found only twice elsewhere in the Old Testament. God shared his high ideals for these developing cities. He planned that the new communities should be devoted to human justice (4:41–43; 19:2–13), spiritual integrity (13:12–18), ecological concern (20:19–20), moral responsibility (21:1–9; 22:13–24), family stability (21:18–21) and social compassion (25:5–10). The Lord longed that his people would 'be blessed in the city' as well as in the country (28:3) but that ideal would be realized only as people within cities acknowledged the uniqueness of his nature and the supremacy of his word (28:1–2, 14). God is still concerned about social, moral and economic issues, and Deuteronomy's insights continue to be relevant. They cannot be automatically transferred to contemporary urban contexts but they provide us with an important and graphic paradigm of God's unchanging values for life in the modern city.

B.   Expounding the covenant (4:44 – 11:32)

Deuteronomy 4:44 – 5:22
6.   Proclaimed in a loud voice

With the book's main introductory section behind us, we have now come to a series of further expositions which Moses gave to his fellow-Israelites before they entered the land. They extend throughout the greater part of the book (from 4:44 – 29:1) and their style, language and structure may well have been influenced by contemporary treaty-patterns, well-known throughout the ancient Near East at this time.

We recall that, following the description of historical relationships which opened such a treaty (1:1 – 4:43), it was usual then for the suzerain or dominant sovereign to list the agreed conditions of the covenant so that the dependant (or vassal) would be in no doubt whatever about his commitments. If the structure of this next section owes anything to these treaties, then chapters 5 – 11 outline the general principles, leaving chapters 12 – 28 to expound the more specific obligations of the covenant.

The central feature in this important passage is the Ten Commandments, sometimes called the Decalogue; they are the covenant obligations in embryo. To *hear, learn, do* (5:1), *keep* (29) and *teach* (31) these commandments, honestly and compassionately applying them to everyday conduct, is to *fear* God (29) and *live* (33) well in the land he has given. There is a sense in which the Decalogue is the main 'text' from which Moses preaches about the covenant. Later sections of Deuteronomy amplify, expound and apply these commandments to the new circumstances the Israelites will face when they enter the land. When interpreting the message of the commandments it is important to examine their context, source, appeal, style, nature and basis, so that we can better appreciate their relevance in late twentieth-century society.

1.   Their historical context

In common with other treaties, this covenant describes the previous relationships between the two parties and the historical background of the agreement (4:44–49; 5:2). The acts of God in history are highly significant for the Israelite people; the God who demands their allegiance is the one who has met their needs. The Lord has done something for them before he asks anything of them. He has delivered them from the power and dominion of a cruel suzerain in Egypt (5:6) and they are glad to be under totally different ownership, 'the people of his inheritance' (4:20). Moreover, he did not only help them *when they came out of Egypt* (4:45) but, more recently, has continued to give them victory over their enemies (4:46–49). The God who speaks is a God who saves.

The covenant made at Horeb (5:2) was now being renewed in the presence of all the people before they went on to make new conquests. The agreement is set within a clear historical framework. It describes something which actually happened, at a precise location and at a given time. The nations which surrounded them had endless stories to relate about the activities of their gods but they were mere fanciful tales, passed on from one generation to the other. They described the adventures of gods and goddesses whose favour could be won by performing certain religious acts, even made happy by the offering of human sacrifice. But none of the stories was true because none of the gods was real. Israel's God, the only God, spoke to his people at Sinai. It was a true story of what actually happened in history and a story of a God who gives before he commands.

2. Their authoritative source

Unlike the treaties and agreements between the surrounding nations, this was not a contract of human design; it was not a covenant between equal parties. Everything in the narrative emphasizes the majesty and glory of the God who initiates the agreement. The physical setting in which the obligations were given to Moses for the people is described in graphic and arresting detail (5:4–5). A sense of awe and widespread fear pervaded the camp. God was speaking with Moses, and the Israelites kept away, afraid even to approach the foothills of the mountain. For most of the time, the heavy clouds and *thick darkness* (22) hid most of the scene from their view, but occasionally there were glimpses of the beyond. Then they could see that the summit was ablaze with a great fire (a detail constantly repeated throughout this chapter, 4–5, 22–26) and the people were terrified of the consuming flames (25). In addition to these visible manifestations of God's presence there was the inescapable message, the *loud voice* (22) of God's word. The suzerain was speaking and his vassals were compelled to listen. The visible phenomena of cloud, darkness and fire conveyed to the people an unforgettable sense of God's greatness and transcendence, his holiness and uniqueness. Here was no neighbouring monarch, making a convenient agreement with a dependent nation. This covenant had five features; it was to be binding (*You shall . . . You shall not*), exclusive (7–8), compassionate (*showing love*, 10), reciprocal[1] (*two tablets*) and permanent (*. . . of stone*, 22). It must be honoured because of its origin and source. God gave the covenant and it must be neither mutilated (4:2) nor manipulated.

3. Their inclusive appeal

This covenant was for *all Israel* (1), a phrase found in the opening and closing sentences of Deuteronomy and one which constantly recurs throughout the book (11:6; 13:12; 18:6; 21:21; 27:9; 29:1; 31:1, 7, 11 [twice]; 32:45). It reminds the people that the unity of their nation is the gift of God. There is *one* God (6:4) who by this unique agreement has made them into his own people, formed them into *one* nation, giving them this *one* law. God has set down these covenant-conditions for his people and the stipulations govern the lives of *all*. There was no opting out, and no room for the individual Israelite to determine his own ideals in isolation from the rest. The rules are for everyone. The people are bound together with strong chords of loyalty to God and to one another. To break this covenant was not only to grieve God but to harm one's fellows. Moses is a realist, however. The later teaching of the book anticipates the rebellious and arrogant independence of groups and individuals who, either publicly or secretly, will argue vigorously for their freedom to worship idols (*e.g.* 13:1–18; 29:18). As far as such people are concerned, the covenant may well be for many, or for others, but not for *all*.

The idea that God sets basic standards for everybody is hardly popular in today's world. People will argue vigorously for the right of the individual to behave exactly as he or she wishes, without any interference whatever from any outside party. They will claim that circumstances differ, and insist on far more flexible patterns of conduct, 'situation ethics' rather than fixed norms. Joseph Fletcher's influential book of that title[2] claimed that nothing is universally

---

[1] Meredith G. Kline suggests that the Decalogue was, in accordance with current treaty practice, recorded fully on both stones, one for each party to the covenant, *cf. Treaty of the Great King: The Covenant Structure of Deuteronomy* (Eerdmans, 1963), pp. 17ff., and the same author's *The Structure of Biblical Authority* (Eerdmans, 1972), pp. 113–125.

[2] J. Fletcher, *Situation Ethics* (SCM, 1966).

77

right or wrong, or intrinsically good or bad. The only thing which is intrinsically and invariably 'good' is love, and everything must be judged by love, and by Fletcher's second principle, justice. By this reasoning, the Ten Commandments may be respected but also discarded if, in the light of individual experience, any or all of them seem to inhibit the exercise of love and justice. But how can men and women with limited knowledge, inevitable bias, or unhelpful presuppositions decide what is 'loving' and 'just' in any given situation without the help of fixed norms and divinely ordained values?

In recent years New Age teachers have promulgated ethical views which are similarly dismissive about objective moral standards, maintaining that 'right' and 'wrong' are merely human illusions which enlightened people can disregard. One of their leading writers, Marilyn Ferguson, insists that 'Human nature is neither good nor bad, but open to continuous transformation and transference'.[3] Such people naturally hold that, uninhibited by a divine code of human behaviour, men and women are totally free to shape their own standards of morality, especially if, along with most New Agers, they believe they are part of God anyway.

The outstanding feature about God's covenant, however, was that in the Decalogue it presented firm irrevocable ideals for *all* God's people, not for a select minority who might be attracted to them. There was to be no variability. David was not exempt from the charge of serious adultery[4] simply because he wore the crown. When God sets his standards there are no favoured exceptions.

4. Their didactic style

The covenant must not only be heard but learnt, not merely to imbibe religious information but in order to convey these timeless truths to the next generation. Other people have the right to hear as well as ourselves, not least our children. Education is an important feature in Deuteronomy. If the message is to be passed on to succeeding generations then it needs to be cast in a form which is easily transmissible. Memorizing the Ten Commandments, the heart of the law, may even have been aided visually in a nomadic community by using the fingers and thumbs of both hands. Verbally, the covenant's terms are succinctly presented in terse sentences, easily recalled by the person who has taken the trouble to *learn* (1) them. We have a responsibility to convey these standards to our contemporaries. Millions of children in our world are ignorant of God's unchanging values for secure and happy living.

[3] M. Ferguson, *The Aquarian Conspiracy* (Paladin Grafton Books, 1988), p. 30.
[4] 2 Sa. 11.

Although initially these were the rules for God's covenant people, they address people of all races. Here, the world's Creator[5] confronts mankind in general with instructions for life which any modern community ignores at its peril. History testifies to the grim truth that those societies which reject these laws end in death. God's reiterated word, *that you may live* (33; 4:1; 8:1; 16:20; 30:16, 19), is an encouragement to the obedient and a warning to the rebel.

5. Their obligatory nature

Although it clearly has immense educative value, the covenant demands more than a well-stored memory and the spirit of eager communication. It presents us with things to be *done* as well as words to be said: *be careful to do them* (1, RSV). The truth must be put into practice. God knew that throughout the succeeding generations there would be people who would be intellectually conversant with these obligations but indifferent to their claims. Disobedience is probably the worst of sins, and warnings about its dangers are given special prominence in New as well as Old Testament teaching. Achan knew that theft was wrong but he did it.[6] Gideon knew that covetousness was forbidden by the law but it still became his 'snare'.[7] David must have known the commandments and cannot possibly have been in doubt about God's mind on covetousness (his neighbour's wife), theft, adultery and murder, yet he still went in to Bathsheba, and ordered the death of her husband.[8] Ahab knew the offence of idolatry, covetousness, false witness, theft and murder in the sight of God, but he was still partner to these sick sins.[9] These sad stories are told in Scripture as a warning. None of these people sinned in ignorance. They knew *the statutes and the ordinances* well enough but were not *careful to do them* (1, RSV).

6. Their theological basis

Moses had a clear priority in his preaching. He was not allowed to accompany the people into Canaan but he could at least educate them. One of the finest things he could do for his contemporaries was to provide them with a majestic concept of God. We noted in chapter 4, for example, Moses' portrayal of God as a generous Giver, sovereign Lord, merciful Deliverer and incomparable Lover (4:1–43), and here in this passage the Ten Commandments present us with further descriptive pictures of the nature and attributes of God. There are as many portraits of God in the Decalogue as there are commandments, and the ethics of believers are their practical

[5] Ex. 20:11.   [6] Jos. 7:21.   [7] Jdg. 8:24–27.   [8] 2 Sa. 11:1–27.
[9] 1 Ki. 16:29–34; 21:1–26.

response to all they know of the character of God. It is a theme which belongs to the New Testament as well as to the Old. Christians are to be holy, loving, merciful and pure because the Lord himself is all those things.[10]

So, even within the narrow compass of the Decalogue, the Lord is portrayed as the unique God: *I am the LORD your God* (6). 'I am' recalls the very name by which God revealed himself to Moses as he had stood in the desert, forty years earlier, arrested by the unusual sight of a bush blazing with inextinguishable fire.[11] He is their powerful God, able to act redemptively for downtrodden and disheartened people: *who brought you out of . . . the house of bondage* (6, RSV). He is a personal God, for throughout these commandments the Lord is described as '*your* God' (6, 9, 11–12, 14–16); they are people who enjoy an intimate personal relationship with him. But they only do so because he has chosen them. He is the sovereign God who set his love upon them. The story of Israel's redemption did not begin with their choice of him.

A doctrinal reason is given for the prohibition about idolatry; it is because the Lord is a *jealous God* (9). Those who disobey that commandment will also prove that he is a righteous God, *visiting the iniquity of the fathers upon the children to the third and fourth generation* (9, RSV). We cannot, in other words, play 'fast and loose' with God. Human behaviour has moral consequences and, above all things, the various corrupt and damaging forms of idolatry will have a disastrous effect on future generations.

The Lord, however, is also a compassionate God who delights to show *steadfast love to thousands of those who love me and keep my commandments* (10, RSV). That word translated *steadfast love* is one of the most important in the whole Hebrew vocabulary. It is essentially a covenant word; it denotes the kind of dependable love which is characteristic of a totally reliable partner in an agreement. In other words God says 'I am not a capricious kind of God like the Baals of the land you are about to enter, gods which might do you a particular favour in return for something special you might sacrifice to them, gods whose love can be bought or earned. I am a faithful God who not only says he will show steadfast love to future generations, but does.'

Moreover, the commandments present a picture of a holy God whose name is to be honoured and revered (11). He is also a benevolent God who longs that all may *go well* for his people in the land which the Lord their God *gives* (16) them. He is a vocal God who constantly addresses his people about the most important issues in life. They are not spiritually and intellectually bereft, left to

---

[10] Lv. 11:44–45; 1 Pet. 1:15–16; 1 Jn. 4:11; Lk. 6:36; 1 Jn. 3:3.   [11] Ex. 3:14–15.

pursue an isolated theological quest or expected to discover basic essential truths for themselves. God speaks to them authoritatively, attractively, persuasively and effectively. The people are told to do *as the LORD your God commanded* you (16).

The Decalogue, therefore, is not simply a compact code of human behaviour; it is an arresting portrait of God. God is a God of truth, so the people must not indulge in lies (20). He is the giver of life[12] so they must not murder (17), ruthlessly snatching what is God's property. He is generous, so they must be kind to needy people in society as well as to their more familiar relatives and neighbours. God has been loving to outcasts of conventional society (like helpless Israelite slaves in Egypt, for example, 15), so they must be equally loving to similarly disadvantaged people in the land he is about to give them – social outcasts like widows, orphans and aliens. He is the unique Creator who not only gives life but sustains it. He is concerned about necessary rest not only for humans but for animals as well (13), and his children must not ignore such practical needs in local communities. All the demands of the Decalogue are a reflection of the nature of God. The image of God and the standards he expects of his people are inseparably woven together in the fabric of the Ten Commandments.

7. Their contemporary relevance

Although it originated in the world of antiquity, the Decalogue is never out of date; it is for us as well as for them. The people who listened to this word prior to their march towards Canaan are here reminded that the Lord their God *made a covenant with us* (not them) *in Horeb* (2), and to emphasize the point Moses went on to say, *Not with our fathers did the LORD make this covenant, but with us, who are all of us here alive this day* (3, RSV). The fact, security, blessings and obligations of the covenant were not simply for the people who saw the theophany and heard the voice in the Sinai desert. *All Israel* (1:1) did not merely mean 'everybody present at Sinai' any more than it restrictively meant everybody present at the law's second promulgation by Moses. It was, of course, given to them but not only to them; this truth was for all who would follow them in the covenant-community.

The message of the Ten Commandments is highly relevant in the more sophisticated and complex structures of modern society. The most important thing about them is that they explain who we *are* and not simply what we should do or not do. Their teaching makes it clear that in our different, but no less sinful, world we are people

[12] Gn. 2:7.

81

who have been made by God the Creator to live as committed worshippers, caring partners and dependent children.

a. Committed worshippers

There is a God-shaped vacuum in every human life, and uncultured, illiterate, uneducated people in the most remote tribes of the world have a desire to reach out beyond the limited confines of their own lives to confess their dependence on someone or something greater than themselves. The introduction to the Decalogue (6) and its opening commandments (7–11) deal with the relationship of men and women to their Creator. Nobody can possibly live the kind of satisfying and fulfilled life for which they were made unless they are rightly related to their Maker. The commandments are, as one writer has described them, 'the Maker's Instructions'.[13] People have seriously damaged valuable and delicate equipment because they have used it for some purpose other than that for which it was made. Our lives can be seriously, even eternally, ruined if we totally neglect the Creator's purposes for them. The Decalogue's initial instructions concern our relationship to the Maker; once they are honoured there is every likelihood that the rest will be obeyed. They tell us that men and women must acknowledge, exalt, reverence and remember their Creator.

Committed worshippers acknowledge God's uniqueness. The worshipper's basic requirement is to know who God is. The Israelite people are about to enter a land with its own deities. In their journeys they have passed through or alongside territory littered with a bewildering variety of local or tribal gods, and in their later history they were to meet many more. Before they can offer their adoring worship to God they need to know who he is. Which God are they to honour? The Lord here begins the instructions by identifying himself to all who would offer their worship to him: *I am the Lord your God, who brought you out of Egypt, out of the land of slavery* (6).

The God we are to worship is the God of *revelation* (the 'I am' of the desert encounter with Moses, Ex. 3:14) and *redemption* (who delivered his people from tyrannical enslavement). Once in Canaan, they will be constantly confronted by hilltop Baal shrines, and the strong and insidious temptation will be to worship these novel gods of the new land. They will only overcome that alluring danger by reminding themselves of the only true God, the one who had brought them out of Egypt and brought them into Canaan, a God who had spoken authoritatively to them at Sinai and acted savingly

[13] Eileen Bebbington, *The Maker's Instructions: Six Bible study outlines on the Ten Commandments* (Bible Society, 1986).

for them throughout their history. So the commandments begin not with a command but with a description. People who want to obey God must first be persuaded of his nature, word and deeds.

Committed worshippers exalt God's transcendence. Because he is unique they must not have any other gods *before*, literally 'in front of' him or 'before his face' (7). It describes the effrontery of some-one who can sin blatantly in the presence of the God who has clearly forbidden it. The Israelites are told that God can never be one, even a favourite one, among several deities. Such teaching ran counter to the popular religious ideas in their day, for other religions were not remotely exclusive in their demands. Syncretism was widely permissible. Israel must not imagine, however, that they can worship him alongside the Baals, gradually accommodating their worship to the religious practices of their new neighbours. There is nothing antiquated about this prohibition; it has a strik-ingly modern ring about it. In a pluralistic society we are in danger of tacitly acknowledging the uniqueness of God but at the same time honouring other claimants to our loyalty.

If there are to be no rivals, then the Israelite people must not make *an idol in the form of anything . . . You shall not bow down to them or worship them* (8–9). Ours is an idolatrous age, though modern idols are ideas rather than statues. The gods of the late twentieth century are surprisingly like those old Canaanite deities. Baal was the god of self, power, sex and things, and these four highly relevant contemporary idolatries are starkly exposed within the narrow compass of the Decalogue – egotism, despotism, sen-sualism and materialism.

The idolization of self (adoring ourselves) is a common form of contemporary worship. Baal was the pragmatic god of self-interest; you worshipped him for what you got out of it, good harvests, large families, increased herds and successful battles. Egotism is not the antiquated peculiarity of Canaanite religion. The Ten Command-ments address the problem of idolatrous worshippers in every cen-tury, people who put self before God, others, love and truth. We worship at the shrine of 'self before God' whenever our avaricious 'I want' screams louder than God's 'You shall not'. The cult of 'myself before others' insists that personal interests have priority over kind-ness to others, as, for example, if Israel ignored the prohibition about compelling slaves and animals to work on the Sabbath. It is 'self before love', for example, when we want our own way instead of honouring parents, and the marriage bond; or 'self before truth', when someone is prepared to give a false testimony in a court of law in order to guarantee some personal gain.

The idolization of power (asserting ourselves) is another form of contemporary worship. Baal was the military god of war and aggression. The commandments about the misuse of the divine name referred not only to blasphemy but also to any attempt to misuse God's name for one's own ends (as in a curse), and the idolization of power was certainly exposed by the prohibition of murder.

The idolization of sex (pleasing ourselves) is conspicuously relevant in our late twentieth-century world. Baalism was a fertility cult, notorious for its pornographic idols and sexual permissiveness; its ritual acts included degrading forms of both male and female prostitution. This is not only behind the prohibition about adultery but also about covetousness – *your neighbour's wife* is first in that list. In other words, the stories of the sexual activities of the Baals must not be re-enacted in the behaviour of Israelite marriage partners. Their God is holy, righteous, loving and dependable. He has entered into a love-contract with his people, and if they are to worship him then they must live like him. Modern society has become sex-obsessed and the divine gift of sex, exclusively reserved for the marriage relationship, has been seriously misused, perverted and degraded by pre- and extra-marital sexual relationships.

The idolization of things (satisfying ourselves) is forcefully addressed in the prohibitions about theft and covetousness. Canaanite religion was unashamedly materialistic. Baal was an agricultural god who would reward his worshippers with a substantial harvest even though the cost might be grossly excessive like child sacrifice (18:10). Deliberately opposed to all that, God's people must not be grasping materialists, but generous like the God who created and redeemed them.

The most serious aspect of contemporary idolatry is that this world has already been given a perfect image of God in the person of his Son, Jesus Christ. The early Christians had no need whatever of carved idols for they had seen God in the face of Christ. For true believers, he alone is 'the image (literally *eikon*) of the invisible God'.[14] To set up an idol, either physical, social or conceptual, is to dishonour, disregard or displace Jesus.

At its beginning, therefore, the Decalogue insists on God's exclusive right to our total allegiance. If the Israelite people were to enter in to this covenant-agreement with him then they must understand from the start there can be no other gods whatever.

Committed worshippers reverence God's name (11). Blasphemy has become one of the desperately sad features of contemporary life. The Lord's name is constantly dishonoured, and many thousands of children in our society only hear the name of God's Son in blasphemy. I have a teacher-friend who, talking about Jesus to an

---

[14] Col. 1:15; 2 Cor. 4:4.

entrants class, was politely rebuked by one of her children for swearing. Christians certainly need to be alert to the danger of serious relaxation in Blasphemy Laws, and be ready to take appropriate initiatives whenever related matters come under parliamentary discussion.

The prohibition about misusing God's name in Israel, however, did not relate solely to blasphemy. In fact, the Israelites had such an innate reverence for God that they were reluctant even to mention his name and, whatever the provocation, no devout Hebrew would dream of blaspheming; the issue was more subtle than that. Once on 'Baal territory' with its moral indifference, they might easily misuse the Lord's name by including it in a cruel curse or even to support a blatant untruth in a legal case. In ancient Near Eastern society, the curse was regarded as an irrevocable verbal missile, a fierce destructive weapon, and the Lord was concerned that his children did not resort to damaging abuse of that kind. The Canaanite world was preoccupied with spiritism, occultism and various forms of witchcraft, and here the Hebrew people were being warned in advance not to misuse God's holy name by using it in a spell or any form of magical ceremony; his children must never engage in such corrupt, abominable and forbidden practices (18:9–13).

Committed worshippers remember God's goodness (12–15). He has given them a special day on which they should deliberately recall his mercies as Creator[15] and Redeemer (15). The God who made us knows only too well that rest and relaxation must form a necessary part of the rhythm of each week, and honouring him on that day will also mean that we refrain from secular work, giving time to think about spiritual things, exalting him by our worship, witness and service.

Those who take this commandment seriously also recognize that daily work is his choice gift to us (*Six days you shall labour*, 13), so we will not take employment for granted. Wide-spread experience has shown that unemployment can give rise to a serious loss of human dignity, gnaw away at our personal respect, create boredom, and can even change one's personality, thereby endangering family life. Christians who experience redundancy must remember, however, that other forms of 'work' may honour God far more than remunerated service. Nobody can possibly deny the incomparable value of the housewife's work, but it is never undertaken with a weekly or monthly pay-packet as its constant incentive. Most of us will for ever be indebted to unsalaried mothers. 'Unemployed' people may find unique opportunities for invaluable service within the local community through compassionate voluntary work, or in

[15] Ex. 20:11.

the local church by serving faithfully amongst the elderly, sick, lonely, disabled, or with children and young people. Some churches have pioneered imaginative ventures to create employment opportunities, even on a modest scale, for deprived people in the local community. Other Christians have organized day-centres where unemployed men and women can meet for friendly contact, support, advice and worthwhile activities. Such beneficial work may be far more glorifying to God than that which attracts impressive salaries.

b. Caring partners

The prohibition about the Sabbath (12–15) illustrates the impossibility of isolating sharply those commandments which define loyalty to God from those which concern behaviour in society. The Sabbath day was every Israelite's opportunity to honour God, not only by giving time to praise, learning, and witness, but also by showing practical compassion for others – members of the family, the household's servants, even its animals, and the refugee who has just arrived in the local town or village. The Sabbath commandment is a striking reminder that God's people cannot separate their adoration of God from their attitude to their fellows. Although the opening commandments deal primarily with the believers' relationship with their Creator, they also relate to matters of social concern – they expose the idolater who might lead his neighbours astray by adopting Canaanite worship patterns, or misuse the divine name for the purposes of a curse, or make his family or employees work on a day of essential rest. In a more direct manner, however, the later commandments deal with life in the community and are arrestingly relevant in our own time.

In Deuteronomy the Sabbath commandment reminds Israel of her redemption (15) while in Exodus it is firmly set within the context of creation. After his work God 'rested', and those who rest on that day follow the divine example.[16] Those words suggest that we are dealing here with a creation ordinance. Whichever context we recall for this commandment, both contain a specific injunction about rest from daily work (14). Employers are not to behave like Egyptian taskmasters, denying leisure, but like God who encourages rest.

Christian believers may not be able to compel their secularized contemporaries to adopt biblical principles on this subject, but they should certainly attempt to persuade them that what is essential for God's people must be beneficial for society. It is not simply that the

[16] Ex. 20:11.

day provides believers with an opportunity for regular worship and witness; it is a weekly testimony to the inviolable necessity of physical rest and regular restoration after a full week's work. Some kind of break is vital or the quality of work will soon deteriorate. All of us need to be diverted from our daily work, however worthwhile, interesting or rewarding it may be, or even that can become a subtle form of idolatry. With its clear prohibition about making people work, the Sabbath commandment reminds us not only that we must worship God but also that we are forbidden to live selfishly in community.

Obsessive self-absorption is a regrettable characteristic of modern life. People act primarily for their own satisfaction rather than in the interests of society. Geoffrey Lean of the *Observer* described the past decade as 'the Egoistic Eighties ... the decade when self-interest became sanctified'. It was the decade when 'we were told on the highest authority that "there is no such thing as society, only individuals"'. The commandments are directly concerned with social life and community health and address some of the most important issues in the contemporary world. Men and women who have been made in the image of a loving and living God must be concerned, as he is, about love and life. Like the God they worship they must be passionately committed to the cultivation of love and the preservation of life.

The loving God is concerned about the cultivation of love. The fifth and seventh commandments take us to the heart of all human relationships, the family unit. It can only work harmoniously if there is proper respect for both parents (16) and partners (18). Parents must be 'honoured', which in Hebrew meant something more than the respectful recognition of the parents' existence, but a dutiful submission to their authority, and a loving provision for their needs. Later in the book this particular commandment is amplified and illustrated in the injunctions given regarding a rebellious and disobedient son (21:18–21). There, the punishment is severe because, despite the parents' pleading, the son deliberately despises the family unit and acts in a manner totally unworthy of someone made in the image of a loving, caring, attentive and generous God. If this profligate son had honoured his parents he would have been their obedient child, compassionate helper and kind supporter.

In practical terms, honouring parents meant making provision for their care in old age, ensuring that they had adequate material resources when they were no longer physically capable of maintaining themselves by daily work. There is little doubt that this commandment also addressed a spiritual priority as well as a social provision. Honouring one's parents meant following their faith.

87

The covenant which God made with his people at Sinai drew them all into a believing community in which the family's spiritual values played an important role. The education of children was entrusted to believing parents and just as the father and mother were to share the truth faithfully with their children, so the children were to receive the truth gratefully from their parents.

Naturally, the cultivation of love was important not only towards elderly parents but for married partners. The adultery prohibition (18) is based on the distinctive holiness of Israel's God who is loving and dependable. If his covenant-partners are to be, as he demands, like him, then they too must be loyal in their relationships. A partner who is committed by covenant to exclusive faithfulness must never violate that agreement by having sexual relationships with another person. This commandment is certainly relevant in our own time. In contemporary society, marriage has been described as a dying institution. The divorce rate rises tragically every year.

The living God is also concerned about the preservation of life: *You shall not murder* (17). God is the giver of life. Breath was his unique gift to newly created mankind[17] and no person has any right to rob another human being of that infinitely precious gift. In today's world there is an alarming disregard for human life. Responsible citizens are naturally concerned about the increase in violence; barbaric acts of cruelty are a constantly disturbing feature in our newspaper columns. The biblical world was familiar with the incidence of human slaughter; both Old and New Testaments begin their story with grim accounts of jealous murder. Neither Cain nor Herod could bear the idea that another human being might have precedence over them.[18] The Bible, however, exposes their sin for what it is and both offenders are brought under the direct judgment of a righteous God.

Three contemporary issues concerning the preservation of life make this commandment forcefully relevant in our own time – abortion, euthanasia and suicide.

The prohibition about taking life must relate to the fate of the unborn child. With the declining popularity of marriage and the increasing social acceptability of cohabitation, unwanted pregnancy is one of the saddest features of modern society. A conservative estimate of the latest abortion figures claims that every time our heart beats an unborn baby dies somewhere in the world. Evangelical Christians base their resistance to indiscriminate abortion on the biblical conviction that every man and woman is made in the image of God.[19] Conceived of the Holy Spirit, Jesus became flesh in the womb of his virgin mother, and from the moment

---

[17] Gn. 2:7.   [18] Gn. 4:1–10; Mt. 2:16–18.   [19] Gn. 1:26–27.

of that conception, shared our humanity. Without exception, every human life has, from the moment of conception to the moment of death, a distinctive dignity which is to be respected. In the light of this sixth commandment Christians should do everything possible to protect unborn children, through personal influence, pastoral care and appropriate political pressure regarding legislation.[20]

Euthanasia is another subject of urgent contemporary debate which, in the light of this commandment must seriously disturb the Christian conscience and, once again, prompt believers to insist on reverence for human life, whatever the personal requests of the person concerned. This commandment prohibits any human being from taking another person's life, whatever the circumstances. Yet, we live in a society where secularist thinkers demand that human freedom be extended to the control of life. The Young Humanists sector of the British Humanist Association urges its school student members to put pressure on religious education teachers to invite speakers to their schools who will defend humanist ideas about voluntary euthanasia. Once again, believing people need to be vigilant in pressing for the regular presentation in schools and elsewhere of Christian ideals about the sanctity of life.

Suicide is self-murder and is firmly prohibited by this commandment. God is the unique giver of life at conception, and only he is free to remove it at death. The early Christian people rejoiced that the keys of death[21] were in the hands of the Lord Jesus alone; their destiny was not at the mercurial whim of some local Roman magistrate who might summarily order their execution. They genuinely believed that they would not pass into eternity until the moment which God has set, and throughout the centuries Christians have rejoiced in that same certainty. However grim the conditions of life, no committed and obedient Christian can seriously contemplate suicide. When life's circumstances are desperately difficult, they present us with a renewed challenge to trust a caring God for promised peace and strength, not a time for blatant disobedience to a divine command which firmly prohibits self-murder.

Because God wants us to cultivate our caring partnership within society, he makes us responsible for maintaining high standards of community conduct. The last three commandments remind us of our accountability to him for our actions (19), speech (20) and

---

[20] For a discussion of these issues see John Stott, *Issues Facing Christians Today* (Marshall, Morgan and Scott, 1984), pp. 280–300, and Francis A. Schaeffer and C. Everett Koop, *Whatever Happened to the Human Race?* (Marshall, Morgan and Scott, 1980), particularly chapters 1 and 4.

[21] Rev. 1:17–18.

thought (21). We must not steal, give false testimony, or covet another person's property.

Accountability for our actions is focused in the commandment about theft (19). No society can organize its life harmoniously and creatively without a mutual respect for the law of property. In the later chapters of the book, the commandment not to steal is applied to specific instances of land-acquisition and similar thieving offences. Men and women need to live peacefully in the assurance that their goods will not be stolen, yet in today's world there are few places where people's minds can be at rest about such matters. Theft of every kind is widespread; crime is on the increase in many societies. Materialism has firm control of the popular mind, and even among men and women with normal moral principles, petty thieving is widely prevalent. In modern Britain, for example, an astonishing number of people are convicted every week of travelling on railways without paying a fare. The numbers of television licence 'dodgers' rises alarmingly every year. In Britain such people are now being tracked down at the rate of 1,000 a day. In May 1991, a Post Office spokesman said that a total of 373,000 had been discovered in the previous twelve months, 50,000 more than the previous year's record figure. It is reliably estimated that 1.8 million households in the UK are still watching television without paying for their licence.[22] In this important commandment a generous God forbids his people to steal.

A truthful God forbids his people to lie (20). In their best moments, the Hebrew people hated deceit of any kind. A 'lying tongue' and the words of 'a false witness who pours out lies' are among the seven things which the Lord finds 'detestable' about human sin.[23] Accountability for our speech is illustrated here in its relation to Israel's divinely appointed legal system. If an offender is brought before their judges, the evidence of reliable witnesses is of crucial importance. The last two commandments envisage the danger of manipulation in an Israelite context of law whereby a covetous judge might accept a bribe and so pervert the cause of justice.

It would be a mistake, however, to confine this commandment rigidly within the legal context in which it is set. Any form of lying is forbidden by this commandment, not solely the deliberate telling of an untruth whilst under oath in a court of law. We also break this commandment if we contribute in any way to damaging verbal traffic about somebody's good name and, as Calvin says, there are few who 'do not notoriously labour under this disease'. For any 'eagerness to listen to slander, and an unbecoming proneness to

[22] *The Times*, 4 May, 1991.   [23] Pr. 6:16–19.

censorious judgment' are alike condemned here.[24] The person who is being slandered may well be guilty of some offence or other, but are we in possession of all the facts? Are we sure that the details pleasurably conveyed to us have not been distorted, manipulated or perverted in order to convince us of the slanderer's sordid opinion? We dishonour the name of our totally trustworthy God if ever we indulge in profitless gossip, or become guilty of wild exaggeration or of spreading damaging rumours. The Bible makes it dauntingly clear that deliberate deceivers have no place in God's heaven,[25] and that should still the tongue of the liar.

The Decalogue ends by emphasizing our accountability for sins of thought: *You shall not covet* (21). The closing commandment exposes humanity's lust for things. It is the sin of our age, a world in which alluring television advertisements portray expensive possessions which may be acquired without effort, and instant credit schemes appeal to the prospective purchaser to 'take the waiting out of wanting'. But, as Joy Davidman has reminded us, nobody can

> reasonably expect happiness from an insatiable appetite ... No matter how many fat sheep the rich man had, it was always the poor man's ewe lamb that caught his eye. No-one who had once learned to identify happiness with wealth ever felt that he had wealth enough.[26]

The other commandments forbid specific actions, but this one challenges the ceaseless mental activity of an envious spirit. It reminds us that sin is spawned in the craving thought before it proceeds to the rapacious action. Behaviour which violated the other commandments could usually be detected, condemned and judged, but the Decalogue's closing prohibition reminds us that sin in its worst forms cannot always be seen. This commandment, however, presupposes the omniscience of God who knows our desires and can read the intents of our hearts. It takes us directly to the inwardness of Israel's faith. The Lord God was not simply concerned about details of formal religious ceremonial or correct moral conduct; he wants our hearts to be right before him.

Once again, this commandment may be preparing the Israelite people for their prospective encounter with Baal-religion, for the Ugaritic texts have shown that Baal was a covetous god. In other words, God is telling his people that they must not live in the way Baal-worshippers do, lusting after other people's treasured things. They must be like Israel's unique God – holy (no other gods), loyal (no idols), kind (not using his name improperly in a curse), loving

[24] Calvin, *Institutes of the Christian Religion*, II, 8. 48.   [25] Rev. 21:27.
[26] Joy Davidman, *Smoke on the Mountain*, pp. 109–110.

(not causing others to work on the Sabbath), protective (honour father and mother), generous (do not steal; do not covet), faithful (do not commit adultery), and true (do not give false testimony). It has been rightly said that the 'imitation of God' is one of the important models for understanding Old Testament ethics; the 'appeal of the Ten Commandments is not just to do what God says but be like him'.[27] Eichrodt maintains that, in Old Testament teaching, God's 'purpose of sanctification is understood as a moulding of man in accordance with his own image'.[28]

The Ten Commandments are strikingly relevant in our own time. They teach us that spiritual obedience must have priority over *self*, that social compassion must transcend the personal lust for *power*, that moral values are more important than *sexual satisfaction*, and that eternal realities are more satisfying than *things*. It is amazing how comprehensive as well as relevant they are, dealing with the right attitude to our Maker (no other gods), to ourselves (the importance of rest), to children, servants, animals (the Sabbath commandment), parents (honour father and mother), one's partner in marriage (no adultery), neighbours and aliens.

c. Dependent children

The Decalogue is a magnificent signpost, clearly showing us the way to live, but it does not impart the power to make the journey. It exposes sin but cannot provide the strength to overcome it. Something more is necessary. The final commandment, *You shall not covet* ... reminds us that sin begins in the human heart. The commandments drive the dependent child of God into the presence of a loving Father for mercy and strength.

First, we need mercy: to read this covenant-agreement is to realize that we have failed to obey (27), keep (29) and do *what the* LORD ... *has commanded* (32) in this law. Luther, Calvin and the English Puritans taught their contemporaries that God's Law in the commandments was like a mirror which shows us what we are really like in the presence of a holy God. The Ten Commandments are like 'the bright glass of the Law wherein we may see the evil of sin'.[29] Our first response to the Decalogue is penitence. The commandments show how far short we have fallen from God's intended standard for our lives, and the only possible way to get rid of our sin is to confess it. With the return to a firmly biblical faith, the sixteenth-century Reformers soon recognized the important place

[27] J. Barton, 'Understanding Old Testament Ethics' (*Journal for the Study of the Old Testament* 9), pp. 44, 59ff.
[28] Walther Eichrodt, *Theology of the Old Testament*, II (SCM, 1967), p. 373.
[29] Jeremiah Burroughs, *Evil of Evils* (1654), pp. 80, 124.

of these commandments in a Reformed liturgy. Both Luther and Calvin produced metrical versions of the commandments with *Kyrie eleison* as a refrain after each verse. The Decalogue confronts us with our need for mercy, and perhaps we need to be reminded of that whenever we meet for worship. In the brief period of the Reformation under Edward VI in England, the commandments were for a time recited at the beginning of the Anglican service,[30] as if to emphasize that this is the first thing we do when we come into God's presence: confess that we are sinners.

Secondly, the Ten Commandments remind us that we need strength. We cannot possibly have the power to obey God's word in this comprehensive law unless he is its donor. The Decalogue's introduction reminds us that God has not only spoken (revelation) but acted (redemption) for his people. If, with his mighty hand, he brought his people *out of Egypt, out of the land of slavery* (6), he can certainly provide us with that moral dynamic which is a vital component in our obedience. Law-loving Israelites knew that moral energy was not automatically conveyed merely by memorizing the Decalogue's words, but it had been generously promised by their author. Like the hesitant Moses, they too could prove that the eternal *I am* (6)[31] not only commands but empowers those who genuinely desire to honour him.

[30] An innovation which may have been due to Bishop John Hooper who regarded the Ten Commandments as 'the abridgement and epitome of the whole Bible'; see John Hooper, *Early Writings* (Parker Society, Cambridge, 1843), p. 144.

[31] Ex. 3:6–15.

Deuteronomy 5:23 – 6:25
7. Truth to tell

Once the Ten Commandments had been given to Moses he was under an obligation to serve the Lord as a responsible communicator, immediately sharing the truths which had been revealed to him. He had been commissioned to listen attentively to God's word and then communicate it faithfully to the waiting people (5:31). Truth is not only to be received but shared. There is a sense in which the teaching of this passage is a more detailed application of the first two commandments. Rich truth about their unique (5:6–7) and jealous (5:8) God is communicated both visually and vocally, as God's people are taught to honour (5:23 – 6:3), love (6:4–5), confess (6:6–9), remember (6:10–12) and serve (6:13–25) the *one* and only (6:6) Lord.

1. Honour the Lord (5:23 – 6:3)

Once they crossed the Jordan, these travellers would soon be immersed in a culture and lifestyle which encouraged belief in a variety of pagan gods. From the start they must understand that the Lord is to be honoured as the one and only true God who had an exclusive claim on their worship and allegiance. Unlike their pagan neighbours, they would honour their God best not by the multiplicity of sacrifices they offered but by their reverence for and obedience to him. These twin truths were communicated to the waiting people visually and verbally.

The Lord would be honoured by their reverence. He chose to convey the sense of his holy and righteous presence by an awesome physical manifestation which would convince them beyond all doubt of the closeness, greatness and glory of God. They needed an outward and visible sign that God himself was speaking to them and that their only appropriate response was to *fear* or reverence him. He had revealed himself in *the fire, the cloud and the deep darkness* (5:22), dramatic visual proof of his immediate presence (frequently

94

symbolized by cloud,[1] authentic voice (4:11–12), holy character (4:24) and unfathomable purposes. The *deep darkness* reminds us that we do not know everything about God – his thoughts far transcend our own.[2] Moreover, God had revealed himself in over-whelming majesty at Sinai not only to demonstrate his holiness but to encourage theirs: 'that the fear of God will be with you to keep you from sinning'.[3] An appropriate sense of awe and reverence prevents evil from gaining a firm foothold in our lives. Those who honour God shrink at the thought of grieving him.

Late twentieth-century spirituality could be greatly enriched by a more sensitive awareness of God's holiness and majesty. We need to remember that irreverence is disobedience. If God commands that we *fear* him then we must. It is rarely easy to achieve the right balance in the matter, but the study of Scripture will certainly help towards it. There must be some balance between that cowering type of awe which so heightens the sense of God's 'otherness' that he becomes remote, detached and distant, and the opposite kind of error, an insulting casualness or patronizing familiarity. The fifteenth-century English mystic, Julian of Norwich, emphasized the importance of an appropriate sense of balance in our approach to God: 'For our courteous Lord willeth that we should be as homely with him as heart may think or soul desire. But let us beware that we take not so recklessly this homeliness as to leave courtesy.'[4] The biblical balance is found in this passage – God is to be loved as well as feared.

The Lord would be honoured by their obedience. That truth was conveyed vocally as the Lord told them with unmistakable clarity that his word was not simply to be heard, preserved, treasured and taught but obeyed. The people promised Moses that they would *listen and obey* (5:27) but God knew their instability, waywardness and disloyalty: *Oh, that their hearts would be inclined to fear me and keep all my commands always* (5:29). Through Moses therefore they were repeatedly urged to *be careful to do* what the Lord had commanded them.

Deuteronomy constantly faces us with its plea for obedience: *fear the LORD your God as long as you live by keeping all his decrees and commands . . . be careful to obey* (6:2–3). The command to 'do' what God says occurs about fifty times in this book. Here, the Lord promised them that their willing response to the word would guar-antee his unfailing provision for their varied needs.

Another key theme in this book frequently presented alongside human obedience is that of divine generosity, vividly conveyed in recurring phrases like *keep all my commands always, so that it might*

[1] Ex. 13:21–22; 14:19–20; 40:34–38.   [2] Is. 55:8–9.   [3] Ex. 20:20.
[4] Julian of Norwich, *Revelations of Divine Love*, ch. 77.

go well with them and their children for ever! (5:29); *walk in all the ways that the* LORD *your God has commanded you, so that you may live and prosper* (5:33); *so that you may enjoy long life . . . so that it may go well with you and that you may increase greatly in a land flowing with milk and honey* (6:2–3).

These verses in Deuteronomy must not be snatched from their original context. They are encouraging these Israelite pilgrims to understand that their *one* and only God (6:4) would provide their physical and material needs, not the crude Canaanite agricultural and fertility gods which they would encounter once they entered the land. He was the generous giver and he would just as certainly withhold those gifts if they failed to honour him by their reverence and obedience. Promises of this kind do not mean that if we *fear* and *obey* God we shall always receive everything we want; far from it. That type of 'name it and claim it' prosperity theology relies on a highly selective use of biblical quotations and has little foundation in Scripture as a whole. Jesus could not possibly have had more reverence for God[5] and yet he had few possessions of his own. Paul and Peter certainly held God in awe[6] and were similarly lacking in material benefits. Reverence and obedience will not necessarily lead to our economic prosperity but they will always work for our spiritual enrichment. We may not be wealthier people because we honour him but we shall certainly be richer ones.

2. Love the Lord (6:4–5)

The Lord desires their loving as well as their reverent and obedient response. These verses have a distinctive place in Judaism. Known as the *Shema* (the Hebrew term found at the beginning of this passage, *Hear*), they still form part of the Jewish believer's daily prayers: *Hear, O Israel: The* LORD *our God, the* LORD *is one. Love the* LORD *your God with all your heart and with all your soul and with all your strength*. They should love the Lord because of his nature, work and promise.

a. His unique nature should inspire their love

The Lord is *one*. He is the only God they can love; there are no others. In times of drought or famine the Israelites may be tempted to turn to Canaan's fertility gods (6:14) but the Lord here reminds them of his uniqueness; there are no rivals. To love other gods is to pursue nothing. They do not exist. He is the *one* and only Lord.

---

[5] Heb. 5:7–8.   [6] 2 Cor. 7:1; 1 Pet. 1:17.

b. His work should inspire their love

He has deliberately chosen them as his elect people. He twice addresses them here by their special name *Israel* (3, 4), emphasizing that they are a people bound to him in the special relationship of covenant-love. The loving initiative is with him, not them (7:8).[7]

c. His promise should inspire their love

That love did not begin with these desert pilgrims about to enter the land; it reached back into their history. He was their *fathers'* God, true to his word, fulfilling what he *promised* them (3). If they love him they are responding to the unchanging love of a reliable God who had been true to their ancestors and would not disappoint them.

Such a unique, generous and dependable God deserves their total, not partial or divided, allegiance. He has pledged to give them so much when they enter Canaan (10–11) and he is surely worthy of their best and highest devotion: *love . . . with all your heart . . . and . . . all your soul and . . . all your strength.* Their love for him must be exclusive; it cannot be shared with other gods.

3. Confess the Lord (6:6–9)

Moreover, this love for God was not to be a secretive devotion, a purely private relationship which did not concern others. From the start it was to involve the element of public confession as well as personal allegiance.

First, this loving devotion to the *one* Lord must be shared in the home. These God-given truths must not only be taught by Moses but also by every parent in Israel (7), so that children and grandchildren would learn and keep *all his decrees and commands* (2). Parents were to *impress* this word on their children's minds and make it the subject of natural everyday conversation within family life.[8] There is a danger in modern Christian homes that either or both parents can be so fervently absorbed in 'the Lord's work' (often among children or young people) that the spiritual welfare of their own children can be seriously neglected.

It has been wisely said that 'the family that prays together stays

---

[7] *Cf.* 1 Jn. 4:10.

[8] For an exposition of the Hebrew family as 'a vehicle of continuity for the faith, history and traditions of Israel', and for its didactic and catechetical function within the life of God's people, see Christopher J. H. Wright, *God's People in God's Land*, pp. 81–84.

together'. In earlier generations family worship was an important aspect of spiritual devotion. Before or immediately after a meal, parents and children met together for a reading from God's word, a brief application of its message, and prayer for the Lord's guidance and help in matters of everyday family concern. It presented a regular opportunity for teaching, the sharing of news, mutual encouragement and united dependence on God. The pressures of contemporary life make it extremely difficult, if not impossible, for many families to eat together at any one time in the day but, in order to obey God and apply these verses to our own home-life, every Christian parent should strive for some opportunity to gather the family together for brief biblical exposition and prayer.

Additionally, this love for God and his word must be shared in the community. Displaying the truth on their doorposts and gates makes it unmistakably clear to their neighbours that this family is committed to God's unchanging yet relevant word. They tell everybody where the household stands. The instructions about carrying the word on the hand and forehead are, by contrast, more personal. They testify to where the individual stands – the hand as the symbol of personal action and commitment; the forehead as symbolizing personal direction and deliberate intent.

It is possible that the words about frontlets and doorposts were intended to be taken metaphorically to indicate that the 'covenant demands were to be the central and absorbing feature' (Thompson) of their entire life. Some Jews, however, came to interpret the saying literally, prescribing the use of phylacteries secured around the forehead during morning prayer, and mezuzahs, small boxes containing a tiny parchment with texts from Exodus and Deuteronomy, which were fixed to doorposts. For many devout households, the mezuzah (the word means 'doorpost') must have served as a timely reminder of every family's need to love and obey God, but in the first century some were using phylacteries as a religious form of self-display, 'done for men to see', a practice criticized by Jesus.[9]

In our very different kind of society, there is still need for Christians to give their neighbours the opportunity to learn something about our personal faith. With an ever-increasing number of people in our communities who never attend a local church, many believers are making more imaginative use of their homes for friendly hospitality, coffee mornings, informal occasions for neighbours to meet a Christian speaker so that those who live around them are not ignorant of the gospel and, in a relaxed context, are

[9] Mt. 23:5.

able to share their doubts and uncertainties in an informed biblical discussion about life's greatest themes.

4. Remember the Lord (6:10–12)

Several of this book's great key-words have already appeared within this passage: *listen* or *hear* (5:27; 6:3–4), *fear* (5:29; 6:2), *keep* (5:29), *teach* (5:31; 6:1), *do* (5:32), *love* (6:5). Another important word in Deuteronomy is *remember*. When they inhabit the land, the Israelites may quickly forget the generosity God has constantly shown throughout some of their darkest years. Careless forgetfulness is here introduced as a serious peril and, as a good teacher, Moses returns to the theme in his later preaching: *when you eat and are satisfied, be careful that you do not forget the LORD* (11–12). The idea has already appeared in different contexts in earlier chapters (4:9, 23; 5:15) and it is presented here as a renewed warning. The Israelites are here told that in the highly materialistic culture of Canaan they will be in danger of forgetting four crucial things – God's gracious promise, incomparable nature, generous gifts and mighty acts.

In the years ahead the people are likely to forget what God said. God had not failed them by forgetting the promise *he swore to your fathers, to Abraham, Isaac and Jacob*, but the Lord knew that they would not remember what he had taught them.

When the people entered Canaan they were also in danger of forgetting who God is: the faithful God (*the God of your fathers* who made and kept these promises, 3, 10), the only God (*one* Lord, 4), and the *jealous God* (15) who cannot be worshipped as one among others.

Moreover, they will soon forget what God gave (10–11). In the days to come they were to enjoy the security of cities they did not build, riches they had not earned, water from reservoirs they had not constructed, fruit from vineyards they had not planted. But there was a danger that when they had eaten their fill, they would forget the giver of all these good things. Throughout history, affluence has often led to spiritual indifference and moral carelessness. In many parts of the western world, people have only perishable assets. They have everything but the things which matter most.

In their new-found prosperity, the Israelities would also forget what God did. He had redeemed them, bringing them out of the bitter experience of Egyptian slavery (12, 20–23), a great and mighty act of undeserved salvation which ought never to be erased from their corporate memory. It was for this reason that the Hebrew people had their great festivals, especially Passover, to keep all these things in the top level of their minds.

Forgetfulness is not a sin confined to the Israelites after they had settled in the prosperous land of Canaan. All God's people have been in danger of forgetting what he has said, given and done, as well (at times) of who he is – Father, Guide, Protector, Comforter, Sovereign. The gifted nineteenth-century hymn-writer, Frances Ridley Havergal, regularly kept a 'Mercies Diary'. At the end of each day she gratefully recorded in four or five words just *one* thing for which she was supremely thankful. A similar practice might save us from the sin of persistent ingratitude. Forgetting God's goodness seriously impoverishes our spirituality; it reduces our thinking to the level of the ungodly pagan.[10]

5. Serve the Lord (6:13–25)

The people are confronted with both a negative and positive exhortation; they are *not* to forget God (12), and they *are* to serve (13) him. There is a deliberate contrast here between God's *service* and Egyptian *slavery* (21). Craigie points out that in Hebrew 'both words are derived from the same root and contrast vividly the old and the new masters of Israel'. In former years they had a cruel suzerain in Pharaoh (who in Egyptian religion was regarded as a god) but God had shown his invincible power against Pharaoh (22) and delivered them. They now serve a better suzerain. Christians rejoice that they have been redeemed from a greater tyranny than anything the Hebrews experienced in Egypt. By Christ's saving work, God has liberated them from 'the dominion of darkness' miraculously transferring them to the 'kingdom of the Son he loves'.[11] They too respond to God's mercy by offering their lives for his work.[12] 'Serving the Lord' is a central theme in Moses' preaching (10:12, 20; 11:13; 13:4; 28:47 and elsewhere). In the passage before us, the Israelites are reminded that service is an act of obedience (13), loyalty (14–19) and gratitude (20–25).

They are to serve him because he says so: *Fear the LORD your God; serve him only, and take your oaths in his name* (13). Swearing by his name probably refers to their vow of total allegiance to the God of the covenant. The treaties to which we have referred usually contained an obligation of this sort. The vassal had to make a solemn promise to obey the suzerain, and in turn the suzerain vowed to keep his part of the agreement.

They are to serve him despite competing loyalties. Their future land would not only be marked by prosperous vineyards (11) but by the corrupt idol-groves of Canaanite worship. We are always exposed to the lure and attraction of rival 'deities', *the gods of the*

---

[10] Rom. 1:21.   [11] Col. 1:13.   [12] Rom. 6:22; 12:1.

people around us (14). Late twentieth-century society has been subtly infiltrated by worthless idolatry – materialism (the god of 'what I can get'), hedonism (the god of 'what I enjoy'), social approval (the god of 'how I am regarded'), vaulting ambition (the god of 'what I must achieve'), and there are many more.[13] The believer's greatest ambition is to serve God and put him first.[14]

Loyalty to God must be expressed in trust. Once more, Moses uses an incident from the past as a warning for the future. The people are reminded of what happened at Massah ('testing') when they were determined to *test the LORD* their God (16). On that occasion[15] the community in the wilderness was thirsty and, in those adverse circumstances, they seriously doubted both the Lord's word and presence among them. They disregarded his word, for he had promised to meet all their needs; it was a time for trusting not complaining. They seriously doubted his presence, saying, 'Is the Lord among us or not?' Theirs was not a casual, careless or thoughtless grumble in an unguarded moment but an act of fierce rebellion. They threatened to stone Moses, saying that God had brought them out of Egypt to kill them, totally rejecting all the good and kind things the Lord had said to them about his provision and their security.

Trusting in dark and difficult times was not an experience required only of the desert pilgrims on their way to Canaan. It would also be expected of their children and their descendants who settled in the land. The land was *flowing with milk and honey* (3) but life would not always be easy and comfortable. Adversity of one kind or another is bound to arise in all our lives. When things go against them, those of God's children who *serve* him and him alone, trust him fully even when they cannot remotely understand his ways.

These verses (13, 16) became important for Jesus immediately prior to the commencement of his earthly ministry. Like the people at Massah, he was in the wilderness and, like them, he too had a basic physical need. They were thirsty; he was hungry. The enemy came to taunt him just as he had tempted them. Jesus refused to put God to the test by responding to the devil's suggestions and quoted these very words.[16] At his baptism, Jesus had been publicly identified as God's Servant-Son. The words from heaven, 'with you I am well pleased'[17] recalled words addressed to the 'Suffering Servant' in Isaiah's prophecy.[18] As God's Son, Christ knew that he had a caring Father. The Father would scarcely have initiated his Son's mission by letting him die in the desert. But because he was

---

[13] Peter C. Moore, *Disarming the Secular Gods* (IVP, 1989).   [14] Mt. 6:33.
[15] Ex. 17:1–7.   [16] Lk. 4:5–12.   [17] Lk. 3:22.   [18] Is. 42:1

determined to serve God and nobody else, Jesus firmly rejected the devil's attack and used these words from Deuteronomy to send him packing! It is always important to *do what is right and good in the LORD's sight* (18), not simply that which seems opportune, reasonable or convenient in the sight of men. Jesus would rather have died of hunger than doubt his Father, but he knew he would not die until the moment of God's choice.

Finally, they are to serve him as an expression of gratitude. They are grateful for his dependable promise (*that the LORD promised on oath to your forefathers*, 18–19, 23) and his saving achievement (20–25). When future generations asked how these *stipulations, decrees and laws* originated, what was their importance, and why must they be studied, the children were told about God's redemption (21–23) and revelation (24–25). This mighty and faithful God, who did and said such unique things, is always worthy of the believer's obedient, loyal and grateful service. Throughout Christian history, believers have regarded their service for the Lord as an immense privilege rather than a biblical obligation. The seventeenth-century minister, John Tillinghast, put it superbly when he wrote: 'It is from you alone that God expects this service; 'tis work the world cannot do ... Christ is never at a loss for instruments when he hath worke to do; that any of you are employed, it is more his free grace towards you, than from any need he hath of you ... 'tis now high time ... to be up and doing.'[19]

[19] John Tillinghast, *Generation-Work* (1654). For this reference I am indebted to G. F. Nuttall, *Visible Saints* (Oxford, 1957), p. 153.

Deuteronomy 7:1–26
8. God's people in a new land

We have now come to one of Deuteronomy's main sections, covering the next five chapters of the book (chapters 7 – 11). The common theme which runs throughout this extended passage is that of God's people, their characteristics, privilege, security, discipline and love. A number of familiar ideas are found here which have already made an appearance in the opening chapters of the book and it will hardly be necessary for us to give detailed attention to topics which we have already discussed earlier. When we come across identical themes in successive chapters, however, we must appreciate that for Moses frequent repetition was an extremely important part of the educative process. The people had to be told more than once that, for example, they must hear, learn, obey and keep the law, that they must not forget the God who had given that word and so many other good things to them, and that they must not worship other gods or bow down to pagan idols. These themes make regular appearances throughout Moses' preaching and are given an equally prominent place in the teaching which believing parents were told to communicate to their children.

Role-definition was particularly significant for the Hebrew people as they stood on the threshold of Canaan. It was of supreme importance that they should know God but they must also know *who they are* and what he wanted them to be. God's plan was that they should live in the land as his holy (1–6a), chosen (6b–16) and secure (17–26) people.

1. A holy people (7:1–6a)

God's people must first understand that they are his exclusive possession, *holy to the Lord* their God (6). Belonging to him, they cannot possibly hand themselves over to anyone else. Anything which was considered 'holy' had been 'set apart' for a distinctive purpose. It was not to be used for less worthy tasks. The priests were holy because they were 'set apart' as God's servants,[1] the Sabbath was holy because it was God's special day (5:12), and sacrifices were holy because they belonged exclusively to God.[2] It was not just religious objects, places and individuals which were 'holy' however. The people themselves – every man, woman and child in Israel – had been 'set apart' for God's use, and they must recognize God's exclusive claim on their lives.

A number of prominent features in this passage illustrate the nature and centrality of holiness for the Lord's people as the Bible defines us. The teaching also provides the essential background for New Testament teaching about Christian spirituality.

First, the holiness of God's people is here announced as an *assured fact*: *For you are a people holy to the* LORD *your God* (6). They are not urged to become holy; they are told that they *are* already holy. They must be what they are. As R. E. Clements points out, holiness in Deuteronomy 'is an established fact, not a spiritual ambition. Israel is holy by virtue of the specially tight bond which binds it to God ... this link was forged by God and not by the members of Israel ... It was commanded to keep the law because it was a holy people, and not because it hoped to become one ... Israel's holiness is an act of God, not an act of man.'[3] Likewise, Christian sanctification begins not with what we do but with what God has done. It is important to observe that one of the most important New Testament names for Christians is 'saints';[4] the word is derived from this same source, 'to make holy'. It denotes those who are set apart, utterly dedicated to Christ. The term is used at the beginning of many New Testament letters to describe *all* the members of a local congregation, not some of them who may have made more spiritual progress than others. Every member has been 'set apart' as God's special agent and instrument in the world. Believers are not to become saints; they are saints. They too must be what they are.

Secondly, the holiness of God's people is here described as a *divine achievement*. God's people belong exclusively to him, just as the land he is giving them belongs to him. Moreover, their possession by him as a holy people does not depend primarily on their special efforts or to any excellent deeds which they may have done; the victory is due to God's work, not human hand. He went ahead of them, fighting the battles for them. This theme recurs throughout the teaching of Deuteronomy: *When the* LORD *your God brings you into the land ... and when the* LORD *your God has delivered them over to you* (1–2). The seven strong nations were *larger and stronger*

---

[1] Lv. 21:6.   [2] Lv. 6:25; 7:1; 10:12.
[3] R. E. Clements, *God's Chosen People*, pp. 32–33.
[4] Rom. 1:7; 8:27; 12:13; 16:2, 15.

(1) than the Israelites and apart from God's mighty acts in vanquishing their foes, the Hebrews would have been entirely wiped out. Humanly speaking, they did not stand a chance of military success. They were decidedly inferior in numbers and skill and, above all, their opponents already had possession of the land. They knew its hills and valleys. It was strange and unfamiliar territory to the invading people. From a purely human point of view, it was an impossible assignment. God, however, worked and did for them something which they could not possibly have achieved for themselves.

In biblical teaching the message of holiness as God's achievement is also a call to resolute action. Here, the people of God are commanded to take by conflict what he had given them by grace. Christian spirituality is often portrayed in the New Testament in terms of combat; there is a fight which must be fought and will be won. Yet, it will certainly not be won purely by our own moral effort or religious zeal. Every Christian has to realize that God himself is our conqueror. He fights for us, as for the Hebrew people many centuries ago, and we enter into the victory he has obtained on our behalf. Christian holiness does not begin with what we do but with what God has done for us in Christ. When Paul sent his letter to the church at Corinth he knew only too well that some of them were living lives far below all that the Lord intended for them, but he begins by reminding them of all that Christ *is* and longs to be towards them. God made Christ Jesus 'our righteousness, holiness and redemption'.[5]

Thirdly, Moses here reminds his contemporaries that the holiness of God's people involves a *specific obligation*. As God's holy people, their relationship with him is a unilateral commitment. Once more we notice the important part played in this teaching by the language and ideas of the treaties used by different nations in the ancient Near East. The Israelite people are told that under no circumstances whatever are they to make a *treaty* or covenant (2) with any of the seven nations which occupied Canaan at that time. They were already bound in covenant-love to the Lord God and they must not break their part of the agreement by entering into an alliance with anybody else. The reference to marriage agreements (3) may well have as its context the common practice in international alliances secured by strengthened relationships through the marriage of leading members of a royal house from both countries. Even this teaching has its parallel in the New Testament where Christians are specifically told that they must not marry unbelievers.[6]

Fourthly, the holiness of God's people confronts them with a

[5] 1 Cor. 1:30.   [6] 2 Cor. 6:14 – 7:1.

serious warning. It is not merely that marriage with these unbelieving people might lead to domestic unhappiness because the two parties had different religious interests. When such treaty-marriages took place, the two parties involved undertook to recognize and accept each other's gods. For the Hebrew people, however, such an arrangement would violate the terms of the treaty and would be a blatant act of both religious and moral degradation. *For they will turn your sons away from following me to serve other gods* (4). The political treaties to which we have referred were always ratified by a recognition of the deities of each participating nation. The Hebrew people, however, had responded to God's invitation to make an exclusive covenant with him, and they must honour its terms and conditions by refusing to become allied with other gods. God tells them that if they make such an alliance, then he will quickly *destroy* them. Divided loyalties are forbidden.

Being 'holy' for the Hebrew people meant that they belonged exclusively to God. The land the Israelites were about to possess was already occupied by seven nations (1), each of which had their own gods. Canaanite religion was not only false; it was immoral. Cult prostitution played a significant part in some of their fertility rituals. Such practices were an offence to a holy and pure God. In these circumstances, the danger of moral as well as religious corruption was particularly acute, so the Lord demanded that their idolatrous statues, pillars and images must be completely destroyed. There is recognition here that the life of any believer can be tragically ruined by the corrupting influence of other people. The apostle Paul reminded the Corinthian church of a familiar saying of Menander: 'Bad company ruins good morals'.[7]

All of us are influenced by others. John Donne was right to remind us that no man is an island and, without maintaining a detached, superior 'holier-than-thou' attitude, Christians need to remember that their witness can be marred and their spirituality severely damaged by wrong relationships. In his *Collected Memoirs*, the renowned accompanist, Gerald Moore, wrote about a world-famous opera singer whose brilliant career was, in its later stages, kept markedly below standard, largely because of an unhelpful relationship. He says that the magnificent singer was 'destroyed by a man she loved deeply, by a man without an atom of music in his soul, cruel and callous, who enjoyed torturing her by telling her she was nothing'. We also have a sinister enemy; he too enjoys taunting us and wants to ruin us. Jesus described the devil as a 'murderer' as well as a liar.[8] He likes to tell us we are nothing and he has partly achieved his destructive purposes when he has involved us in

---

[7] 1 Cor. 15:33.   [8] Jn. 8:44.

relationships which will hinder rather than help us in our Christian lives.

2. A chosen people (7:6b–16)

Holiness and election are twin themes in Moses' preaching about Israel's covenant relationship with God and they are frequently found together in these chapters. The Israelite congregation is here assured that God has deliberately chosen them *to be his people, a treasured possession* (6b), a decision made on the basis of purposive selection (*out of all the peoples on the face of the earth*), not arbitrary choice. Their holiness is entirely due to the divine favour, not their moral superiority. In describing their election, Moses here reminds God's chosen people of their privilege, peril, responsibility and resources.

a. Their privilege

God's *treasured* people are, literally, 'prized more highly' than other nations. The Hebrew term (translated here as *his treasured possession*) has an interesting parallel in some Akkadian words found on a treaty-seal, describing a king as the 'treasured possession' of his god. Moses knew that the only true God had made a unique covenant with his Israel, his greatly valued people. It was not that God lacked compassion for other nations or cared nothing for them; his universal sovereignty and unlimited love are amply illustrated elsewhere in this book. He deliberately chose Israel, however, to be a special instrument of his purposes in the world.

Other passages of Scripture emphasize that God chose his people because he wanted to use them. This aspect of the Old Testament doctrine of election is not given a full exposition in Deuteronomy but we must remember that this book, important as it is, does not contain the whole of the biblical revelation. Like the apostle Paul we need 'the whole will of God'[9] and not fragments of it. If we study both Old and New Testaments, other aspects of the election theme will provide us with additional and complementary perspectives to those we find in these verses. We shall see elsewhere that election is not simply to privilege but to service.

Peter gave expression to this important aspect of the theme when he applied Israel's great names and titles to the church and said that believers are 'a chosen people . . . a holy nation, a people belonging to God' that they might 'declare the praises' of the Lord who has

[9] Acts 20:27.

called them 'out of darkness into his wonderful light'.[10] Biblical election has an evangelistic purpose.

God's plan for Israel was that she should be a blessing to others – 'a light for the Gentiles',[11] a 'kingdom of priests' serving as his representatives among the nations,[12] a missionary people, a moral testimony, a model of God-centred community living, a reflection of his own holy, righteous and loving character. Those additional aspects of the 'chosen people' story are expounded elsewhere in the Old Testament, but it is important to mention them here to provide the necessary perspective.[13] God's people received the truth of their election in stages; all was not revealed at a single moment. At this particular moment in their history it was more important that the Hebrew people should possess the land than convert the nations.

Here in the passage before us, the unique privilege of God's people is based on two key facts, the source and guarantee of their election.

First, the source of their election was in the love of God. When later generations of intelligent Hebrew children asked their parents why their particular nation had been chosen rather than any other, they would be told that, *it was because the LORD loved you* (8). He *set his affection* (7) upon the Israelites because he treasured them as his special possession. The agreement between God and his people was a *covenant of love* (9, 12). It resembled a marriage and that is why the 'covenant' imagery is so appropriate. When a husband determines to set his love upon his wife, it does not mean he has no love whatever for anybody else. There is certainly a sense, however, in which it is an exclusively loyal love, bound by a covenant. He will not love anyone else in the same way as he loves his wife, and that particular love cannot possibly be shared with anybody else. To do that would seriously violate the mutual agreement between them. That is why there is such a repetitive insistence in these verses that there can be no other gods (4–5, 16, 25–26).

Secondly, the guarantee of their election was in the word of God. He *kept the oath he swore to your forefathers* (8). He is *the faithful God, keeping his covenant* (9), not a vascillating, unpredictable God like the changeable gods of the surrounding nations, petulant, fickle, always ready to be coaxed or persuaded by the offering of the right kind of animal or human sacrifice. The God of the Hebrew people is the unchanging, reliable God who honours his promises. Many years before, he had given an assurance to Abraham which he renewed to succeeding generations: one day they would possess the land they were about to enter. He would not say one thing to them

---

[10] 1 Pet. 2:9.   [11] Is. 42:6; 49:6.   [12] Ex. 19:6.

[13] This aspect of the election-theme is carefully interpreted in H. H. Rowley, *The Biblical Doctrine of Election* (1950).

today, only to withdraw it tomorrow. His word of promise is completely dependable.

b. Their peril

There is an inherent danger in any preoccupation with the election-theme, however. It is that the elect begin to assume that God's special favour is all due to some attractive quality or achievement of their own, rather than to God's totally undeserved generosity. Human pride is quick to snatch the glory for itself. The Israelites are told in no uncertain terms that their special role as God's chosen people is not due to anything at all which they have done. It seems as though God anticipates three false arguments which men will use to explain the election and uniqueness of his people, and Moses clearly refutes them in these chapters. In later generations, some Israelites might foolishly imagine that God's choice of them was due to their numerical strength, physical ability or moral superiority. Nothing could be further from the truth and the people are warned about such erroneous ideas and the human pride which produces them.

It was not their numerical strength which determined their election: *The Lord did not set his affection on you and choose you because you were more numerous than other peoples, for you were the fewest of all peoples* (7). Israel had not been chosen because God was in desperate need of a vast multitude in order to achieve his purposes. Far from it; there was a choice array of numerically strong nations in the ancient world. Israel's population was minute by comparison. God deliberately chose Israel because of his affection, not her numbers.

When the Hebrew people entered the land and conquered their foes, some might even wonder whether God's choice of them was due to their physical ability: 'You may say to yourself, "My power and the strength of my hands have produced this wealth for me"' (8:17). The Israelites are reminded that the Lord had given them the strength they needed to achieve such victories. It was not by their unaided efforts that they had come to this highly favoured position. They owned nothing except the resources which God had given them. Christians are equally indebted to God for all they have received and, in the words of Henriette Auber's hymn,[14] gratefully acknowledge the Spirit's gifts:

---

[14] Henriette Auber, *Our blest Redeemer.*

And every virtue we possess,
And every victory won,
And every thought of holiness,
Are His alone.

Some might even have the effrontery to suggest that it was because of their moral superiority that the Israelites had been chosen. Moses says to such people: 'do not say to yourself, "The LORD has brought me here to take possession of this land because of my righteousness" ... It is not because of your righteousness or integrity that you are going in to take possession of their land' (9:4–5).

Pride is a subtle and dangerous sin. It is greedy for the glory which is due to God alone. The psalmist rightfully dismissed all human praise when he cried out, 'Not to us, O LORD, not to us but to your name be the glory'.[15] God has clearly said 'I will not yield my glory to another'.[16] When the apostle Paul was assuring both the Jewish and Gentile Christians at Corinth that they were an elect people, he told them that in choosing the weak and insignificant, God had deliberately by-passed the arrogant, self-opinioned citizens of Corinth so that no-one may boast in the presence of God.[17]

c. Their responsibility

We have already seen that God chose his people because he loved them and was determined to keep his word. The chosen people must respond to the divine initiative with similar qualities. The terms of the agreement call for mutual love and faithfulness. He loves them and they must love him; he keeps his word and they must keep theirs. Theirs is *the faithful God, keeping his covenant of love to a thousand generations of those who love him and keep his commands* (9). He made promises to their forefathers and *swore* on oath that he would be true to his word (12). The people must never forget that they are bound to their loving and loyal God by the terms of an agreement he made with his people at Sinai; they too must be loving and loyal to him.

As they stood in the plains of Moab listening to Moses' compelling preaching, it all seemed so simple and uncomplicated. How could they ever think of doing anything else than love and obey him? But Moses knew of the dangers ahead – a country littered with hill-top shrines to false gods, sickeningly corrupt, immoral religious practices, heathen neighbours with vastly different ethical standards. On innumerable occasions in the succeeding years they would gradually turn away from God's word,

[15] Ps. 115:1.   [16] Is. 48:11.   [17] 1 Cor. 1:26–29.

and allow new, attractive voices to lure them away from their high spiritual and moral values. Easily and imperceptibly, the pagan world around them could begin to make them as materialistic and immoral as any other nation in the Near East, and all because they had lost their love for a loving and loyal God. Centuries later, John warned his friends in the churches of an identical peril, and reminded them of the exclusive claims of God's love: 'Do not love the world or anything in the world. If anyone loves the world, the love of the father is not in him.'[18]

The problem is not confined to the history of ancient Israel nor to the first-century church. The perils are even more prevalent in contemporary society. In most parts of the world Christians are totally outnumbered. Constantly challenged by an alien environment, it is not always easy for believers to maintain a consistent witness. Even in countries with a nominal Christian commitment, the standards are lowered, year by year. In modern Britain, for example, only 10% of the population now attend church; in the mid-nineteenth century it was 40%.[19]

Reliable reports on social trends go on to describe record numbers in prisons, rising illegitimacy, more abortions, growing divorce rates, a mounting drug problem and increasing alcoholism, especially among teenagers. The number of teenage pregnancies in England is proportionately higher than any other European country. Not surprisingly in this environment, the number of illegitimate births has trebled since 1961 and now, one in every four babies is born without the love and security of married parents.[20]

Those who plead for high moral standards are embarrassingly dismissed as antiquated kill-joys or Victorian prudes. Conventional behaviour is outdated and irrelevant for 'liberated' people. In this kind of society, it would be astonishing if the Christian church remained unscathed. Marriage-breakdown is now one of the Christian counsellor's most frequent problems. Christians are, however, by their very name and new nature, called to be different. They are God's holy people, entrusted with a mission to their contemporaries. It demands a radically distinctive and consistent lifestyle as well as courageous vocal witness.

Israel's *faithful God* promised to keep his love-agreement with those who *love him and keep his commands* (9). Lovers of God are loyal to his word. Love and loyalty are inseparable partners; each complements the other. Love without loyalty is verbose religious emotionalism. Loyalty without love is cold, unbiblical legalism. Jesus, as well as Moses, linked the twin qualities together: 'If you

[18] 1 Jn. 2:15.
[19] Peter Brierley, *Christian England* (MARC Europe, 1991), p. 30.
[20] *The Times*, 20 September, 1990. In 1989 the figure was 27%.

love me, you will obey what I command.'[21] He went on to remind his disciples of his own example in the matter. When he linked love with obedience, he was only urging them to do what he always did himself: 'If you obey my commands, you will remain in my love, just as I have obeyed my Father's commands and remain in his love.'[22]

d. Their resources

These verses (12–16) describe God's generous provision for his loving and obedient people. The order of 'events' is important: God takes the initiative in loving, choosing and saving his people (6–8), all without merit as far as they were concerned. He commits himself to them and then expects them to respond by loving him and keeping the covenant he has made with them (9). He then promises that, if they do this, he will meet all their future needs.

It required a venture of faith, however, on their part. The wilderness period had been difficult but, in thirty-eight years, they had at least become accustomed to it. The environment was familiar, the conditions predictable, and their sustenance assured. It would have been strange if, on the verge of this entirely new experience, they had not been fearful (17, 21). Here, God lovingly anticipates their worries and speaks directly to them about their family welfare, material provision, economic stability and physical health (13–15). The Lord knew about all these things and, in his merciful goodness, dismisses their anxieties by pledging his abundant provision. God is like that. He always goes ahead of his people, calming their fears by declaring his promises. Egypt was an alien land and they remembered how, as children, they had been tormented by its endless diseases (15). What if it were to be the same in the land ahead as it had been in the land they had left? About to enter Canaan the people could be haunted by countless fears: 'We might be childless', or 'We might be hungry', or 'We might be sick.' Moses answers their frightened 'We might's' with a confident 'He will'. He assures them that if they love God and keep his word he *will keep his covenant . . . will love . . . bless . . . and increase*, feed and protect them (12–15). They must, however, keep their part of the agreement – no other gods.

Sadly, the attraction of rival deities proved too much for many of them. That *snare* (16) was to hold them tight in its cruel grasp at times when they might have enjoyed their promised freedom and God's immense bounty. Because they loved other gods and disobeyed the only true God they exchanged Egyptian slavery for

[21] Jn. 14:15.   [22] Jn. 15:10.

Canaanite, Philistine, Assyrian or Babylonian slavery – and it was all so unnecessary. They had heard the warning but ignored it. That is why the exhortation to 'Remember' keeps recurring throughout these important chapters. It is a word which needs to fall on our dull ears just as much as on theirs.

3. A secure people (7:17–26)

These verses present us with a mingled account of human fear and divine confidence. We have already seen that God anticipated his people's fears about entering a new land. He knew what was in their hearts, the crippling sense of inadequacy, the awareness that they were totally outnumbered by the nations they were about to encounter (17). He has assured them of his bountiful provision for their future but something more was necessary. Here, the naturally hesitant people are repeatedly told that they must *not be afraid of them* (18) or *fear* (19) or *be terrified by them* (21). They are urged, once again, to *remember* (18) some key truths. Fear is the fruit of forgetfulness. We are to remember in particular how God acts, where God is and what God says.

a. How God acts

They must first remember how he delivered them in the past: *But do not be afraid of them; remember well what the Lord your God did to Pharaoh and to all Egypt* (18). Naturally anxious about their limited resources, God invites them to look back into history in order to remind themselves that he is a saving God. It was a humanly impossible assignment to get them out of Egypt, but their eyes saw (19) what God did for them when they were totally unable to fight for themselves, those *great trials* and plagues which harassed their enemies, *the miraculous signs and wonders* which demonstrated God's power, the deliverance at the Red Sea, when the Lord's *mighty hand* and *outstretched arm* obtained for them a unique salvation (19). When believers are fearful about the way ahead they should reflect on the wonder of their redemption. We too were slaves to sin and self but have been miraculously liberated,[23] and God has done it all. It owed nothing to our puny moral efforts or intense religious zeal. The Father who sent his Son to save helpless sinners will surely not forsake his believing children in their continuing need.

They must also believe that he will go on saving them. Their unique salvation is far more than a dramatic past event; it is a

[23] Eph. 1:7.

113

present, continuing experience. The Lord who 'brought them out' (a favourite phrase in these opening chapters: 4:20, 37; 5:15; 6:12, 23; 7:8, 19; 8:14) will certainly 'bring them in' (6:10, 23; 7:1; 8:7; 9:28). Genuine spiritual experience naturally takes account of God's former blessings. We are grateful for what God has done for us but past victories should inspire present confidence. To *remember well what the* LORD *your God did* (18) is a convincing prelude to what he *will do* (19).

Believers must always remember that their salvation is three-dimensional. We were saved; we are being saved; we will be saved. The letter to the Hebrews declares the truth that Jesus is able to keep on saving those who come to God by him,[24] and the apostle Paul is grateful that for those 'who *are being saved*', the 'message of the cross . . . is the power of God'.[25] Believers look back with gratitude to Christ's sacrificial death in the past, and trust in its efficacy; they have been saved from judgment, the penalty of sin. They genuinely long to be saved in the present from the power of sin, however, and they look expectantly to the future when, at Christ's final triumph, they will be saved from the presence of sin. To be saved from sin's punishment, judgment, death and hell is a miracle not to be minimized. It is only part of God's greater work in the life of his people, however. We must be saved today from those things which spoil our lives and damage our witness – selfishness, greed, impatience, jealousy, pride, lovelessness. The Christian believer's testimony must always be not just that 'Jesus saves' but that 'Jesus saves me now'.

Those hesitant Israelites who are afraid of the future are told that the God who sent *great trials* (19) in Egypt will continue to work wonders for them. His intervention on their behalf is not an isolated miracle in the remote past. He is still determined to work for them and do things which they cannot possibly accomplish for themselves. When their fathers acted without God, the enemy chased them 'like a swarm of bees' (1:44) but their children are told that all that will be reversed for those who obey God. He will *send the hornet* (20) into the land ahead to drive out their enemy. This may be interpreted literally (vast hordes of stinging insects would make it physically impossible for their enemies to concentrate on warfare), or metaphorically (as the 'bees' reference earlier), that God has his own means of stinging their opponents. Some Old Testament scholars have suggested that the word here might even be translated 'panic', 'discouragement', or 'depression';[26] it is an idea which fits in well with other references in Deuteronomy and elsewhere to the 'terror and fear' which the Lord puts upon Israel's

[24] Heb. 7:25.   [25] 1 Cor. 1:18.   [26] Craigie, p. 182.

enemies (2:25; 11:25).[27] By whatever means, God has promised to give victory to weak but dependent people.

b. Where God is

When they feel daunted at the prospect of future conflict they must remember that God does not simply act for them at a distance; he is actually *present* with them as they march into this threatening situation. Unlike the gods of the pagan nations, their God is neither remotely removed (enthroned in some celestial dwelling but unconcerned about events on earth) nor restrictively localized (physically confined to some local shrine or inert statue). He is too majestic for any human being fully to comprehend, the *great and awesome God*, yet too compassionate ever to leave his people on their own: *the Lord your God, who is among you* (21). They will not merely witness (19) his power; they will realize his presence. The earlier promises about what the Lord *will* do (12–15) are continued throughout these verses: *the LORD your God will do the same to all the peoples you now fear* (19); *the LORD your God will send the hornet among them* (20); *the LORD your God will drive out those nations* (22); *the LORD your God will deliver them over to you* (23); *he will give their kings into your hand* (24). And God will do it all not only as their victorious Conqueror but as their ever-present Companion: 'Immanuel', 'God with us'.[28]

c. What God said

God's word to them at this time was of immense significance. As God's spokesman, Moses presents the people with two great truths – an encouraging promise and a renewed warning.

First, the encouraging promise; the Lord says that he will *drive out those nations* before them *little by little* (22).[29] God's repeated assurances of forthcoming victory might create the impression that he had planned a dramatic deliverance which was to be accomplished overnight. The Lord was certainly capable of that, but did not choose to do it. That is an important distinction and we often need to be reminded of it. We are sometimes impatient for God to act dramatically and miraculously with sudden and supernatural interventions. He is able to do such things but he knows that most of his purposes are best accomplished gradually. We like everything to change in a moment and naturally plead for a speedy answer to our prayers. He knows, however, what is best for us and sees the

[27] See also Ex. 15:14–16; 23:27; Jos. 2:9; 2 Ki. 7:6–7.   [28] Is. 7:14; Mt. 1:23.
[29] See Ex. 23:28–30.

complete picture, not the tiny fragment that our limited vision can perceive.

What a marvellous divine achievement if the Canaanites could be vanquished in a day; such an irrefutable testimony to the surrounding nations! In his omnipotence, God could certainly have done it but, in his wisdom, their Father knew it was not for his children's good. He knew Canaan better than they did and realized that it would take his people some time to settle in to a totally different environment. They had children to rear, homes to establish, cattle to feed, fields to tend. Whilst they were preoccupied with these essential tasks, the wild animals could over-run their newly-occupied lands. The Canaanites had years of experience of keeping them down. It was vital, therefore, that the conquest should be gradual rather than instant.

The *little by little* promise continues to be relevant in the lives of believing people. When we are broken and bruised by life's experiences and sometimes feel we have failed to be at our best in them, we dream of a dramatically instant salvation that, once and for ever, will give us constant, effortless deliverance. If only we could lose, in a flash, the downward pull of our 'old nature' and, in one single trusting moment, be free for ever from every insidious temptation and life's unremitting conflict. But that is not how God works. He promises that we shall be saved, but only by continual dependence upon him. The renewing work will not be accomplished overnight. A 'once and for ever' deliverance might make us independent, prayerless and proud. The process of 'being transformed into his likeness' is achieved only as we behold 'the Lord's glory',[30] and looking at him is the work of a lifetime. For those who live for Christ, the transformation certainly happens, but *little by little*.

Some may venture another question: If we are not promised instant Christlikeness, why can we not have instant results in our work for him? Christians who have worked hard and long without the encouragement of evident fruit can be forgiven if they occasionally long for immediate success. Mostly, however, the work is done *little by little*. The finest teacher in the world took three years to train his men and, in that time, there were many disappointments, and one complete failure. A disciple is a 'learner', and learning takes time. Even in his incomparable preaching, Jesus was not always successful as the world judges success. Not everyone responded to his matchless appeal, and even those who did, did not always stay with him. The Lord often chooses to break into life's situations dramatically and unexpectedly, in a sudden moment of time, as he did when he changed that fanatical opponent, Saul of Tarsus, on the

[30] 2 Cor. 3:18.

Damascus road. Usually, however, his work is done gradually, *little by little*. William Carey worked for seven years in India before he saw his first convert. In his anti-slavery campaign, Wilberforce read, studied and researched, week in and week out. There were endless discouragements but he pressed on, enlisting support, planning, praying, diligently preparing hundreds of speeches, and addressing meetings at every opportunity – and went on doing it year after year. It took twenty years to secure the abolition of the slave trade and, once achieved, he immediately began to press for the abolition of slavery itself in all British territories. Lesser men would have given up but, *little by little*, the work went on until, in the year of his death, the cause was won.

Secondly, the renewed warning: *The images of their gods you are to burn in the fire. Do not covet the silver and gold on them . . . or you will be ensnared by it, for it is detestable to the LORD your God* (25–26). Once again, the waiting multitude are told of the same lurking danger. God knows that, like ourselves, they are frightened of the wrong things; they are afraid of mere men: *These nations are stronger than we are. How can we drive them out?* (17). They ought to enter Canaan with two very different fears, the fear of loving other gods and the fear of grieving their own. God regards the graven image as *a detestable thing* and they must have nothing to do with it. They are covenant-people, and such useless and damaging things will lure them away from the love which really matters. Those who grasp an idol lose everything of lasting value.

For some, the silver and gold coverings which embellished Canaan's gods would prove a destructive snare (25). They did not particularly want to gain the idol, but they certainly did not want to lose the money. In that moment, gold mattered more than God. Materialism is still a trap. People develop an appetite for things; it is a sick hunger which can never be satisfied. Paul knew that, and warned young Timothy of materialism's destructive potential:

People who want to get rich fall into temptation and a trap . . . For the love of money is a root of all kinds of evil. Some people, eager for money, have wandered from the faith and pierced themselves with many griefs. But you, man of God, flee from all this.[31]

Those who lust for a fat purse end up with nothing else.

[31] 1 Tim. 6:9–11.

Deuteronomy 8:1–20
9. God's word for a time of change

In earlier chapters we have seen that 'remembering' is a key idea in Deuteronomy. As a good teacher, Moses frequently returns to the theme in order to drive its message home. For his congregation, the years in the desert had been far from easy but he knew that once the people entered the land they would be exposed to entirely different hazards. Life in Canaan would confront them with the temptations of disobedience (11, 20), materialism (12–13), forgetfulness (14–16), pride (17–18) and idolatry (19–20). The future was bright with promise but not free from danger.

In the wilderness they had been tested and tried, but during those dark days the best of them had held on to the promise of a happy future, a land overflowing with tokens of God's unfailing generosity. Life is not all 'milk and honey', however. The Bible's realism is one of its most arresting features. It does not encourage the idea that all life is uninterrupted bliss. It is frequently punctuated by change, and new experiences are not always congenial. Over the years, these Hebrew travellers had heard glowing descriptions by Moses of the plentiful territory which lay ahead, but he made it clear that there were other aspects to the future story. They were about to enter a land with new temptations, noted as much for its corrupt, immoral religion as its flowing streams and abundant harvests. Once they possessed this unfamiliar territory, the prosperous Israelites would be in serious danger of forgetting the Lord's correction (1–6), provision (7–18) and commandments (19–20). These themes are intertwined throughout these verses as God's servant prepares the congregation for life in a new environment.

Life frequently involves big changes and fresh adjustments. Contemporary society is highly mobile; little remains static for long. School must be exchanged for work or further education, and training is followed by full-time employment. All these stages involve change and disruption to our customary routine. For the majority of people, a new job means we have to get used to a totally different life-context during the greater part of a day. New work frequently involves a move to an unfamiliar part of the country; close friends are at a distance, local church support is no longer at hand, family-support has had to take on a different pattern. None of these relationships is likely to be completely severed, of course, but they are no longer as close and available in ways we used to appreciate. Compulsory redundancy has meant that many men and women are suddenly uprooted from the work they know best. Many have to train for new jobs, which often involves a geographical change as well as a vocational one. Others have to cope with periods of unemployment, with all the painful adjustments which that demands. This chapter has some important things to say to people in a time of change. In such circumstances, forgetfulness is a serious danger. When we are confronted with new, possibly unwelcome, experiences we must take care that we do not *forget the Lord our God* (11, 14). In such circumstances believers must deliberately *remember* (2, 18) God's fatherly training (1–6), undeserved generosity (7–16) and sovereign demands (17–20). The chapter invites us to value his discipline, acknowledge his goodness and obey his orders.

1. God's fatherly training (8:1–6)

Life is about learning. As they look into the uncertain future, the Israelites are told to remember the past. If they think about the way God has helped them through difficult experiences in years gone by, they are not likely to be terrified about the way ahead. The Puritan preacher, Stephen Charnock, reminded his friends who were suffering fierce persecution in the late seventeenth century that 'if we did remember his former goodness we should not be so ready to doubt ... his future care'.[1] Moses tells the Hebrew people that those *forty years* in the desert had been difficult years, but not wasted ones. Disobedience had kept a whole generation out of a land they might have enjoyed, but God had been with them just the same. When people grieve him, he does not utterly forsake them. If rebels run away from him, he lovingly pursues them, as Bunyan reminded us, 'with a pardon in his hand'.[2] God's people looked forward to a rich and prosperous land ahead, but they must not forget that God had also been good to them in the barren desert. They had learnt lessons there which prosperity could never have taught them. Through those bleak wilderness years, he had been like a compassionate father who occasionally has to discipline his children for their

[1] Stephen Charnock, 'A Discourse of Divine Providence', *Works* (1864), Vol. I, p. 114.
[2] John Bunyan, *Grace Abounding to the Chief of Sinners*, para. 173.

119

own good (5). Some lessons can only be learnt in trouble.

One of the most important things we all have to learn is what life is all about. God longs for his people to enjoy life. We have already seen that the phrase *that you may live* recurs throughout the book and it appears in this chapter also (1). But these desert pilgrims had to learn that 'life' consists of more than eating and drinking. When they were hungry in the wilderness, they cried out for food and God gave them *manna* (3) as his choice gift to meet their daily needs. Without it they would have perished physically, but if they had also been denied even more satisfying food, they would have died spiritually. The manna would feed their earthly bodies, but nothing more. They were spiritual people, with a capacity for receiving the most necessary food of all, God's word. Only as they made an obedient response to that word could they truly 'live'. God spoke to them in the desert and it was that which kept them truly 'alive'. By his word he presented them with great, unchanging spiritual realities, essential both for this life and for eternity. To eat and drink is merely to exist; only as men and women receive and obey God's truth can they really 'live' as God intended – lives which bring them lasting satisfaction and eternal security. In order to make us aware of the priority of spiritual over material values, God sometimes temporarily 'holds back' physical necessities to remind us of the supremacy of spiritual ones.

This passage in Deuteronomy was familiar to all devout Jews and the Lord Jesus must have known it by heart. Life was not easy for him. Immediately after his signal experience of the Holy Spirit and prior to the beginning of his public ministry, he was led by the Spirit into the wilderness. There, he was severely tested. After forty days (surely an intended reminder of the *forty years* in this passage) utterly without food, he was desperately hungry. The devil invited Jesus to work a miracle. Why not turn those light brown stones of the Judean desert into fresh, warm loaves so that he might immediately satisfy his natural hunger? If he did so it would prove that he was God's Son, as the voice from heaven had clearly declared at his baptism. Jesus was not simply invited to transform stones into bread; it went much deeper than that. The devil confronted him with the temptation to doubt God's word: 'If you are the Son of God.'[3] It recalled the first temptation in the garden: 'Did God really say . . .?'[4] Jesus knew that the voice from heaven at his baptism was absolutely true and completely dependable. He had known from his youth of his unique relationship with the Father[5] and the voice from heaven confirmed it. He was God's Son and, if he was, then he could certainly trust his Father. With that seemingly innocent

[3] Lk. 4:3.   [4] Gn. 3:1.   [5] Lk. 2:49.

suggestion that Jesus turn stones to bread, the devil was inviting Jesus to doubt both God's word and God's nature.

Jesus refused to doubt God's word. God had said, clearly and unmistakably, 'You are my Son, whom I love.'[6] Jesus knew that was so, and refused to do anything which might suggest that the saying needed some further support or visible evidence. There was no need whatever to prove it. If God had said it, then that was enough.

Moreover, Jesus refused to doubt God's nature. If he had referred to Jesus as his beloved 'Son', then God must certainly have been his caring Father. With a destiny of ministry and sacrifice which he had prepared for his Son, God would hardly let him die in the desert. When he was hungry, Jesus trusted his Father to supply the food, but, if not, he would not adopt the devil's suggestions.

God cared for his Son just as he had fed (3) and clothed (4) his people in the wilderness centuries earlier. He sometimes led them through adverse experiences, however, so that they might realize how much they needed him. When Jesus was hungry in the Judean desert he quoted these familiar words from Deuteronomy. He answered the devil's doubt of God's word by quoting the very word the enemy rejected: *man does not live on bread alone but on every word that comes from the mouth of the LORD* (3).

God continues to discipline his children. He sometimes leads us through difficult, bewildering, even bitter experiences to prove our dependence upon him. Such times can be used to strengthen our faith, determine our priorities, enrich our witness and increase our usefulness to others. When we encounter new situations or come up against adverse circumstances, we must remember that these times may not be as threatening or destructive as, at first sight, they often seem. The Lord may be using such events to 'discipline' us, to show us how much we have been relying on our own resources, or how prayerless we have become, or how we have allowed our lives to be determined by materialistic values, and a host of other things. Testing times are learning times. Writing from his prison cell in 1943, Dietrich Bonhoeffer said, 'Much as I long to be out of here, I don't believe a single day has been wasted . . . something is bound to come out of it . . . We shall come out of it all much strengthened.'[7]

Moses here tells the people that during periods of chastisement or corrective discipline we must remember to do three things: *Observe the commands of the LORD your God, walking in his ways and revering him* (6). During life's dark and puzzling experiences we are to obey the word (*observe*), live (*walk*) in a manner which pleases God, and hold him in reverence. We will not complain or grumble

[6] Lk. 3:22.
[7] D. Bonhoeffer, *Letters and Papers from Prison* (Collins, Fontana, 1960), pp. 29, 34.

during such periods but fear him, acknowledge his sovereignty and recognize that he alone is God, fully entitled to control every aspect of our lives.

2. God's undeserved generosity (8:7–16)

The theme of 'change' is here presented with an arresting word-picture which makes deliberately bold contrasts. The barren *desert* (2) of the past is sharply contrasted with the *good land* (7) of the future, the *forty years* of constant mobility (2) with the settled years in Canaan's security, their moveable tents with the *fine houses* (12) of the land ahead, the temporary existence with the permanent. The *hunger* (3) of the desert is exchanged for *bread ... not ... scarce* (9) but, sadly, the days when they were *humbled* (3) give way to the years when they are proud (17). Moses here makes special mention of two serious dangers in any time of change – forgetting God's former mercies and ignoring his continuing favour.

God's former mercies are forgotten. In the forty years which had gone by he had redeemed (*brought you out ... of the land of slavery*, 14), guided (*led you through the vast and dreadful desert*, 15), protected (*with its venomous snakes and scorpions*, 15), and sustained them (*water out of hard rock ... gave you manna*, 15–16). Even the times of adversity had all been lovingly designed, that he might do them good *in the end* (16). Those unwelcome decades in the wilderness had been years of beneficial humbling (2–3), purposeful testing (2, 16), and necessary learning (*to teach you ... Know then*, 3, 5). But the constantly repeated experiences of God's earlier blessing had quickly faded from their memories. When we are preoccupied with the present, it is easy to forget the mercies of the past.

God's continuing favour is ignored. The Lord knows that, once they settle in such a fruitful land, prosperity will quickly rob them of their earlier dependence upon him. During those long years in the desert, they were compelled to rely on God. Circumstances demanded it; there was nobody else to whom they could turn. The daily collection of manna (3) is specially mentioned. Perhaps more than any other event, it drew attention to their utter dependence upon God. The regular morning activity of gathering it in hardly presented the Israelites with much of an opportunity for boasting. He gave, they took – it was as simple as that. Once they settled in Canaan, however, the contrast was overwhelming and the temptations immense. The sandy waste, the vast, wind-swept desert was a thing of the past. Now they could enjoy the *good land* (10) around them with its attractive physical features (*streams, pools of water, springs, valleys, hills*), rich agricultural produce (*wheat, barley*), abundant orchards (*vines, fig trees, pomegranates, olive* trees) and useful resources (*a land where the rocks are iron and you can dig copper out of the hills*).

God's purpose was that they should welcome these blessings and recognize his goodness; they did the former without attempting the latter. Instead of remembering, they forgot (11, 14). Widespread prosperity led to gross ingratitude. The Lord intended them to do three things – enjoy his benefits (*when you have eaten and are satisfied*), offer their worship (*praise the LORD your God*) and acknowledge his generosity (*he has given you*, 10). Instead, however, they forgot him (10, 14), disobeyed his commands (11) and became arrogantly self-sufficient and proud (14) – even in the presence of such a generous God. Once they began to disregard his kindness it was not long before they disobeyed his word (11).

3. God's sovereign demands (8:17–20)

Once the abundant prosperity became an established feature of life in the land, two further dangers would seriously damage their spiritual lives – pride and idolatry. Once they became wealthy, they exalted themselves (17–18) and insulted their God (19–20). They committed two acts of blatant theft – they stole from God the glory due to his name (*it is he who gives*, 18), and robbed him of his exclusive right to the worship of their lives. They followed *other gods* and worshipped them (19).

First, they foolishly imagined that all this prosperity was due to their own efforts: *You may say to yourself, 'My power and the strength of my hands have produced this wealth for me'*, 17). Self-glorification is a sinister transgression. It takes full credit for all life's achievements. It forgets that without the breath God gives, the motivation he inspires, the intelligence he provides, the strength he imparts, the perseverance he encourages, none of these things would be possible. He did not give these rich qualities to his people in order to feed their pride but because he was determined to honour his word, confirming *his covenant which he swore to your forefathers* (18). He can be relied upon to keep his word, but they certainly do not keep theirs. In the covenant they agreed not to worship other gods but, forgetting God's word, they broke their promise.

Once God is not acknowledged as the supremely generous Giver it is an easy step to look elsewhere for the source of life's gifts and blessings. The Canaanite people were deeply persuaded that the rich harvests of their land were the special gifts of Baal, the agricultural god *par excellence*. He gave the rains which watered the earth. The Lord's warning to his people was a necessary one. In the long years ahead they did *follow other gods* to *worship and bow down to them*

(19). God here issues his warning that if they begin to follow idols they will perish. The fulfilment of that threat became a sad feature of their later history. This land which lay ahead of them would one day be taken from them. They endured the bitter experience of the Babylonian exile for *not obeying the LORD* their God (20).

God is sovereign and, for our own good as well as for his own glory, he will not allow his unique place to be taken by another. He is a 'jealous God' (5:9) and there can be no rivals. In late twentieth-century society, these two perils are specially prominent – pride and idolatry. Mankind exalts itself and dethrones its God. Such arrogance can only end in judgment. Sometimes, in his mercy, the Lord can bring low a proud man or woman to *humble* (2, 3) them and teach them that there is more to life than material possessions or social prestige or intellectual attainments or vocational ambition. The greatest thing in life is not to rely on *a land where bread will not be scarce* (9) but to recognize that *man does not live on bread alone.* The only food which lasts is the eternal provision of God's unchanging word, that which *comes from the mouth of the LORD* (3). Those who obey (20) that word will live for ever.

In this chapter God's people are confronted with Canaan's inevitable change of circumstances. In such times they are to remember that God is a Teacher to be heard (1–3), a Father to be obeyed (5–6), a Giver to be thanked (10), a Deliverer to be remembered (14–16) and a Sovereign to be honoured (19–20). Those who acknowledge such a generous and caring God rarely take his blessings for granted and never look elsewhere (idolatry) for an answer to their deepest needs. Preoccupied with their new situation, however, the Israelites forgot what God had done (2–4, 14–15), given (3, 7–10, 16, 18) and said (1, 3, 6, 11, 18–20). Their later story is a saga of continuing forgetfulness and necessary correction. However, another passage in this book (10:10) makes it abundantly clear that these sad, spiritually disloyal events are also a testimony to the Lord's unmerited mercy. He does not deal with us as we deserve: 'the Lord listened to me at this time also. It was not his will to destroy you.'

Deuteronomy 9:1–29
10. When rebels are forgiven

In the preceding chapter the main sin of the Israelite people was a serious negative one – forgetfulness; here the trouble is a positive one – rebellion. At this point, the people are reminded of the invincible God (1–5), the rebellious pilgrims (6–24) and the dependent intercessor (25–29).

1. The invincible God (9:1–5)

The Lord had anticipated what the Hebrew people would say once they took possession of the land. They would claim that the dramatic victory and its consequent prosperity was entirely due to their own strenuous efforts: 'My power and the strength of my hands have produced this wealth for me' (8:17). In the light of this false assertion of Israel's might, the Lord deliberately emphasizes Israel's weakness. It is the Canaanite people who are strong, not the Hebrews. The words *greater and stronger* (7:1) are used to describe Canaan's seven *nations*, large fortified *cities* and individual *people*. The Israelite invaders have not been chosen because of their superior strength but on account of their evident weakness (7:7). The potentially proud and arrogant Hebrews are told how small and insignificant they are. It was their opponents who had the strength. The notorious *Anakites* were men of enormous stature. Physically (and derisively) they could look down on these relatively puny Israelites who had dared to enter their country. How could this crowd of untrained desert nomads possibly gain possession of the land ahead?

The secret of effective conquest was certainly not in Israel's self-assured boasting. The miracle of victory would be achieved only by confessing their weakness, acknowledging God's greatness and expressing their dependence. The true power of the invading army would not be in its prodigious strength but in its divine resources. The Lord would equip them – that was the secret. In order to fortify their spirits as they embarked on this entirely new experience, Moses assured the people that God was among them as they crossed the Jordan (1). Four pictures of God are presented to the waiting soldiers before they march forward. He is not simply with them; he has already gone ahead of them as their Advance-Guard (*the one who goes across ahead of you*, 3), conquering Warrior (*a devouring fire*), dependable Lord (*He will destroy them . . . as the LORD has promised you . . . to accomplish what he swore to your fathers*, 3, 5) and righteous Judge (*it is on account of the wickedness of these nations that the LORD is going to drive them out before you*, 4). Their victory will be on the basis of his intervention, not their skill; the conquests will be due to God's strength not theirs.

The Lord knows, however, that, once their enemies have been vanquished, the Israelite people will quickly snatch the glory for themselves. Some among them will argue that if the victory was not due to their military expertise then it must have been because of their moral excellence. God had certainly been the victor, but surely the conquest must be seen as a well-earned prize – a public recognition of their holiness, obedience and good deeds: *The LORD has brought me here to take possession of this land because of my righteousness* (4).

They agree that the conquest is not a human achievement, so they insist that it must be a divine reward. Nothing could have been further from the truth. They find it impossible to admit that it is a totally undeserved gift, generously given on the basis of God's reliable promise to *Abraham, Isaac and Jacob* (5). This universal human tendency to earn our own salvation is the reason why so many people cannot put their trust in Christ. If they could gain a place in God's heaven by their own *righteousness* or *integrity* (5), they would certainly do it and prefer it that way. They cannot forsake their trust in human effort. The road to eternal judgment is littered with tragic monuments to self-salvation – 'a few more good deeds, a few more prayers, a few more pilgrimages, and all will be well'. Those who accept God's *gift* of new life in Christ recognize that they can do nothing at all to earn their salvation. Christ has done it all. It has been said that the only contribution we can make to our own salvation is the sin which made it necessary. Augustus Toplady expressed it perfectly in his famous hymn:

> Nothing in my hand I bring,
> Simply to Thy Cross I cling;
> Naked, come to Thee for dress;
> Helpless, look to Thee for grace;
> Foul, I to the fountain fly;
> Wash me, Saviour, or I die.[1]

---

[1] Augustus Toplady, *Rock of Ages*.

God was to *give* the land of Canaan to the Hebrew people because he had *promised* it to the patriarchs and because he was *judging* the evil nations who had occupied it previously. Their future occupancy of the land was, therefore, a token of his merciful generosity, an expression of his righteous judgment and the fulfilment of his reliable promise. It was nothing whatever to do with their works.

2. The rebellious pilgrims (9:6–24)

Moses drives home the point that the land is not a reward for good behaviour by explaining that, far from being righteous, the Israelites have been persistently unrighteous. If they imagine for a moment that they deserve such a generous gift, it is time for them to think again. They must be living in a self-flattering, make-believe dream-world, if they seriously believe that Canaan is God's special prize for virtuous conduct. In order to make the point abundantly clear, the people are made to look at themselves as they really are, not as they vainly imagine themselves to be. Moses illustrates the fact of Israel's unrighteousness in two ways: first he presents a general description, then he quotes some historical examples.

First, knowing the error of their self-righteous delusion, Moses describes the people as God sees them. He shows that God is giving the land not to a righteous nation but to people who are arrogant (4), stubborn (6, 13, 27), rebellious (7, 23–24), provocative (8, 18), corrupt (12), idolatrous (12, 16), sinful (16), evil (18), unbelieving (23), disobedient (23) and wicked (27), eleven characteristics which are hardly the marks of a 'righteous' community.

In case these sweeping generalizations are not acceptable, Moses then goes on to quote some specific examples of the nation's unrighteous conduct. Actual places, precisely located on the pilgrims' route, are remembered as the scenes of Israel's widespread disobedience. They were not isolated acts of disappointing behaviour in an otherwise harmonious relationship. Arrogant defiance had marked the start of their journey and it had persisted throughout the decades: *From the day you left Egypt until you arrived here, you have been rebellious against the L*ORD *(7)*. They are reminded of five specific acts of gross rebellion.

At Horeb (8), when Moses was at the top of the mountain and God was confirming the covenant with his people, they made the golden calf. It was an act of blatant disobedience, making an idol (which had been strictly forbidden) and doing it at the very time when the Lord was declaring his love for his people. Surely if ever there was a time for loyal and adoring love, that was it. It was like a young and flirtatious wife constantly diverting her attention to

127

other men, only days after her wedding. On his descent from the mountain, Moses saw that they had broken the commandment about idolatry. Moreover, his own brother, Aaron, had led the rebellion saying that it was this newly manufactured image which had brought them out of Egyptian slavery. When Moses saw the idol he threw down the tablets (17) on which the law was written – not in anger but in grief. The people had broken the agreement and God's servant smashed the tablets. It was like one of the symbolic actions of Israel's later prophets.[2] It was a visible public sign of the people's appalling disloyalty.

The disobedience at *Horeb*, however, was only the beginning of sorrows. At *Taberah* (22)[3] the rebels complained about their difficulties. At *Massah* (22)[4] they 'found fault with Moses' to such an extent that he feared for his life. They wished they had never left Egypt and doubted the presence of God among them. *Kibroth Hattaavah* (22)[5] was the place where they reflected wistfully on the rich variety of Egypt's food. They contrasted its plentiful supply of fish and vegetables with their monotonous diet of daily manna. Craving for meat, they grumbled yet again. At Massah Moses worried that the people might kill him;[6] at Kibroth Hattaavah he wished he could die.[7]

When they were within easy striking distance of the promised land, *Kadesh Barnea* (23–24) became another scene of rebellion, unbelief and disobedience. There the rebels paid the highest price for continuing insurrection. They were kept out of the land and left in the wilderness until, thirty-eight years later, every offender had died. The revolt at Kadesh was the worst scene of all. God had repeatedly assured them that the land was theirs, and he had ordered them to possess it. They dismissed the promises (*did not trust him*), however, and rejected the commands (*or obey him*, 23). It was hardly appropriate conduct for people who claimed to be distinctively righteous.

This stark realism is one of the most compelling features of biblical teaching. The Scripture does not spend time flattering a few special favourites. Sin is sin whoever commits it. Although the Israelites were his 'chosen people', the Lord did not overlook their iniquities. Their election was an example of his grace not a reward for their works. Christians are equally aware of all that they owe to God. They are accepted by him on the basis of his immense generosity, not on account of their religious practices or moral achievements. Salvation is a totally undeserved gift, not a spiritual reward.[8]

---

[2] Je. 19:1–13.   [3] See Nu. 11:3.   [4] See 7:16; Ex. 17:1–7.
[5] See Nu. 11:4–34.   [6] Ex. 17:4.   [7] Nu. 11:15.
[8] Rom. 3:24; Gal. 2:16; Eph. 2:8–9.

3. The dependent intercessor (9:25–29)

This sad catalogue of Israel's rebelliousness is relieved by a moving account of Moses' role as the community's intercessor. The narrative leaves the rebellion at Kadesh and returns to the idolatry at Horeb. God threatened to *destroy* the people and *blot out their name from under heaven* (14). He said that he would make a totally fresh start by making Moses the father of a new race, *stronger and more numerous than they* (14). When Moses heard this he went in to plead with God for the disobedient people. The story of Israel's intercessor offers some important insights into our ministry of prayer for others. The intercession of Moses was submissive, persistent, sacrificial, specific, compassionate, comprehensive and effective.

a. Submissive

Moses' total subjection to God's will was expressed both in posture and language. Before he began to speak he *fell prostrate before the LORD* (18, see also 25). It was the attitude of a surrendered servant, an adoring worshipper and a loyal subject. The people had been arrogant and *stiff-necked* (6, 13), fiercely and foolishly rebellious, but Moses gave outward physical expression to a totally different frame of mind.

He did it also in the words he used as he began to pray. *Sovereign LORD* (26) is a title reserved in Deuteronomy for an introduction to prayer (3:24); it was used earlier by Abraham[9] and later by Joshua[10] in times of special need. It affirmed at the start God's complete lordship and unrivalled dominion. The rebels had worshipped the golden calf. Moses had no other god but the Lord alone. He was determined to surrender himself, and this tragic situation of Israel's rebellion, to the only ruler of the world. Their destiny was under the control of a mighty ruler, not at the mercy of a man-made idol. Genuine intercession begins by confessing God's right to act as he wishes in the lives of those for whom we are praying. It does not attempt to order God about or tell him what is best in any particular situation. Some prayer can be commendably strong in faith but seriously lacking in reverence; the true intercessor does not obtain one at the expense of the other. However great our need, when we approach God we must never forget who he is.

[9] Gn. 15:2, 8.   [10] Jos. 7:7–9.

b. Persistent

Moses knew better than anyone the seriousness and urgency of the situation. The rebels were under sentence of divine wrath and he must give himself to earnest and continual prayer. It was a matter of life and death. He gave time to it; nothing was more important than his plea for the people. He spent *forty days and forty nights* (18, 25) in God's presence, beseeching the Lord to change his mind about the threatened extermination of the disobedient and disloyal rebels. The New Testament teaching about prayer similarly insists that we should 'pray continually'[11] and must 'always keep on praying'.[12] We are meant to 'devote ourselves'[13] to it, yet there are many occasions when we 'give up'[14] far too quickly. Persistent prayer is a confession of dire need and utter dependence; we keep on asking because there is no-one else to whom we can go.[15]

c. Sacrificial

Moses refused to eat until he had done his utmost for the needy people: *I ate no bread and drank no water, because of all the sin you had committed* (18). Abstaining from food or drink for this long period was a sign of penitence. The people had been casual about their sinning but Moses could not take it lightly. He grieved deeply for them and was as distressed about the nature of their sin as they were about its consequences. His refusal to eat was *because of all the sin* which they had committed (18), not solely because they were about to lose their lives. The absence of Moses from the meal table for almost six weeks was a testimony to his genuine grief over the sins of his heedless contemporaries. In Old Testament times, fasting was an outward expression of inward sorrow.[16] Fasting is also given a place in the New Testament understanding of prayer.[17] The Lord Jesus clearly expected his followers to use fasting as an aid to prayer[18] and that, additionally, should cause us to think deeply about its meaning.

In our extremely busy world, occasional fasting may release some additional time for prayer. We could profitably spend half an hour in prayer instead of having a meal. In contemporary society food has become such a ridiculous obsession that many people live to eat instead of eating to live. Fasting might be viewed as a silent witness to our conviction that 'man does not live on bread alone' (8:3), though we must certainly not be ostentatious about it. Jesus

---

[11] 1 Thes. 5:17.   [12] Eph. 6:18.   [13] Col. 4:2.   [14] Lk. 18:1.
[15] Lk. 11:5–13; 18:1–8.
[16] Ezr. 8:23; Ne. 9:1; Est. 4:3; Ps. 35:13; Dn. 9:3.   [17] Acts 14:23.
[18] Mt. 6:17–18; Mk. 2:20.

condemned that kind of objectionable religious showmanship.[19] Moreover, in a time of world hunger, the regular or occasional fast may be a contemporary Christian obligation. The money we would have spent on a meal might be given to support the missionary or Christian worker we are praying for, or relieve the plight of those homeless people whose crying needs rightly disturb our consciences. Refugees dying of starvation need something more than our uncostly prayers.[20] Fasting could be one of the ways by which the Lord answers our prayers for the hungry.

d. Specific

Although content to accept God's will, Moses came to the Lord with a bold and definite request. It was bold because God had said, *Let me alone, so that I may destroy them* (14). Moses, however, did not want to leave God alone on the matter. Too much was at stake. Reverence and boldness were beautifully harmonized in the life of this man of God. It was a definite request because he knew exactly what he was asking for. Here was no vague, uncertain prayer, hovering about in some pietistic void. He pleaded with God in precise terms, *do not destroy your people, your own inheritance* (26).

In God's mercy, generalized prayers ('Lord, bless the missionaries') may well be answered, but they hardly fall into the category of intelligent intercession. In today's world ill-informed prayer is unnecessary and unworthy. Most Christian societies regularly provide their supporters with helpful information to encourage prayer. Any Christian who wishes to intercede for modern missions can be well equipped by means of up-to-date prayer letters from overseas workers as well as excellent books to provide wider perspectives, like Patrick Johnstone's *Operation World*.[21] Moses asked for something definite and God was pleased to grant it to him.

e. Compassionate

He was naturally concerned about the people as a whole but he was particularly distressed about his sinful brother, Aaron. *And the Lord was angry enough with Aaron to destroy him, but at that time I prayed for Aaron too* (20). During those six weeks of earnest prayer, he did not only consider the plight of the thousands. He was grieved that a member of his own family had allowed that idolatry to take place. Aaron does not seem to have initiated the apostasy[22]

---

[19] Mt. 6:16.   [20] Jas. 2:14–17.

[21] Patrick Johnstone, *Operation World: Handbook for world intercession* (STL/WEC, 1986).

[22] Ex. 32:1.

but he certainly encouraged it. Moses must have been overwhelmed with sorrow at the thought that his own brother could be so unreliable (when left in charge of the camp), disloyal (to go along with their request), disobedient ('fashioning it with a tool'),[23] cowardly ('You know how prone these people are to evil'),[24] and dishonest ('I threw [the gold] into the fire, and out came this calf')[25] – what a ridiculous explanation. Moses, however, still prayed for him. This narrative is a reminder that we must not only intercede for people we like but also for people who disappoint us or make life difficult for us. Jesus said we should even intercede for those who oppose us.[26]

f. Comprehensive

It is important to see how carefully the intercessor marshalled his facts and presented his case to the sovereign Lord. Moses certainly had no occasion to appeal on the basis of Israel's merit. They were a crowd of rebellious idolaters. He made his request on the basis of five aspects of God's uniqueness. He appealed to God's election of Israel (*your people, your own inheritance*, 26, 29), his saving achievement (*that you redeemed*, 26), unchanging promise (*Remember your servants Abraham, Isaac and Jacob* and *the land ... promised them*, 27–28), personal repute (lest the Egyptians say, *Because the LORD was not able*, 28) and unrivalled power (*by your great power and your outstretched arm*, 29).

It was totally unfitting for Israel to boast but it was equally inappropriate for the Egyptians to brag and, worst of all, get a distorted impression of God's dealings with his people. If they did not enter Canaan, it would be an act of God's judgment on them. The Egyptians, however, would not see it like that. For them it would be a confession of God's weakness. Therefore, Moses pleaded, God's glory was at stake; that was far more important than Israel's reputation. If the multitude died in the desert, it would seriously reflect (28) on God's power (*not able to bring them*), word (*which he promised*) and nature (*because he hated them*). Moses genuinely feared that pagan nations might well be misled if God visited his people with the judgment they deserved.

g. Effective

The time which Moses spent in God's presence was abundantly worthwhile. He did more by praying for them than reasoning with

---

[23] Ex. 32:4; see Ex. 20:4 'You shall not make for yourself an idol'.　　[24] Ex. 32:22.
[25] Ex. 32:24.　　[26] Mt. 5:44.

them. At the end of those six weeks of persistent intercession, the Lord renewed the covenant with his disobedient people. Moses was commanded to bring another two tablets of stone up to the top of the mountain. The sin had been pardoned, the relationship restored, the prayer answered. Thanks to a merciful God,[27] the people were enabled to forget the past and begin again. What a good thing that, among such a vast array of unsubmissive rebels, there was a man like Moses to pray for them. God is still looking for surrendered people to exercise that kind of intercessory ministry, even in a rebellious age like ours.

[27] Ex. 33:19.

Deuteronomy 10:1 – 11:32
11. Love matters most

Moses continued to speak to the people about the sad events at Horeb. By making a golden image, their fathers had grieved the God who loved them. The sins of infidelity and ingratitude had seriously damaged the covenant-relationship. Moses, their sacrificial intercessor, was concerned, however, both for God's honour and the people's salvation. He had 'stood in the breach'[1] between an angry God and a sinning people. Their iniquity was pardoned and the relationship restored; the renewed community could continue their journey, facing the future with gratitude and confidence.

Moses did not tell the story to the children of the offenders simply to open sore wounds. He was using their history as a warning device. Our worst sins are not a total disaster if we can learn something from them. If they are completely pardoned, yesterday's mistakes will surely encourage greater dependence, serve to make us more alert and possibly far less presumptuous. In years to come, that grim apostasy at Horeb would be recalled both in the Old Testament and the New, not simply to condemn the idolaters but to warn later generations of similar dangers.[2] It was not the last time that the Israelite people were to worship a golden calf.

God is generous in his love and mercy, however. Although Moses uses the incident to alert the waiting people to similar dangers in Canaan, they are not left in any doubt whatever concerning the dependable, forgiving love of God. In the teaching of the next two chapters, 'love' is the central theme. This extended passage brings Moses' historical review to a close. The people must not be left simply with a depressing account of human sin but with a reassuring exposition of God's love. As this main address moves to its conclusion, Moses refers to God's love for his people (10:15), and their love for him (10:12; 11:1, 13, 22). He also describes God's love for

[1] Ps. 106:23.   [2] Ne. 9:16–19; Ps. 106:19–21; Acts 7:39–41.

the alien (10:18) and the consequent responsibility of the Israelites to love them as well (10:19–20). The people who are about to enter Canaan are therefore reminded of love's generosity, initiative, priority, obligation and pledge.

1. Love's generosity (10:1–11)

Whilst recalling the Horeb story, Moses speaks to the congregation about God's generosity to Israel's people, Aaron's family and Levi's tribe.

a. Israel's people (10:1–5)

Moses makes sure that the people remember how God told his servant to chisel out two more stone tablets *like the first ones*, an observation which is made four times in as many verses (1–4). Although the first tablets had been broken, the Lord invited Moses to make a new record of the agreement, and the freshly made tablets were to be placed in the ark of the covenant. Although the people had sinned, breaking the *commandments* (4), God was giving them an entirely new beginning. They did not deserve to be pardoned, but it is love's nature to forgive, and to do so fully, completely and immediately. Those repeated words, *like the first ones* (1), are a striking reminder of God's generous pardon.

b. Aaron's family (10:6–7)

Aaron had sinned. There was no doubt about that. The first two *commandments* had made it clear that the Israelites were to have no other gods nor were they to make any graven image (5:8). The people had said 'Come, make us gods' and, in response to their demands, Aaron's own hands had fashioned the golden-calf.[3] The prohibition against idolatry plainly said that those who rejected God's love by worshipping images would encounter the wrath of a 'jealous God' who would punish 'the children for the sin of the fathers to the third and fourth generations' (5:7–10). Yet, in God's mercy, Aaron was permitted to assume his leadership responsibilities once again and, after his death, his son, Eleazar, *succeeded him as priest* (6). The sins of that particular father were not visited upon his children. Aaron's great transgression was generously forgiven.

---

[3] Ex. 32:1, 4.

135

c. Levi's tribe (10:8–9)

The new tablets on which the commandments were written were preserved in an ark, made with poles so that it could be carried (8) on the journey by a specially appointed team of priests from the tribe of Levi. The ark was overlaid with gold and its lid was known as 'the mercy seat'.[4] When the people sinned, the sacrificial blood was sprinkled on the mercy seat to 'make atonement'[5] for the sins of the people. Moreover, the ark was to be a visible reminder to the people of God's presence in their midst. It was there, at the ark in the tabernacle, that God 'met' with Moses.[6] Images, or representations of God, were strictly forbidden but the Lord knew that the people would be helped by symbols or outward signs of his presence and power. The Lord also knew that his people could easily lose their spiritual and moral values, so a particular tribe (Levi) was set apart to become God's ministers to remind them of holy things. As the Levites carried the ark on the long pilgrimage across the desert they were witnessing to the fact of God's presence, word (the two tables of the law) and mercy.

The tribe of Levi was, in itself, a symbol of the importance of spiritual realities and the generosity of God in making such rich provision for their basic human needs. They were to serve the Lord (*stand* – the posture of a servant) and *pronounce blessings* on the people (8), making them aware of the things which mattered most of all. The Levites were not to be given an allocation of land like the other tribes. They were to be supported by the people. If they gave themselves wholeheartedly to their teaching, pastoral and intercessory ministries among the Israelites,[7] divine resources would always meet their daily needs. The devoted priest was God's 'messenger' to the people. The Lord himself undertook to be his special *inheritance* (9). He would be as generous to them as to all the other tribes. They would certainly not suffer any deprivation because they had put God's work first.

In a brief description (10–11) of his intercessory ministry on the mountain, Moses reminded the people of five important aspects of God's generosity. He answers prayer (*the LORD listened to me*), forgives sin (*It was not his will to destroy you*), provides guidance (*Go ... and lead the people on their way*), guarantees help (*enter and possess the land*) and fulfils promises (*that I swore to their fathers to give them*).

---

[4] Ex. 25:21.   [5] Lv. 16:15–16.   [6] Ex. 25:22.   [7] Mal. 2:4–7.

2. Love's initiative

The preacher returns to some familiar themes as he closes his historical survey of God's dealings with his people. We recall that Near Eastern treaties frequently began with an account of earlier relationships between the two parties making the agreement. This historical introduction to the treaty was usually followed by some general principles, a description of qualities and attitudes which were to govern the relationship in the years ahead. The language of 'love' was often given a prominent place in this section of these documents. It is certainly of supreme importance in the covenant God made with his people.

He is the creator, sustainer and ruler of the entire universe (14) yet the sovereign Lord chose one very small nation, Israel, to be the instrument of his special purposes in the world. The people are told that, though there were so many other nations he might have used, *the Lord set his affection on your forefathers and loved them, and he chose you, their descendants, above all the nations, as it is today* (15). The covenant-relationship was based on his commitment to love them, not on their decision to follow him. The initiative was with God and it still is. The apostle John shared the same truth with the early Christian people in the first century: 'This is love: not that we loved God, but that he loved us and sent his Son as an atoning sacrifice for our sins.'[8]

God does not simply love in word. His love is practical not theoretical. It is expressed in his everyday relationships with his people. These two chapters expound the visible outworking of God's love in human experience. The divine love was manifested not simply in Israel's election (15) but in his constant protection throughout the years. The *great God, mighty and awesome* (17) has never failed to come to their aid (21; 11:2–4). He has loved not only the vast community but also the bereaved family. His love has been constantly displayed in his providential care for widows, orphans and aliens. He is specially concerned for those who are easily forgotten, the despised minorities (18, 22). He expresses his fatherly love not only by giving to his children (11:8–15) but by correcting (11:2, 5–7) and teaching them (11:1, 8, 13, 16–21).

3. Love's priority

God's love for his people is the foundation of the covenant. Although the initiative is with God, however, there are two parties to the agreement. Israel must respond to God's love by loving him

[8] 1 Jn. 4:10.

in return. Moreover, just as the Lord demonstrates his love in his practical deeds, so they must do the same. They must not love in word only either. The covenant requirements are undeniably explicit: *And now, O Israel, what does the LORD your God ask of you but to fear the LORD your God, to walk in all his ways, to love him, to serve the LORD your God with all your heart and with all your soul, and to observe the LORD's commands and decrees* (10:12–13).

The Lord expects them to give expression to their love for him and their commitment to his covenant in several ways. People will know that they love God because of their reverential worship (*fear*), holy living (*walk in all his ways*), willing obedience (*observe the LORD's commands*), active service (*serve*) and wholehearted devotion (*with all your heart and with all your soul*).

These covenant obligations are not tyrannical rules, oppressive regulations, designed for God's pleasure but human's pain. They have all been planned for his people's *good* (10:13). God is no kill-joy. He wants them to *live long* (11:9), to *eat and be satisfied* (11:15), to be happy and secure in the land he has prepared for them (4:40; 5:33; 6:2, 18, 24; 12:28; 13:17–18). This passage pays particular attention to God's generosity to his people. The narrative of the exodus and its aftermath recalled in 11:3–7 deliberately contrasts what God did for his people and what they did to him in return. He delivered them but they rebelled against him. In that story, Dathan and Abiram described Egypt, not Canaan, as 'a land flowing with milk and honey'.[9] Forgetting the agonies of Egyptian slavery, they became obsessed with the security of the past and the uncertainty of the future. Did those rebels seriously imagine that God would deliberately lead them into a total disaster? So, Moses also heightens the contrast between Egypt and Canaan. The land ahead will not be like Egypt, totally dependent on artificial irrigation, *where you planted your seed and irrigated it by foot* (11:10). During the years of slavery many thousands of them worked in the Egyptian fields where irrigation channels were in constant use. Once a channel had sufficient water, it was customary to move some earth with the feet to close off the channel. Hebrew slaves would have often done such menial work and without it they would have died of starvation. Moses assures the people, however, that God has better things in store for them. They are told that the *land you are entering* is infinitely better than the land *from which you have come*. It *drinks rain from heaven* (11:11) and throughout the entire year, God's eye is upon it continually (12). But although God has good things in store for his people, they will never be happy if the quest for good things comes first. Earlier in the book the point has been made that lasting contentment is not to be found in material prosperity: 'Man does not live on bread alone' (8:3).

Here, Moses also makes it clear that it is not to be found simply in religious ceremonial either. The Lord is specially concerned about those things which cultivate the *inner* life of the individual believer and the covenant community to which he belongs. The covenant's first obligation, clearly stated in this passage (10:12), is not that they obey the rules but that they *fear* the Lord. Moses' reference to the Lord's electing-love for their *forefathers* (10:15) naturally recalls the story of how the covenant-sign of circumcision was given to the patriarchs.[10] Here, however, as the people are about to enter the land promised to the patriarchs, Moses tells them that it is far more important to *circumcise* their hearts (10:16; 30:6) than their bodies. In the teaching of this book, attitudes and motives are of greater spiritual value than correct ceremonial observance. R. E. Clements has pointed out that the 'personalising and spiritualising of worship is a very marked feature'[11] of Deuteronomy. '*Loving*' God (11:22) is infinitely preferable to performing rituals. '*Walking in all his ways*' (22) is better than offering all our sacrifices. Love for the Lord is to be genuine and earnest: *with all your heart and with all your soul* – a recurrent phrase in Moses' teaching (4:29; 6:5; 10:12; 11:13; 13:3; 26:16; 30:2, 6, 10).

A later passage makes it clear that, even when they come to offer their sacrifices, inner attitudes are of greater importance than the outward ritual. In the ancient world, other nations offered their sacrifices to feed the gods, but this book emphasizes that it is the priests and people who eat the sacrifices, not the Lord: 'Eat the tithe of your grain . . . so that you may learn to revere the LORD your God always' (14:23). So, although the sacrifices are appropriate offerings to God as tokens of his people's love, they are presented 'in order to satisfy the religious needs of the worshippers and not the physical needs of God'.[12] Reverence is more important than ritual.

4. Love's obligation

Although the Lord chose Israel and *set his affection* (10:15) upon them, they were not the only people he loved. His love was certainly extended to Israel's bereaved families but his practical love was also shown to the resident alien within their borders. The helpless (*the fatherless and the widow*) and homeless (*alien*, 18) were both assured of his special care. Moreover, because God loved them, his covenant-people must love them too (19). Caring for deprived and depressed people was part of the agreement and such

[10] Gn. 17:9–12.   [11] R. E. Clements, *God's Chosen People*, p. 82.
[12] *Ibid.*, p. 87.

obligations figure prominently in this book (24:14, 17; 26:11–13; 27:19). They are to *love those who are aliens* not only because God says so but because there was a time when the Hebrews were 'resident aliens' as well: *for you yourselves were aliens in Egypt* (19).[13]

In the global village we inhabit, there are countless *aliens*, people who are literally homeless, others who have a roof over their heads but are far from 'home'; thousands of overseas students for example. Additionally, and more seriously, there are the world's starving refugees, numbered by their millions. Those who say they love God must not allow that love to remain at the level of the emotions. The New Testament as well as the Old reminds us that we ought to express our gratitude for God's love by loving others. Moreover, that love will never be merely vocal; it will be strenuously and sacrificially practical. It will be love that costs something, like God's love which was not without price. It will mean offering a meal to someone away from home, making a regular gift for the world's hungry, doing something for a person in trouble, befriending someone bereft of other help. John had all this in mind when he urged his readers not to love 'in words or tongue, but with actions and in truth'.[14] Love which is merely emotional or vocal is not the kind of love which God exemplified in the giving of his Son.

5. Love's pledge

Moses concludes this address by saying that if the people genuinely love the Lord, then their wholehearted devotion will be characterized by obedience, witness and commitment.

a. Obedience (11:13–17)

So if you faithfully obey the commands I am giving you ... to love the LORD your God ... I will provide (13–15). Moses knows that the danger of disobedience in the matter of idolatry is not a failure which belongs to the past. Horeb's sin is likely to be repeated: *Be careful, or you will be enticed* (16). To *worship other gods* (16) is to violate the terms of the covenant and breaking the treaty is an act of blatant disloyalty. In such circumstances, the *good land* (17) will soon become a barren land for only thus will his people be brought back to their former love.

b. Witness (11:18–25)

God's word must therefore be learnt (18), shared (19–21) and per-

---

[13] See Ex. 22:21; Lv. 19:33.   [14] 1 Jn. 3:17–18.

formed (22–25). The truth must not be left as an external statement, written on stone tablets, and deposited in the ark; it must be committed to memory, carefully stored in their *hearts* and treasured in their *minds*. Jesus is our supreme example in this discipline; because he memorized some of this book's great words, he could quote them in a moment of severe testing, when no scroll was remotely at hand.[15]

The word must be shared within families, using life's many opportunities to make it known – in the intimate conversations of home (*when you sit at home*), during journeys away from home (*when you walk along the road*), at the end of the day (*when you lie down*), as well as at its beginning (*when you get up*). Indoors, outdoors, morning and evening, these great truths must be faithfully communicated to the next generation. In contemporary society, we all have a special responsibility to share God's word with children. Unlike former generations, the majority of them no longer attend Sunday School or Bible classes. In England only 14% of children under the age of fourteen attend a Christian church on Sundays.[16] In such a context, the ministry of religious education teachers in schools is of strategic importance but, inevitably, the Christian teacher's opportunities are limited. Children who live around us may hear very little about God's word unless we find some opportunity to share it with them through children's work in our churches and youth organizations. Some people have gathered small groups of children in their homes on a weekly basis for simple Bible teaching and activities, and from such modest beginnings many young people have been won for Christ.

The word was to be displayed on the *door-frames* of homes and the *gates* of cities (6:9), which may, as we have seen (p. 98), be metaphorical imagery rather than a visual display. Whatever is intended, one thing is certain: the Hebrew people were told not to be secretive about their love for God. Their neighbours, friends, visitors and aliens were all meant to know how much he meant to them.

There are times, however, when it is easier to display the word than obey it. Those who love God must *carefully observe all these commands . . . love the* LORD *. . . hold fast to him*, literally 'clinging closely' (10:20; 11:22) to him. In the days ahead of them, those who practised Canaan's idolatrous religions would constantly attempt to lure them away, but they must keep near to God. The imagery of 'cleaving' is vivid, indicating (as Craigie observes) 'a very close and intimate relationship'. In the Old Testament the same verb is employed to describe the love of a man who is 'united' to his wife[17]

[15] Lk. 4:4, 8, 12.
[16] Peter Brierley, *Christian England* (MARC Europe, 1991), p. 52.
[17] Gn. 2:24.

and Job uses it to depict the way human bones and skin 'cling' together on an emaciated man.[18] Those who cling to God do not lust for lesser things.

c.   Commitment (11:26–32)

The people are told that there can be no neutrality. If they do not love him then they hate him. They are either destined for blessing or consigned to the curse. The language is deliberately uncompromising. Once they took possession of the land, there would be those who had no desire to forsake the Lord entirely but who would try to mix the worship of God with the idolatrous practices of their neighbours. No such syncretism is permissible. They are either completely for God or totally against him. So, the congregation are confronted with stark alternatives. It is a device used more than once in this book. They either *obey the commands* or *turn from the way*. If they do not *cleave to him* they will certainly *go after other gods*. They must decide their destiny: do they want a *blessing* or do they prefer a *curse*?

In order to present the truth in graphic terms and emphasize the need for such a radical decision, Moses portrays two mountains which would stand on either side of them as the pilgrims entered the land: Gerizim and Ebal. One typified blessing, the other cursing. They were, as Thompson says, 'two silent witnesses' to the Lord's demand 'for Israel to choose where her allegiance would be placed'. The two-mountains imagery recurs later in the book (27:1–26) where, once again, Israel is reminded of the necessity of total allegiance. Those who love God give themselves to him unreservedly. With Frances Ridley Havergal they express their commitment in radical terms – 'Ever, only, all for Thee'.[19] Their surrender to his will is permanent, exclusive and total.

[18] Jb. 19:20.   [19] Frances Ridley Havergal, *Take my life.*

C. Applying the covenant (12:1 – 26:19)

Deuteronomy 12:1 – 14:29
12. Honouring God

We recall that in the ancient treaties which may have been a model for the structure of Deuteronomy, the general principles of the covenant were followed by specific regulations. We have now reached that part of the book where there is a clear transition of that kind. The teaching moves from a general statement of the law to an applied interpretation of its precise demands. We are not confronted, however, with a coldly formal, detailed law-code or a set of rules and regulations. What we have here is 'preached law' (von Rad). It is a sermon, preached by Moses, an application of the law or covenant given forty years earlier, and now related more closely to their new life in a totally different environment. The changed context demands a fresh interpretation of the covenant for people who are about to settle in either agricultural or urban communities and are called to live in a way which pleases God.

When Moses preached about these *decrees and laws*, he began by reminding them, once again, that the land was a divine gift in fulfilment of a dependable promise to a privileged people. It was *the land that the LORD, the God of your fathers, has given you to possess* (1). The gift precedes the demand. Moreover, the preaching must not only be heard, it must be obeyed. They must *be careful to follow* what the Lord required of them (1; 10:13; *cf.* also 11:32; 12:32; 13:18). In other words, obedience was to be the obligatory response to the Lord's generosity – a way of acknowledging God's goodness, not a means of earning his favour. Moses here tells the people that their obedience to God will be expressed in their corporate worship (12:1 – 13:18), daily conduct (14:1–21) and generous giving (14:22–29).

1. Honouring God by our worship (12:1 – 13:18)

We have been made for God and unless that God-shaped vacuum is filled by God, other things will always be out of perspective.

Augustine gave eloquent expression to this basic truth at the beginning of his famous *Confessions*: 'You made us for yourself, and our heart is restless until it find rest in you.'[1] Those who honour God are given both the motivation and ability to live as he demands and deserves.

The precise summary of the covenant given in the Ten Commandments begins with worship, true and false. Its opening instructions define our relationship with God, and only then do they deal with our responsibility towards others. The first four commandments establish the fact that God must come first. Jesus had precisely the same priorities; during those wilderness temptations, he repeatedly insisted on putting God first. Neither his own appetite (turning stones to bread), nor his immense capacity to influence people for good (ruling the kingdoms), was allowed to take precedence over his submission to God. In his preaching he told his followers that in daily living, they must 'seek first' God's kingdom, then other things would fall into their correct place. If that is wrong, little else will be right.[2] Nothing, therefore, is of greater importance than acknowledging his prior claim on our lives, and that is precisely what we do when we worship. Moses here presents six aspects of corporate worship. He tells the people that, if they genuinely put God first, their worship will be acceptable, unifying, sacrificial, joyful, compassionate and consistent.

a. Acceptable worship

The Canaanites had an essentially pragmatic approach to worship. They wanted abundant harvests, so at their hilltop shrines they indulged in practices which they considered might encourage fertility and growth. Their worship-patterns became little else than sexual orgies with a religious scenario, but such an approach to worship is utterly offensive to a pure and holy God. His people are told that they must not allow their worship to be corrupted by Canaanite traditions. God laid down the terms on which he is to be approached by his children. Their worship will not only honour God's word; it will reflect God's nature. He is holy, so their worship can never be impure. He is consistent, so their worship can never be contradictory, worshipping in one way but behaving in another. He is loving, so their worship will never have a harmful effect on others. He is righteous, so their worship must never ignore moral values. Therefore, right at the beginning of this detailed interpretation of the covenant, God insists that there is no true religion without good morality. Double standards are totally

---

[1] Augustine, *Confessions*, I:1.   [2] Mt. 6:33.

unacceptable as far as God is concerned. As R. E. Clements has observed, 'What was at stake was ultimately the union of morality with religion, and what we find in Deuteronomy is the refusal to accept that God could demand of men, in the name of religion, what the conscience of society condemned as immoral.'[3]

Once they settled in Canaan, it would be perilous if they compromised on these essential spiritual principles. The command is direct and explicit: *You must not worship the Lord your God in their way* (4). So, on entering the land, they must *Destroy completely all the places on the high mountains ... where the nations you are dispossessing worship their gods. Break down their altars, smash their sacred stones and burn their Asherah poles in the fire; cut down the idols of their gods and wipe out their names from those places* (2–3). The prohibition is absolute and emphatic; it literally reads, 'Destroying, you will destroy.'

In the days ahead, the Israelites may not be tempted to abandon the worship of the only true God, but they would certainly be tempted to worship him in Canaanite ways. Here, the preacher makes it clear that Canaanite worship was totally unacceptable to God. It had a number of serious defects: it was religiously false, morally corrupt, physically brutal and socially destructive.

It was religiously false because the gods of Canaan were meaningless nonentities, mere nothings, the sick projection of unclean minds. God had forbidden the manufacture of idols because he is the only and unique God. There are no others. Statues and images suggest the existence of other deities, represented by their idols. The commandment was clear: 'You shall have no other gods before me' (5:7).

The worship of the Canaanite people was morally corrupt. Their religious practices were degrading and damaging to human life and experience. It was widely held that these agricultural deities demanded certain cultic acts in order to promote fertility and ensure that the seed sown in their fields would grow and multiply. Their worship included sacred prostitution, both male and female. Sexual practices of that kind frequently took place at the shrines and temples of most ancient Near Eastern religions, apart from Israel.[4] Moses tells his congregation that *the Lord hates* (12:31) that sort of worship. It is 'detestable' (18:9), and people who promote and participate in such degrading acts are nothing other than shrine-prostitutes (23:17–18).

Moreover, at times, their worship was physically brutal and cruel, involving the offering of human sacrifice: *They even burn their sons and daughters in the fire as sacrifices to their gods* (12:31). The

[3] R. E. Clements, *God's Chosen People*, pp. 73–74.
[4] Nu. 25:1–9; 1 Ki. 15:12; 2 Ki. 23:7; Ho. 4:14.

teaching of Deuteronomy is specially concerned about the welfare of children. They are to be taught, fed and protected (4:9; 6:7; 10:18; 11:19, 21; 21:15–17; 22:8; 24:19–21). The thought that they could be murdered in the name of religion was horrific in the extreme (18:10) and totally dishonouring to a God who had impressed upon his people the unique value of human life.

Canaanite worship was socially destructive. Its religious acts were pornographic and sick, seriously damaging to children, creating early impressions of deities with no interest in moral behaviour. It tried to dignify, by the use of religious labels, depraved acts of bestiality and corruption. It had a low estimate of human life. It suggested that anything was permissible, promiscuity, murder or anything else, in order to guarantee a good crop at harvest. It ignored the highest values both in the family and in the wider community – love, loyalty, purity, peace and security – and encouraged the view that all these things were inferior to material prosperity, physical satisfaction and human pleasure. A society where those things matter most is self-destructive.

Although the practices of Canaanite religion belong to the ancient world, even twentieth-century people may be tempted to insist on their own way of worshipping God, rather than accept the biblical norm. In the contemporary world there are endless varieties of self-determined worship patterns. There is, for example, the familiar 'I worship God in the open air' pattern. Nature-worshippers of this kind idolize their enjoyment of the created world but are not prepared to listen attentively to the Creator. That is one of the marks of self-centred paganism,[5] not genuine Christian belief.

Then, there are the 'I don't go to church because I'm as good as those who do' people. Nobody wishes to deny the moral qualities of the non-churchgoing millions but Christian worship is an expression of submissive obedience not an assertion of superior morality. Christians attend public worship because they desire to follow the example of God's people in Old Testament times and, even more importantly, of God's Son. Jesus worshipped with God's people. His local synagogue was not packed to the doors with Nazareth's righteous citizens. But Jesus went to worship there 'as was his custom'[6] because God demanded it, not because his fellow-worshippers were perfect. After Pentecost, Peter and John went up to the temple to pray because it was 'the time of prayer – at three in the afternoon',[7] not because all those who prayed with them were examples of moral excellence. Among that crowd in the temple were a good number who, weeks before, had demanded the execution of Jesus. The apostles, however, went to pray with God's people

---

[5] Rom. 1:25.   [6] Lk. 4:16.   [7] Acts 3:1.

because God's word required it. It is not appropriate for us to tell God how he is to be worshipped. We are to respond to what he describes in his word.

Others belong to the 'I prefer to do it my way' type. Although for centuries western society has acknowledged an intellectual dependence on biblical Christianity, many people in contemporary society have religious loyalties which are not submitted to the scrutiny of God's word. In our contemporary culture, alongside the marginalization of the Christian churches, new religions are on the increase every year, and in many countries the old eastern religions are being widely promulgated. A recently advertised university extra-mural department course on New Religions claims that there are 500 new religions in Britain today and in many of them, there is an explicit rejection of any concept of authority. Some are in direct rebellion against the use of reason. The general emphasis is on self-divinization and the ultimate transformation of mankind through some form of promised spiritual evolution, practically attained by meditation techniques, the use of yoga, hypnosis, chanting of set-phrases, all designed to bring us to some other level of consciousness. In this teaching, evil is reduced merely to ignorance, and faith is replaced by 'knowledge' of a set of ethereal concepts or vague propositions. Syncretistic New Age teaching follows this pattern of belief with its spiritually arrogant self-idolatry, its total rejection of the deity and atonement of Christ, and its determined indifference to biblical authority.

At a different level, there has scarcely been a time since the Middle Ages when people have been so interested in those damaging religious ideas associated with the occult, black magic, witchcraft and spiritism. Such practices are an offence to God as this book's later teaching makes abundantly clear (18:10–14). Only *biblical* worship is acceptable to God – worship which is defined and described in his word, and reflects the character of the God who is worshipped. It encourages purity, obeys truth, pursues righteousness and promotes love.

b.   Unifying worship

The Israelites are forbidden to worship at the Canaanite's hill-top shrines and groves. They are to *seek the place the LORD your God will choose from among all your tribes to put his Name there for his dwelling. To that place you must go* (5). The harmonious unity of God's people was essential to their spiritual vitality as well as their national security. During their long travels through the desert, they had been compelled to keep close to one another. Daily food was given to the whole community as it camped together with their portable tabernacle at the centre of the camp. The pillar of cloud by day and the column of fire by night did not guarantee guidance and protection to individual Hebrews who wanted to 'go it alone'. These were corporate blessings not individual rights. Once they settled in the land, the danger of disintegration was very real indeed. Later, in the period of the Judges, a significant phrase is used to describe the people's lack of cohesive unity: 'everyone did as he saw fit'.[8] The same words are used in this passage about worship (8).

It was important for the preservation of their unique faith that Israelite worship be gathered around an approved sanctuary so that it could be seen to be pure, regularized, uniform and acceptable to God. If the old Canaanite sites were used, anything might take place at those hill-top shrines, so it was essential that they be totally destroyed. This directive about an authentic meeting-place is important in contemporary religious life where, in a pluralistic society, Christian believers are sometimes expected to take part in inter-faith services of worship. In such acts of public worship the reading of a passage of New Testament Scripture may precede a selection from the Koran chanted by a Muslim leader. A Sikh participant may address prayers to his lord, while a Buddhist contribution extols the Krishna, offering his worshippers the prospect of nirvana. It is this kind of syncretistic approach to worship which is directly opposed by the teaching of Deuteronomy.

No thinking Christian would wish to deny the crucial importance of dialogue with adherents of other world-religions, nor the value of participating in community projects alongside people of other faiths. It is important for Christian believers to work harmoniously with all sorts of people regardless of their ethnic background, religious allegiance or political convictions. We are under an obligation to guard their religious liberty as well as our own. We must be eager to learn from others as much as we can so that we do not consciously misrepresent their views, and so that we might point them more effectively to the unique Christ. With our own treasured beliefs firmly rooted in Scripture, we shall be the first to acknowledge that God clearly uses people of other religions for his sovereign purposes.[9] It is surely misleading, however, for Christians to share in any service of worship which creates the impression that the various world religions are all valid approaches to the one God, and that to select any of them would be equally acceptable to the God and Father of our Lord Jesus Christ. In the context of first-century religious pluralism, the early Christian preachers rightly insisted on the uniqueness of salvation in Christ alone,[10] as did Jesus himself.[11]

[8] Jdg. 17:6; 21:25.   [9] Is. 10:5; 44:28; Ne. 2:4–8.   [10] Acts 4:12.
[11] Jn. 14:6.

Believers in the modern world also have a 'central' sanctuary. It is neither at Rome, Geneva, Canterbury, nor anywhere else which can be located on a map or described from some historical association. Wherever in the world they happen to live, Christian believers have a Trinitarian meeting-place. They gather in adoration before the throne of God, at the feet of Christ and in the presence of the Spirit. Moses said that the Israelite people were to worship at the place where God had *put his Name* (5), an expression which probably indicates 'a claim to sovereignty'. God wishes to be worshipped wherever he chooses to 'assert his sovereignty' (Thompson). The *place* which the Lord our God has chosen is at his throne and in the new temple of Christ's presence.

Jesus described his body in terms of a new meeting-place between God and men: '"Destroy this temple, and I will raise it again in three days." . . . But the temple he had spoken of was his body.'[12] That is the new temple where believers meet. He is the only way by which we can approach God.[13] Jesus once told a religiously argumentative woman that the day would come when true worship would be offered neither at her Samaritan shrine at Mount Gerazim nor in the revered temple at Jerusalem.[14] He said that in that day, the spiritually acceptable 'place' of worship would unite believers – not divide them as Jews and Samaritans. Those who gather for worship, fellowship, teaching and correction 'in his name' are assured of his living presence: 'there I am with them'.[15] In an ecumenical age, Christian believers of all denominations rejoice that their true unity is not attained by merging their ecclesiastical structures, or by finding some point of acceptable compromise about their doctrinal differences, but by worshipping and confessing their one Lord. Paul made that discovery in the very different churches of the first century and asserted its reality in the context of a potentially serious division.[16] The unity of churches and of Christians is *in Christ* – nowhere else. Those who recognize his uniqueness, acknowledge his centrality, glory in his redemptive work and anticipate his certain return, *are one* – it is a present fact, not a future dream.

c. Sacrificial worship

The Israelites were to bring their different sacrifices to the appointed *place*, where God was to *put his Name*. The burnt offering (6) is mentioned first; that was the sacrifice which was given to God in its entirety. The priest was required to 'bring all of

---

[12] Jn. 2:19, 21.   [13] Jn. 14:6.   [14] Jn. 4:21–24.   [15] Mt. 18:20.
[16] Gal. 3:26–28.

it'[17] – nothing was kept back either for the officiant or the worshipper. It typifies the believer's complete dedication to God.

Other offerings were 'shared' sacrifices; part was presented to God, the remainder offered to the priests or the people: *There, in the presence of the LORD your God, you ... shall eat* (7). They typify the believer's privileged communion with God.

Ours is a very different culture but our worship must be no less sacrificial. We are not required to offer animal sacrifices. Something far more costly is demanded of us. We are to offer ourselves, the bodies which God has entrusted to us, so that they can be used in the service of Christ. These are 'living' sacrifices; not the offering of dead animals. This total surrender is 'acceptable' in the sight of God. It is genuinely 'spiritual worship'.[18] We must also present the sacrifice of our praise and the offerings of 'good' deeds, our service for others.

These Christian sacrifices, pleasing to God,[19] must be made in the power of the Spirit for the glory of Christ. They are inspired and motivated, however, by the essential, complete, sufficient and unrepeatable offering of himself which Christ presented 'once for all time' when on the cross he made 'one sacrifice for sins'.[20] A distinctive characteristic of genuine Christian worship is a sustained focus on that unique sacrifice of Christ at Calvary.

d. Joyful worship

Worship was never meant to be a dreary affair, tedious, monotonous and boring. When the Hebrew people came together to present their gifts to God, it was an extremely happy time. With grateful hearts, they appeared before God with a sense of unpayable debt. The Lord had been good to them: *There ... you and your families shall eat and shall rejoice in everything you have put your hand to ... there rejoice before the LORD* (7, 12). Worship is acknowledging God's worth. In the first century, the winning athlete at the games would run a lap of honour during which all the spectators would call out excitedly *Axios! Axios!* ('Worthy! Worthy!'). The runner had proved himself worthy of all their admiration and jubilant applause. That is the very word used to describe the worship of the company of heaven as they exalt God their Creator and Christ the Redeemer:

---

[17] Lv. 1:13.   [18] Rom. 12:1.   [19] Heb. 13:15–16.
[20] Heb. 10:12.

'You are worthy, our Lord and God,
to receive glory and honour and
power . . .
Worthy is the Lamb, who was slain.'[21]

In the contemporary church scene it is important for Christians to recognize that worship is designed by God as a radiantly happy, not a divisive, experience. Sadly, in some churches, differing worship-patterns and styles of music have led to serious disharmony. It is tragic when the joyous adoration of God becomes a source of painful schism.

In this debate, which can be a healthy as well as necessary exercise in Christian maturity, traditionalists who love familiar patterns need to recognize the immense enrichment to the worship of hundreds of congregations of an equally thoughtful but less predictable approach to worship. They must remember that even in the Jerusalem temple there must have been occasions when a new psalm was introduced to the people. Every century has produced gifted writers and composers, and there is nothing uniquely sacrosanct about the music or verse of earlier centuries. In the majority of cases, the outstanding merit of the new material is its biblical content; many of the best songs are settings to music of uniquely inspiring words of Scripture.

Similarly, those who dislike older hymns need to appreciate the sense of helpful spiritual progression, and the more detailed exposition of a great theme, which can take place within a hymn which is hardly possible through a brief song. The older hymns also serve to remind us of the historical dimension to our faith. Those who have worshipped centuries before us are not antiquated figures of an irrelevant past; they are our brothers and sisters in Christ, *living* partners in that heaven to which we are travelling. Their experience of God in Christ is something to be appreciatively enjoyed, not impatiently dismissed. Both sides in this debate have so much to learn from each other, and good worship in the contemporary scene ought to be able to combine older and modern material, to the enrichment of all.

Whatever their style of worship, whenever Christians meet together for adoration and praise, they are rejoicing in the unique worthiness of God and the matchless beauty of Christ. Their worship is an expression of their infinite indebtedness to the God who loved them, the Christ who died for them, and the Spirit who has made these great truths effective in their personal experience. No wonder they are joyful. They can express their worship not only in the hymns or songs they sing, in the prayers they offer, in their attention to the exposition of God's word, in the presentation

[21] Rev. 4:11; 5:12.

151

of their monetary gifts for the Lord's work, but also by their personal surrender and their kindness to others. Worship is not an activity for the occasional hour on Sunday morning or evening. It is the adoring preoccupation of a lifetime. When the Israelites met for worship, they exalted the name of their God, the One who had done so much for them. Moses' words in this book give perfect expression to their gratitude:

> 'Blessed are you, O Israel!
> Who is like you,
> a people saved by the LORD?' (33:29)

e. Compassionate worship

Moreover, genuine Christian worship is not an exercise which encourages our retreat from the world of everyday life. It must never become a spiritual escape mechanism, so totally devoted to the adoration of God that it ignores the people he loves. If the God we worship is a God of unlimited compassion, then our worship of him can only be acceptable if it practically reflects his loving nature. Believers cannot love God without also loving others.[22] The provisions of the covenant about worship insisted that, on such occasions, love must be shown to the family, employees and the Lord's servants.

God is concerned about family life, so these acts of worship were intended not only to unify the nation but also to bring its families together. Any family which had suffered some difficulty in relationships was compelled by God's law to meet together in worship and in this way everything was done to heal divisions and break down barriers. The disintegration of families is one of the most serious aspects of contemporary social life. Jonathan Sacks devoted one of his 1990 Reith Lectures to 'The Fragile Family', pointing out that the family is not simply one of our social institutions; it is *the* one on which all others depend. The Chief Rabbi reminds us that the Hebrew Bible is 'above all a book about the family ... The heroes and heroines of Genesis are simply people living out their lives in the presence of God and the context of their families.' The family is 'that enclosed space in which we work out, in relation to stable sources of affection, a highly differentiated sense of who we are'.

Sacks uses an illustration from Communist China to show how totalitarian regimes have minimized the priority of family values. In 1976 the Chinese press reported a post-earthquake rescue operation by a man who had brought a local Communist officer to safety, even at

[22] 1 Jn. 4:20–21.

the cost of ignoring his own child's cry for help. He saved the officer because he considered him to have greater social value, and by the time he returned to the wreckage, his own son was dead. Newspapers described the incident as an example of commendable behaviour. The loss of family-priority, however, is a tragic aspect of contemporary social life.[23] In the century when Freud and others first emphasized the determinative psychological influence of early childhood, we have witnessed the disintegration of the British family. Marriage statistics in the European Community show that the United Kingdom has the second highest divorce rate in western Europe. Our divorce figures have doubled in the past twenty years. On current trends, 37% of new marriages are expected to end in divorce proceedings, which means that about three million people will experience a broken marriage this decade. Current research has shown that a large proportion of people regret their divorce. One recent study showed that 51% of divorced men who have not remarried wished they had stayed with their former spouse.[24] These figures confront the Christian church with an immense challenge. Many of these breakdowns in relationships might be avoided if the people concerned were welcomed into a friendly, compassionate, healing community with good resources of well-trained pastoral care.

All this surely demonstrates the immense importance of a spiritual dimension to marriage and family life, an aspect of social conduct which was prominent in the provision God made for his people. If, by their worship, they were to put him first, then they would not only be drawn nearer to him but closer to one another. Moreover, in this context, the family would frequently be reminded of moral and spiritual values, as well as their indebtedness to God in everyday life and work. Passages such as this one about Israel's worship underline the importance of spiritual priorities as a crucial component in a happy and effective married life.

Some families, however, in treasuring these values can be selfishly insular. In Israelite life, the worshipping family was not allowed to neglect their employees. When they met for worship, the *menservants* and *maidservants* in every Hebrew family were to be as welcome as any of the *sons* and *daughters* (12). This says something to us about the sanctification of work, and underlines, once again, the refusal of the Hebrew people to draw sharp distinctions between the sacred and the secular. For them, anything which was 'secular' was simply an area of life which, unfortunately, had not yet become sacred. If that transformation could not happen naturally,

---

[23] Jonathan Sacks, *The Persistence of Faith: Religion, Morality and Society in a Secular Age* (Weidenfeld and Nicolson, 1991), pp. 48–58.
[24] *Facing the Future Together: Relate Annual Review 1990–91* (Relate National Marriage Guidance, 1991), pp. 12–13.

then the area was not simply 'secular'; it was sinful. Their God was passionately interested in the whole of life, not just 'religion'.

Furthermore, the inclusion of employees in family worship said something crucial about the value of every individual. We are all made by God and for God, and for that reason nobody must be despised or disregarded. People were not to be excluded on either economic or social grounds; limited means or inferior status within the community were of no significance whatever. Worship was designed not only to honour God but also to bring all God's people closer together so that there are no differences between them. Any pattern of life and work which encourages class divisions is not appropriate activity for Christian worshippers. The early church received plain and direct teaching on the scandal of superiority.[25]

Moreover, these times of worship were occasions when Israel's spiritual leaders could also be assured of loving, practical support. Those Levites who served as priests in local communities were to be welcomed to the sacrifices so that they could share the meals with the other worshippers. As we have noticed, they had no tribal *allotment or inheritance* (12) so, without fields of their own, they were completely dependent for their upkeep on the freewill gifts of God's people. They too must be fed: *Be careful not to neglect the Levites as long as you live in your land* (19). Christian worship is also a time when we present to God our gifts of money for those who are engaged in the Lord's service, at home and overseas. Giving to his work is a theme which figures in other contexts later in the book. It was far too important for Moses to dismiss it in a sentence or two.[26]

f. Consistent worship

This remarkable passage also makes it clear that biblically defined worship is not restricted to specific places and ceremonies; it pervades the whole of life. Inconsistent conduct negates the most ardent and correct activity in public worship. God is not simply interested in what we say on Sundays but how we live on the other days. As part of his address, Moses' reference to sacrifices leads him naturally to the important matter of killing animals for daily food. God tells the people that when they enter the land, *you may eat as much of it as you want* (20). They are God's gifts to the people (15) not, initially, their gifts to him. The killing of animals for domestic consumption would not, therefore, be part of a cultic ritual for which those participating had to be ceremonially clean. It could be

[25] Jas. 2:1–9.
[26] For a fuller discussion of tithes and its relation to Christian giving, see 26:11–19.

performed and eaten by *unclean and clean* (15, 22) alike. Moreover, animals like the *gazelle* and *deer*, not permissible offerings for the sacrifices, may be used to feed the Hebrew people.

Only one regulation governed these dietary laws – when the animal has been killed, it must be completely drained of all blood before it is eaten (16, 23). The repeated command to *pour it out on the ground like water* (16, 24) was intended to emphasize that life belonged essentially to God. For the Bible, 'the life of a creature is in the blood'.[27] Just as God had given it, so it must be returned back to him and this idea was symbolically portrayed by the action of ritually pouring the blood on to the ground. It was a particularly vivid way of giving it to him, just as David poured the water from Bethlehem out on to the ground because his friends had risked their lives to bring it to him.[28] It was far too precious to drink; it must be given to God. So, even when animals were slain for food, there was an element of sacrifice and thanksgiving in it all, a recognition that God was the creator and giver of all good things. Perhaps it also preserved the idea that worship must never be confined to distinct places. That would make a false distinction between sacred and secular. All life should be worship. Our homes as well as our churches ought to be places where God is honoured, loved and served.

Before concluding his exposition of worship, Moses returns to the theme of false worship (12:29 – 13:18). Idolatry is not likely to disappear with the departure of the Canaanite people. The temptation to make images and worship false gods will continually return in one form or another. Yet, if the people ignored God's word on this matter, it would virtually mark the end of their distinctive relationship with God. These issues are of the greatest seriousness and the congregation must be warned of insidious temptations which may lie ahead. Some dangerous people may well arise in any community to lure them away from God's explicit commandment on this matter. Several traps will be laid for them: *be careful not to be ensnared by enquiring about their gods, saying, 'How do these nations serve their gods? We will do the same'* (12:30).

Moses warns (13:1–18) that the temptations may come from three different quarters; idolatry may be presented as an attractive option in a religious (1–5), domestic (6–11) or community (12–18) context. Later generations may be troubled by public, secret or forceful enticing.

The public enticing (1–5) which may appear to be genuine, may come from the oracle of a local *prophet* or *one who foretells dreams* who invites the people to *follow other gods*. This kind of influence is

---

[27] Lv. 17:11, 14.   [28] 2 Sa. 23:14–16.

particularly dangerous, especially if this prophet has already given to the people a *miraculous sign or a wonder* (1–2), presumably to demonstrate the authenticity of his message. The occurrence of supernatural manifestations does not automatically authenticate the message of the prophet. The passage emphasizes that theology must always have priority over 'miraculous signs and wonders'. By inviting the people to worship idols, this miracle-working prophet is turning the people away from their exodus God.

It is in this context that God's people are told that they are not to *add to* or *take away* from God's word (12:32) as given in the covenant-commandments. Even a miracle or a sign which *takes place* does not warrant a change of mind on this vital issue. After all, idolatrous Egypt had its magicians and on several occasions, they worked 'signs' quite as effective as those done by Moses. Certain 'signs' or miracles may take place within black-magic circles or in Spiritism but activities of that kind are totally forbidden by God. The 'signs' do not sanctify the practices. The 'wonders' only heighten the danger. God has not changed his mind on what he said.

God has plainly said that there must be no other gods, so if the prophet invites them to disobey God's revealed word on the matter he is an imposter, a teacher of *rebellion* (5). If they refuse to do what the prophet says, they have passed a crucial test by demonstrating their utter loyalty to the Lord. The offending prophet, who has used religious means to achieve an immoral purpose, must be executed. The sentence is deliberately severe and uncompromising. If that man continues his evil and sinister work, he may mislead thousands of innocent people who genuinely believe that he has had a 'further word' from the Lord. His presence in the local community is a pernicious evil which must be purged from their midst. He professes to speak for God but is an agent of wickedness. He must be *put to death* so that others may live. He is not leading people into God's presence by his pretentious revelations; he is deliberately causing them to *turn from the way* in which God had commanded them to walk.

The 'secret' enticing (6–11) takes place within the secure intimacy of family life or within some close relationship with a treasured friend. What happens when those closest to us invite us to *go and worship other gods* (6)? However close this friend or member of the family may be he or she is a destructive influence who has tried to *turn you away from the LORD your God* (10). If such an offence takes place, the execution of the offender will serve as a deterrent within society: *Then all Israel will hear and be afraid, and no-one among you will do such an evil thing again* (11).

The 'forceful' enticing (12–18) is quite different. It is not the seductively appealing word, quietly whispered by some trusted friend. That which is envisaged here is the more strident, even terrorizing, activity of *wicked men* (13) who eventually lead an entire city into idolatry.

It is important to see how the basic principles of justice are outlined in these three narratives. In the first instance, the passage describes the seriousness of the offence. It makes it abundantly clear that the crime is against God. Idolatrous practices are *rebellion against the Lord* (5). Secondly, idolatry is a sin against the people. It causes them to *turn ... from the way* of God's commandments (5). Further, it is an expression of gross ingratitude for its draws them away from the Lord who has redeemed them (5, 10). They have been brought out of one form of *slavery*; they must not exchange it for a greater tyranny. It is, moreover, a crime committed in direct opposition to God's law. That is why these warnings are expressed so forcefully, and also why the punishment is so severe. It is hoped that idolatry will not have any place within Israel, but if it does the offenders cannot possibly say that they were unaware of its seriousness.

Even though the offence is widely known to be religiously, morally and socially destructive, however, the crime must be proved before sentence is passed: *then you must enquire, probe and investigate it thoroughly* to discover whether it is *true and it has been proved that this detestable thing has been done* (14) in the community. The Lord is a God of truth and those accused of idolatrous practices must have an opportunity to defend themselves; they may have been misrepresented or blatant lies may have been deliberately manufactured in order to damage them. If the offenders are proved guilty, however, then they and those who have followed them must be punished by death and every shred of their idolatrous trappings must be burnt along with the city which has forsaken God: *It is to remain a ruin for ever, never to be rebuilt* (16). If such tragic apostasy ever did take place, later generations must know how serious it is so that they would *obey the Lord* [their] *God, keeping all his commands ... and doing what is right in his eyes* (18).

2. Honouring God in our conduct (14:1–21)

Do not ... for you are a people holy to the Lord your God (1–2). The Lord expects his people to be different from their neighbours but before the unique differentia is explained, their special relationship is defined. They are his covenant people – greatly loved (*children*), set part for his use (*a people holy to the Lord*), elect (*the Lord has chosen you*), and uniquely valued (*out of all the peoples on the face of the earth ... to be his treasured possession*). Consequently, their

157

lives must bear the marks of God's special ownership. Here and elsewhere in Scripture, God's children are urged to be what they are. They must not allow their standards and values to be shaped by the world around them. If they are truly God's sons and daughters, then certain things will follow as far as their daily conduct is concerned. Two specific issues emerge here – what they do to their bodies, and what they bring to their tables. Basic to both prohibitions (one brief, the other extensive) is the holiness of the body. It reflects the distinctive attitude of the Bible to the human body. For the Greeks the 'soul' was the most important aspect of human personality; the body was a prison where the soul was held in captivity. For the Hebrew people, however, the body was not to be despised. God made it and saw that, like the rest of his creation, it was not evil but 'very good'.[29] The body is still 'good', the human sphere of operations within which God can be glorified.

a. What you do to your bodies (14:1–2)

The very first effect of being holy is a prohibition concerning the body which obviously reflects the heathen customs of the Canaanite people and the nations around them. It forbids the practice of self-mutilation in time of bereavement: *Do not cut yourselves or shave the front of your heads for the dead* (1). A commandment of this kind follows naturally after the previous chapter's serious warnings about idolatry, and may even anticipate the danger of ancestor-worship. Even if they do not erect forbidden images they may be tempted to adopt some of the pagan customs and godless traditions of their neighbours.[30] One of these was to cut the body with sharp stones or knives, or remove all the hair in times of mourning or great distress.[31] A text from Ugarit vividly describes a Canaanite grief ritual:

> He cuts cheeks and chin, lacerates his forearms.
> He plows the chest like a garden;
> like a vale he lacerates the back.[32]

Heathen customs of this kind are still practised as in some parts of New Guinea where a joint of a finger may be removed by the bereaved person as a sign of grief.[33] In the ancient world, these forms of self-mutilation were clearly part of pagan religion and were

[29] Gn. 1:31.   [30] Is. 15:2; 22:12; Je. 16:6; 41:5; Ezk. 7:18; Am. 8:10.
[31] Lv. 19:27–28; 1 Ki. 18:28.
[32] Ugaritic Textbook, tablet 67, VI, lines 20–22. For this reference I am indebted to Elmer B. Smick, 'Israel's Struggle with the Religions of Canaan', in W. Robert Godfrey and Jesse L. Boyd III, *Through Christ's Word: A Festschrift for Dr Philip E. Hughes* (Phillipsburg, NJ, 1985), p. 117.
[33] Thompson, p. 177.

thought to achieve magical results. God directly forbids this way of responding to bereavement.

This teaching is strikingly relevant in the late twentieth century. We are hardly likely to indulge in funeral rites of the kind described here but there are more ways than one of mutilating the body. Why are such practices, ancient or modern, forbidden by God? They dishonour God, harm ourselves and mislead our neighbour.

In the first place, these practices are dishonouring to God himself. He gave the body and his priceless gift must not be mutilated and damaged. The apostle Paul described the body of a Christian in Trinitarian terms. God should be glorified in it, it can serve as the limbs of Christ and is the temple of God's indwelling Spirit.[34] Sadly, it is possible to desecrate these temples. God gave these bodies to us and these choice gifts must not be misused.

Secondly, such practices can do irreparable harm to ourselves. It is physically improper to misuse God's gift and act with indifference to the fact that God created it. We are his stewards. The human body is his property and God expects us to 'manage' it properly and respectfully. For this reason, any activity which may cause damage to the body must be offensive to God.

Our temptations to self-mutilation are utterly different from those of the Canaanites, but they are no less real. Drug abuse is one of the most serious tragedies of our time. A recent obituary in *The Times* concluded the account of a successful pop star's life with these words: 'Thereafter his career continued, but increasingly fitfully, until his addiction to drugs finally got the better of him.'[35] Smoking is known to be harmful and is one of the main causes of lung cancer. Alcoholism is on the increase. In the United Kingdom more than seven million people are drinking more than the recommended weekly alcohol limits, and about half a million of these consume dangerous amounts. The problem is particularly acute among teenagers. We must remember that nobody begins to drink with the specific ambition of becoming an alcoholic. In such a society, many Christians deliberately abstain from intoxicating drinks so that they do not cause anybody else to stumble.[36] Inadequate, excessive or unwise eating habits can also be harmful to our bodies; these are serious contemporary forms of self-mutilation, often leading to unnecessary illness. Sexual relationships outside marriage can be physically as well as morally, psychologically and emotionally damaging. In times like ours, with the spread of AIDS and the increasing seriousness of sexually transmitted diseases, such misuse of the body may prove totally self-destructive.

Thirdly, practices which misuse the body mislead our neighbour.

[34] 1 Cor. 6:15, 19–20.   [35] *The Times*, 6 June, 1991.   [36] Rom. 14:13–23.

The Lord expects us to be different – and so does the unbelieving world. Believers should not be conformed 'to the pattern of this world' but 'transformed' by the inward renewal of our minds. Those who belong to Christ have a different scale of values. We no longer live for ourselves but for the Christ who died for us.[37] If we ill-treat our bodies, we are conducting our lives on exactly the same basis as an unbeliever.

We recall that these pagan customs of self-mutilation were performed *for the dead* (1). That was how pagans behaved when death had robbed them of someone they loved. The way in which Christians react to bereavement can be a most persuasive testimony to their confidence in Christ. If we 'grieve like the rest of men, who have no hope',[38] we are acting as if there were nothing beyond the grave and as though Christ had not been raised from the dead.[39] Unbelievers watch us carefully when we are in any kind of trouble. They 'read' our faith much more carefully when we are going through hard times. If we react in precisely the same way as non-Christians, they find it hard to believe that our faith is worth anything at all.

b. What you bring to your table (14:3–21)

This section introduces us to the food laws which governed the daily life of the Israelites: *Do not eat . . . you may eat* (3–4). We may be puzzled or intrigued by dietary restrictions of this kind though they do testify to the fact that spiritual principles were as important in people's homes as when they met for public worship. They did not believe in compartmentalized religion – some things being sacred and the rest secular. Obedience to God was as necessary for family life as it was for the worshipping congregation gathered in the tabernacle or the temple. God was interested in life as a whole, not just religion.

New Testament teaching makes it clear that we are no longer inhibited by food restrictions of this kind.[40] We cannot be absolutely sure why for the Israelites certain animals, fish and birds were regarded as *clean* (11) and others *unclean* (7), but there must have been sound reasons for the prohibitions. The choice of specific foods cannot possibly have been arbitrary. All creation was 'good' but the precise regulations may have been determined by health or religious considerations.

The physical health of the Israelites may have been specially in mind. The explanation that the *clean* animal is that which *chews the cud* (6) certainly suggests the possibility of hygienic reasons for the

[37] Rom. 12:2; 2 Cor. 5:15.   [38] 1 Thes. 4:13.   [39] 1 Cor. 15:12–19.
[40] Mk. 7:19; Acts 10.

various prohibitions. Swine and predatory birds, for example, would be easily infected foods. Insufficiently cooked pork is still a health hazard. Medical experiments have shown that there is a far higher level of toxic substances among the prohibited food in this list than in those which were considered suitable for human consumption.[41] The command that the Israelites were not allowed to eat anything they found already dead (21) was probably determined by the earlier regulation about not eating blood (12:23). For that reason, such food might be passed on to those who were not bound by the rules of the covenant: *You may give it to an alien living in any of your towns.* The prohibition about eating unslaughtered animals may also lend further support to the idea that God was specially concerned here for his people's health. Moses was one of the world's earliest public health officers. God is concerned about such issues as social hygiene. Contaminated foods are a special danger to the well-being of any society and the Lord wanted to protect his people from physical harm.

Others suggest that these regulations were to protect them from spiritual perils. The rules may be due to religious factors. Many of the prohibited animals, fish and birds are known to have been associated with heathen religions and their sacrificial rites. The pig played a significant part in some Canaanite and Syrian religions. The Hittites used to slaughter a small pig to protect worshippers from an evil curse. Certain fish were venerated in Egypt. The snake was regarded as a goddess of fertility in various parts of the ancient Near East. The prohibition that they must *not cook a young goat in its mother's milk* (21) probably reflects Canaan's fertility rites. Such heartless and corrupt religious practices must be avoided. The text governs the Hebrew practice of separating meat and milk foods, still part of dietary law in contemporary Judaism. Christians do not find it necessary to have such restrictions[42] but most believers would wish to applaud the principle behind these conditions; every time an Israelite family sat down for a meal, they would be reminded of spiritual realities and of the necessity of obedience.

Most important of all, these regulations may quite simply be one further means by which the Lord enforced upon his people the duty of having a different lifestyle from their pagan neighbours. The rules were a vehicle for recurrent testimony; they regularly witnessed to the priority that God's will must always come first. If the Lord required something of them, then, whether they understood it fully or not, it must most certainly be done.

---

[41] Craigie, p. 230.   [42] Col. 2:20–22.

3. Honouring God through our giving (14:22–29)

The covenant's obligations concerning worship concerned the believer's relationship with *God*. The food prohibitions related to the proper care of *themselves*, physically and spiritually. These verses remind us that our spiritual lives have a further dimension – our responsibility towards *others*. The Israelites were required to set aside their tithe (*one tenth*, 22) of their produce as an offering to the Lord. Best quality food was to be taken to the appointed sanctuary, *the place he will choose* (23), to be eaten and enjoyed (26) by all the members of the family.

When they came to the celebration meal, they were to eat it gratefully. It is all too easy to take life's blessings for granted. They were told that this was a reminder of how they had been *blessed by the* LORD *your God* (24). Here was an opportunity to acknowledge before others that he had helped them with their daily work (29). He had given them the soil in which the food would grow, the strength to till the ground, the sun and the showers. Without his help there would have been no harvest. So, the meal must be eaten not only in the company of each other but *in the presence of the* LORD (23) as a public acknowledgment of his goodness and generosity. If they were too far away from the sanctuary to carry their food, they must exchange it for money (25) and then purchase the necessary commodities for an excellent meal together as a family at the sanctuary. Whatever they desired (26) was to be set upon their tables to recall the Lord's provision of their family's needs. They were times for families to *rejoice* (26) together at the recollection of the Lord's abundant blessing.

Moreover, when they came to this celebration meal, the families were to share it generously. The previous section in the chapter emphasizes that because the Lord is holy, his people must also be holy (2). The Lord is generous, so his people must also be generous (27, 29). These occasions were times when God's good gifts must be shared with others. The Levites, the local priests, must be invited to the meal because, as we have seen, they had not been given their own tribal territory for cultivation. If the food was to be eaten at one central sanctuary, then those priests who served such an important place of worship would certainly receive sufficient food. Local priests would not share those benefits, however, unless special provision was made for them. In his love and generous care, the Lord thought of that and the people are given explicit instruction concerning the care of priests from the local community: *And do not neglect the Levites living in your towns, for they have no allotment or inheritance of their own* (27).

Every three years this celebration meal was to be held locally. The

Hebrew people were told to bring their produce and *store it in your towns* (28). On those occasions, the meal must not only be shared with the local priests but also with *the aliens, the fatherless, and the widows who live in your towns.* They must also *come and eat and be satisfied* (29). God was deeply concerned about the welfare of all his people, rich and poor alike, and all the people must make God's concern their own. We have already seen that God's care for the needy has an important place in this book. To neglect them is not merely thoughtless or loveless; it is sinful (24:15).

These legal obligations were based on firm doctrinal foundations. They reminded every member of the local community of the Lord's providential care and faithfulness. Whatever their circumstances, all would be made aware of their continuing dependence upon God – the healthy worker by what was given to the Lord, the needy dependant (*alien, fatherless, widow*) by what was received from others.

Deuteronomy 15:1 – 16:17
13. Festivals of praise

1. Every seven years (15:1–18)

This passage gives added emphasis to two important principles which have already emerged in the book – God's concern for the individual and his compassion for the needy.

One might have thought that, with such an insistent appeal to the well-being of the *whole* community, the individual Israelite might easily have been overlooked. Although the Lord was creating a 'people' (14:2), that did not mean that individuals were disregarded or devalued. In God's sight every single man, woman or child, rich or poor, was of infinite worth (for everyone belonged to him),[1] and special care must be taken over their distinctive needs.

Moreover, although this book has a great deal to say about the promised well-being of God's people, it also anticipates the needs of the destitute and the oppressed. Scripture is remarkable for its realism; it certainly does not guarantee the material success of those who put God first. Some of the holiest people in Christian history have encountered times of economic hardship and serious deprivation.

Those who honour God readily accept his priorities as their own. If he cares for the needy, so will they. The 'celebration meal' teaching of the previous chapter illustrates his special provision for the alien, fatherless and widow, but he is also concerned about other disadvantaged people who may be found in any Israelite community. Three classes are here singled out for special mention – the debtors, the poor and the servants. Such people were to benefit from the year of release which was held *every seven years* (1).[2] It guaranteed their practical help and relief.

---

[1] The Old Testament emphasizes 'God's ultimate ownership of all creation, including persons', Christopher J. H. Wright, *God's People in God's Land*, p. 181.

[2] For a discussion of the exegetical difficulties of 15:1–2, see *Ibid.*, pp. 147–148, 167–173.

a. The debtor (15:1–6)

Debt in the ancient world was rarely due to irresponsible spending. A poor harvest in any year could throw hundreds of families into serious trouble. Sudden death might rob a reasonably affluent home of a hard-working husband. After some time, the mother might find it extremely difficult to support her young children. Under such circumstances, it would be all too easy to fall into debt. Once they became old enough, the children could even be sold as slaves to pay off the debts. Bereft of her husband, the widow was then robbed of her children also.

Such a situation is not an imaginary one. That combination of debt, poverty and prospective slavery is exactly portrayed in one Old Testament narrative which describes how the prophet Elisha was instrumental in giving practical help to one particular family in a time of grave financial crisis.[3] It was to meet such a situation that God gave these instructions to his people, compassionate rules and regulations which Thomas Cameron once called, 'The Kindly Laws of the Old Testament'.[4]

At the close of every seventh year *every creditor shall cancel the loan he has made to his fellow Israelite* (2). The law insisted that in that seventh year the land must lie fallow[5] testifying to the fact that the Lord was the true owner of the property.[6] It was his right to order a sabbath rest. In such a year it might be difficult for debtors to earn enough money to repay debts, so there must be a 'letting go' (the literal meaning of the Hebrew word for *cancel*, or 'release' RSV) at that time.

Some suggest that in that year the cancellation of debt was total and complete. Whatever the amount, the debt was totally removed from the creditor's books and debtors were 'let go' from any further responsibility for payment. Others believe that debtors were only released from responsibility to pay in that particular year, thus giving them more time to pay off the creditor without him constantly breathing down their necks or threatening to take their children into slavery. Four reasons are given why creditors are to be generous to their fellow Israelites – they must remember God's kindness, obey God's word, trust God's promise, and love God's people.

---

[3] 2 Ki. 4:1–7.

[4] Thomas Cameron, *The Kindly Laws of the Old Testament* (1945).

[5] Lv. 25:3–4.

[6] Lv. 25:23: 'The land must not be sold permanently, because the land is mine and you are but aliens and my tenants' insists that the land belongs to God 'and the directness of this relationship ought to be restored every seventh year'. Martin Noth, *Leviticus* (SCM Old Testament Library, 1965), p. 186.

They must remember God's kindness

All the creditors are debtors in God's sight. Without his generous gifts they too would be in abject poverty. They only have materialistic possessions themselves because the Lord has blessed them in a land which he has given them (4). If he has dealt bountifully with them, they must not be unkind to others.

They must obey God's word

This was not an exhortation; it was an order. The creditors are told they must *fully obey the* Lord *their God* and be *careful to follow all these commands I am giving you* (5). The Lord had kept his part of the covenant by giving what he agreed (*as he has promised*, 6); they must keep theirs by doing what he said. Their obedience could entirely banish all poverty within the community. God anticipates a time when all the people care for one another. Then, *there should be no poor among you . . . if only you fully obey* (4).

They must trust God's promise

Obedience to the command called for an act of faith on the part of the creditor. If, during that year, he did not persist in his endeavours to collect debts, how could he be sure that his own needs would be met? The promise is clear: *For the* Lord *your God will bless you as he has promised* (6).

They must love God's people

The matter of relationship is supremely important. The creditor must not regard his fellow Israelite as a tiresome debtor, an expensive irritant in his business affairs. Although the debtor owes money he must not be made into an enemy. The unfortunate debtor is a *fellow Israelite* and, even more, a *brother* (2, 3), bound by ties of love and loyalty. Creditor and debtor alike are joint members of God's family with one Father caring for them all.

We need to ask whether this passage has anything to say to us about debt in our entirely different economic and social context? Personal debt is now said to stand at £2,300 per household (excluding mortgages) in the UK, so this is certainly a problem-area in contemporary society. Although the provisions and stipulations of these verses cannot be mechanically transferred from an Israelite agricultural milieu to late twentieth-century technological society, it has presuppositions and priorities which are just as important as when they were first given.

First, we ought to do everything possible to live as responsible stewards of the resources which God has given us and endeavour to live within our monetary limits. Although the words *borrow from none* (6) are in this passage a vivid way of describing Israel's promised prosperity, they also portray God's ideal – that in our financial affairs, we do not become dependent on others. We all recognize, of course, that in modern society most people who wish to buy a house are compelled to borrow by taking out a mortgage but, given that necessity, individuals and families need to ensure that such an arrangement does not become a pattern for irresponsible borrowing, thus incurring increasing debt.

Secondly, Christians need to help others to manage their financial affairs. Those who work among young people ought to include some regular teaching on issues of this kind, so that the ethical content of the Christian message is not totally preoccupied with negative issues, but is practically orientated. Much ethical teaching among Christians does not include nearly enough help about how to handle some of the big social problems of our time – family life, severed relationships, stress, drinking, sex, and the use of money. On the monetary issue, it is estimated that less than 15% of people in contemporary Britain know how to budget, so there must be an alarming number of the remainder in our churches as well as outside them. Good courses are available for Christians on money management and the Scripture itself offers perceptive insights into the right use of our resources. Such teaching can challenge, inform and encourage many Christian believers who are struggling with problems of serious debt, as well as help others (especially young people) to avoid these hazards in a world where many are lured into compulsive buying. Some churches have set up advice centres on their premises where people with serious money problems can obtain necessary guidance.

Thirdly, in the light of this passage it is surely unbiblical, inappropriate and unkind to do anything which actively encourages anyone to go into debt. That may mean that, within home relationships, we do not strive for lifestyles which are beyond our predictable income. It may also have repercussions at work. Christians should do everything possible to ensure that their employment does not deliberately encourage people to adopt instant credit schemes which can later become intolerable burdens, thus making us agents of serious domestic unhappiness long after the necessary forms have been signed.

b. The poor (15:7–11)

Poverty is not remotely necessary in God's economy (4) but the Lord knows that everyone will not obey his word on the matter: *There will always be poor people in the land* (11). Human sin is such that some people will always be greedy and selfish. Adequate

167

provision must therefore be made for those who are destitute: *If there is a poor man among your brothers ...* (7). The Lord knows that kind-hearted and generous people will not always be in the majority so the passage tends to address the innate miser rather than the potential benefactor. Stingy people in the Hebrew community are told to avoid four dangers – a hard heart, a closed hand (7), an evil thought (9) and a grudging spirit (10).

Israelites who have been blessed by God are told that, if they become aware of the poverty of one of their *brothers*, they must *not be hard-hearted* (7). It is a serious offence against God (9) if the needs of any *poor brother* are deliberately ignored (7). If God constantly cares for the poor, the rich must not studiously avoid them.

Nor must the rich man hold back any help he can give to his brother. He is told not to be *tight-fisted* but *open-handed* (7–8, 11), gladly making help available, albeit by a loan, to a needy member of the same spiritual family.

Anyone who is really mean will be hesitant to loan anything if the 'year of release' is approaching because he might not get the money back! He is therefore warned against such a *wicked thought*, and urged to be generous-hearted, whether the money will be returned quickly or not. Not to do so is to *sin* against the Lord (9). Even if he decides to give, however, the spirit in which he gives is also important.

If the person with plenty decides to help the poor, it is not sufficient merely to give them the money they need. The manner in which assistance is offered is as important as the help itself. God is concerned about what is in our hearts as well as what is in our hands. The benefactor must not adopt a grudging spirit towards the *poor brother* he intends to help. God is concerned about motivation as well as obedience. He does not want people to help others in a totally unwilling spirit: *Give generously to him and do so without a grudging heart* (10). The apostle Paul reminded the Corinthians that 'God loves a cheerful giver'.[7]

Teaching of this kind is not simply restricted to the conduct of pre-conquest Israelites. The eighth-century prophets took up these themes with passionate social concern, and they are equally relevant in our own time. Homelessness is one of the acute social problems of our generation, and committed Christians cannot possibly ignore the Lord's command in these verses. In the UK the rate of home-lessness has doubled in the past eleven years and the problem is ten times worse than it was thirty years ago with over 1,000 families a day turning for help to local authorities. Compulsory redundancy

[7] 2 Cor. 9:7.

and widespread unemployment result in the daily repossession of homes. Over half a million of Britain's 9.1 million home-loans were at least two months in arrears, many of these being first time buyers. Believers who take God's word in these verses seriously must express their concern in practical ways by encouraging responsible attitudes to money management, as well as by active participation in local initiatives and community enterprises for homeless people. Christians need to use their influence to relieve this alarming social problem of the late twentieth century, and offer church and personal help whenever possible to people in need.

c. The servant (15:12–18)

It is important for us to realize that when we read about provisions for 'slaves' in Israelite society we must not think of these people as victims of ruthless oppression, like those who suffered such cruel indignity in later centuries. It was more in the nature of 'living in' employment in an extended family situation. We must remember that God's provision for a foreigner bought as a 'slave' was that he be circumcised, that is, he became a brother and a fellow inheritor of all the covenant promises and protections.[8] As these verses make clear, many who began their household service under compulsion were far too happy to leave the household of a beloved master when their required contract came to an end.

Those Hebrews whose financial circumstances compelled them to go into this form of domestic service were only allowed to serve for a period of six years. The seventh year was to be the year of their release. Moreover, when the servant left the service of his master, he must be sent on his way with a generous farewell-present. If the servant was released without adequate provision for the immediate future, it would not be long before new debts were incurred and another period of enforced service could follow. The released servant must therefore leave the master's house having been treated liberally (14) with generous food and drink supplies. The servant must be allowed to leave his master's house in style, with worthy gifts to adorn his departure. If, at the end of the six-year period, the servant does not want to leave his master's employment, then he must submit himself to a simple ceremony whereby the ear is pierced as a sign of willing submission. These simple laws concerning the treatment of servants are governed by three spiritual principles:

First they are to remember what they have received: Supply him liberally . . . Give to him as the LORD your God has blessed you (14). The Lord's generosity to them will surely inspire them to be good to others. But for the Lord's bounty they too would be in poverty.

[8] Gn. 17:12–13; Ex. 12:44.

Secondly, they are to remember what they have suffered: *Remember that you were slaves in Egypt and the LORD your God redeemed you* (15). Moses told the people that their hearts ought to go out to anyone in servitude for, only a generation earlier, the entire nation had experienced the cruelty, poverty and humiliation of Egyptian slavery.

Thirdly, they are to remember what they have heard. God was speaking to them on the matter, giving them clear instructions about the way servants should be treated at the time of release: *That is why I give you this command today* (15).

The law even anticipates the complaint of a miserly employer who grumbles about letting the servant go free after he has had only six years work out of him. Such a mean man is told that he has no possible ground for complaint. After all, the resident servant's wages have only been half of what he would have had to pay a *hired hand* (18), so he has certainly not been cheated.

2. Year by year (15:19–23)

The *firstborn male* of every Israelite flock must be consecrated to the Lord. The animal must not be put to work, nor shorn. It is to be taken to the appointed sanctuary so that, *at the place he will choose* it can be offered to the Lord as a sacrifice and then eaten by the whole family as a celebration meal. If the *firstborn* had any kind of blemish, it was not to be offered as a sacrifice but could be eaten locally, like any other meat, though the animal must be drained of all blood. It was not fitting to offer to the Lord that which was substandard, though at a later period of Israel's life, some careless priests dared to do just that.[9]

These laws were a further reminder of the truth that the Lord deserves the best and they also testify to the importance of family life and worship. The sacrificial meal was to be eaten *in the presence of the LORD* by the entire household (*you and your family*) in gratitude for God's many blessings.

3. Three times a year (16:1–17)

The idea of 'celebration' played a prominent part in the worshipping life of the Hebrew people. The people owed more to the Lord than any of them realized. He knew that it would be harmful for them if his mighty acts were allowed to slip from their memories. Yet, the pressure of life was such that, all too easily, the people could forget what he had done for them. Without intending to do

[9] Mal. 1:7–10.

so, they would gradually become preoccupied with materialistic things and begin to adopt an ungrateful, selfish and loveless lifestyle. It still happens. When people have plenty they often care little about God. It is when unexpected disaster sweeps down on them that they begin to think about things money cannot buy. Throughout Deuteronomy we constantly hear the plea that the nation 'remember' what the Lord has done for them and said to them. It was not only necessary to keep the nation aware of its debt to the Lord but to remind the people also of their responsibilities towards each other. Yet without specific occasions in the annual calendar these things would soon be forgotten. Therefore, the Lord commanded his people to hold three great festivals each year, specially designed to keep the great facts of creation and redemption to the forefront of their minds – the feasts of Passover, Weeks and Booths.

Each of these great national festivals was to be held at the appointed sanctuary, *the place which the LORD your God will choose* (6, 7, 11, 15), bringing the people together from various tribes and different parts of the country. That, in itself, was no mean blessing. Left in relative isolation, they could easily become indifferent to the needs of others. Primarily, the three festivals would be periods of worship, but they would also be periods of necessary rest and recreation, 'holy days' (hence our word 'holiday') as well as occasions which gave expression to the solidarity and unity of God's people. The feasts provided God's people with special days set apart for spiritual, physical and corporate renewal. These three outstanding festivals would help the people to remember God's saving deliverance (1–8), abundant generosity (9–12) and continuing faithfulness (13–15).

a. Remember God's saving deliverance (16:1–8)

Passover, the 'feast of unleavened bread', lasted a full week. The people were to hold this Spring (*Abib* means 'the month of the green ears', 1) celebration each year to mark the deliverance of the Israelites from Egypt. The eating of *unleavened bread* (3) may have been instituted as a reminder of either the need for their release or the urgency of their escape from captivity. It may simply recall their food during Egyptian slavery (*the bread of affliction*) or it may have been the bread they ate on that particular night of their redemption. Their departure from Egypt *in haste* meant they could not wait for leavened bread to rise.[10] The order (4) to remove *yeast* and meat at the festival time may have originated as a safety precaution as both

[10] Ex. 12:34.

171

were prone to decay in excessive day-time heat; once decayed it would symbolize impurity, and therefore be improper for a holy festival. Everything at the festival was designed to recall the great exodus events – the month (of their redemption, 1), the offering of the passover lamb (2), the food that was eaten (bread without yeast, 3) and the time of the sacrifice (*in the evening when the sun goes down*, 6).

Jesus kept the Passover[11] before he was crucified and since that time Christians have made the celebration of the 'Lord's Supper' their great 'Passover' celebration. We recall a greater deliverance than the exodus from Egypt. When Christ became our Passover Lamb, he was sacrificed for our eternal salvation.[12]

b. Remember God's abundant generosity (16:9–12)

The *Feast of Weeks* (10) was later known as Pentecost because it took place fifty days after the Sabbath which began Passover. It was the period between the start of barley harvesting (*from the time you begin to put the sickle to the standing corn*, 9) and the close of wheat harvesting. This feast also recalled the deliverance from Egypt (*Remember that you were slaves*, 12) but its emphasis on the produce of the land draws attention to the Lord's evident goodness to his redeemed people. He did not only bring them out of Egypt; he has cared for them ever since. The people were to bring *a freewill offering* and, when they were considering the size of the gift they ought to offer, they were told to give *in proportion to the blessings the* LORD *your God has given you* (10).

An important feature about this feast and the next one is that special provision is made not only for the family but also for deprived people in the local community. The sacrifice was a time when the family would *rejoice before the* LORD (11), but they must not keep the joy to themselves. The meal must be shared with the servants in the household, the local priest, *the Levites in your towns*, as well as those who could easily be overlooked in a time of general rejoicing – *the aliens, the fatherless and the widows living among you* (11). The Festival of Weeks reminded the Israelites that because God's gifts are bountifully received they ought to be generously shared. If ever the Hebrew people were tempted to be indifferent to the needs of others, these festivals reminded them of the time when they were in dire straits: *Remember that you were slaves in Egypt* (12). Those who had suffered such appalling deprivation in the past, would surely not want others to go through hardship of any kind, especially if it was caused by the negligence of the Lord's redeemed people.

[11] Mt. 26:1–2, 17–30.   [12] 1 Cor. 5:7; 1 Pet. 1:19.

The Levites were God's ministering servants in the local community and they were to be supported by the gifts of God's people. Christians also have a responsibility to further the Lord's work by their gifts of money in their church offerings on the first day of the week. Such weekly sacrifices are both pleasing to God and encouraging to his servants.[13] They make a gift similar to that presented at 'Weeks' each Lord's Day. We are to give in proportion to the Lord's goodness toward us.[14] God has given his most costly gift to us by giving his Son. We must not hold back anything from God's altar. C. T. Studd put it perfectly when he said: 'If Jesus Christ be God and died for me, then no sacrifice can be too great for me to make for Him.'[15]

c. Remember God's continuing faithfulness (16:13–15)

The third feast (*Tabernacles*) which took place each year in the autumn was similar to a 'harvest thanksgiving' occasion. It was a time for general rejoicing, a factor specially mentioned at the beginning and end of this short account: *Celebrate ... Be joyful at your Feast* (13–14). Once again (as with Passover), the festivities were to last for a full week and needy people (14) in the locality were to share in the special meals to mark the occasion. No Israelite was encouraged to *be joyful* if others were desperately hungry. This festival was a special reminder of the Lord's continuing goodness to his covenant people. Other accounts of the feast in the Old Testament link it specially with the years when the Israelites were refugees, homeless pilgrims, travelling through the wilderness. They recalled the experiences of those forty years, and their utter dependence upon God, by making booths or tents[16] in which they lived for a full week.

If God had not continued his faithfulness to his people through that long pilgrimage they would have perished in the desert. Many Christians like to give thanks to God every time they sit down at their meal table. This 'grace' or thanksgiving prayer need never degenerate into a religious formality. We ought to think in such moments not only of what we continually receive but of the food supplies which others constantly lack. The Feast of Booths was a time for sharing with the needy. We ought to pray intelligently and provide regular financial support for those who suffer from hunger and deprivation all over the world.

These three feasts were times for recalling God's acts (1), enjoying God's rest (8), obeying God's word (*all your men must*

[13] Phil. 4:18.   [14] 1 Cor. 16:2; 2 Cor. 9:6–15.
[15] Norman P. Grubb, *C.T. Studd* (1937), p. 141.
[16] Lv. 23:40–43; Ne. 8:13–18.

appear before the LORD, 16), remembering God's goodness (*the way the* LORD *your God has blessed you*, 17) and sharing God's gifts (*No man should appear before the* LORD *empty-handed*, 16).

Deuteronomy 16:18 – 18:22
14. Responsible leadership

Moses recognized the crucial importance and lasting influence of exemplary leadership. Aaron's failure to discipline the crowd at the foot of Horeb resulted in the golden-calf incident.[1] A man with stronger convictions and less cowardice might have saved Israel from a disaster it was never to forget. The later wilderness period also witnessed a number of serious crises regarding the leadership of God's people, and Moses' teaching in Deuteronomy makes no attempt to hide them (11:6). Good leaders can raise the spiritual and moral life of a community to high levels of commitment, obedience and love, while poor or indifferent leadership can set a people on a downward path of corruption, immorality and apostasy.

Almost two chapters of the book are now devoted to four important leadership roles within the life of the Israelite people – judges (16:18 – 17:3), kings (17:14–20), priests (18:1–14) and prophets (18:15–22). The four leaders were given distinctive roles within the covenant community. Ideally, judges were meant to serve as the covenant's administrators, kings its guardians, priests its exemplars, and prophets its interpreters. These chapters indicate the qualities of leadership expected within the life of God's people and therefore have continuing relevance in today's world.

1. Judges (16:18 – 17:3)

It seems strange to us that this book's teaching leaps suddenly from annual religious festivals to the community's legal system, but for the Bible there is nothing remotely incongruous about the transition.[2] The Lord they worshipped was as concerned about

---

[1] Ex. 32.
[2] 1 Cor. 16:1 is a New Testament example of the same principle. Biblical truth about physical resurrection and financial responsibility are of equal importance to the Lord of the church.

175

what was decided in the law courts as about what was offered at the sanctuary.

The teaching about the three festivals had emphasized the joy and happiness of the community, but things can go wrong in the best of societies. Deuteronomy began by reminding the congregation of the earlier responsibility of Israel's judges (1:16–18). The Ten Commandments anticipate social offences (murder, theft, adultery) and the consequent need of legal procedures which are just and righteous: 'You shall not give false testimony against your neighbour.' Those who were called to administer the law had both a spiritual and moral function within Israelite society. A corrupt legal system would be abhorrent to a God who loves truth and righteousness. So, when the people (18) appoint a judge, four characteristics must be borne in mind. He must be available, impartial, upright and dedicated.

a.   The judge's availability to the people

The festivals were to be held at a central sanctuary but *judges and officials* would be based locally, *in every town* (18), where people can have easy access to them in times of unexpected stress and urgent need. Their work is to be allocated to the different *tribes* so that every local community had proper legal help.

Those who give themselves to the Lord's work must begin by discovering opportunities for service in their immediate neighbourhood. All too often local (and sometimes unspectacular) Christian work suffers because of the alluring appeal of more attractive projects in other places. The eighteenth-century Baptist pastor and hymn writer, Robert Robinson, was spiritually indebted to George Whitefield's itinerant evangelistic ministry and, when Robinson became minister in Cambridge, he used every opportunity to evangelize in the surrounding villages. He also realized, however, that if his work was to have lasting effect, his local pastorate must have priority: 'A man may work in a neighbour's field but he must learn to cultivate his own.' Some believers spend valuable time tentatively seeking what they might do somewhere else, when there is a crying need on their own doorstep. A Christian man may be dedicated to work which promotes family welfare, but neglects his own family. A gifted woman might spend valuable time instructing children whilst her own are left without help. The demand that Israel's judges commit themselves to ministry in the local scene is of challenging relevance to us all.

b.   The judge's impartiality in the execution of justice

Determined not to *pervert justice*, the people entrusted with these responsibilities must follow *justice and justice alone* (18–20). An earlier passage in the book had described God's character with the aid of distinctively legal imagery; the Lord 'shows no partiality and accepts no bribes' (10:17–18). God was the perfect example of a righteous judge, so there must be no favouritism in the execution of justice. In later periods of Hebrew history, the nation's legal system became seriously perverted by those who used their legal status to obtain favours for their friends or excuse them from condemnation. The eighth-century prophets frequently spoke out against such corrupt practices.[3] These practices were highly offensive to a God who has the same standards for everyone.

c. The judge's upright character

He will not be tempted to accept bribes. Corrupt practice of that kind *twists the words of the righteous* (19). The *bribe blinds the eyes of the wise*; there can be no true justice if money is allowed to come between the judge and what is 'right'. Greed spawns innumerable sins, and bribery is but one. Once again, Deuteronomy's preacher is issuing another stark warning about the perils of materialism.

d. The judge's dedication to his vocation

Follow justice and justice alone (20). He must be single-minded and thorough, paying careful attention to detail, and not go about his work hurriedly or carelessly. It will not be easy, and will demand his best.

As if to emphasize some of the spiritual problems which will confront Israel's leaders, the text abruptly confronts us with the dangers of corrupt worship in any locality (16:21 – 17:7). Leaders will legislate about spiritual offences as well as moral misconduct, and Israel's judges and priests in any locality may have to deal with blatant syncretism, stubborn disobedience or secret idolatry.

The people are warned not to set up alongside the Lord's altar *any wooden Asherah pole* (21) of Canaanite religion with its depraved sexual connotations. God *hates* syncretistic religion of that kind: 'You shall have no other gods before me' (5:7). The warning was certainly necessary, for in their subsequent history Israel's pure faith was constantly endangered by Baalism.[4]

Moreover, their worship might be imperilled not simply by alien elements but by disobedience and insincerity. It is always possible to do the right thing in the wrong way. People might reject Baalism and worship the only true God, but offer him a sacrificial animal marred by a *defect or flaw* (17:1), when they were meant to offer

[3] Is. 1:23; 5:23; Am. 5:12.   [4] Jdg. 3:7; 6:28; 1 Ki. 16:32–33; 2 Ki. 13:6.

their best.[5] That would also be *detestable to him*. Even as late as the late post-exilic period, this kind of flaunting hypocrisy marred the worship of God's people. The prophet Malachi (1:8) rebukes his contemporaries for offences of this nature.

Idolatry was to be a recurrent threat to the purity of Israel's spiritual life. In times of religious apostasy, economic success and materialistic preoccupation, the people could ignore the covenant's clear prohibitions, and secretly set up in their homes idolatrous shrines in order to secure abundant harvests from pagan deities. The faith of God's people would quickly be corrupted if such conduct were ignored, and Israel's leaders were to keep a close eye on the local community to ensure that such corrupting behaviour did not go unnoticed (17:2–7).

With serious problems of this kind, and many others, the local judge must know when any particular case was beyond him, and needed the perspective and impartiality which only an objective assessment can bring. It is a good thing when God's servants realize that they need fellow-workers, and cannot do everything themselves. Precise legislation is here laid down (17:8–13) concerning *cases ... before your courts that are too difficult for you to judge* (17:8). In such circumstances the case must be brought to the central sanctuary where it will be heard by those priests in office there at that time and by central legal officials (17:9). Their judgment must be followed: *Do not turn aside from what they tell you* (17:11). Those who treat the judgment of this highest court in a contemptuous way will be exposed to the death penalty (17:12–13).

2. Kings (17:14–20)

The time would come when the Hebrew people would want a king just like the nations around them. The Lord was Israel's true king (33:5)[6] but he permitted them to be governed by a king who would be God's representative on the throne of Israel. It was important, however, for the right man to rule, for there were enough despots ruling the surrounding nations without God's people providing another. It would be fatal if these dictators were used to provide God's people with models of national leadership.

Israel's king must always belong to Israel's people. A *foreigner* (15) must never usurp his authority over the Hebrew people by claiming the crown. Doubtless, this provision is intended to guard the spiritual life of the Israelite people, for the introduction of a *foreign* monarch would inevitably lead to the adoption of pagan

---

[5] Lv. 22:20–22.   [6] See Ex. 15:18.

worship. It is possible to discern in these verses seven important features regarding kingship.

a. The king must not be pretentious

He must be the man *the Lord your God chooses* (15). The people appear to have been responsible for selecting their own judges but the other three leaders in society (kings, priests and prophets) had to be called by God alone. Self-appointed demagogues would be acting contrary to the divine purpose and could not therefore expect the blessing of God during their reign.

b. The king must not be afraid

Israel's monarch *must not acquire great numbers of horses for himself* (16). *Egypt* was renowned for its horses[7] and the Lord did not want his people ever to return to that country again. Although the Egyptians had superior military skills, they had suffered a humiliating defeat at the exodus; the horse and its rider had been thrown into the sea.[8] In this period of history, Israel's battles had to be fought on foot. Supplementing infantry with cavalry involved far more sophisticated forms of military encounter and one which was more costly. The Hebrew people had been told that when they were on the battlefield they must rely on God's presence, not on Egypt's horses.[9]

Some scholars believe that this prohibition may also refer to the practice of trading Israelite mercenaries for horses. We do know that, at a later period, the community at Elephantine in Upper Egypt had garrisons of Israelite mercenaries.[10] This form of trading men, however, was like sending Israel's people back into the old slavery; it was unthinkable. Such action did not only betray a lack of confidence in God on the Israelite's part; it showed a lack of compassion for their fellow-men. It suggested that military strength was more important than the people's welfare. Israel must not be led by a king devoid of humanitarian and social values.

c. The king must not be disloyal

The prohibition that the king *must not take many wives* for himself (17) is not addressed primarily to a moral issue, though that naturally enters into it. It refers to the common practice of entering into marriage contracts in order to strengthen political alliances. This would also involve bringing the pagan images into the royal court

[7] Ezk. 17:15.　[8] Ex. 15:1, 21.　[9] Is. 31:1; Ho. 1:7; 14:3.
[10] G. von Rad, *Deuteronomy*, p. 119.

and accepting other gods as part of the palace's religious life. The warning that *his heart will be led astray* anticipates what happened during Solomon's reign.[11] Such behaviour was an act of gross unfaithfulness to the Lord God, and a breach of the covenant which specially forbad the making of such alliances: 'You shall have no other gods before me' (5:7).

d. The king must not be materialistic

These political treaties may also have been designed to increase the king's wealth – another problem in Solomon's time. The king who decides to *accumulate large amounts of silver and gold* (17) is relying on things rather than God alone. Israel's various God-substitutes are forcefully condemned in these prohibitions – Egypt's horses, foreign wives, political alliances, monetary wealth. All these can take God's place. There must be no rivals.

The love of money can still be ruinous in Christian leadership. It appears to have been a problem in the early church[12] and it has not disappeared from the contemporary scene. Some ambitious extension and growth ventures appear to owe more to patterns of worldly self-aggrandizement than Christian humility. Any form of expansionism always needs to have its motives purified, especially when large sums of money are expected from the Christian public. We all need to ask ourselves whether, in a day of crying world need, the resources ought to be directed elsewhere – the starving millions, the homeless refugees of Third World countries, the furtherance of world mission, the vast physical and material needs of developing nations, the work of smaller Christian churches, and other worthy causes.

e. The king must not be ignorant

He must *write for himself on a scroll a copy of this law ... It is to be with him, and he is to read it all the days of his life* (18–19). This appears to be an order that the king himself copy the covenant out by hand to impress it more deeply upon his memory, though it may simply mean that he makes sure that a copy is provided by the scribes for his own use. It is important for him to have the law readily available and he needs to know it thoroughly for himself. Some Old Testament scholars believe that this instruction means that the king is required to copy not the entire covenant but the specific part (*this law*) that relates to kingship so that he will not forget his moral and spiritual responsibilities.

---

[11] 1 Ki. 11:1–4.   [12] 1 Tim. 3:3, 8; 6:10; Heb. 13:5; 1 Pet. 5:2; Rev. 3:17.

f. The king must not be disobedient

The possession of a law scroll, or a selected part of it, does nothing to guarantee the holiness of the monarch. He must not only know the covenant; he must obey it. He needs to *revere the LORD his God and follow carefully all the words of this law and these decrees* (19). The biblical test of effective leadership is not doing what the people like, or what the leader wants, but what the word demands. The reliable leader will not *turn from the law to the right or to the left* (20).

g. The king must not be proud

He must remember that although the people are his subjects, they are also his *brothers*. The term appears twice in the passage (15, 20). Love must be the motivating factor in his leadership. He must not *consider himself better* than those who belong to the same family of brothers and sisters.

In our own day, it is all too easy for Christians to be influenced, albeit unconsciously, by the world's self-assertive leadership patterns. Jesus warned his disciples of that serious danger and it is still with us: 'You know that those who are regarded as rulers of the Gentiles lord it over them, and their high officials exercise authority over them. Not so with you.'[13] God's best leaders are slaves. That is precisely what Jesus said: 'Whoever wants to be first must be slave of all',[14] and Jesus is the perfect model for such lowly service and willing slavery.[15] In the same way, there was no room whatever for the tyrannical king in Israel. They had suffered enough pain at the hands of enemy rulers without having another in their own royal house.

3. Priests (18:1–14)

The priests were not simply men who performed the various rituals in the nation's worship. They were Israel's pastors, and four topics are brought to the attention of the people concerning these important spiritual counsellors.

a. The dependence of the priest on God's provision (18:1–2)

The people are again reminded that the Levites would not be given the usual allocation of land which the other tribes had to till in order to live. They were to give themselves completely to the Lord's work

---

[13] Mk. 10:42–43.   [14] Mk. 10:44.   [15] Mk. 10:45.

in pastoral care, teaching, the leading of worship, discipline and other spiritual responsibilities. The earlier saying (10:9), *the LORD is their inheritance* (2) is repeated again; these spiritual leaders were to rely on the Lord to meet their needs. Their main job was to concentrate on the spiritual needs of other people. If they put that first, the material things of life would not be denied to them.

b. The support of the priest by God's people (18:3-4)

The Lord planned to meet the material necessities of the priests through the offerings of his people. Moreover, they were told that the priests were to be given the best, not the unwanted left-overs: *You are to give them the firstfruits of your grain, . . . the first wool from the shearing of your sheep.* We must not be mean in our support of the Lord's work. That, however, means far more than willingness to give money.

The congregation had already been told that they must not 'neglect the Levites' (12:18–19). It was not an imaginary danger. God's servants can still be neglected. In most churches there is an initial excitement and sense of privilege when anyone is called to full-time Christian service but it is all too easy to forget the Lord's servants once they have embarked upon their work, either at home or overseas. They need our continuing strong support and that means something far more sacrificial than writing the occasional cheque. Missionaries, for example, can be seriously neglected. Once they are abroad only a limited number of people write regularly to them, send out interesting magazines and newspapers from home, respond seriously to their prayer requests, take practical steps to help with furlough arrangements and so on. When they return home, local church members do not always turn out in encouraging numbers to hear about their work. God's servants have crossed the world to share the good news and some people will hardly cross the road to hear about it. A missionary's occasional discouragement is perfectly understandable.

c. The responsibility of the priest in God's work (18:5)

The Levites had been *chosen* by God *to stand and minister in the LORD's name always.* That word *stand* is a graphic one. It is the term used to describe a loyal and devoted servant who stands in the presence of his king or master, waiting for his orders and ready to run immediately on his errands. The word is used in the Bible to describe prophets,[16] priests[17] and angels[18] – those who serve the

---

[16] 1 Ki. 17:1, RSV; Je. 23:18, 22. [17] Zc. 3:1; Heb. 10:11–12. [18] Lk. 1:19.

Lord attentively, submissively and obediently.

Under the new covenant, every believer is a priest. We all belong to a 'royal priesthood'.[19] Through Christ's redemptive work, we have been made 'priests to serve his God and father'.[20] That means that we spend time in God's presence not only (as the Levites) to intercede on behalf of others but also to receive from our king the orders he wants to give to us. Genuine prayer consists of more than persistent asking; it makes room for attentive listening.[21] 'Standing' before the Lord means discerning God's will by spending time in his presence, and then (like slaves) making ourselves ready to do whatever he commands.

d. The protection of the priest as God's servant (18:6–8)

We have noticed earlier that the Bible is outstanding for its realism. It does not encourage us to engage in fanciful dreams and idealized pictures. It deals with life as it is, as well as how it could be. The Lord knew that some of the local Levites who served as priests might not be properly cared for when they went to the central sanctuary. They would normally be given enough for their needs in their home locality, where they were known, loved and respected. In the larger and more impersonal context of the main centre of worship, however, they *might* be regarded as outsiders, even intruders, people who did not count for much, and were not always welcome. The law provided for the Levite's care and maintenance wherever they happened to be. After all, if others were expected to attend the main sanctuary for the great festivals, then the Levites must do the same with their wives and children. On such occasions, they must not be overlooked by the more prominent, possibly even arrogant, central sanctuary priests. The local priest must be free to attend worship at the main sanctuary when he desires, and be allowed to serve the Lord there alongside the other priests. He must be given the same opportunities for service and be assured of similar material provision.

A passage like this is a stark warning against pride and haughtiness in the Lord's work. The Bible itself has more than one example of this kind of arrogance which is specially offensive. Diotrophes was severely criticized in one of John's letters because he 'loves to be first'.[22] Jesus said that only those who are 'meek' will experience true happiness.[23] After all, they will be following the example of Christ himself who is 'gentle and humble in heart'.[24] He did not strive for prominent places in the religious or social structures of his

---

[19] 1 Pet. 2:9.   [20] Rev. 1:6.   [21] Ps. 85:8.   [22] 3 Jn. 9.   [23] Mt. 5:5.
[24] Mt. 11:29.

day. He knelt as a servant at the feet of those he longed to help.[25] Self-assertiveness is an ugly and inconsistent characteristic in the life of anyone who claims to follow Christ. It is particularly obnoxious in leaders.

Occultism

In Old Testament times the priest was expected to 'deal gently with those who are ignorant and are going astray'.[26] One of the most dangerous expressions of the people's waywardness and ignorance was to seek God's help by the wrong means. Most of Israel's neighbours gave a prominent place in their religious life to magic and sorcery, witchcraft and soothsaying. It is appropriate that, in discussion about priesthood and authentic spirituality, there should be some mention of unacceptable rites and forbidden religious ceremonies. If people in the ancient world wanted to know whether any proposed course of action was favoured by the gods, it was common for them to consult a witch or a wizard. This kind of prohibition is certainly relevant in late twentieth-century society where there is increasing commitment to witchcraft, black magic and Satanism. Thoroughly dissatisfied with materialistic lifestyles and secular humanism, some of our contemporaries are beginning to explore new and dangerous paths of 'spiritual' discovery. This passage (9–14) offers some important teaching on these forbidden occult practices.

First, such practices are *offensive to God*. Here God's people are told that the activities of the person who *practises divination or sorcery, interprets omens, engages in witchcraft, or casts spells, or who is a medium or spiritist or who consults the dead* is *detestable to the LORD* (10–12). These evil rites were the cause of God's judgment on Canaan. It cannot be right for any believer to indulge in practices which God despises.

Secondly, occult activities are *harmful to us*. The black magic of those days included human sacrifice. The Israelites were told that anyone *who sacrifices his son or daughter in the fire* (10) cannot be numbered among the Lord's people. There is no doubt whatever that some of the forms of modern witchcraft are physically harmful; there is undeniable evidence in contemporary Britain of ritual abuse. Moreover, this sinister and Satanic activity is eternally damaging. The work of a *medium* is among this grim list of forbidden occupations and the *spiritist* also, who claimed to make contact with the dead. Bereavement is a time of intense personal distress and, during such dark and painful times, the bereaved person may long

[25] Jn. 13:3–5.   [26] Heb. 5:2.

to be reassured in some way about the one they have loved and lost. Modern day Spiritism is as serious a danger now as it was in the ancient world and can have devastating effects in the lives of totally innocent people. The Bible makes it abundantly clear that we are never to attempt any form of contact with those who have died.

Thirdly, occult practices are *forbidden by Scripture*. We cannot hope to benefit from anything if the Lord has prohibited its use. Canaan was littered with such evil practitioners but the warning about their destructive activities is unmistakably clear: *do not learn to imitate the detestable ways of the nations there . . . Let no-one be found . . . who practises sorcery or divination . . . The* Lord *your God has not permitted you to do so* (9–10, 14).

It is significant that this warning about *divination*, discovering the divine mind, is set between passages concerning the appropriate and acceptable way for the Israelites to discern God's will – through the ministry of priests and prophets. The priest entered the Lord's presence on behalf of the people. They were to consult him about what was pleasing to God: 'True instruction was in his mouth and nothing false was found on his lips . . . from his mouth men should seek instruction – because he is the messenger of the Lord Almighty.'[27] The prophet came out from the audience-chamber of the Lord into the presence of the waiting congregation. He is the one appointed to speak 'in the name of the Lord' (18:22). If the people wanted to know what God thought about any particular issue, they must listen carefully to the words of God's prophet, not the damaging and inane ramblings of a degraded wizard.

The Canaanite preoccupation with such evil practices meant that they were guilty before the Lord, and their unacknowledged guilt had issued in God's judgment – their expulsion from their land. Witchcraft was one of the specific reasons why they had been driven out (12). The Israelites must *be blameless* of such conduct or they too will incur the divine wrath. The privilege of being God's chosen people does not entitle them to a different standard of morality. If they turn to witchcraft they too will be thrust out of Canaan.

4. Prophets (18:15–22)

God will provide his people with a chosen prophet – *You must listen to him* (15), not soothsayers. Moses had served the people as God's prophet[28] and, when his life came to an end, the Lord would continue to give them prophetic leaders of great distinction with a rich persuasive ministry. Throughout Israel's history, however, the nation was frequently plagued by false prophets, not people who

[27] Mal. 2:6–7.   [28] Ho. 12:13.

spoke for false gods but men who said the wrong things about the true God. An earlier passage in Deuteronomy had already alerted the people to the peril (13:1–5). Jeremiah was particularly concerned about such men and their dangerous 'peace at any price' message. They gave the people the words they wanted rather than the truth they needed.[29] Moses here shares with the people three characteristics of an authentic prophet.

a. An authentic prophet obeys God's call

Like the priests, the prophets would not be self-appointed spokesmen. The Lord God would *raise up* (15, 18) such gifted people and equip them for their strategic work. Their place in the ministry of the word would be due entirely to the divine initiative. Those who engage in the ministry of preaching in our own world need to do so out of a strong sense of spiritual compulsion. Nobody ought to pursue a course leading to ordination, or embark on a career like the Christian ministry, for example, without the strong conviction that this is what the Lord wants. In a sense, they must not decide to become ministers; they must feel that the decision has been made for them already – by God himself.

b. An authentic prophet welcomes God's word

The Lord says, *I will put my words in his mouth* (18). The words anticipate the call of Jeremiah to the prophetic ministry when the Lord said to that young and initially reluctant man, 'Now, I have put my words in your mouth'.[30] For the contemporary preacher, nothing is of greater importance than the painstaking study of that word in Old and New Testament Scripture. The preacher's task is not to confront the congregation with his own ideas but with the authoritative word of God. In the early fifth century, Augustine of Hippo testified to the centrality of the word when he said, 'I am never so happy in speaking as when I have ample support in the Scripture.'

c. An authentic prophet imparts God's message

Moses says that, having received God's word, the true prophet will not regard it as his exclusive possession. The truth has been given to him so that it can be shared with the people: *he will tell them everything I command him* (18). There was no room in Israel for a

<hr/>

[29] Je. 5:12–13, 30–31; 6:13–14; 8:10–11; 14:13–16; 23:17; 29:8–9.
[30] Je. 1:9; 5:14.

highly favoured class of select people who received esoteric messages for themselves which were not to be communicated to other people. God's word was for everybody, not the favoured few.

The teaching about the prophet's role in the Israelite community closes with a warning about two different people: the disobedient listener (19) and the presumptuous speaker (20–22).

The disobedient listener (19), who merely hears the word but does not put it into practice, will be accountable to the Lord for his stubborn resistance to the truth. The prophet's task is to communicate the message faithfully. It is unlikely that everyone will respond, and the prophet will not be accountable for the people's refusal to do what God says. To use Ezekiel's vivid word-picture, the prophet is like a watchman appointed to do duty on the walls of a city and alert its citizens to any approaching danger. If, through preoccupation with lesser things, carelessness or laziness, the watchman fails to warn the people, and they perish, then God 'will hold the watchman accountable' for their blood. He will face eternal judgment for his failure to save the people by issuing the warning. If, however, the people hear his urgent warning and take no notice, then he is not remotely responsible should any of them lose their lives in a subsequent disaster.[31] The apostle Paul must have had this 'watchman' passage in mind when he told the Ephesian elders on the shore at Miletus that he was 'innocent of the blood' of all of them.[32] He had faithfully and lovingly preached the gospel in pagan Ephesus. What the people did about it was their responsibility. Those who hear the good news must understand that God's word conveys an explicit warning as well as an earnest appeal. Obedience guarantees life; disobedience invites death.

The presumptuous speaker (20–22) is one who dares to *speak* in the Lord's *name* (implying that it is an authentic word) when that word has not been given to him by God. He will be equally guilty of divine condemnation. The disobedient listener rejects what God has said. The presumptuous speaker trades in things which God has not said. Such a person has spoken *presumptuously* (22) – a word which means to 'seethe, bubble, or boil up'. It describes someone who gives a message which is supposed to come from God while it is merely an emotional or carnal experience with no divine authority whatever. There are several ways whereby we can distinguish true from false prophecy. The problem was acute for Jeremiah and he identified three tests. The true prophet *stood* in God's presence (as a servant), *heard* the divine message and was *sent* by God.[33] A further test is given here in Moses' address to the people – fulfilment is the test of authenticity. The validity of a prophetic message is not a

---

[31] Ezk. 3:16–21; 33:1–9.   [32] Acts 20:26.   [33] Je. 23:18, 21.

subject confined to the Old Testament period. It became an important issue in early Christian times, and it is still relevant in our own.

A deeply sincere Christian may genuinely believe that he or she has been given a specifically worded message for other believers, a 'prophetic utterance'. Recognizing that God can and does speak in such a way,[34] it is important to emphasize that all such prophecies need to be submitted to two Spirit-inspired checks, God's word and God's people. The utterances need first to be tested by God's perfect revelation in Scripture; that is the unique standard by which all other 'truth' must be tested.[35] The Holy Spirit has already spoken in the Bible.[36] Such prophecies must also be considered prayerfully by the local church to discern by the Spirit that they are truly of God.[37] Not all which claims to come from him does so. Infallibility belongs to the Lord alone. We are only human and can easily be mistaken.

Far more seriously, in the contemporary world, scores of new religious sects come to birth in every year. All of them claim to have some new word from God. The New Age movement, Transcendental Meditation, the Church of Scientology, Eckankar, the Divine Light Mission (Elan Vital), the Hare Krishna movement with their rejection of biblical authority and their humanistic spirituality, are but a few of many hundreds of novel sects which have emerged comparatively recently. These movements can seriously mislead innocent people, for some of them have some familiar 'Christian' elements as part of their teaching. Christians need to realize that there are false as well as true prophets.[38] God's unique revelation in Scripture, the exemplary life of Jesus, and the teaching ministry of the Holy Spirit, are the Lord's appointed 'tests' to help us if we want to distinguish reality from sham, truth from error. Does the Bible, God's word, support this new truth? Does this new truth encourage Christlikeness? Does the indwelling Spirit of God confirm this new truth? In a day when there are so many competing voices, that searching Trinitarian test can help to save us from false and spiritually damaging teaching.

Before we leave this important passage, we need to remember that these particular words (18) came to be treasured by Jewish and Christian people as one of many predictions regarding an inimitable leader or promised Messiah. In other words, *the prophet like you* was not simply a reference to any prophet but to a particular prophet. Some Jewish people held that the words were of special importance as they looked for the coming of *the* prophet of the last times. The Qumran community, for example, who preserved the

---

[34] 1 Cor. 14:1–40.   [35] 1 Thes. 5:20–21.   [36] 2 Pet. 1:20–21.   [37] 1 Jn. 4:1–3.
[38] Mt. 7:15; 1 Jn. 2:18.

now-famous Dead Sea Scrolls, remembered this saying and anticipated the coming of an outstanding prophet. The Samaritans gave special prominence to these verses in their teaching. Their version of the Pentateuch places these verses about *the prophet* immediately after the account of how Moses received the Law.

Christian believers maintain that these words found their perfect fulfilment in the coming of Christ. He was *the* prophet and those who despised his word would be accountable to God for their disobedience (19). In their preaching both Peter and Stephen referred to this passage and saw Jesus as its unique fulfilment.[39] He was the greatest of all the prophets for the entire Old Testament revelation was brought to its perfect fulfilment in his birth, life, ministry, death and resurrection. As the letter to the Hebrews puts it, 'God spoke to our forefathers through the prophets ... but in these last days he has spoken to us by his Son'.[40] The word of Moses comes to us across the centuries: *You must listen to him ... If anyone does not listen to my words that the prophet speaks in my name, I myself will call him to account* (15, 19). The Lord God repeated that appeal during Christ's ministry on earth when he said 'This is my Son, whom I love; with him I am well pleased. Listen to him.'[41] Those who listen and obey receive new life. Attentive and responsive listeners will live for ever.[42]

[39] Acts 3:22–23; 7:37.   [40] Heb. 1:1–2.   [41] Mt. 17:5.   [42] Jn. 3:36; 5:24.

Deuteronomy 19:1–21
15. When things go wrong

God's realism is more vividly portrayed in Deuteronomy than anywhere else in the Bible. He makes careful provision for life as it is, not how some would like to to be. The people are about to enter a 'land flowing with milk and honey' but the Lord knows that, however beautiful the land, it will be inhabited by sinners. There will be times when its soil will be stained by blood. Judicial matters have already been under discussion in the book (16:18 – 17:13) and this passage provides instruction about the right way to deal with three offenders – a manslayer, a thief and a false witness. In treaty language, here is an example of the transition from general to specific regulations. The Decalogue says that the covenant people must not kill, steal or bear false witness against their neighbours. Those three general commandments are now applied to the three specific offences in question.

1. The killer (19:1–13)

What if anyone *kills his neighbour unintentionally, without malice aforethought* (4)? Moses provides an example: an accident takes place whilst two men are cutting down trees. The axe head slips from the handle, hurls through the air and mortally wounds the neighbour. The forester had no intention of killing the man who was working alongside him but in a part of the world where blood-feuds were common, the offender's life was now in serious danger. The unwritten laws of kinship and blood-ties were so strong that some member of the deceased man's family would feel immediately obliged to *avenge the blood* (6) of the dead man. What can be done to ensure that the case is properly heard, the offender protected and justice done in respect of the dead man's family and the community at large? After all, the offender may have been guilty of gross negligence regarding his axe. If he had not taken the trouble to ensure that the head was properly secured, his carelessness ought to be exposed and properly dealt with by the judges. *The rage of the avenger of blood*, however, might be such that the offender could be killed before the case could be brought for a legal judgment.

Before the Hebrew people crossed the Jordan three 'cities of refuge' (as they are called elsewhere)[1] were marked out for those Israelites who were in the same dangerous circumstances as the offender we have just described. These were places to which a person could run when his life was at risk because of an impending blood-feud. Once the entire congregation had entered the promised land, three more cities must be provided on the other side of the Jordan and, should their territories expand (8–9), then another three need to be built so that there are nine places in different geographical locations where an offender might find shelter and safety from his angry pursuer. The place of refuge must be reasonably accessible for, if the offender has to travel too great a distance, he is likely to collapse on his journey and be slain by the avenger. God loves his people so much that he anticipates the kind of disaster which might happen suddenly in any community, and then makes full provision for such emergency situations.

The law said plainly, 'You shall not kill' (5:17) but what of a person who kills his neighbour accidentally? He must be protected or the situation will get worse. If the offender's blood is also shed, however transparent his innocence, then within a matter of hours two innocent people have died and the feud would inevitably spark off further trouble between two families which had earlier been at peace.

The divine realism is extended, however, not only to the innocent person but to the guilty. It envisages an entirely different situation where, in a carefully premeditated act, a local man murders his neighbour. The tragedy is compressed within a single sentence (11) so that human sin can be seen for what it is. The narrative describes three clearly defined stages of transgression, each one progressively worse than the one before: *a man hates . . . lies in wait . . . and kills* (11). The brevity with which it is told heightens the sense of horror; everything happens with devastating speed once sin is allowed to run its evil course.

The man hates. The story starts with a thought, not a deed. As a man thinks, so he is. The wrong begins first of all in the heart, and disobedience is the initial offence. It does not start with a sin against man; it begins with a sin against God. The man *hates his neighbour*; that is the first offence. He has been clearly told by God to 'love' his neighbour and that precise commandment in Leviticus is set in the context of potential damage in relationships. The command is not

[1] Nu. 35:1–34.

191

an appeal for pietistic emotionalism. It is far more down-to-earth than that, for it spells out the serious dangers of *not* loving: 'Do not hate your brother in your heart . . . Do not seek revenge or bear a grudge against one of your people, but love your neighbour as yourself. I am the LORD.'[2]

The man waits; he does not do what the Lord requires of him. He bears a grudge and refuses to reason with his brother; he waits for an opportunity to get revenge. That is the second offence. The unsanctified thought has given birth to an evil deed. Yet, even at this stage there was time to turn back. If any such person had honoured God's word the Lord would have pursued him, even there, as he waited in the shadows with his dagger in his hand. But the revengeful man lets sin have its way.

The man strikes. Sin was there, crouching[3] near him in the darkness, waiting to pounce not only on the victim, but on the murderer; not only on the victim's family, but the murderer's also; not only on the two families but on the whole community as people hear the news, begin to talk, and take sides. What hatred and bitterness was let loose as the man waited to kill, his heart burning with bitter rage. If only the temptation had been mastered,[4] the devastation could have been averted. That, of course, is the terrifying thing about sin – its awful power to go on reproducing itself, not only in our own lives but in the lives of other people. The Bible recognizes the destructive power of sin and that is why it insists that evil and impenitent people must face the consequences of their transgression. The sin must be dealt with. It must end its cruel course somewhere or other; people must be able to see that offences against human life cannot be overlooked.

Christians are divided over the death penalty (12–13). Some maintain that this law of Moses still stands and that this principle of retributive justice has never been superseded. Others, equally submissive to biblical truth, hold that though this law was certainly God's word, it was not his last word. They argue that the principle of divine compassion must always be determinative; now that Christ has come we must see things as he saw them. 'For the law was given through Moses; grace and truth came through Jesus Christ.'[5] Such people will ask us whether we wish to stone idolaters to death as well as execute murderers, while their opponents will argue for a distinction between the two offences. In one case the Old Testament law ought to be retained, for the other abandoned.

Whatever our view, one thing is certain. Sin must be dealt with, one way or the other, so that society recognizes the unique value of human life. God gave life and he alone has the right to take it. In the

---

[2] Lv. 19:17–18.   [3] Gn. 4:7.   [4] Gn. 4:7.   [5] Jn. 1:17.

late twentieth century, the columns of our daily newspapers are seldom free from stories of violence and aggression. If such stories were simply presented factually, and only featured in news bulletins, perhaps we should see the horror for what it is. There are times, however, when violence is dramatized, even idealized, in films, television and novels. Five minutes in a video-shop will convince most unbiased onlookers that many people in our society enjoy violence enough to pay money to watch it. Our children are growing up in a world where physical assault is the normal way of sorting out life's problems. Mugging in the street and highjacking in the air are violent means of getting your own way. Cruel and callous revolutionaries who put a low value on human life are given all the media publicity they need, and all under the guise of individual freedom and essential tolerance. Political ambitions are given a higher rating than human life. These forms of aggression are condemned in the teaching of Moses to the people. God is the living God, the God who gave life.[6] Human life is irreplaceable and must be prized above all other values.

2. The thief (19:14)

The eighth commandment (against theft) is here interpreted with reference to land rights. It is important enough to be repeated later in the book (27:17). Once the various parts of the country have been allocated to the different tribes, each clan[7] will be given a certain area, and each family in the clan will then have their particular fields carefully marked out. The *boundary stone* shows where one person's territory begins and ends. In an ideal world, that is how it would be left and one generation after another would keep within their allotted boundaries. But men and women are sinners, and greed is likely to dictate another story. The prosperous person who wants some more land may be tempted to move his poor neighbour's landmark so as to extend his own possessions at someone else's expense.[8]

A healthy respect for the law of property is an essential ingredient in the life of any peaceful society. God tells his people, 'You shall not steal' (5:19). Moreover, he warns them about the danger of even *thinking* about claiming another person's possessions: 'you shall not covet your neighbour's ... land' (5:21). In fact, the entire land is God's property.[9] He has given some of it to our neighbour. Therefore, we have no right to snatch God's gift from him. God is the generous God. A person's property must be respected.

[6] Gn. 2:7.　　[7] Jdg. 6:15.　　[8] Pr. 23:10.

[9] For the theological implications of landmarks and property owners' rights, see Christopher J. H. Wright, *God's People in God's Land*, pp. 128–141.

3. The false witness (19:15–21)

At some time or other, cases of both manslaughter and theft were bound to come before Israel's judges for legal settlement. On such occasions, witnesses were naturally of supreme importance and the law here makes it clear that an offender cannot be convicted (15) on the testimony of a single witness. Moreover, a *malicious witness* (16) who gives *false testimony against his brother* (18) was to be subjected to the same punishment he had hoped to inflict upon the one he has accused. Such a sentence, however, could only be imposed after the judges and priests had made *a thorough investigation* into the details of the case from both parties of the dispute. These legal matters were of immense importance within the life of the community. Any society is sick if people within it will lie deliberately in order to inflict harm on others. The Lord is a God of truth; he does not deceive us by anything he says. Therefore, the word of those who belong to the covenant community must also be reliable and trustworthy.

No Christian is likely to take the course of deliberately giving a false testimony in a court of law in order to damage his neighbour. There are other forms of false witness, however, apart from those which might involve legal procedures. Anyone making an untruthful or unverified statement about someone with the intention of damaging their character is a false witness. Destructive and malicious gossip can inflict immense pain on others and the practical letter written by James warns Christian readers about the dangers of an unbridled tongue. Iago in Shakespeare's *Othello* describes a 'good name in man and woman' as 'the immediate jewel of their souls'.

> Who steals my purse, steals trash; 'tis something, nothing;
> 'Twas mine, 'tis his, and has been slave to thousands;
> But he that filches from me my good name
> Robs me of that which not enriches him,
> And makes me poor indeed.[10]

The familiar *eye for eye, tooth for tooth* saying (21), with which this chapter closes, sounds exceptionally harsh, but we need to note three things about it.

First, an examination of other passages where this saying is found makes it clear that the words were not meant to be taken literally. It was designed to encourage exact and fair compensation in cases of physical damage. Exodus 21:23–27 provides an example. A slave-owner strikes his slave so fiercely that he robs the man of his sight.

---

[10] Shakespeare, *Othello*, III, iii, 159–165.

If this principle of *lex talionis* (as it is called) was applied literally, then the slave would be given the opportunity to damage his master's eye as well. The context, however, shows that physical retaliation is not remotely in mind here: 'When a man strikes the eye of his slave, male or female, and destroys it, he shall let the slave go free for the eye's sake. If he knocks out the tooth of his slave, male or female, he shall let the slave go free for the tooth's sake.'

Secondly, even in cases where *malicious* and *false testimony* was proved beyond doubt, this saying was not an open invitation to engage in forms of vindictive punishment. Indeed, it was meant to be exactly the opposite. In a day when reprisals could be harsh and extreme, this saying imposed strict limitations on the type of physical penalty which could be imposed. Thompson makes the point that the principle here 'was thus not licence for vengeance, but a guarantee of justice'. Indeed, instead of 'encouraging vengeance it limits vengeance and stands as a guide for a judge as he fixes a penalty suited to the crime'. In eighteenth-century England two hundred offences were punishable by death; that was because this law of *lex talionis* had been forgotten or ignored.

Thirdly, we remember that Jesus quoted this saying in the Sermon on the Mount[11] not, as often supposed, to abolish an item of Old Testament legal procedure but to limit its application to courts of justice. Over the centuries, its original legal context tended to be overlooked and it had come to be applied to the level of personal relationships. As John Wenham says, the saying 'was being interpreted Shylock-wise, as though it gave every man the right to demand his pound of flesh when wronged. It was being used as an instrument of personal revenge.' In the famous sermon Jesus says that the citizen of the kingdom is 'forbidden to seek vengeance for personal wrongs and is told to do good to his enemies. Our Lord is not giving directions to the civil judges, telling them to stop punishing evil doers.'[12]

[11] Mt. 5:38–42.   [12] J. W. Wenham, *The Enigma of Evil*, pp. 93–94.

Deuteronomy 20:1–20
16. Soldiers with a difference

Israel's geographical location exposed its people to constant danger. The land was hemmed in on one side by the Mediterranean sea, on the other by mountainous desert. Those who journeyed from Egypt in the south to the Assyrian and Babylonian nations in the north were normally compelled to travel through Canaan. Israel's conquest of the land was regarded as an act of divine judgment on its inhabitants for their persistent evil and, as we have seen, there was to be no compromise with their idolatry and its worshippers (16–18). The regulations given in this chapter look beyond the initial conquest to future times when, for their own safety and security, they will be compelled to go out to war against their oppressors.

Although conflicts of this kind would be both varied and (in a sinful world) inevitable, there was likely to be one common factor in Israel's military encounters – they would be totally outnumbered. Here is the advice and help they need for those many occasions when they will meet *an army greater than yours* (1). Their opponents were likely to have *horses and chariots* whereas, until Solomon's time, Israel relied solely on its infantry. Although they were lacking in numerical strength, necessary equipment and military skill, however, they can still have the qualities which matter most in God's sight. They are always likely to be a minority force but, when Israel's troops are compelled to confront large armies in war, they must march out as a confident, dedicated and compassionate minority.

1. A confident minority (20:1–4)

Their greatest enemy is internal not external. Fear is likely to do more damage in the ranks than any fierce onslaught which can be organized by their opponents. The soldiers are told right at the start: *Do not be faint-hearted or afraid* (3) and they are given three

196

reasons why fear is unnecessary and inappropriate. These three truths are better resources in conflict than the finest armour of their enemies; each soldier who goes out to fight is reminded of a fact, a testimony and a promise.

a. A fact in the present

They need *not be terrified* because they are clearly assured of the Lord's presence with them on the battlefield. Their families had to be left at home, but they have not left the Lord behind. He plans to be close to them in their most dangerous moments, and the assurance is repeated for special emphasis: *the LORD your God . . . will be with you . . . For the LORD your God is the one that goes with you* (1, 4). Christians rejoice that in life's inevitable conflicts, this promise is equally for them, God's new Israel.[1] Throughout history, vulnerable individuals as well as threatened communities have proved the reality of the Lord's presence.[2]

b. A testimony from the past

Before they march forward they are to look back. They must remember how good God has been to them in the past. The One who is with them on the battlefield has accompanied them in other dangerous situations. He is *the LORD . . . who brought you up out of Egypt* (1). In those days there was no human hope of deliverance. Egyptian soldiers had the best weapons, the finest equipment and the right strategy, and they pursued the Hebrew slaves to the very point where there was no possible escape.[3] The Hebrews were hemmed in, hopelessly trapped with a totally impassable mass of water ahead of them. But because God was with them they crossed that seabed which, only hours later, became the grave of Egypt's sophisticated cavalry and their chariots. The Lord simply blew with a wind: 'By the blast of thy nostrils the waters piled up.'[4] If God could overcome their former enemies, he could do the same for their future opponents.

c. A promise for the future

When Israel's soldiers approach the battlefield they are specially told that they must listen to the words of their spiritual leader: *the priest shall come forward and address the army* (2). Some might be tempted to say that it was no time for a sermon, but the troops were told to give their best attention to the word which would sustain

[1] 1 Pet. 2:9.　[2] Jos. 1:5; Je. 1:8; Mt. 28:20; 2 Tim. 4:17.　[3] Ex. 14:1–3.
[4] Ex. 15:8.

them through the hours ahead. The priest had a promise: God would be with them. Given that fact, conquest could never be in doubt: *the Lord ... goes with you to fight for you against your enemies to give you victory* (4).

2. A dedicated minority (20:5–9)

When the priest had finished speaking, it was the officer's turn to address the troops. His main job was to thin out the ranks! Israel's enemies would always have larger armies but for the Hebrew soldiers, quality is infinitely more important than quantity. With God, what we are is always more important than what we've got. There was no point whatever in marching a great army to the battlefield when most of them had their hearts somewhere else. The ranks must be drastically reduced; only the best are left for the conflict so that the nation would put its trust in the invincible God and not in its superior armies. It was important first to single out people who ought not to be in the ranks (5–7) and then some others who did not want to be in the ranks (8–9).

a. Those who ought not to be in the ranks

The officers in charge of the campaign must begin by sending home any man who has just finished building a house but has had no opportunity to live in it and dedicate it to the Lord (5). It was no time for such a man to be away from his family. He must settle his wife and children in their new home. If the house remained empty and he died in battle, someone else might take possession of his property and his family could be destitute. We have already seen from other passages in this book that the Lord is deeply concerned about the preservation of family life.

A man who owns a recently established vineyard must also be exempt from warfare (6). For the first three years there would be no fruit on the vines and in the fourth year its fruit must be offered to the Lord. So, until the fifth year its owner *has not begun to enjoy* its fruit. If he lost his life in the conflict, another person might easily take his property and just at the time when he and his family were likely to benefit personally from it. What then would happen to his wife and children who relied upon its produce for their income?

Anyone who has *become pledged to a woman* (which means someone firmly engaged and about to be married) must not go out with the troops (7), and a later passage makes it clear that the exemption was to continue throughout the first year of marriage. The Lord is concerned about the establishment of good, secure relationships. He wants the husband 'to bring happiness to the wife he has married' (24:5).

b. Those who do not want to be in the ranks

Once the officers had singled out the three types of people we have noticed, it was necessary for them to speak further to the people in order to discover whether any of the remainder were *afraid or faint-hearted* (8). Those who were, literally, 'soft of heart' were best left at home. The Israelites were not a war-faring people by nature; these instructions were not given to a permanent standing army. Most of these men were hesitant conscripts, not eager volunteers, and all of them were poorly equipped for a fierce encounter with well-trained soldiers. In such circumstances, fear was natural enough. There were three dimensions, however, to the prospective soldier's fear, and any one of them could make the soft-hearted man a liability in the camp rather than an asset. First, fear is debilitating – a soldier paralysed by fear could hardly do justice to himself in military conflict. Moreover, fear is contagious. A fearful soldier could seriously damage the morale of the troops so that *his brothers . . . become disheartened too.* Then again, fear is symptomatic; it is due to lack of faith in God. The power of fear is nullified when a man has confidence in God.

The instruction to send home the fearful anticipates the Gideon incident over two centuries later where the same word is used to describe those who were afraid.[5] There, Gideon was told to reduce the number of his soldiers so that 'Israel may not boast' against the Lord, saying 'that her own strength has saved her'.[6] A similar danger may have been envisaged here in Deuteronomy. Those who know that God alone is their conqueror are unlikely to snatch the glory for themselves.

3. A compassionate minority

The law made it clear that an invading army of this kind has a responsibility both to the present and to future generations.

As far as the present generation was concerned, the first thing which the troops must do on reaching an enemy city is to *make its people an offer of peace* (10). Only if its inhabitants resist such an overture are the Israelites to *lay siege to that city* (12). The terms of peace and the sparing of some life only applies to the *cities that are at a distance* (15) from Israel, cities which have threatened national security through frequent raids and persistent onslaught. These are

[5] Jdg. 7:3.   [6] Jdg. 7:2.

wars of necessary defence not of selfish expansion. The *cities of the nations* in Canaan itself must be exterminated because of the serious danger of religious compromise. Accommodation to morally corrupt and idolatrous Canaanite religion would imperil Israel's uniqueness as the Lord's holy people. It would ruin them, exalt idols and grieve God. The land was being taken from the Canaanites because of all the *detestable things they do in worshipping their gods* (18). If Israel is taught to do similar things they will *sin against the LORD*, their unique and jealous God.

There is no reason whatever why future generations, however, should suffer because their forefathers had lived immoral and corrupt lives, so Israel's troops were ordered not to *destroy its trees by putting an axe to them* (19). A four-fold objection to such practice is being expressed here. God is concerned about the trees, the land, the people, and the future.

First, as Lord of Creation, he is concerned for the trees: *Are the trees of the field people, that you should besiege* (same word as in 12, 19) *them?* (19). Whatever the iniquity of the city, its trees are innocent enough – why should they suffer because men are at war? He made the trees and wants to preserve them. Secondly, as Lord of the universe, he is concerned for the land. It may not be Israelite territory but it needs trees, just as our lands do, and to cut them down is to rob the countryside of its necessary resources. Thirdly, as Lord of the nations, he is concerned for its people. Both the besieging army and the citizens which are left after the attack need the trees so that the people can *eat their fruit* (19). Finally, as Lord of history, he is concerned for the future. The children and grandchildren of those who live in the city will need the fruit which should come from those trees. It is devastatingly cruel to make innocent children suffer by not making adequate provision for their future happiness and security.

A passage of this kind has striking contemporary relevance. In our very different world, every country desperately needs its trees and the present ecology debate has reminded us all of their unique contribution to our life. Their presence beautifies a landscape, their leaves guarantee a continual supply of oxygen for the air we breathe, they provide a rich variety of fruit, they shelter birds and animals, and their roots help to secure the stability of the soil. Their self-propagation is God's thoughtful provision for their essential continuance.

During the Great Leap Forward planned by Chairman Mao and implemented in 1959, vast numbers of trees were cut down to clear land for agriculture and supply timber for the smelters to increase the nation's iron production. In the second half of this century, soil erosion in China has increased disastrously by 32%. Much of its surface soil is being washed into the country's great rivers systems as silt. The bed of the Yellow River is rising at a rate of four inches a year and is already standing twenty-three feet above the east China plain. 'Yet this impending disaster in the most populous nation on earth goes almost unmarked in the western world.'[7] Since the beginning of recorded history, more than half the earth's topsoil has been lost. In 1979 it was predicted that by the end of this century 30% of the remaining half of our soil deposits will be gone. When God told the Israelites not to cut down the fruit trees he, as Creator, knew their strategic importance in the ecological scene.

We are frequently reminded of the serious dangers of widespread de-forestation in various parts of our global village. The hunger for land and timber in the Himalayan foothills means that when the snows melt and the monsoon comes, water cannot be retained, the surface soil is washed away, and Bangladesh suffers disastrous flooding. Unwittingly, the poor of Nepal have inflicted crippling devastation on the refugees of Bangladesh. When one country acts irresponsibly other nations will suffer. The widespread removal of trees from north Africa centuries ago has served to extend a vast desert and is not unrelated to that continent's present tragic famine conditions. In the early Christian centuries North Africa was the granary of Rome but during the past fifty years the Sahara has engulfed more than 250,000 square miles of arable land. The extensive destruction of trees in South America will ultimately impair the lives of people in distant parts of the world. The 'ozone effect' must be a matter of concern to all who honour God's word. God thought 'Green' long before we did, and this passage is but one example of it.

Even when we have taken these humanitarian and ecological factors into account, we may still find ourselves uneasy about Israel at war. We must remember, however, the context of the times. They lived in a part of the world and at a point in history when smaller nations were severely threatened by great world powers. They literally had to fight for survival or they would have been totally exterminated as a minority nation. These laws tell them that, though defensive warfare may be necessary, they are not to behave as their neighbours. It is their radically different approach to warfare that we must notice here. One cannot imagine a crowd of Egyptian soldiers being given the opportunity to go home if they were seriously inconvenienced by military service or if they were personally afraid of conflict! The important factor about this passage

[7] For this data, and other important perspectives on a Christian approach to ecology, see John Biggs, *For Such a Time as This* (Baptist Union Presidential Address, 1989), pp. 1–2, and the same author's *Stewardship of the Soil* (Baptist Men's Movement, 1989).

lies in the complete contrast between these laws and the military practice of Israel's neighbours.

The cruelty, havoc and devastation caused by invading armies from Egypt, Assyria and Babylon were notorious. During their long period of enforced slavery, the Hebrew people must have heard of the ruthless conduct of Egyptian soldiers against enemy cities. An account survives of one of their campaigns into Asia where the conqueror plainly says, 'I took away the very sources of life for I cut down their grain and felled all their groves and all their pleasant trees . . . I destroyed it.' The report says with pride that the ravaged territory became a land 'upon which there are no trees'.[8] An Egyptian temple mural depicts one such attack and shows some soldiers scaling the city's walls with ladders whilst others are felling trees. Commenting on the features of this particular scene, one scholar says that the 'destruction of the fruit groves surrounding the Syrian towns was a regular part of the attack upon one of their fortified places'.[9] At a later period, the vicious cruelty of Assyrian troops was notorious throughout the Near Eastern world and it was not restricted to the devastation of natural resources. Men and women were subjected to barbaric and sadistic punishments.[10] Israel is plainly told that its soldiers cannot behave like that. God's people must be different from their neighbours.

[8] J. B. Pritchard, ed., *Ancient Near Eastern Texts*, p. 240.

[9] Harold H. Nelson, *Medinet Habu Reports I: The Epigraphic Survey 1928–31: University of Chicago Oriental Institute Communications No 10* (Chicago, Illinois, 1931), p. 31.

[10] J. B. Pritchard ed., *Ancient Near Eastern Texts*, pp. 276–279, 288, 299–300.

Deuteronomy 21:1–23
17. Families in need

Deuteronomy has given earlier expression to God's deep concern for family welfare. This new chapter deals with a number of sad situations which might arise within the life of the Israelite community. The Lord knew that, in a sinful world, tragedies of this kind were likely to occur. Each of them would have the most serious ramifications within Hebrew families. The Lord wants his people to be aware of the right way to react to some of these heartbreaking circumstances should they arise in any of their towns. Five classes of people are portrayed in distinctive trouble. The different forms of their personal anguish are described in the passage together with some basic instructions regarding the help they or the community are to receive in their sorrow. The distress concerns a murdered man (1–9), a captured woman (10–14), a deprived son (15–17), a depraved son (18–21) and an executed criminal (22–23).

1. A murdered man (21:1–9)

The first tragedy concerns any locality where the body of a murdered man or woman is found *lying in a field* (1). The situation describes the consequences of a grim action already outlined in the book concerning the angry man who 'lies in wait' for his neighbour and kills him (19:11–13). That earlier law presumed that the murderer had been identified, proved guilty and punished. The verses now before us portray a local situation where the dangerous offender has not yet been discovered. There is concern for the entire community, not solely because a violent criminal is at large but because the land itself has been seriously defiled by the shedding of human blood. Several features emerge from the narrative and they are markedly relevant in our world. Although the outward form in which the ideas are conveyed (sacrifice and ritual lustrations) belongs to an entirely different thought-world from our own, the underlying principles are still of inestimable worth. The unusual procedure to be adopted emphasizes five important themes – responsibility, solidarity, substitution, confession and forgiveness.

First, one of the nearby towns must take full *responsibility* for the ceremonial cleansing of the people. The elders from adjoining communities must measure the precise distance from their own cities to the spot where the dead body has been discovered. The one *nearest the body* (3) is responsible for the ritual purification of the community and its land. The town's leaders had not committed the murder but all the people felt the pain and guilt of it. The murdered man's suffering family was part of the local community; innocent children had been robbed of a father, a widow was destitute. The sin which started in one man's heart was spreading like an ugly disease through the entire body. Everybody felt the pain of it. It is an emotional response not confined to the ancient world, though they may well have felt it more acutely than we do.

In the modern world, a group of football hooligans, with no love of sport, become bent on destructive behaviour. They travel to another country, creating havoc and destruction wherever they go. People are killed, others are injured. The number of criminals involved is minute when contrasted with the club's supporters but the sense of responsibility is such that the club is ashamed and, to some degree, the country itself feels guilty. Is this how people behave when they are guests in another land? The sense of responsibility is acute, inescapable and painful.

Although one Israelite town comes to accept responsibility for atoning this cruel murder, the crime has affected the entire Hebrew community. *Solidarity* is also emphasized here. When the elders seek the Lord's cleansing they ask that all *Israel* will be cleansed and will not be held *guilty of the blood of an innocent man* (8). Somewhere in an Israelite town one person is directly responsible for the hideous crime but he has not been found. The sinner is still at large and he may strike again. Guilt, not fear, however, is the strongest factor. The dominant need is for the community to be forgiven, not protected. Although in the strictest sense one unknown individual is the offender, the guilt cannot be confined to one person. The nation's solidarity is such that the entire community carries some sense of responsibility for what has happened.

Criminals are accountable for their crimes but they are not *solely* responsible for them. The murderer grew up in a family and in a wider community which accepted some responsibility for his welfare and education. Was the life of his family happy and harmonious? Did his parents love him deeply? Was he made to feel secure, treasured and wanted? Were his mother and father always at peace with one another and their neighbours? Before he could read a word, the example of his parents was eloquent. Was he taught

God's word: 'You shall not murder', 'Do not hate your brother', or 'bear a grudge . . . but love your neighbour as yourself'?[1] Did the murderer first learn hatred from an angry look in his father's eyes? Was he nurtured in a local community where people constantly damaged relationships by petty quarrelling? Was covetousness the cause of his anger and, if so, who in Israel failed to tell him that things are infinitely less valuable than people? Hatred is rarely silent; was there no-one in the community brave enough to talk to him about his bitterness? Someone must have heard him say cruel things about his enemy; that was the moment to have spoken to him lovingly about the serious wounds he was inflicting on his own soul. If those ugly gashes had been gently healed, there would have been no dead body in the open field. Wherever he lived, there had been priests in the community and it was their work *to decide all cases of dispute* (5). Was there no godly priest in Israel to offer spiritual counsel, and help the man to see that he was heading for disaster?

When things go wrong, people soon point the finger of bitter accusation. A public crime has been committed and such sins of commission must be punished. But what of those serious sins of omission which may have led up to the crime? Many things may not have been done for the offender, or they may have been poorly done. If he had been helped lovingly, that solitary man, hiding in the community, tormented by his guilt, might have been in peace. When anybody sins, we all bear some responsibility. John Donne reminded us that 'no man is an island, entire of itself; every man is a piece of the Continent, a part of the main'. He expressed it movingly when he wrote:

Any man's death diminishes me, because I am involved in Mankind; and therefore never send to know for whom the bell tolls; it tolls for thee.[2]

Substitution is the next theme which emerges in the passage. The offender cannot be found but atonement must be made. Guilt hangs over the community like a dark cloud. The punishment must be borne. A sacrifice must be offered, so a young heifer is slain, one *that has never been worked and has never worn a yoke* (3). The purification ceremony must take place in an area *that has not been ploughed or planted*, in a valley where there is a flowing stream. The animal is young, the ground unsown, the fresh water moves freely; each portrays the element of 'newness'. There must be an atonement and that calf must be the substitute. The people long to put the sin away from them and try to begin again. In the first century a unique

[1] See Lv. 19:17–18.   [2] John Donne, *Devotions*, XVII.

sacrifice was offered for what was, at the time of the death, unacknowledged and unconfessed sin. Jesus, God's Son, took the condemnation we deserved and obtained our eternal forgiveness. Christ died, 'the righteous for the unrighteous', that he might bring us to God.[3]

There has to be *confession* as well as substitution, however. The elders of the city clearly act in a representative capacity when they *wash their hands* at the place of sacrifice. In a legal sense they publicly testify that they are not personally responsible for the crime nor, to their knowledge, is anyone else in the city. They are also, however, making a spiritual confession. Grieved over the sin, the ritual is a visual aid and a public testimony. Necessary washing (6), the plea for forgiveness (8), purging the guilt (9) and doing *what is right in the eyes of the LORD* (9) are all part of the nature and vocabulary of atonement.

Once the sin is confessed, the *cleansing* is immediate and complete. The word translated *atonement* here (8) is derived from a Hebrew term meaning 'to cover' and 'signified an obliterating or cancelling of sin' (Thompson). In this way they *purge* away the guilt (9) which is in their midst. Sin is like a fatal infection which quickly spreads from one person to another. The importance of purging evil away is a prominent feature in this book (13:5; 17:7; 19:13). In their better moments, the Israelites knew that God's children must be clean people. Moreover, biblical truth and personal experience alike had taught them that, if sincerely confessed, their sins could be forgiven. We know that too – for 'if we confess our sins' God is 'faithful and just and will forgive us our sins and purify us from all unrighteousness'.[4] Unrelieved guilt is the result of unconfessed sin. It is harmful to us, damaging to our relationships, and grieving to God. It is persistently acting as though no provision has been made for our pardon.

2. A captured woman (21:10–14)

The woman who has been captured in war is still a human being and must not be exposed to inhumane degradation – as she would certainly have been if she had fallen into the hands of pagan conquerors. If her Hebrew captor wishes to marry her, then the covenant-law insists that he must have a proper respect for her as a person. She must be given appropriate shelter (*into your home*), decent clothing (*put aside the clothes she was wearing when captured*), complete security (*in your house*), and an unhurried opportunity to grieve (*mourned her father and mother for a full month*).

---

[3] 1 Pet. 3:18.   [4] 1 Jn. 1:9.

Our natural sympathies are with the woman that she should be taken into slavery at all, but we must remember the historical, social and cultural context in the Near Eastern world and realize that if she had been captured by heathen oppressors, it would have been a very different story. The instruction to *shave her head* and *trim her nails* (12) may refer to acts accompanying her bereavement (but see 14:9) or, more likely, they may indicate her change of religious allegiance. The woman begins her new relationship by removing the outward symbols of her former paganism.

The law provides further protection for the woman should the Hebrew husband become unhappy about their marriage (14). In such circumstances, the wife must be fully released to begin a new life as a completely free woman. She can never be transferred back from the status of wife to that of slave, nor can her husband sell her to anybody else for that purpose. The prohibition not to *sell her or treat her as a slave* (14) can be translated 'treat her as merchandise'; the verb is only used once elsewhere in the Old Testament (24:7). The Lord will not allow people to be treated as things. The rejected woman has had enough sadness in her life already; the discontented husband is not permitted to add anything further to her sorrows. Israel's God cares for the slave, the foreigner and for those who have lost the support of their husbands, whether they are Israelites or not. In his mercy, the Lord makes special provision not only for their welfare but also for their protection from people who might otherwise treat them casually if not cruelly.

Although we live in an entirely different world, a passage of this kind is not without its importance for our late twentieth-century society, at times obsessively preoccupied by sex. It is perfectly clear from this humanitarian law that there was no question whatever of pre-marital sexual relationships: *After she has ... mourned ... for a full month, then you may ... be her husband and she shall be your wife* (13). Had the woman been taken by pagan conquerors an attractive woman would probably have been humiliated, publicly degraded and raped, but in Hebrew law the captor was not permitted to act in such an immoral and heartless manner.

Even if he wished to marry her, the soldier must not *go to her* until the period of her mourning had come to an end. The Hebrew captor had no 'rights' whatever in the matter. The physical, moral and emotional welfare of the Gentile woman was of far greater importance than the sexual desires of her conqueror. His 'love' in such circumstances might be impulsive, crude and ungenuine. The slave woman must not suffer because the man is capricious and unreliable. No man loves a woman as deeply as he says he does if he insists on pre-marital sexual relationships with her. The average man still hopes that his future wife will come to their marriage as a virgin. How can such a basic ideal be realized if other men do not respect human chastity, God's law regarding the sanctity of sexual relationships, and the uniqueness of the marriage bond? God is holy and people must live responsibly. God is love and we must act compassionately.

3. A deprived son (21:15–17)

The story of potential family sadness continues. In his love and concern for justice, the Lord God envisages a situation where a first-born son is about to be deprived of the inheritance to which he is entitled. The father has fallen out of love with the son's mother. It is not simply that he no longer has any interest in her, she is thoroughly 'disliked' (15, rsv) by him. His natural preference is to favour the child of his second marriage, the son of the woman he now loves. But Hebrew law was unequivocal on the issue: the first-born son must receive the greater part of the inheritance, and the son cannot be deprived of what is legally his right simply because his father is no longer in love with his mother. The interpretation of God's laws cannot possibly be at the mercy of mercurial human whims and emotional instability. What God has said must be done, whatever the feelings of the man and his new wife. Why should the first-born son suffer because his mother is no longer in favour? God is just and people must live justly.

4. A depraved son (21:18–22)

The obedience of children to their parents needs to be seen within the context of divinely ordained, creative and supportive family relationships. The covenant between God and his people upheld the privilege, responsibility, sanctity and security of Israelite family life. All was reasonably good while children respected the basic standards and discipline of their parents but what was to happen when *a stubborn and rebellious son* refused to listen to parental advice concerning his increasingly damaging lifestyle? If the young man refuses to *obey* either *father* or *mother*, however much they plead with him and if, despite their attempts to *discipline him*, he persists in being *a profligate and a drunkard* (20), then the matter must be referred to the elders of the local city. For several reasons, the misconduct cannot be overlooked. Although the death penalty is severe there are four distinct issues which must be borne in mind.

First, the procedure emphasizes that *the Lord must be obeyed*. By his persistently insulting and corrupt behaviour, the offender was breaking God's law. The covenant plainly said that parents must be honoured (5:16). Stubborn and persistent disobedience is an act of

208

unloving defiance towards the God who framed that law specially for his children's benefit. It was for their 'good' (10:13) and ours; to reject it is to insult the God who demands our obedience, and such blatant rebellion invites serious repercussions, not least upon ourselves.

Then, *the offender must be challenged.* He has disregarded the earnest appeal of both his mother and father. The normal channels of affectionate pleading have broken down. The son insists on continuing in his stubbornness, rebellion, gluttony and drunkenness. This law confronts the young offender with the dire consequences of his persistent rebellion. Life is a responsibility as well as a privilege. Nobody ought to be free to damage himself, grieve his parents, corrupt others and damage society without being checked. If the drunken, rebellious glutton will not change his destructive life, he must face the consequences.

Furthermore, *the parents must be supported.* The elders of the city have a clear responsibility towards the distressed mother and father.[5] Naturally, human love alone would ensure that no mother or father would dream of bringing such a matter before the elders until they had done everything possible to sort the trouble out within the intimacy of family life. They are probably distracted at their repeated failure to improve the situation at home. They must not take the punishment into their own hands, however, as parents could in Roman society for example. It is a matter for a higher and more objective judgment than they are able to bring to it. By laying down a series of severe warnings, the law sought to protect parents from the physical and verbal assaults of rebellious children (27:16).[6] The elders must see that the parents are given all possible help in time of severe trouble. The stark warning contained in this law was surely intended as a support for parents who could warn their rebellious children of the possible outcome of their uncorrected behaviour.

Finally, *the community must be protected.* If such an unworthy member of a family was allowed to continue his corrupt lifestyle unchecked, it would not be long before he would be joined by others. Sin has a sick way of reproducing itself within communities and everything must be done to halt its rapidly depraving influence within society. This law was intended to serve as a severe deterrent. We have no evidence anywhere in the Old Testament that any

[5] Note the co-authority of both parents on this issue as in 25:15ff. The mother is not 'confined to the passive role of "being respected"', but takes 'an active part alongside her husband in legal proceedings . . . the charge is made jointly'. The part played by the mother 'represented an added element of protection for the son', Christopher J. H. Wright, *God's People in God's Land*, pp. 219, 231.

[6] See Ex. 21:15, 17.

Israelite son suffered death by stoning for this offence. These verses provide a stark warning about what could happen in such a case and not a description of what did happen.

There are two further issues here, both of contemporary relevance. The first concerns the damaging example of the offender. He was guilty as a *profligate* (glutton, RSV) and a *drunkard*. Gluttony and alcoholism are two of the most common sins in western society. Both are an offence to God. In a starving world, over-eating cannot be much less serious than compulsive drinking. It is reliably estimated that nearly one billion people in today's world can be accurately defined as 'the absolute poor', adults and children whose daily existence is characterized by malnutrition, illiteracy and disease.[7] When vast numbers of people are dying because they do not have enough food, it must grieve God that millions eat far more than is good for their health, and spend vast sums on intoxicating drink, totally unconcerned about the devastating problem of world hunger.

The rebellious son's greatest mistake was to ignore the advice, appeal and example of his parents. Alexander Solzhenitsyn claims that one of the clear signs of decadence in any society is when it loses a healthy sense of respect for the older generation. It is a serious warning to late twentieth-century men and women. Some contemporary management ideals are modelled on the conviction that once men and women have passed middle-age, they are no longer suitable for positions of creative and energetic leadership. The story of human achievement, however, hardly supports this outlook. When John Wesley was eighty-eight years old he was still alert and preaching the good news twice every day. Monet was still producing great masterpieces after his eighty-fifth birthday. Michelangelo was sixty-nine when he painted his famous 'Last Judgment', and it was not until Titian was eighty-nine that he painted his 'Battle of Lepanto'. If Winston Churchill had died before his sixtieth birthday, some would have described his life as a failure. Yet, a recent Gallup survey on ageism in the workplace revealed that 8 out of 10 employers regard the under-thirty-fives as the ideal age group for all jobs except cleaner and company director. That may be a commonly accepted principle for the unbelieving world but it will be tragic if such thinking is ever allowed to influence, let alone determine, appointments to Christian leadership. God will not be confined to such rigidly inflexible norms. Some of his finest leaders during the biblical period and since have been either exceptionally

[7] J. D. Douglas, *Proclaiming Christ until He comes: Calling the Whole Church to take the Whole Gospel to the Whole World*, Report on the International Congress of World Evangelisation, Manilla, 1989 (Worldwide Publications, Minneapolis, 1990), p. 157.

young or unmistakably elderly. He uses people he can trust, not those who are suitable from a merely human viewpoint. Worldly opinion has only marginal relevance when spiritual issues are at stake.

5. An executed criminal (21:22–23)

When an execution had to take place within the Israelite community, the people were not at liberty to inflict further emotional pain on the victim's family. The offender's body must not remain *on the tree* after dusk; it must be buried by the end of the day. The people knew that *anyone who is hung on a tree is under God's curse* and the land would be defiled if the corpse remained exposed to public view after a few hours. Whilst the holiness of the land is primarily in mind here, a deep humanitarian concern is also implicit in this law. In a natural environment where a body left overnight would certainly be preyed upon by wild beasts and carrion, this prohibition is deeply sensitive to the emotional strain on the victim's wife and family. Why should they suffer further because of his crimes?

In many New Testament contexts, early Christian writers often reflected on the fact that on that first Good Friday, Jesus suffered as an innocent victim for crimes he did not commit. The apostle Paul reflected on these particular verses from Deuteronomy when he was writing about the death of Christ.[8] God's Son hung upon the cross as a common criminal.[9] He suffered a death he did not deserve and bore the punishment of our sins.[10] Paul says he became 'a curse for us, for it is written "Cursed is every one who is hung on a tree"'. By that unique, once-for-all, atoning death he obtained our complete pardon and eternal redemption.

[8] Gal. 3:13.   [9] Acts 5:30.   [10] 2 Cor. 5:21; 1 Pet. 2:24.

Deuteronomy 22:1 – 23:16
18.   Loving the neighbours

The next four chapters of Deuteronomy (22 – 25) provide us with further detailed interpretation of the law on matters of everyday life and conduct. They cover a wide variety of different (and, on the first reading, unrelated) topics: lost property, unacceptable clothing, raiding birds' nests, town planning, agricultural prohibitions, marital difficulties, sexual offences, public health, and many more. Although the topics are diverse, the unifying theme is clear – the covenant community must consist of good neighbours. God is generous and loving; nobody who believes in him is allowed to live selfishly and carelessly within society. Every believer has a responsibility towards his neighbour. The person who lives in the adjoining Israelite farm or who occupies the small house across the street, is far more than a fellow-countryman – he is a *brother* (22:1–4; 23:19–20) who belongs to God's family. Even an Edomite is a *brother* (23:7) and must therefore be treated with compassion. Love draws no boundaries.

1.   Lost property (22:1–4)

'Finding's keeping' was not part of Israel's law. To hold on to property which plainly belonged to somebody else was a form of theft and must not be tolerated within the community. The eighth commandment (5:19) was just as applicable to things which had been found as to possessions which might be stolen. The straying ox, sheep or ass must be returned to the *brother* to whom it belonged. If he lived too far away, or if the owner was not known, the animal must be cared for until it was claimed: *Do not ignore it* (1, 3, 4). If an Israelite discovered an animal in trouble he must always go to its aid, whoever its owner happened to be. The members of the covenant community must help each other and they must always be kind to animals. When the law about lost property is given in Exodus, it states that even an enemy's animals must be cared for.[1] Why should the animal suffer because the neighbours are at variance? The same principle is then applied to lost property – clothing, possessions or anything else. The neighbour may be in urgent need of those items and they must not be claimed by anybody else.

The Israelite is told that he must *not ignore* the issue or 'withhold ... help' (rsv), which can be translated 'You must not hide yourself' (1, 4). The one who makes the discovery that a neighbour's sheep has fallen into a pit, must not look the other way because he has a busy day and has several things to do. Admittedly, rescuing the animal will cost him time and effort, and he will not gain anything personally from the deed – but it must be done because God says it, the animal needs it and the *brother* deserves it.

There is a serious danger in the contemporary world that Christians 'withhold help' by an apathetic attitude to the moral and social evils of our time. Believers must not be indifferent to the grave problems which confront us in modern society – alcoholism, drug abuse, abortion, homelessness, pornography, sexual deviance, child abuse, and so on. It will be tragic if believers 'hide themselves' rather than become informed, pray for improved legislation, lobby appropriate authorities, write well-argued letters, and take appropriate steps to bring about change. Alert Christians are urgently needed in the contemporary world as 'salt' and 'light'[2] in a social environment which needs action as well as intercession and example. The saying attributed to Edmund Burke is highly relevant in late twentieth-century society: 'The only thing necessary for the triumph of evil is for good men to do nothing.'

2. Improper clothing (22:5)

The extremely forceful language regarding inappropriate clothing for men and women (*the Lord your God detests anyone who does this*) sounds strange to us but there are two likely reasons for the uncompromising prohibition.

First, there was probably a serious moral issue at stake here. Sexual promiscuity was rife in Canaan, and transvestite practices were all part of the corrupt and immoral context of the land Israel was about to inherit. This prohibition is a warning to the Hebrew people not to identify with the degrading sexual and homosexual practices of the Canaanites. The law does not simply relate to clothing but to any typical possessions normally worn or carried by the opposite sex. It emphasizes that gender-distinctions are part of the created order and must not be obliterated.

[1] Ex. 23:4–5.   [2] Mt. 5:13–16.

213

Secondly, it is also likely that there were religious reasons for this regulation. Some pagan religions in the ancient Near East demanded that men and women exchange their clothing as part of their fertility rites. A couple who wanted to have a child would be expected to engage in magical ceremonies which included this kind of behaviour, and Israel is here warned not to be remotely involved in degrading conduct of this kind. The biblical testimony was that a couple who wanted to have their own child were expected to pray earnestly[3] and rely on God's power, not on pagan magical customs.[4]

3. Protecting birds (22:6)

Anyone finding a bird's nest was not allowed to kill the mother bird. In cases of extreme hunger, it was permissible to use the eggs or even take the young for food, but not the mother bird. She must be spared so that she can lay again. These matters of conservation are of great importance in Deuteronomy and reflect the Lord's concern for the continuity of life. As Craigie observes, the 'large-scale killing of any species can lead to a serious diminution of its numbers and to eventual extinction'. Men and women are meant to serve as responsible stewards in the world which God has made for our enjoyment. 'The earth is the LORD's, and everything in it.'[5] We have no right to plunder God's property.

4. Protecting others (22:8)

But rules about animal conservation are followed with specific instructions concerned about the preservation of human life. In the eastern world, the flat roof of a house was regarded as an additional room.[6] Access was by means of an outside staircase and the area was conveniently used by Israelite households as either a bedroom, workroom, entertaining room, or play area – often a mixture of all four. Without a parapet, however, the additional room could become a serious hazard. It was easy for anyone, especially a child, to step off the edge, and an accident could prove fatal. Although at the conquest the Hebrew people took possession of Canaanite homes, there were sure to be times in the future when it would be necessary to build new houses. This law rightly insisted on the provision of an adequate railing around the roof-top to prevent serious accidents and consequent family grief.

Building regulations and planning permission begin with God.

[3] 1 Sa. 1:11; 2:15.
[4] For a further discussion of this subject, see H. A. Hoffner, *Tyndale Bulletin* 20 (1969), pp. 48–51.
[5] Ps. 24:1.   [6] Jos. 2:6; 1 Sa. 9:25–26; Ne. 8:16; Acts 10:9.

He is as concerned about the conditions in which people live as about all the other matters of human life. Using this Scripture, John Calvin insisted that similar provisions about parapets should be made for houses in sixteenth-century Geneva and gave himself tirelessly to matters of public health and social hygiene in order to arrest the spread of illness and disease in the city. He pressed for the introduction of regulations concerning adequate ventilation and effective drainage so that people could live in reasonably healthy conditions. Similarly, at the time of the Industrial Revolution in nineteenth-century Britain, Lord Shaftesbury and his colleagues worked strenuously over many years to ensure that men, women and children were given adequate protection from dangerous machinery in factories, reasonable hours, proper periods of rest, and the like. Their campaign about working conditions was a practical expression of genuine Christian concern.

Believers in the modern world cannot be indifferent to such urgent contemporary issues as homelessness, inadequate housing and family welfare. In the face of unjust inequality it is not remotely appropriate for Christians to 'hide themselves' (22:1, 4) from the appalling housing problems of the world's derelict and deprived areas. Many of our neighbours have to live and rear their children in such grim conditions and we cannot remain indifferent to such degradation. Books such as the Archbishop of Canterbury's Report, *Faith in the City* and Colin Marchant's *Signs in the City*[7] remind us of the tragic social problems of Britain's inner-city areas. The same can be said of other countries throughout the world. A God who insists on adequate safety precautions in Israelite homes cannot possibly be less concerned about poor housing in the late twentieth-century world. It will be tragic if, aware of God's concern, Christians 'hide themselves' from responsibility in the face of these evils, or (to borrow imagery from Christ's teaching) 'pass by on the other side'[8] when others are in grave need.

5. Mixing the wrong things together (22:9–12)

There are four distinct laws here, two which relate to work (9–10) and another two which concern everyday clothing (11–12). The Hebrew people were not permitted to sow different kinds of seed between the rows of grapes in their vineyards (9), or put dissimilar animals together for ploughing (10). They were not allowed to wear garments made of different material, *clothes of wool and linen*

---

[7] *Faith in the City: A Call for Action* (The Archbishop of Canterbury's Commission on Urban Priority Areas), and Colin Marchant, *Signs in the City* (Hodder and Stoughton, 1985).
[8] Lk. 10:31–32.

woven together (11), but they were to sew *tassels* (12) on the corners of their cloaks. We may be puzzled by this form of meticulous legislation and find the scrupulosity extremely difficult to understand. One thing is certain – every item was of particular importance at the time it was given and we do well to look beneath the precise detail to the underlying principles which may have dictated these regulations in the first place.

These particular rules, and some others in the covenant, may simply be one effective way of telling the Israelites to *be different*. In many cases these laws are likely to have been governed by religious factors. They probably relate to magical customs and pagan ceremonial practices which are no longer easy to trace or recover. The Egyptians mixed vegetables and grapes in their vineyards. Perhaps in these practical and visible ways, God was urging Israel to be different from her pagan neighbours. In the original text, the word translated *woven* or 'mingled' (11, RSV) is not Hebrew; it seems to be borrowed from an Egyptian term. We know that some cloth-weaves in Egypt were likely to have had magical associations and that may well lie behind the prohibition about mixed fabrics.

These unusual covenant obligations also remind them that they must *be obedient*. They might not always understand why they are asked not to do certain things, but they must trust the God who made the rules. The Lord would certainly not have forbidden his people to do anything unless the thing was positively harmful to them. 'No good thing does he withhold from those whose walk is blameless.'[9] If the Lord had forbidden certain customs and practices, they cannot possibly have been 'good' for them. They were not to quibble and argue as to why such things were denied them; they were to do exactly what the Lord required and be content in their obedience. One item of their clothing was to bear testimony to their loyalty to God. Instead of being like their heathen neighbours, the Israelites were to make their distinctive witness by wearing *tassels on the four corners* (12) of their cloaks. The *tallith* or prayer-shawl is still used in orthodox Judaism. The tassels were a visible reminder of their obligation to obey the Lord's word:

> You will have these tassels to look at and so you will remember all the commands of the Lord, that you may obey them and not prostitute yourselves by going after the lusts of your own hearts and eyes. Then you will remember . . . and be consecrated to your God. [10]

For most Hebrew people, the cloak with the four tassels served a dual purpose; it was an outer garment by day and a heavy blanket at night.

---

[9] Ps. 84:11.   [10] Nu. 15:37–41.

In other words, at all times the tassels were there at each of the four corners to confront them, day and night, with the priority of obedience.

Additionally, one of these rules may have been given to remind them that they were to *be compassionate*. The farmers are told that they must *not plough with an ox and a donkey yoked together* (10). God does not wish a strong and a weak animal to be yoked together during their work. The surrounding nations regularly combined the two animals for ploughing so it is possible that this prohibition may simply be another summons to adopt different practices from their pagan neighbours. Moreover, the ox and ass represented that which was 'clean' and 'unclean' in their food laws (14:3–8), which may have been yet another reason why the two animals were to be kept separate. Three of the regulations in this passage (animals, seed and clothing) are found together in one verse elsewhere[11] and in that context the prohibition relates to mixed breeding. There could, of course, be more than one reason for the rule but, in view of the emphasis on animal welfare elsewhere in the covenant (22:1–4, 6)[12] it is quite possible that behind this particular obligation is a concern to protect animals from any kind of pain or cruelty whilst they were working. In Britain today there is widespread concern about increasing cruelty to animals. God made them, and cares about them even if some humans fail to do so.

6. The sanctity of sex (22:13–30)

The law now deals with a group of six regulations concerning personal and community morality. They emphasize that God's purpose is that physical sexual relationships are to be confined to marriage and to marriage alone. The passage indicates how important it was for the Hebrew people to preserve high standards of morality within the community.

The first law (13–21) envisages the complaint of an Israelite husband who claims that his wife has deceived him concerning her virginity at the time of their wedding. It is extremely serious if he *slanders her and gives her a bad name* (14) and the accusation must be dealt with so that either the husband is exposed for defamation of character or the wife is punished for her pre-marital sexual relationship.

The second law (22) is an uncompromising condemnation of adultery – sexual relations with a partner who is married to somebody else. It is a sin which breaks three commandments – those which forbid covetousness ('your neighbour's wife'), theft

[11] Lv. 19:19.   [12] See Ex. 23:10; Lv. 25:7.

and adultery. The third law (23–24) is equally condemnatory. Here, the partners include *a virgin pledged to be married* who did not resist the sexual advances of the man concerned. Although *she was in a town*, the woman already engaged to be married to someone else *did not scream for help*. The fourth law concerns the rape of a betrothed woman *out in the country* (25–27). In this case the woman *screamed* but *there was no-one to rescue her*. As in the earlier cases, the punishment must be by death but, naturally, only the offending rapist is condemned. The fifth law (28–29) deals with another case of pre-marital sex. Here, a man seduces a young woman *who is not pledged to be married*. The offender was ordered to make financial compensation to the family, marry the girl and never be free to *divorce her*. The final law (30) in this group concerns a man who has sexual relationships with his stepmother. To *dishonour* or 'uncover' (RSV)[13] means 'to encroach on his father's marital rights' (Thompson). Incest was explicitly forbidden. Such behaviour was under the divine curse (27:20).

These laws were specifically designed to preserve the sanctity of marriage and maintain the general well-being of Hebrew family life. In our own time, whilst not wishing to adopt the punishments which are prescribed, we need to expose the transgression. We live in a period of widespread moral decadence, and sexual permissiveness is openly applauded in news-items, theatre, films, videos and novels. A recent issue of an international news magazine carried a comment by a Belgian legislator, Jean-Pierre Detremmerie, on European reaction to allegations of marital infidelity on the part of American politicians: 'In Europe, extramarital affairs are considered a sign of good health, a feat.'[14] It is astonishing that, in today's world, anyone could equate sexual permissiveness with healthy behaviour when contemporary society is confronted with the serious increase on a world scale of a fatal sexually-transmitted disease. The AIDS crisis confronts men and women in every continent with an undeniable medical deterrent which needs to be set alongside the Bible's persuasive ethical teaching and its unequivocal demand of personal morality.

Commenting on this passage, J. A. Thompson reminds us of two important things: the warnings of history and the teaching of Jesus. 'Great nations in centuries past lost their nationhood in considerable measure because of their unrestrained licence in sexual matters. For the Christian, at any rate, nothing less than the standard set by Jesus can be regarded as the norm.'[15]

In the first century, with these particular verses in their minds, the Pharisees brought an adulterous woman to Jesus. It was not out

[13] See Ruth 3:9 and Ezk. 16:8.   [14] *Newsweek*, 10 February, 1992.
[15] Mt. 5:28–29.

of concern for public morality that they made an exhibition of her, but because they wanted to have 'a basis for accusing him'. Jesus refused to stone the woman but he did not condone the offence: 'Go now and leave your life of sin.'[16] Another woman, whose morals were hardly commendable, came to experience Christ's transforming power. Released from her guilt, she publicly confessed that Christ had not only exposed her sin but changed her life. On the basis of her testimony other people came to realize that he was indeed 'the Saviour of the world'.[17]

In today's world, those who have ignored God's law regarding sexual purity have more need to fear the onset of incurable disease than the pelting of stones. We live in a different world, but sin is no less serious in its ramifications and effects. God's word makes it clear that all who are guilty can be forgiven immediately, but the penitence must be genuine and the sin abhorred. All sins are offensive to God. Unlike us, he does not choose to grade them in order of seriousness. Sexuality is God's gift. Within the marriage relationship it is to be valued and treasured as the deepest physical expression of human love. Tragically, however, any of God's gifts can be misused and diverted to evil rather than good purposes. Sexual sin (like any other kind of sin) needs to be seen for what it really is – a damaging power which grieves God, ignores warnings, ruins us and damages others. Nobody in their right mind can afford to be casual about such a sinister and destructive force.

7. Clean worshippers (23:1–8)

A series of rules follows at this point which govern the composition of the covenant community at worship. Certain people were not permitted to *enter the assembly of the* LORD (1, 2, 3). The prohibition of a man who has been physically mutilated (1) is probably a further reference to the corrupt ceremonies of Canaanite religion which practised castration, as is that to the child of *a forbidden marriage* (2) which probably describes the son or daughter of a Canaanite temple-prostitute (17–18). At birth, the child will have been dedicated to a pagan god and it would be both disobedient and harmful to attempt to mix paganism with the worship of the only true God. These two classes of people were sad evidence of the physically and morally damaging practices of heathen religions and it was not appropriate for them to share in the worship of a holy people. Such restrictions were aimed at preserving Israel's distinctive testimony to God's holiness and were designed to guard the Hebrew worshipping community from alien pagan influences.

[16] Jn. 8:1–11.   [17] Jn. 4:17, 29, 39–42.

The Ammonites and Moabites were also forbidden entry to the congregation (3); the former because of what they did not do, the latter because of what they did do. The Ammonites' sin was one of omission – they did not show compassion to the Israelites during their wilderness journey (4). The Moabites' offence was one of commission – they made strenuous (but unsuccessful) attempts to pull Israel down through the prophetic oracles of Balaam (4–5). We do well to remember that we can grieve God as much by what we fail to do as by what we do. We imagine that sins of commission – flagrant acts of transgression and disobedience – are the more serious. The Bible, however, does not support such a view. The three failures portrayed in the parables of Matthew 25 are sins of serious omission – the lamps were not filled; the talents were not used; the needy were not helped. The prohibition not to *seek a treaty of friendship with them* (6) refers to foreign alliances. It was the kind of language used in their political treaties.

Although the Moabites had tried to use Balaam for sinister purposes, God had thwarted their design. He *turned the curse into a blessing for you, because the LORD your God loves you* (5). There are times when Christian people find themselves opposed and oppressed by those who are intent on damaging them in one way or another. In his sovereignty, the Lord is still able to turn curses into blessings, and he continues to do such things because he loves us. In the late nineteenth century, Tom Barnardo's work among the homeless boys of London's East End was brought to the brink of ruin by a smear-campaign. A 62-page booklet was published which brought slanderous accusations against Barnardo and the subsequent troubles (stretching over three years) caused him intense personal distress. He was fully exonerated, however, and the newspaper coverage of the case brought the needs of London's orphans to the attention of people all over the country. Money came pouring in to support him in his work. Yet, but for the publicity, his essential ministry among destitute children would hardly have been known beyond London. Because God loved Barnardo and the work he was doing he *turned the curse into a blessing*. God goes on doing that.

Conversely, the Edomites and Egyptians were not to be rejected. The Edomite is to be regarded as a *brother*[18] and the earlier role of the Egyptians in the history of the Hebrews was not to be forgotten (7). This verse tends to support the view that, although Israel's later years in Egyptian slavery were severely painful and unpleasant, the initial years may have been extremely good (26:5). In years of serious famine, when everyone in Israel was a needy *sojourner*, there

---

[18] Gn. 36:1–19.

was food in Egypt and many of its people must have been generous, protective and supportive. The kindness of those days was not to be forgotten. Therefore, the children of *the third generation* of Edomites and Egyptians may be admitted to *the assembly of the LORD* (8). By that time the Israelites would be able to see whether such people were genuine in their desire to belong to God's holy people.

8. Personal hygiene (23:9–11)

Two rules follow at this point which relate specifically to Israelite military expeditions. On such occasions, the soldiers would need to set up camp and it is important that the camp-site be kept *from everything impure* (9). The general injunction about cleanliness is followed by two specific commands – one relates to personal hygiene, the other to public health. The first probably concerns a nocturnal emission,[19] though Craigie thinks it possible that it may refer to the act of a soldier who urinates either involuntarily in his sleep or deliberately, because he is too exhausted to go outside the camp. Such an *unclean* man was not a moral offender; his act was considered to be unhygienic and therefore unworthy of God's presence. He was therefore commanded to wash himself thoroughly before returning to the camp at sunset.

9. Public health (23:12–14)

Each camp must have appropriate toilet facilities. God is not only concerned about the cleanliness (and 'holiness') of the individual soldier but also that, in the intense heat, disease was not allowed to spread throughout the community. Profound theological reasons are given for this personal care and public welfare. The rules are given to remind the people of God's holiness as well as their health. The camp is a place where *the LORD your God moves about* (14); his presence among them makes the camp *holy*. The Hebrew people do not want the Lord to see anything which is unfitting as he walks around their tents. This statement (14) about Israel's holy God provides a threefold testimony to his omnipresence (*in your camp*), omnipotence (*to protect you*) and omniscience (*that he will not see among you anything indecent and turn away from you*). For the Hebrew people, their everyday conduct was determined by the nature of God. Because he is holy they were to be like him: 'Consecrate yourselves and be holy, because I am holy.[20]

---

[19] As explicitly stated in Lv. 15:1, where the Hebrew is different.
[20] Lv. 11:44–45; 19:2; 20:7–8; 1 Pet. 1:15–16.

221

10. Helping the helpless (23:15–16)

An injunction based on God's holiness is followed by another which is inspired by his mercy. The runaway slave was to be offered protection and security. The person envisaged here was probably a foreign refugee. He must not be intimidated, exploited or extradited, nor must he be sold again into slavery. Nobody must be allowed to make money out of this person's sad misfortune. His days of compulsory service were over; he can now enjoy his freedom by living in any Hebrew town *he chooses*. He is utterly at liberty to live *wherever he likes*. The Israelites had once been slaves themselves and they will surely want to be kind to others.

This compassionate regulation is in marked contrast to those found in the political treaties and pagan law-codes of the time. Some treaties made explicit provision for the extradition of refugees.[21] Here, it is clear that Israel must not enter into such agreements. As a nation, her only commitment was to the Lord. He loved the 'sojourner', and people must always come before politics. In the Babylonian Code of Hammurabi anyone harbouring a runaway slave could be executed.[22] Within the borders of Israel such compassion was an obligation not an offence. God's purpose was to create a community where it was not difficult to be loving.

[21] J. B. Pritchard, *Ancient Near Eastern Texts*, pp. 200–205.
[22] Laws 15–19 in J. B. Pritchard, *Ancient Near Eastern Texts*, pp. 166–167.

Deuteronomy 23:17–25
19. More about the neighbours

The passage before us covers an extraordinarily wide variety of diverse themes such as worship, economics, religious vows, divorce, military service, slavery, disease and general social concern. It is not easy to understand why they appear in this particular order, but the literary structure of the laws is hardly as important as their doctrinal and ethical teaching. Although they deal with life in an entirely different context from our own, these rules frequently have striking relevance for late twentieth-century individuals and communities.

1. Pure worship (23:17)

For those who treasured Israel's unique relationship with God, the greatest fear was that the nation's distinctive spiritual life could be corrupted by Canaanite religious practices, most of which were sickeningly immoral.[1] Cult prostitution played a significant part in their fertility rites and was utterly abhorrent to the Lord. No Israelite was permitted to engage in acts of ritual immorality. Religion must never be divorced from morality; genuine belief must go hand in hand with consistent behaviour.

2. Clean money (23:18)

The Lord *detests* deviant sexual practices and does not want immoral earnings in the offerings of his people. Money must not be brought *into the house of the LORD* which had been earned by either female or male prostitution. The words used here are not the same as those in the previous verse which describe cult prostitutes. The way we earn our money is important. Believers must ensure that their wages are not obtained by employment which is either degrading to themselves, damaging to others or dishonouring to

[1] Nu. 25:1–9; 1 Ki. 15:12; 2 Ki. 23:7; Ho. 4:14.

God. In the early Christian period certain occupations were considered unsuitable for Christians and, in the late second century, the North African writer Tertullian took the trouble to mention some of them. It is important in our own times to ensure that we are not earning our money at other people's moral or emotional expense. Some high-pressure salesmanship, for example, encourages thoughtless people to purchase goods they can ill-afford on deferred payment schemes. In some situations, high unemployment levels could drive some desperate, high-principled people into unsuitable and unhelpful work. Believers will want to subject their daily employment to divine scrutiny and so make sure that their daily work is not displeasing to the Lord.

3. Generous help (23:19–20)

Life was precarious for many in Israel. During hard and difficult times any member of the covenant community might find himself financially impoverished. Natural disasters (storms, earthquakes), drought, famine years, illness, bereavement, a dramatic change in domestic circumstances, and other serious adversities could mark the sudden end of normal income. But severe poverty could be relieved and a person's children fed if a *brother* in Israel would come to his aid. A loan would tide the impoverished family over until a better day when the money could be repaid. But no Hebrew man or woman must make money out of another Israelite's misfortune. Interest must not be charged except in cases when the money is on loan to a *foreigner*. To exact interest would only increase the trouble for the destitute man or woman. If a Hebrew has been blessed by God so that he is in a strong enough position financially to help his brother or sister, then he must do so as an expression of his gratitude to God and not as a way of increasing his wealth.

4. Dependable words (23:21–23)

Two statements are made here concerning *a vow to the LORD*. First, it is not sinful to refrain from making vows and, secondly, if a vow is made then it must be honoured without unreasonable delay. This rule emphasizes the importance in biblical teaching of the spoken word. Once again, their own conduct was determined by what they knew about God's nature. God's word was utterly reliable. If God said something, it was done.[2] If he made a promise it would certainly be fulfilled.[3] Their word must also be trustworthy and dependable. In no sense does the Lord expect us to make vows to him but

---

[2] Gn. 1:3.   [3] Nu. 23:19; Jos. 21:45; 23:14; 1 Ki. 8:56.

if we do make them then we are under a spiritual obligation to do what we have promised. If we do not keep our word, what began as a high resolve can end as a serious offence: *you will be guilty of sin* (21). This saying needs to be seen in the light of its covenant setting. In any treaty, both parties had to be assured that each would keep his word and that the promises outlined in the covenant would be honoured.

Jesus once referred to this passage from Deuteronomy when he spoke to his disciples about the importance of reliable words: 'You have heard that it was said to the people long ago, "Do not break your oath, but keep the oaths you have made to the Lord." But I tell you . . . Simply let your "Yes" be "Yes", and your "No", "No".'[4] Therefore, although this covenant obligation relates primarily to vows made to the Lord, it is also a reminder of the incalculable potential (for good or evil) of our everyday conversation. We must not speak carelessly, rashly or harshly. The believer's words need to be truthful, wise, helpful, dependable and loving.

5. Grateful sharing (23:24-25)

Although the covenant specially emphasized the law of property, there was also provision within its teaching for people with little or no property – the hungry traveller or the destitute neighbour. Nobody must be hungry within the covenant community. So, if any deprived men or women had to make a journey, they could help themselves to grapes in a vineyard or corn in the fields, on the firm condition that they did not take any of the produce away with them. In other words, the law provided for the meeting of an immediate need. In the sweltering heat, a homeless person could eat some grapes as he stood in the vineyard, and he could rub the ears of corn together, as Jesus did,[5] so that he might at least have a little food. A law of this kind brought immediate help to the hungry or the refugee without encouraging the idle thief; to remove either grapes or grain would be stealing and a violation of the eighth commandment (5:19). God had been good and generous to the owner of the vineyard and the cornfields. He could afford to share that bounty with others.

By this simple provision in the law, the Lord made sure that Israel's poor would not die of starvation. The vineyards and fields of their neighbours were always open to them. The cry of the hungry was not to be heard within the borders of Israel. In the contemporary world, millions of our global neighbours are dying of

---

[4] Mt. 5:33, 37.   [5] Mk. 2:23.

starvation. Every believer has a moral as well as a spiritual obligation to do something practical every week to help those who long for food. To ignore their cry is to be deaf to the Lord's plea.

Deuteronomy 24:1 – 25:4
20. Basic rights

The next section of legislation covers a number of different issues which could arise at any time within the Israelite community. The unifying theme is the Lord's protection of his people. God is concerned about the welfare of a woman involved in a broken marriage, the security and stability necessary for a newly married couple, and the embarrassment of debtors. There are prohibitions concerning compulsory slavery, rules which govern the health of the community, the wages of hired servants, as well as care for the hungry and destitute. They highlight the Lord's concern for every aspect of human life and emphasize that for God's people 'no-go' areas are prohibited. Everything we do should be glorifying to him.[1]

1. Protecting women (24:1–4)

Women counted for little in the social structures of the ancient world and the law which controlled the arrangements for divorce stands in marked contrast to the provisions of Israel's neighbours. In most of the surrounding nations, a woman could be divorced on almost any pretext. If a husband tired of his wife, it was not difficult to have her banished from the home and there was little by way of redress. Amongst the Canaanite people there was scant regard for the sanctity of marriage; divorces were common and remarriage frequently took place. This particular law states that a man who divorced his wife may not remarry her if she had married again after leaving the home. Such teaching controlled divorce, protected women and guarded marriage.

First, the law controlled divorce. There are no laws in the Old Testament which actually establish divorce. Divorce was a common practice throughout the Near East and is almost taken for granted here in Deuteronomy. Once, when Jesus commented on

---

[1] 1 Cor. 10:31; Col. 3:17.

this very passage, he said that it was only permitted by God because of mankind's 'hard hearts'.[2] Here in this law, however, the divorce conventions of the time were strictly regulated and controlled. The woman could not be dismissed from the home simply because her husband was no longer interested in her or because he had now turned his attentions to another woman. The husband could not divorce his wife unless he found *something indecent about her* (1). The same term (literally, 'nakedness of a thing') is found in the previous chapter describing impurity in the camp (23:14) and it is not easy to know precisely what it was intended to convey in this marriage context. It could mean that she was found to be impure in some way, or had been guilty of some improper conduct (but not adultery, which was punishable by death) or simply that she was incapable of child-bearing. The wife, however, could not be sent away at the changeable whim of a thoughtless and heartless husband.

Secondly, the law for divorce arrangements protected women. Throughout the ancient world, women were seriously disadvantaged in cases of marital breakdown. It would seem that in Israel, as elsewhere, only the husband could commence divorce proceedings. He may have behaved despicably and, by his own misconduct, brought his marriage to utter ruin but his wife was powerless to do anything about it. The woman had no rights whatever. If a man had set his mind on terminating his marriage, however, at least this law imposed strict limits on what he could do. The discontented husband was required to obtain *a certificate of divorce*, which presumably had to be properly issued and legally authenticated. These provisions would cause any man to hesitate before taking precipitate action. Whatever the trouble which had damaged the marriage-relationship, the man could not simply dismiss his wife from the home. When she left she was required to have this certificate 'in her hand' (1, RSV) to prove that she was free to remarry and that she had not been sent away from home on grounds other than those permitted by the bill of divorce. Without such legal protection, any homeless woman could easily become the victim of slanderous attacks, especially by a malicious husband and his friends who might even accuse her of adultery, thus putting her life at risk.

Thirdly, the law guarded marriage. Thompson says that 'there is some value in the proposal that these laws were intended to preserve the second marriage'. In other words, they are not simply a check on the discontented husband, but also on the mercurial wife. She might become tired of the second husband and put pressure

[2] Mk. 10:5.

on him to allow her to return to her first one. This law makes it clear that even if her second husband was prepared to release her by issuing a bill of divorce, or even if the second husband died, she could not re-marry her first husband. Ideally, marriage was for life and, if partners thought for a moment that they were free to change their marital allegiance backwards and forwards, they had to know that such conduct would be *detestable in the eyes of the LORD* (4).

We have already noticed that Jesus once quoted this law in the course of a conversation with some lawyers who were trying to 'test him' about divorce. He said that God's purpose was that nobody should be allowed to separate two partners in marriage. They had 'become one' and their union was for life.[3] Moreover, on another occasion, Jesus limited this law still further by saying that divorce was permissible only 'on the grounds of unchastity'.[4] Some first-century Jewish teaching about divorce was cruelly lax – a woman could be divorced because her husband no longer liked the look of her or because she had burnt his food. It was also grossly unfair – a woman could be guilty of committing adultery against her husband but not vice versa. As in other places in the Sermon on the Mount, Jesus lifted this Pharisaic interpretation of the Mosaic law on to a higher level altogether. A woman must not be divorced for trivial or flippant reasons. In his teaching Jesus emphasized the sanctity, moral obligations and permanence of marriage.[5]

2. Protecting newly married couples (24:5)

The next law is also concerned about the uniqueness, privilege and responsibilities of marriage. It is clear from these verses that marriage is God's designed relationship for men and women, but this choice gift can be grossly misused. Concerned about the preservation of marriage and the establishment of a happy family life, the Lord God commanded that the newly married man *must not be sent to war*, nor must he have *any other duty laid on him* which might threaten the stability of his married life. He was to be excused from such responsibilities for a full year so that he could give his best to the new relationship and *bring happiness to the wife he has married* (5). Moreover, it sought to protect the young bride from the dangers of an early widowhood. If her husband had to go out to fight within weeks of their wedding, he might easily lose his

[3] Mk. 10:2–9.   [4] Mt. 5:31–32.
[5] Mt. 19:3–9. See J. R. W. Stott, *The Message of the Sermon on the Mount* (IVP, 1978), pp. 92–99, the same author's *Issues Facing Christians Today* (Marshall, Morgan and Scott, 1984), pp. 258–279, and Norman L. Geisler, *Christian Ethics* (Apollos, 1989) for a fuller discussion of this important subject.

life on the battlefield, leaving her (and possibly an unborn child) destitute.

3. Protecting debtors (24:6, 10–13, 17)

A group of laws are found in this passage which concern the welfare of people in debt. Anyone in serious financial difficulty might gain immediate relief by obtaining an interest-free (23:19–20) loan and in such cases it was customary to make a *pledge* available to the lender – some item of furniture, clothing, jewellery, or other personal effects which the lender could 'redeem' should the loan not be repaid. Two laws are introduced governing the use of pledges within the covenant community. One controls the kind of article which can be offered, the other relates to the collection of them.

The first concerns some items which were forbidden pledges. In the first place, one piece of equipment could not be removed from an Israelite home. Nobody was allowed to accept *a pair of mill-stones . . . as security* (6). Some hard-hearted lender might want to take one of the two stones between which the grain was ground, but without both it would be impossible to perform the task. These two stones were essential household items for grinding the corn each day and without them any family could be in serious difficulties; a woman in debt would not be able to prepare the most basic food for her already deprived children.

Moreover, two items of clothing were also on the 'forbidden pledges' list. If a poor man's *cloak* (12–13) was offered as a pledge it could not be retained by the lender after nightfall. A man would have had to be utterly destitute even to consider offering his cloak as a pledge. In such circumstances a borrower would have had nothing else to offer as security. The law protected him, however, for that cloak also served as the quilt on the poor man's bed. Although extremely hot during the day, in many parts of Israel it could be bitterly cold at night. The debtor was in enough trouble without having to shiver through sleepless nights because of the severe drop in the temperature. Whatever his financial difficulties, the Lord wanted the debtor to have a good night's rest so that he could work properly on the following day and help to pay back his debts. The fact that a cloak had to be returned at dusk would naturally discourage a creditor from taking one as a pledge. Acts of kindness, such as ensuring that a poor man had a good night's sleep, were 'right' in God's sight and would prompt the grateful borrower to seek God's blessing on the one who had helped him. His prayers might obtain treasures for the creditor which money could not buy.

Additionally, the Lord ordered that *the cloak of the widow* (17) was not to be accepted as a pledge. The man's garment could be left with the lender during the day but the widow's cloak could not be taken at all, day or night. She was specially needy and the person who tried to relieve her distress by loaning money to her must have compassion on the borrower, just as the Lord has had compassion on the lender. Everyone must remember that at one time all Israel was as deprived and powerless as that poor widow – *Remember that you were slaves in Egypt and the LORD your God redeemed you from there. That is why I command you to do this* (18).

The second law concerning pledges relates to their collection from the home of the debtor (10–11). The Lord was concerned about the deprived man's feelings as well as his poverty. It was difficult enough for him to cope with his financial problems; there was no reason why he should also be exposed to unnecessary emotional strain. The creditor who loaned him the money must *not go into his house to get what he is offering as a pledge* (10). He must *stay outside* the poor man's home so that the debtor could bring the pledge out to him. That someone should enter his poor home in order to take away his few remaining possessions would be a degrading act, and God protected the debtor from such pain by promulgating a law which prohibited such a thoughtless action. We see from these laws that the Lord was concerned about the poor man's financial deprivation (no interest on the loan, 23:19), social embarrassment (24:11) and physical comfort (24:13).

4. Protecting vulnerable people (24:7)

The next law was against kidnapping. Stealing was plainly forbidden by the commandments (5:19; 19:14; 23:24–25; 25:13–16; 27:17) and this was specially so if the theft involved robbing men and women of their freedom. If an Israelite was caught *kidnapping one of his brother Israelites* in order to take him into slavery or to sell him, the robber was to be punished with the death penalty. People of that kind, who were prepared to degrade a fellow human being in order to be served by them or to acquire financial gain, were unworthy of a place within the covenant community. The *evil* they committed by such avarice and cruelty must be purged from the midst of the community. Such blatant disregard for the dignity of human life was an act of rebellion against God, the Creator (who made all men and women equal in his sight), Lover (who values one as much as another) and Redeemer (18) of his people. Those who do not value their fellow human beings are an *evil* menace in any society.

In our world, kidnapping has assumed some highly sophisticated forms – highjacking aeroplanes, the taking of hostages, the continuing confinement of 'political' prisoners, and the incidence in places like Northern Ireland, parts of the Middle East and elsewhere, of 'political' executions. All these forms of activity are forbidden by the God who treasures the men and women he has made and loves, people for whom Christ died.

Mercifully, however, for most of us, these acts of human aggression and degradation remain at a distance from our everyday lives; they come to our attention only through newspaper and television and we have no personal experience of them. This verse, however, still has something important to say to us. The offender here is guilty if he maltreats another human being and *treats him as a slave*. In the light of this teaching, we also grieve God if ever we look down on other people, or manipulate them for our own purposes, or treat them as if they were our property.

5. Protecting the community (24:8–9)

The Bible describes any form of skin disease, infectious or contagious, as leprosy.[6] The priests served as local medical officers of health within these Israelite communities. It was of the utmost importance that the regulations[7] regarding the isolating of victims and their readmission to the local community be scrupulously observed. The people are here given a serious warning. If anyone became careless or apathetic about the basic health rules given in the law, diseases of this kind might spread rapidly throughout the towns and villages of Israel. Therefore, the people are told that they must *be very careful to do exactly as the priests . . . instruct you*. The Lord has *commanded them* and has provided them with basic teaching about community care. They must listen to such teaching and obey it.

The covenant people are given a stark illustration to remind them of the necessity of obedience in this matter. The name of *Miriam* is mentioned and the people are asked to recall what the Lord did to her *along the way after you came out of Egypt* (9). She was stricken with leprosy because she would not accept the unique authority of God's word.[8] She thought she knew better than her brother Moses, God's servant, and blatantly questioned his authority. This passage warned the Israelites that those who ignore the word contained in the law, and as mediated through God's servants (the Levitical priests) might suffer a similar fate.

6. Protecting the employee (24:14–15)

Once the people entered the land and settled down to their new life, there was always the likely danger that some oppressive landowner

[6] Stanley Browne, *Leprosy in the Bible* (Christian Medical Fellowship, 1979).
[7] Lv. 13–14.
[8] Nu. 12:1–16.

might misuse a needy employee, either *a brother Israelite* or a refugee, *an alien living in one of your towns.* When sin and greed become entrenched in human lives, its victims are quite prepared to treat their fellows harshly in order to acquire financial, material or social improvement for themselves. This law insisted that, on the day he earned it, every labourer must be given his full wages before sundown so that he could buy the food he needs to take home to his hungry family. God is concerned about the wage packet. He would not dream of leaving such matters to the goodwill of the individual farmer. He knows he is dealing with sinners. Therefore, the employer is not advised but bluntly told that the wages of the *hired man who is poor and needy* must be properly (*not take advantage of*) and promptly (*before sunset*) paid.

If such a matter is neglected, the poverty stricken worker may *cry to the Lord* against his employer. Such a breach of the law would be a serious *sin* for which the negligent, greedy or preoccupied farmer will be accountable to God. The employer neglects his duty; the poor man's family is hungry; the worker cries to God in his need and the Lord will not overlook the sin. There is a deliberate contrast here with the earlier passage (24:13) where instead of crying against his fellow, the poor man blesses his creditor for his generosity, thoughtfulness and kindness. Whereas the employer's indifference becomes 'sin' in him, the creditor's deed is *a righteous act* (acknowledged as what is right) *in the sight of the Lord.*

We live in a very different society and the payment of wages at the close of every day is not normally necessary. There is a word here, however, for men and women in the contemporary world. It reminds all employers of the importance of just and fair wages in return for honest work, and it reminds all wage-earners of the importance of settling our accounts so that we do not run ourselves into debt. Many lives, homes and families are wrecked by financial mismanagement. No Christian can afford to be careless about basic matters of this kind. His or her personal integrity and testimony as a Christian are at stake. More importantly, it is dishonouring to God if we drift into debt. Like the Hebrew employer, it is important that we also do what is 'right' before the Lord so that other people are not able to point at *sin* in us as far as our financial affairs are concerned.

7. Protecting the innocent (24:16)

Throughout the Near Eastern world, the punishment of crime could be totally unjust and cruelly vindictive. If, for example, a person had been murdered in a community, once the offender had been identified, a bloodthirsty vendetta could be applied to his entire family. The criminal's wife, sons, daughters, wider family, and even their servants could be slaughtered in merciless revenge. Therefore, the Israelites were told that under no circumstances must such blood feuds or mass reprisals take place within the borders of Israel: *Fathers shall not be put to death for their children, nor children put to death for their fathers.* There was no reason whatever why innocent children should suffer because their parents had broken the law, nor why a father or mother should be executed because of crimes committed by a violent and aggressive son. God insists that *each is to die for his own sin.*[9] A law of this kind needs to be seen in the context of other judicial procedures for offenders in Israel's neighbouring countries. In Babylon, for instance, if the work of a careless builder led directly to the death of the house-owner's son, the son of the builder was executed. Such vindictive reprisals were directly prohibited in Israel.

8. Protecting the weak (24:17–22)

Further laws are here introduced which were specifically designed to help those people in Israel's towns and villages who, without such legislation, might be in danger of serious neglect. The *fatherless, widow* and *alien* were the deprived members of any local community but they were the objects of God's special love and care. He was father to the orphan, husband to the widow, and friend to the homeless. If the Lord cared about such weak people, nobody in Israel must allow them to be forgotten. Three basic human rights are treated here, their right to justice (17), clothing (17) and food (19–21).

First, from time to time, such people would naturally have cause to seek legal aid. There was always the danger that these dis-advantaged members of the community could suffer at the hands of a corrupt judge. For example, on the death of a husband, a close relative might offer attractive bribes to a judge in order to gain material advantages, but all at the widow's expense. Such behaviour was an offence to God for he had said that any form of bribery is strictly forbidden (16:19). If there was a disobedient and dishonest judge in the community, children were in particular danger. Defenceless children (like aliens) were without proper legal status. Somebody must be their helper. The *fatherless* could not plead effectively for themselves so Israel's judges were firmly told that under no circumstances must they *deprive the alien or the fatherless of justice.* Even if such disadvantaged people have money, life is still hard for them so God is specially concerned to see that they have a fair deal (10:18).

[9] For further comment on the prohibition of collective judicial punishment in Israel, see Christopher J. H. Wright, *God's People in God's Land*, pp. 235–237.

In contemporary society, many children are tragically exposed to danger, and rapidly increasing numbers of these young people are emotionally deprived, spiritually ignorant, and morally vulnerable. In the light of teaching such as that found here and elsewhere in Deuteronomy, God's people have a responsibility to respond to the challenge of this serious problem. With the tragic escalation of marriage breakdown, the emotional deprivation of children is inevitable. In years of crucial psychological formation, many of them are denied the right of support from both parents; an increasing number belong to one-parent families. The Christian church has the opportunity to provide for many hundreds of children the love, security and practical support which they have lost through a broken marriage, and any initiatives to help such children would certainly honour the intention of God's word in these verses.

We have already observed that a large proportion of children in contemporary Britain are spiritually ignorant, being totally out of touch with any congregation of Christian believers. Those Christians are to be applauded who have risen to the challenge of dispelling this widespread ignorance of biblical truth on the part of thousands of children in the modern world, and one hopes that more and more believers will discover imaginative and creative ways in their own neighbourhood of attractively presenting this generation of children with the stories of the Bible and the claims of Christ.

Many thousands of people, Christians and unbelievers alike, are concerned about the moral vulnerability of children in modern society. Bereft of responsible parental care and good moral example, exposed to pornography, victims of physical, emotional and sexual abuse, a frightening number of British children have lost their innocence in their earliest years. God's purpose was that the years of infancy and early childhood should be crowded with happy memories, but many children have never known the love, peace and protection of a secure home. Those who deliberately corrupt little children in this life can certainly anticipate God's severe judgment in the next. A poem by Stewart Henderson gives powerful expression to the wrath of God upon those who molest his 'little ones':

> And these, all these are mine
> I know each sinew of their small frames
> I hear their fear of night
> I watch their fun
> and when they laugh, so do I
> in joy I see them invent themselves
> even their shyness is a delight to me
> I cherish their innocence

And these, all these are mine.
And if, when I return,
I find just one who has been defiled
One desecrated by your corruption
One invaded by your lust
One chained to your perversion
One burgled of purity
One dominated by your tyranny
One diseased through your indulgence
One famished by your inequity
One reliant on your base favours
One separated from Me through your wicked fancy,
One, who once was Mine
Then I promise
You will never see the sun again
All you will receive is darkness
It will have no end
And you will not know peace
It will be terrible and just on that day
Because these, all these are mine.[10]

Warnings about corruption, tyranny and inequity were certainly necessary in Israel. On many occasions the Hebrew prophets exposed the corrupt practices of materialistic judges and their heartless indifference to the cry of the widow and the fatherless. In the eighth century BC, Amos criticized people in the northern kingdom who would go to any length to acquire a bit more silver and even 'sell ... the needy for a pair of sandals'. Such greedy citizens 'trample the head of the poor into the dust of the earth'. They 'afflict the righteous' and 'take a bribe'.[11] In the southern kingdom (Judah) Isaiah grieved over those sick materialists who loved a bribe and would run after gifts: 'They do not defend the cause of the fatherless, and the widow's case does not come before them.' He knew of judges who would 'acquit the guilty for a bribe, but deny justice to the innocent'. They were so set on the acquisition of riches that they 'deprive the poor of their rights ... making widows their prey and robbing the fatherless'.[12]

Moreover, God insists that deprived citizens have the right to adequate clothing (17). We have already seen that the warm outer garment could only be accepted as a man's pledge on condition that he could collect it at nightfall. The widow's garment must not be taken at all. She was likely to belong to the elderly members of the

[10] Copyright 1989, Stewart Henderson. From the Tear Fund video and stage production: *Broken Image*. Used with the author's permission.
[11] Am. 2:6–7; 5:12.   [12] Is. 1:23; 5:23; 10:2.

town or village and must at least have warm clothing and be allowed to retain some measure of dignity within the local community. Even if dire circumstances had driven her to borrow money, she must not be reduced to physical discomfort, potential illness through cold weather, social embarrassment and outward degradation.

These disadvantaged people were also entitled to sufficient food (19–21). Special provision was made for their meals at harvest time. If a farmer has overlooked a sheaf in the field he is forbidden to *go back to get it*. The remaining sheaf shall be for *the alien, the fatherless and the widow*. Similarly, when the olives were gathered, the trees must not be completely stripped of fruit. Some must be left for destitute people in the locality. Under no circumstances must the owner *go over the branches a second time*. God has intended the remaining olives to be left for the oppressed and needy. The same principle must also operate when the time comes to *harvest the grapes* of the vineyard. The owner must *not go over the vines again*. These gleanings of corn, olives and grapes were to be for aliens, widows and orphans, people who, in the joy of harvesting, might easily be forgotten.

That sheaf still speaks. Even for those of us who will never see it, its message is unforgettable. Innumerable families in our global village long for the gleanings though they deserve far more. In today's world there are still more than a billion people in absolute poverty. Forty million people a year die from hunger and hunger-related diseases. Forty thousand Third-World children die each day from hunger. That heart-rending cry of the hungry millions must reach 'the ears of the Lord Almighty'.[13] In the contemporary world, there is enough for all if only we would not hoard every grain for ourselves, strip the boughs bare, and clutch each single grape. Without the gleanings, millions more will perish. A compassionate God must be grieved about that, especially when he has said so much about our responsibility to the needy.

The appeal in these verses is not primarily to humanitarian principles, however. It is based on the initiative of God, not the benevolence of man. Those in Israel's community who were in a position to help others are reminded of what God has both done and said. They are confronted with the twin themes of redemption and revelation (18). The Israelites must meet the needs of the oppressed because of their past experience and because of God's present command.

a. Their past experience should encourage kindness to others

Only a few decades earlier they too had been *aliens*. Their fathers and forefathers had been slaves in Egypt *and the Lord your God*

---

[13] Jas. 5:4.

redeemed you from there (18, 22). When they were utterly without freedom, security and protection, God came to their help, and intervened as their Saviour and Deliverer. Now, they too must act mercifully and generously towards others. Whilst they were in captivity, God's love for the Israelites was not limited to comforting words; it was expressed in compassionate deeds.

Moreover, this appeal to God's mighty acts was a forceful reminder of their solidarity as God's redeemed people. Their salvation from Egypt was a testimony to the infinite value of every individual within their community. Every soul was worth saving, therefore they must not do anything which devalues human personality – treating people as things, denying their basic right to clothing, food and shelter. When, in Luther's day, the sixteenth-century peasants drew up their 'Twelve Articles', they based their appeal for freedom on Christ's saving work. In their charter they urged the abolition of bond service, 'since all men were redeemed by Christ'.[14] If Jesus believed that every soul was worth dying for, then surely every man and woman is of special worth in God's sight and not to be trampled upon by men.

b. God's present commandment insists on kindness to others

Speaking of the Lord's unique intervention in Egypt, Moses said: *God redeemed you from there. That is why I command you to do this* (18, 22). God's word about leaving the gleanings was not a suggestion; it was an order: *do not go back to get it . . . do not go over the branches a second time . . . do not go over the vines again.* This same commandment is twice repeated in Leviticus and there it is in terms of deliberate giving, not accidental forgetting: 'do not reap to the very edges of your field'.[15] The avaricious farmer who insisted on removing every single sheaf from his harvest-field was guilty of rank disobedience. Every harvest confronted the landowner with a stark decision; he could come away from his fields either as a submissive servant or a determined rebel. Those who persistently ignore the cry of the needy have forgotten Christ's redemption and rejected God's word. The oppressed are souls for whom Christ died and God has plainly commanded us to answer their cry.

9. Protecting the offender (25:1–3)

It was necessary also to guide Israel's judges regarding the administration of corporal punishment. In a case where a person has

[14] B. J. Kidd, *Documents illustrative of the Continental Reformation* (Oxford, 1911), doc. 83.
[15] Lv. 19:9; 23:22.

been found guilty of crime, he must be punished, but strict controls were to be introduced so that an offender was protected from acts of vicious and violent aggression. Seven principles are given to the community's legal officials so that they do not simply rely on their own ideas about right and wrong.

Firstly, the offender must have a proper trial. People were not allowed to take the law into their own hands and punish criminals in any way they thought fit. No man or woman accused of an offence must be left at the mercy of an angry (and possibly misinformed) community. If trouble arose in any town, then the parties concerned must seek legal advice and *take it to court* (1).

The case must be heard by more than one judge. The law refers here to *judges* in the plural. It is their responsibility to *decide the case* between them how the controversy may be resolved, *acquitting the innocent and condemning the guilty* (1).

The judges must be absolutely sure that the defendant is really guilty. After all, he may be the victim of some personal vendetta or local smear-campaign. Even if he is found guilty, they may decide that he can be punished by some means other than beating. He might be required simply to make restitution, pay a fine (22:19) or be punished in some other way.[16] It is only if *the guilty man deserves to be beaten* (2) that corporal punishment is to be inflicted.

Israel's judges must guard against excessive punishment. They must determine how serious the crime is and then ensure that the punishment is 'in proportion to his offence' (2, RSV). The criminal may have enemies in the community and he must not be repeatedly flogged for a crime which, although an offence, was not serious enough to deserve such a heavy punishment.

If the offender is to be beaten, the punishment must be inflicted in front of a judge (*in his presence*, 2) so that the guilty man is not in danger of being handed over to men who might commit acts of vindictive cruelty. The judge is personally responsible for seeing that the offender does not suffer more than the crime deserves.

Even if it is a serious offence, the number of stripes must never exceed forty.[17] If he has broken the law, the criminal must face the consequences. For his own sake and that of the community, it is appropriate for him to be punished but not publicly humiliated. Under no circumstances must the man *be degraded in your eyes* (3). In a later period, the Jewish people were so afraid of accidentally

[16] 2 Ch. 16:10.
[17] Christopher Wright observes that forty strokes 'was the *maximum* penalty; the law assumes that fewer than that, at the judges' discretion, would be normal. The fact that in a few specific cases the law prohibits any reduction of penalty (for deliberate murder, Nu. 35:31, idolatry, Dt. 13:8, and false testimony in court, Dt. 19:19–21) suggests that lesser penalties were permissible in other cases' (*Tyndale Bulletin*, 43.2, 1992, p. 218).

exceeding this number that they reduced the upper limit to thirty-nine stripes. On several occasions this maximum punishment was inflicted on the apostle Paul,[18] probably for 'breach of the peace'.

Finally, in this law there is an insistence on compassion. The judges, the plaintiff, any others who have suffered because of the crime, and every member of the community must remember that the offender is still a *brother*. They may well be angry about his misconduct, but they must not forget that he still belongs to the family of God's people and must be treated with love as well as with justice.

10. Protecting animals (25:4)

Although all the other laws in this passage concern human rights, a commandment is suddenly introduced which protects animals from owners who are more concerned about working them hard than feeding them well. Once the Hebrews settled in the land, they would soon make use of ox-drawn threshing sledges which served to isolate the grain from the chaff and stalks. This law insists that the farmer shall *not muzzle an ox while it is treading out the grain*. The animal had to serve its owner but in return its owner must care for his animal. The God who wanted the widow, orphan and alien to have food on their table was also concerned about animal welfare. The ox must not be muzzled as it worked. It deserved to be rewarded by sufficient food to renew its energy and maintain its health. To see the grain but be prevented from reaching it because of a leather muzzle, would be a cruel punishment for a beast which was as deserving of proper care as any other worker in the community. Deuteronomy has been called 'the animal lover's law'. We have already had occasion to notice that God is deeply concerned for his creation and that certainly includes the animal kingdom.

There were two occasions when the apostle Paul referred to this law,[19] in both instances spiritualizing it to support the conviction that God's servants ought to be financially supported by God's people. Whilst there is no doubt that that is true, we must remember that the Hebrews were originally given this commandment because the Lord was determined to prevent the suffering of animals in Israel. Naturally concerned about Christian giving, Paul asks a question about this text, 'Is it about oxen that God is concerned?' The answer must surely be, 'Yes, Paul, certainly. That is why God gave this order in the first instance.' It is both imaginative and appropriate to apply it to the support of the Lord's workers but it

---

[18] 2 Cor. 11:24.   [19] 1 Cor. 9:9; 1 Tim. 5:18.

must never be restricted to that when it first concerned kindness to cattle. In interpreting Scripture, the original intention of the writer must always be paramount.

Deuteronomy 25:5–19
21. Community care

In this section of the book the Israelite people are made aware of their responsibilities in four different areas. Although they concern distinctive situations they have an important feature in common – each concerns the continuing harmony of Hebrew society. The first two affect that all-important unit of Hebrew social life, the family, the third deals with a seriously disruptive social offence, theft, and the fourth anticipates the danger of a military invasion by an old and ruthless enemy. The teaching is about a bereaved wife (5–10), a violent brawler (11–12), a dishonest tradesman (13–16) and a cruel opponent (17–19).

1. A bereaved wife (25:5–10)

We have already seen that the covenant frequently emphasizes the importance of the family in Israel. The provision made in this particular law is for a widow whose husband *dies without a son*. It envisages a situation where two *brothers are living together* and their families are under the same roof. In such circumstances, the brother of the deceased man was expected to enable the widow to have a child in the hope that a son would be born to take her husband's name. There are several things which need to be said about this law of 'Levirate marriage' as it is called.

First, we need to realize that in the Near Eastern world it was a social stigma for a woman not to give a son to her husband. A widow would be grieved enough that she had lost her husband but to that agonizing hardship has been added the intense personal shame of not bearing a male child. Families were close-knit units and the birth of a baby boy gave a deep sense of security as well as pride to the parents. When he grew up and was able to earn his own living he would accept responsibility for the welfare of his parents when they were no longer able to look after themselves.

Then, the continuity of the family name was an extremely

influential factor in Hebrew life. The presence in both Old and New Testaments of genealogies or 'family trees' illustrates the importance of a 'known' family background which can trace its ancestry back for many generations. A family without a male heir or successor to the line would know that the social awareness of their particular family would perish in Israel. This law is designed to ensure that the deceased man's *name will not be blotted out from Israel* (6).

Though alien to our culture, a law of this kind would have been an immense comfort to a dying husband in Near Eastern society. His great anxiety would be that his wife might be without proper care in the years ahead. In a terminal illness, he would be relieved of worry if he knew that his brother would accept a measure of responsibility for the care of his wife and the provision of a male child.

We must also realize that this law was designed to protect the widow as well as continue the family line. It was important that she did not have to add to her natural sorrow the further anxiety of finding enough money to keep herself. This law begins with a prohibition, emphasizing how wrong it would be for the bereaved woman to have to go outside the family seeking another husband (5). The family must accept some responsibility for her welfare and, in their culture, the most important thing initially was for her to have her own baby boy to love, rear and care for in the years ahead.

This matter does not simply concern the continuance of a name. It also enters into the realm of property rights. If a woman was compelled to seek a husband outside the family, she would naturally remove various items and ancestral possessions belonging to the family, taking them outside the family circle. Such items were extremely important in Israel, providing the owner with some sense of continuity and security. Moreover, in times of adversity or penury, they could be offered as pledges.

Historically, this practice of 'Levirate marriage' had a long tradition which reached back to the patriarchal period[1] and was an utterly familiar custom in various parts of the ancient Near East. The Hittites and the Assyrians both practised it. In the Assyrian tradition even a betrothed woman could expect to be taken by her prospective husband's brother.

The detailed provision made in this law concerning the brother who does not wish to perform this function for his sister-in-law indicates how deeply rooted the tradition actually was, and how much the local community, represented by the *elders*, expected a man to accept this responsibility. It is likely that, in the ancient

[1] Gn. 38.

world, the reluctance of such a man would be determined by financial rather than moral considerations. If the bereaved woman produced a male child, her boy would legally inherit the property, but in the absence of a child, the property well might pass to the surviving brother. For this reason, the uncooperative brother-in-law was publicly disgraced (9). The sandal was used in Israel to symbolize property – it may simply indicate one who has walked over the owner's fields. Therefore, to hand over a sandal would indicate that property-rights had been transferred.[2] The removed sandal was a sign that the heritage had been totally renounced.

2. A violent brawler (25:11–12)

The covenant anticipates a time when a woman might intervene during a bitter fight between her husband and another man; she *reaches out and seizes* her husband's attacker *by his private parts.* The term employed here in the Hebrew text is one which would only be used to describe a violent act. Any woman who does so must suffer a severe punishment: *you shall cut off her hand. Show her no pity.* The sensitive reader is naturally stunned to think that such a thing could happen in the first place. The event obviously suggests an incident occasioned by extreme provocation but we are even more shocked by the harsh legislation. We need to remember some important contextual issues.

First, we must recall the Bible's extremely lofty view of the sanctity of the human body. It does not regard the body as an entity which could be distinguished or separated from the soul or the spirit, but emphasizes the essential unity of the whole person. The body is not an encumbering load from which we need to be liberated. Scripture has no room either for the notion of the body as a 'prison' for the spirit in this life (as in Greek thought) or of disembodied spirits in the next. In the Bible the human body is a unique gift, perfectly designed and made, a divinely created vehicle or instrument through which God's will and purpose should be served and honoured. The idea of a woman misusing her body to inflict harm on somebody else's body was unthinkable.

The dignity of womanhood is another important factor. It would be totally unfitting and improper for any Israelite woman to behave in such a gross manner. Womanhood is an important theme in Deuteronomy and in a variety of different contexts, the book frequently underlines a woman's rights and privileges. The female captive must not be abused (21:10–14). The wife who is no longer in her husband's favour must not suffer further grief by seeing her son

---

[2] Am. 2:6.

robbed of his rightful share of the inheritance (21:15–17). When a woman is slandered regarding pre-marital sexual behaviour, her honour and reputation are carefully protected (22:13–19). The newly wed husband must not go off to war in the first year of married life; it is the Lord's will that he 'bring happiness to the wife he has married' (24:5). It certainly looks as though, once the Hebrew people had settled in the land which God had given them, the rights of women were to be a significant aspect of their new social structure.

Where there are privileges, however, there are also responsibilities. This law stated that the woman who takes advantage of her rightful new status by abusing it in public, and to somebody else's detriment, must be exposed and punished. One of the sad features of human sinfulness in its corporate aspect is that appropriate freedom can quickly degenerate into harmful licence. Citizens are given the immense privilege of peaceful protest about any issue in society but it will not be long before someone turns the quiet march into a violent demonstration in which people are either hurt or killed. The priceless liberty has been seriously abused.

The importance of testimony is another issue which must also be borne in mind. The Hebrews were about to enter a land where sexual behaviour was largely a matter of indifference, even in religious circles. Far from maintaining high standards of sexual purity, Canaanite religion included male and female prostitution as part of its fertility rites. Baal-worship was an offence to the Lord God because it encouraged low standards of morality and even tried to dignify such corrupt behaviour in the name of religion. Castration even played a part in some of their ceremonies on the 'high places' and anything which approximated to such appalling conduct was despised. The Canaanites felt free to behave in these ways; after all, their gods were immoral. But the Hebrews must live differently; they must be holy because their God is holy.

The continuity of life is a further relevant theme here. The offence is serious not simply because it is undignified; it is dangerous, for by so doing the man may be robbed of the ability to produce a family. The continuance of the family line was of immense significance in Hebrew society; about the worst thing which could happen to any family man in Israel was to have his name 'blotted out from Israel' (25:6). The provision of a large family would ensure that the name would be continued in the community and, from an economic point of view, it also gave a strong sense of security to ageing parents. A violent attack of this kind must have been motivated by a desire to cause the man permanent damage by destroying his ability to procreate.

There is an additional factor which may help in understanding the

245

severity of the punishment. The legislation is to some extent an application of the *lex talionis* provisions. Unlike their pagan neighbours, the Hebrews were not allowed to mutilate the human body. The verse before us is the only instance of punishment by mutilation in the covenant. In contrast to this restriction, the Middle Assyrian laws insist that where any permanent damage is done to a man's testicles, both the offender's eyes were to be torn out.[3]

Although any form of suggested mutilation is unbearably harsh (however modified by contrast with surrounding nations) we must remember that this law, like others, was designed as a forceful deterrent in view of the totally different moral, social and religious environment the Israelites were about to enter. There is no record in the Old Testament or elsewhere that any person was ever guilty of such improper conduct or that any community had to witness such punishment. That may well have been due to the high standards which were demanded by their Covenant God.

Two final things need to be said. The first is that, although this severe law is described in the Old Testament, it is obviously not prescribed as a pattern for modern legislation. We are rightly horrified to hear about penal practice of this kind in some parts of the contemporary world. Like all other Old Testament teaching, this law needs to be seen in the light of the New. The Lord knew that such a code was vital for the well-being of his people at that particular stage of their history in order to maintain their distinctive witness to his holiness. Christ has come, however, and the fuller revelation of God's nature in him not only removes the necessity for such legislation but actually negates any harsh punitive measures which inflict pain and permanent physical damage on offenders.

There is a vital principle, however, which we may and must learn from this verse. In any action we may take, the end does not justify the means. We must never forget that it is possible to do the right thing in the wrong way. It is perfectly understandable for the woman to want to protect her husband in this brawl but she is not at liberty to end the conflict in any way she chooses. Members of any community are not free to act indifferently to the needs of others.

3. A dishonest tradesman (25:13–16)

Do not have two differing weights in your bag – one heavy, one light ... For the LORD your God detests anyone who does these

[3] J. B. Pritchard, *Ancient Near Eastern Texts*, p. 181; see also mutilation punishments in the Babylonian Code of Hammurabi (Laws 195–200), in Pritchard, *op. cit.*, p. 175.

things, anyone who deals dishonestly. This particular covenant-obligation is essential from five different perspectives – doctrinal, legal, social, exemplary and spiritual.

Once again, this law (as others) is firmly based on Israel's doctrine of God. We have seen already that because the Lord is holy, his people must also be pure. Similarly, because he is a God of truth, those who belong to him must not be untruthful or unreliable. Any form of commercial dishonesty is unloving, greedy and deceitful. God's covenant-partners must have a lifestyle which clearly reflects his nature and attributes.

From a legal perspective, these verses are an amplification of the Decalogue. The covenant plainly forbids any kind of theft (5:19) and stealing is a major offence in the agreement. It lies at the root of other breaches of the law: the theft of honour (robbing parents of the respect and obedience which is their covenant privilege, 5:16), the theft of life (murder, 5:17), the theft of property or money (as in this verse), the theft of love (adultery; deliberately stealing the loyalty of another's partner, 5:18), and the theft of reputation (as in slander, for example, or the covenant offence of 'false testimony', 5:20). To have different kinds of weights and measures and use these to increase one's profits at someone else's expense is a calculated breach of the eighth commandment.

Moreover, it was socially essential for Israel to develop as an honest community. Covenant partners are not merely accountable citizens; they are compassionate brothers belonging to the same family. The word 'brother' is found throughout this book, constantly emphasizing the close relationship which the Lord intended for his people (1:16; 15:2–3, 7, 9, 11; 17:15; 19:18–19; 22:1–4; 23:19–20. Even an Edomite is a 'brother', 23:7). A right sense of the law of property was an essential ingredient for Israel's social harmony. If 'brothers' cheated each other by acts of calculated deception, how could they hope to build a strong and trusting community? It is important to notice here how this law addresses itself not only to the travelling salesman who might be tempted in his journeys to carry different weights in his bag, but also to the domestic tradesman who has *two different measures . . . one large, one small* in the shop. The law applied to all forms of business transaction, peripatetic and local, large and small; everyone must be honest, down to the smallest detail.

The moral example to Israel's neighbours, however, is also important here. How can they hope to be 'a light for the Gentiles'[4] if their commercial dealings are corrupt? Once the people settled in the land and began to develop their economic and commercial life,

[4] Is. 42:6; 49:6.

they had frequent opportunities to trade with other nations. After their establishment in Canaan, the Hebrews became highly gifted in trade. Their newly acquired agricultural skills were soon put to good use as they met not only local needs but went on to sell their provisions in neighbouring markets both in their own country and beyond it. The Phoenicians looked to Israel for the regular supply of grain, oil and wine.[5] Under normal circumstances, Egypt in the south had its own liberal supply of grain but was pleased to import olive oil and wine from Israel. As the country developed its industrial skills, the metals promised in Deuteronomy (8:9) became available for export to other nations. We know that David made iron available to Egypt[6] and Solomon sold copper to buyers in Arabia and Africa. The Lord knew that his people would later have extensive commercial dealings with other nations. If they became so greedy that they would cheat an unsuspecting pagan neighbour, their witness would be damaged and the Lord's name dishonoured. Later, the Jewish people became renowned for their economic and business skills. When they were trading in the busy markets of the ancient world, it was perfectly in order for them to be highly competitive but they must never be dishonest and deceitful.

Finally, this particular law has arresting spiritual as well as moral appeal. The covenant people must behave in honest ways, not merely so that their 'brothers' will not be cheated but, even more importantly, so that the Lord will not be grieved; dishonest practices are detestable to him (16; cf. 18:12; 22:5). It is exactly the theme which, in days of commercial prosperity, was later taken up by the prophets. In the eighth century Amos, Hosea and Micah all preached against those tradesmen who used 'dishonest scales' and 'false weights',[7] each making it clear that such behaviour was utterly offensive to a God of righteousness, justice and truth. Anything was unacceptable if it was inconsistent with his character.

4. A cruel opponent (25:17–19)

The Hebrews are told: *Remember what the Amalekites did to you along the way when you came out of Egypt . . . you shall blot out the memory of Amalek from under heaven. Do not forget!* This covenant stipulation is linked to the previous laws by the common theme of 'safeguarding society'. This law appears harsh, even vindictive, but a number of important issues must be borne in mind.

The Amalekites were cruel tribesmen who attacked the Israelites soon after their miraculous escape from Egypt. At such a precarious time, the Hebrew refugees were not remotely equipped for a sudden

[5] 1 Ki. 5:10–11.   [6] 1 Ch. 22:3.
[7] Am. 8:5; Ho. 12:7; Mi. 6:11; cf. Ezk. 45:9–10.

attack of that kind and, but for another supernatural intervention by God, thousands of them would have perished at the hands of the marauding Amalekites. The battle was won by prayer[8] and the Hebrews were commanded there and then to make a written record of the divine judgment on Amalek's brigands for such a vicious raid. It seems that the enemy had attacked the people in the rear of Israel's long column of *weary and worn out* travellers. Those pilgrims were in the most vulnerable part of the huge caravan. It was the men, women and children who *were lagging behind*, the sick and elderly, the weak and infirm, who the Amalekites planned to kill and plunder – people who could do nothing to defend themselves. Several important aspects of biblical truth emerge in this seemingly severe law.

Firstly, here is a provision for Israel's future. The Lord knew that though the Amalekites were conquered in the desert at Rephidim, the Hebrew people had not seen the last of them. They swept down on the Israelites later in their journey and at a time when the Hebrew people were clearly out of the will of God (1:41–46).[9] In the period of the judges they inflicted further havoc on the Hebrew people by combining with other raiders to form large companies of ruthless brigands. Once, they joined with the king of Moab in a direct attack on Israelite territory.[10] In Gideon's day and later their already large numbers were inflated, 'like swarms of locusts', by combined harvest-time raids for which they were joined by Midianites and other plunderers.[11]

At the beginning of Saul's reign, the king only partially honoured the Lord's command about their necessary conquest. Saul's covetousness cost him his kingdom.[12] Years before, Balaam had prophesied that one day Amalek would 'come to destruction'[13] but, though he had the opportunity, Saul was not obedient enough to become God's instrument for that necessary mission. Consequently the Amalekites continued their plundering raids and, centuries after the promulgation of this covenant-law, they brought recurrent misery on the Israelite nations.[14]

By making this law the Lord was seeking to protect his people from future suffering. He was particularly concerned about those Israelites who would come to settle in the southern border areas where the Amalekites would be a persistent threat to local security. The command to *blot out the memory of Amalek from under heaven* may seem terribly harsh, but the deprivation, misery and loss of life consequent upon the disobedience of this law dwarfs any earlier suffering which may have been incurred by Amalekite

[8] Ex. 17:8-16.   [9] See Nu. 14:43-45.   [10] Jdg. 3:13.
[11] Jdg. 6:3-5, 33; 7:12; 10:12.
[12] 1 Sa. 15:1-35; 28:16-18.   [13] Nu. 24:20.   [14] 1 Sa. 30:1-20.

raiders. In a morally corrupt and sinful world it is not always possible to choose between what is either simply right or wrong. Sadly, we are sometimes compelled to choose between a course which may inflict some pain and another which would certainly bring much more.

Furthermore, these verses preserve a warning to Israel's neighbours. The idea of writing 'as a memorial in a book'[15] is to place on record the inevitable judgment of God. Israel was in an exceptionally vulnerable geographical position and constantly exposed to attack. The surrounding nations are hereby warned by this treaty that those who cut down weak and defenceless people may triumph at their easy, immediate success but they will eventually incur God's inflexible and righteous judgment. The Amalekite raiders acted in the way that they did because they *had no fear of God*. This law, however, reminds them that his judgment upon such ruthless people is certain and inescapable.

So, this law is also a picture of Israel's God. He is concerned for the *weary and worn out* and those who, because of age and weakness, are *lagging behind*. He is loving but he is also just, a God who does not turn an indifferent eye to human suffering. When Amos preached in the market place at Bethel those who listened must have been astonished (and reassured) to hear him pronounce divine judgment on Israel's pagan neighbours for their gross cruelty to men and women, near and far.[16] In their appalling inhumanity, these barbaric oppressors disregarded 'a treaty of brotherhood',[17] and the enormity of their sins would not be overlooked by a righteous and compassionate God. He was not a parochial God, merely concerned about sins against Israel. In our own time we need to remember that God is the universal and sovereign Lord. His interests are not restricted to religion. When we read the news headlines and feel helpless in the face of tragic sufferings inflicted upon innocent people by cruel overlords, we must remember that the cry of anguish is not unheard. A day of judgment is fixed when books will be opened.[18]

One final comment is of supreme importance. As with an earlier passage in this section (25:12) these verses are descriptive, not prescriptive. They clearly command what Israel ought to do, not what *we* are to do. This is certainly God's word but it is not his final word. Though this particular law has a great deal to teach us, it does not tell us how we are to treat *our* enemies. Since the promulgation of this law, God's Son has entered our world; for professing Christians, personal relationships must be conducted in the light of his

---

[15] Ex. 17:14. [16] Am. 1:3–15. [17] Am. 1:9. [18] Rev. 20:11–12.

perfect and now complete revelation. We are to love our enemies, not kill them, and we are to pray for those who treat us harshly.[19] God is merciful, and we must be as well.[20]

[19] Mt. 5:43–48.   [20] Lk. 6:36.

Deuteronomy 26:1–19
22. What happens when we worship

Worship is a central theme in Deuteronomy. At this point in its narrative we are given a unique account of Israelite praise; the occasion is the presentation of 'first-fruits', that season when the Hebrews brought their early and best produce as a thank offering to the Lord. These verses describe a simple yet moving ceremony, with a liturgical pattern of Hebrew worship, not elsewhere recorded in the Old Testament. The worshipper takes *some of the firstfruits . . . from the soil of the land*, puts it in a basket and goes to the place which the Lord *will choose* so that, in the presence of the officiating priest, he can make a verbal confession of his indebtedness to God.

This colourful narrative not only describes what was to happen in an agricultural community at a time of 'harvest thanksgiving'; it also embodies some important spiritual principles about worship. Like any great literature (though more so with Scripture) the narrative speaks far beyond the limited confines of its own immediate context. As we read of these times when God's people brought their gifts, we can discern some outstanding features of true adoration, praise and thanksgiving. Whenever we offer sincere worship to the Lord we acknowledge his generosity, recall his faithfulness, honour his uniqueness, obey his commands, and affirm his truth.

1. Acknowledge his generosity (26:1–4)

When the worshipper visits the appointed sanctuary with his attractive basket of freshly grown fruit he is aware above all else of the abundant goodness of God. The man who brings his gift knows only too well that unless the Lord had been generous to him, he would have nothing to offer. The initiative has been with God and this simple liturgy provides a vehicle for the worshipper's recollection of three truths about the divine generosity expressed in revelation, history and nature.

The primary aspect of the Lord's generosity was that he had

chosen the Israelites as his special people and made himself known to them by unique revelation. He had spoken to the patriarchs and they had been the privileged recipients of the reliable promise: Canaan was their *inheritance* (1). Every worshipper could say that they had entered the land which *the* LORD *swore to our forefathers to give us* (3). The promise had come to fulfilment; the word was reliable and effective. The worshippers had not simply heard about the land; they had *taken possession of it and settled in it* (1). The land was God's gift to them (1) and he had chosen to make *a dwelling for his Name* among them (2).

With a personal sense of gratitude each worshipper went on to make a verbal confession of his own indebtedness to God's power manifest in history. Addressing the priest he said: '*I declare today to the* LORD *your God that I have come to the land that the* LORD *swore to our forefathers to give us*' (3). The fathers heard the promise but the children reaped the blessing, and it was all because God had revealed his power to act sovereignly in history, overcoming his people's adversities and vanquishing their enemies. In the bleak days of their Egyptian captivity such a miracle would have seemed beyond their wildest dreams. It was not an inspiring tale, locked away in a remote past; each individual could say by personal testimony, *today . . . I have come.*

As Lord of nature, it was their open-handed God (not the capricious Baal) who had provided the rain to water the earth and the bright sun to ripen the fruit (2) which they now presented in their baskets. He was generous in what he had said, done and given, and such generosity must be personally and publicly acknowledged in adoring worship and grateful thanksgiving.

2. Recall his faithfulness (26:5–9)

As the genuine worshipper carries his basket and presents it to the priest he is encouraged to think not only of his grapes and olives. In this liturgy his mind is directed much further back, to the beginnings; not to the present harvest but to the past mercies of a God who had been good to the Hebrews long before the worshipper was born. The Israelite not only has an offering to bring but something to say. He must 'solemnly recite' (5, NEB) some important words which deliberately bring to mind three outstanding personalities of Israel's early history, Abraham, Jacob and Moses, and recall God's faithfulness as the reliable Provider, mighty Protector and promised Redeemer.

When the grateful believer presents himself at the appointed sanctuary he confesses with joy that the land he has possessed is *an inheritance* (1) which was promised to his *forefathers* (3). The words

253

would forcefully remind every Hebrew of the dramatic story from their earliest traditions, the promise made to Abraham. Here the worshipper recalls the Lord's faithfulness as *the reliable Provider.* God told Abraham on oath[1] that he would give them the land and the people to live in it, and he had not let them down.

When the basket of fruit is laid at the altar a precise liturgical formula must be used which does something more than stir the memory. It publicly identifies the individual worshipper with those miraculous events: '*My father was a wandering Aramean, and he went down into Egypt with a few people and lived there and became a great nation, powerful and numerous* (5). The confession names Jacob as 'father' of the privileged community. The Lord's faithfulness is portrayed as *the mighty Protector.* It is a story of vivid contrasts, capturing within a few sentences the adverse experiences of homeless Jacob. Aram often emerges in the story of the patriarchs.[2] The word *wandering* may also be translated 'perishing' and is particularly suited to Jacob whose vulnerable existence was often in the balance. Jacob became a landless traveller who, despite the onslaught of enemies, proved God as his shield and defence. In arresting phrases the confession highlights the radical transformation experienced by Jacob and his family. The contrasts are deliberately heightened in the confession – the homeless refugee and the resident worshipper, *down into Egypt* (5), and up into the land (1; 1:21), the small company, *a few people,* and the numerous throng, the weak, homeless tribes and the *great nation, mighty and numerous.* God is to be praised by his people for what he does in history as well as for what he gives in nature.

In the confession, however, the drama moves on to Moses. God is faithful as *the promised Redeemer.* He continues to change grim situations into those which vibrate with hope. Although ill-treated and humiliated by their Egyptian oppressors, the powerless Hebrews could at least pray,[3] and the worshipper's harvest confession draws special attention to their distressed cry. All the language recalls the memorable encounter with Moses at the burning bush. It reminds them of the Lord who *saw* their distress and hardship, and the unique achievement of a God who, *with a mighty hand and an outstretched arm,* effected their deliverance, doing so at the great exodus event with *great terror and with miraculous signs and wonders.* They were *brought . . . out* (8) of oppressive bondage and brought in (9) to the land of Canaan whose rich soil had produced the fruits they now wished to offer to the Lord. The *land flowing with milk and honey* (9) was a treasured phrase, first on the lips of

---

[1] Gn. 13:14–17; 17:8; Heb. 6:13–18.   [2] Gn. 25:20; 28:5; 31:20.   [3] Ex. 3:7.

Moses[4] at a time when the Israelite captives could scarcely dream of such a thing.

Milk and honey symbolized a life of peace and stability. It stood in sharp and painful contrast to the intensified slave labour, the cries of their oppressed women and the slaughter of innocent children. At the close of many a day, broken and bewildered, they prayed themselves to sleep: 'If only God . . .'. Those who go through dark times must not imagine that the God of light has left them. He might even be closer than in the bright sunshine: 'Moses approached the thick darkness where God was'.[5] Like the Hebrew slaves, we must trust during the long night and prove that strength will certainly be given, hope renewed, promises fulfilled and a new day yet dawn. Throughout the centuries God has been faithful to his people and we should worship him for that.

3. Honour his uniqueness (26:10)

The Lord kept his promise. The 'land flowing with milk and honey' was more than sentimental words. They did not only hear about the prosperous land; they entered it. It is now important, however, for them to acknowledge that the God of their historical destiny is the Lord of their agricultural success. For centuries the Canaanites had maintained that Baal, their fertility deity, was 'the God of storm and rain'.[6] All the produce for their fields was the work of his hands. So, this presentation of first-fruits challenged every Israelite worshipper about the dangers of idolatry and syncretism. Under subtle local pressures they might easily come to utilize the now abandoned hilltop shrines with their immoral poles. In any community a minority of the people might secretly worship the Baals. Although that sounds unthinkable, certainly by Elijah's time, and even more by Jeremiah's, the Baal teaching, rites and ceremonies had been widely accommodated to the worship of the only true God.

In order to counteract these serious dangers at an early stage, the true worshipper is required to make a crucial public confession which challenges any attempt to combine Israel's worship with that of Baal. As surely as historically the Lord God had brought them into the land, so he, and he alone, had provided their abundant crops: *And now I bring the firstfruits of the soil that you, O LORD, have given me.*

Religious syncretism is one of the subtle temptations of our own day. Some contemporary church leaders seem embarrassed by New Testament teaching which emphasizes the unique and distinctive character of Christianity. Jesus, however, did not die on the cross in

[4] Ex. 3:8, 17.   [5] Ex. 20:21.
[6] H. Ringgren, *Religions of the Ancient Near East* (SPCK, 1973), pp. 131–135.

order to save some people who might come to God by way of Christianity, leaving others to come to him by way of Islam's prophet and Koran, and others by way of the teaching of the Buddha. The apostolic message is as relevant now as when it was first proclaimed in the religiously pluralistic environment of the first-century world.

4. Obey his commands (26:11–19)

Worship is meant to be a radiantly happy experience for the people of God: *you shall rejoice in all the good things the Lord your God has given to you and your household.* The good things which the Lord has given, however, are not to be indulgently enjoyed or greedily hoarded, but generously shared. They are also for *the Levites and the aliens among you* (11). Each year at this special time of rejoicing, the deprived and easily neglected members of each local community must also benefit from the celebration of first-fruits. In offering them to God, the worshipper must also share them with others. It was the Lord's purpose that worship should not be an individualistic and insular experience which locks a believer in a secure and detached ghetto of self-satisfied experience. In looking up to God, worship must also look out in love to the world which he has made. He is not only worshipped by our words and music; he is adored by our lifestyle, by our passionate concern for others, and by our desire to reflect his unique qualities of generosity, love and mercy. It is not nearly enough to thank God for his totally undeserved kindness to us; we must be similarly uninhibited in our compassion for others. This was one of the most searching aspects of Christ's teaching about benevolence: 'If you love those who love you, what reward will you get? Are not even the tax collectors doing that?'[7] The God who 'causes his sun to rise on the evil and the good, and sends rain on the righteous and the unrighteous'[8] does not expect us to be calculating and restrained in our liberality.

In order to encourage the Israelite people to have open-handed lifestyles, the worshipper is reminded that the Lord's gifts are for *the Levites and the aliens among you.* On this same topic of generous sharing, the narrative goes on to mention the triennial tithe. God's provision for needy people was that they must receive a full tenth of all the local produce every three years. By the time any three years had elapsed the local farmer had been given ample opportunity to consolidate his own business, but he must now take care that his working life does not revolve entirely around his own family's needs. The priests were God's appointed servants and they

[7] Mt. 5:46.   [8] Mt. 5:45.

must be supported and the descendants of the homeless Aramean in the past must not neglect the homeless alien in the present.

Once the Israelites took possession of the land they were to offer a tenth of their produce to the God who had saved them and provided for their needs. But for his goodness, their eyes would be looking out on shrivelled plants, blighted corn and withered trees at harvest time. Without his generosity there would be no nine-tenths, so why selfishly and disobediently retain that part which belonged to the Lord? Of course, there are ceremonial features in the Mosaic Law which are no longer relevant, appropriate or applicable since the coming of Jesus, but that is no reason for summarily dismissing everything. As we have seen in earlier chapters, the teaching of the Mosaic Law has many strikingly up-to-date practical implications for ourselves.

Another illustration of the importance of the tithe can be seen in the fact that the priests (who received the tithe) are plainly told that when obedient Israelites bring their obligatory tenth, those gifts must also be tithed.[9] If the Hebrew people kept back part of their offerings and were blatantly disobedient about tithing, then the Levites could not possibly give as generously as they wanted to because only a paltry amount had been given to them. In other words, tithing is not a pattern for certain individuals; everybody is expected to do it. The spiritual leaders must set a good example by doing themselves what they clearly expected from others.

The practice of tithing is a vital spiritual principle. If Old Testament believers willingly offered a tenth, it is sad if contemporary Christians deliberately choose to offer less than is realistic. We who are greater debtors ought to present more, not less. Many believers maintain that the tithe is our basic minimum and, in addition we should all seek opportunities from time to time to give more than that as occasional, extra 'offerings' when the Lord has blessed us with his own extra-generous bounty.

5. Affirm his truth (26:16–19)

The concluding verses of this chapter bring to a close the 'stipulations' section of this book's treaty-structure by summarizing some of the outstanding covenant-themes which have been expounded earlier in the book. Whilst underlining the necessity of total obedience (16) this reiteration of key ideas emphasizes the correlation of commitment and privilege.

In the covenant between the Lord and his people, the Israelites publicly affirmed their commitment as they *declared* that the Lord

[9] Nu. 18:25–32.

was their God and that they would *obey* him (17). He had spoken (*The* L᷊ᴏʀᴅ *your God commands*) to them and they must respond immediately (*this day*), unreservedly (*all your heart and . . . soul,* 16), obediently (*walk in his ways,* 17) and totally (*keep all his commands,* 18) to him.

These committed people were privileged partners, however, in a covenant which would last for ever. Those who confessed their loyalty to God knew that he had affirmed his commitment to them: *And the* Lᴏʀᴅ *has declared this day that you are* his secure (*his people*), loved (*treasured possession*), privileged (*set . . . high above all the nations*) and dedicated (*holy*) people.

It is now time for us to glance back over this important passage and note, by way of summary, that this teaching is pointedly relevant in our own time. It illustrates for us a number of principles of genuine worship.

a. The exclusiveness of worship

The provision of a special sanctuary, *the place that the* Lᴏʀᴅ *your God will choose as a dwelling for his Name* (2), was designed to divert the Israelite people away from the hilltop Baal-sanctuaries. Here is a further echo of the basic covenant obligation: 'You shall have no other gods before me' (5:7). Jesus made a similar claim: 'No-one can serve two masters . . . You cannot serve both God and Money.'[10] Regular attendance at Christian worship is a necessary antidote to worldliness, secularism and materialism, the faceless gods of contemporary society. When we meet with God's people we are forcefully reminded of the poverty of any life which ignores God's existence, nature and generosity. True worship is a public confession that, though we are aware of rival allegiances, the Lord alone is our God.

b. The responsiveness of worship

When you entered the land . . . Then go to the place . . . your God will choose as a dwelling for his Name (1–2). The initiative in worship is not with either the genuine or merely dutiful worshipper. It is with the gracious God who always takes the first step towards them in generosity (he gives them the prosperous land), goodness (he provides its bountiful harvests) and grace (by meeting their spiritual needs as well as their material resources). Whenever we worship either individually in our own homes or corporately with the Lord's people we are acknowledging that before we ever

---

[10] Mt. 6:24.

thought about him, the Lord God thought lovingly about us. We love because, first of all, we were loved.[11]

c. The reflectiveness of worship

It demands thought. In worship the emotions may well be stirred – and, with a love-relationship, that is both natural and right – but the intellectual processes will also be at work. This simple ceremony of the first-fruits provided the Israelites with a regular opportunity to think deeply about the origin and source of all their blessings. It did something to prevent them from taking God's many gifts for granted. After all, it was God who had given them the deliverance (6–8), and security (9) they needed. Genuine worship reminds us that we are debtors. It releases us from the sick and insular preoccupation with ourselves. Self-idolatry is a constant danger. Worship points us away from our own petty achievements to the God who, in generous love, has made every good attainment possible. Worship honours God with the psalmist as it exclaims, 'Not to us, O Lord, not to us but to your name be the glory.'[12]

d. The commemorative nature of worship

At this festival the Hebrew people did not merely think of their present harvest, symbolized by the basket of fruit in their hands. They thought gratefully about the mighty acts of God in the past. Many people are either obsessed with the present or apprehensive about the future. Worship deliberately looks back. Here they publicly rehearsed the achievements of a God who had acted with unique power in shaping their destiny. They reflected on what he had done for the nation in former days (5), a recurrent feature found in many different contexts throughout this book (4:37–38; 6:12, 20–23; 7:7–8, 17–19; 8:13–16; 11:2–7; 12:5, 10; 15:15; 16:1–12; 20:1).

In the modern scene far too much Christian worship is almost painfully subjective; it lacks the objective adoration of a God who is majestic and sovereign in his world. True biblical worship cannot be confined within narrowly interpreted personal and present experience. Worship fails to match the biblical norms if it does not leave us with an enlarged vision of our mighty, universal and transcendent God. Some church services may be disappointing in this respect; they scarcely relate to life in the contemporary world. The concept of God is small; his interests scarcely look beyond the church, in some instances rarely beyond the local church. Huge

[11] Rom. 5:8, 10; 1 Jn. 4:10, 19. [12] Ps. 115:1.

national and international issues can take place in a week and on the following Sunday they are passed by without a mention even in the intercessions. It is not a biblical way of worshipping God. The Hebrew people believed he was Lord and Judge of all the earth, not simply of Israel.[13]

e. The corporateness of worship

This presentation of the first-fruits was certainly not an occasion for narrow reflection simply on what the Lord had accomplished for the worshipping individual. At this harvest season they deliberately rejoiced that, however much they loved God, he was not restricted to the limited range of their own experience. However deep and genuine its personal reality, worship belongs to the whole community of God's redeemed people. There is great value in meeting together and not simply as isolated individuals.

We have already seen that unless the Israelite people were brought together for these corporate and centralized acts of adoration, they might, by dabbling with Baalism, compromise their distinctive message of God's uniqueness. There is more to it than that, however. By meeting together each individual Israelite was thereby reminded that he or she belonged to a supportive company. They were not alone in their allegiance and commitment to the Lord. If personal affliction, sickness, adversity or bereavement had made life painfully difficult, they were comforted by the assurance that they were not on their own in the sanctuary, tormented by solitariness. Although the lamp of their personal faith was flickering, they were surrounded and fortified in worship by fellow-believers who openly confessed their renewed confidence in a God who had seen the Hebrew people through difficult times. When they recalled the *wandering Aramean* (5), the *hard labour* of Egypt (6), the *misery, toil and oppression* (7) of those agonizing years, they testified to a faith which could bring a believer through dark times. It was not fair-weather religion which was being expressed at the offering of first-fruits. It was a robust, resourceful and resilient faith, a faith which was being made vocal by others, even if the individual Israelite here or there happened to be weighed down by sorrow.

This sense of the corporate dimension of our faith in God is something which has not always been at the centre of evangelicalism. Many of our friends in the Orthodox churches are upheld by it and, for some of them in difficult parts of the world, it has brought them immense peace to realize that they are not alone. Luther was also encouraged by this theme of the solidarity of God's

[13] Gn. 18:25; Ps. 94:2; Heb. 12:23; Rev. 19:6.

people. At one time, his barber, Peter Beskendorf, was not finding prayer easy so Luther wrote a book specially to help him. In *A Simple Way to Pray*, the reformer encourages his friend to

> Remember that you are not kneeling or standing there alone, but that all Christendom, all devout Christians are standing there with you and you with them in one unanimous, united prayer which God cannot ignore.

f. The personal nature of worship

So the Lord brought us out of Egypt ... and now I bring the first of the firstfruits ... that you, O Lord, have given me (8, 10). Scripture is so perfectly balanced; the corporate and personal elements are sensitively blended. Although the ceremony vividly recalls God's goodness to their forefathers in the past and to their many contemporaries in the present, Israelite worship had to include the personal element as well as the corporate. Without the balance it might easily degenerate either into a crowd-conscious, empty ritualism on the one hand, or self-centred religious individualism on the other. To be acceptable to God the ceremony must be meaningful to each worshipper because it gave expression to their distinctive needs and personal faith. Although huge numbers of Hebrew people thronged the courts of the sanctuary presenting to the priests their baskets of specially picked fruit, the liturgical response required every individual member of the congregation to make this simple act of worship his own: *I declare ... that I have come ... I bring ... what you ... have given me ... I have given ... I have not turned aside from your commands ... I have obeyed ... I have done everything you commanded me* (3, 10, 13–14). The *I* and *me* testify to the necessity of vibrant personal faith over against cold religious ceremonialism.

g. The sacrificialness of worship

It must make some demand upon the worshipper. In offering the first-fruits, they were presenting their best, and that best must be shared with others. It must not only be given to the neighbouring Levite to whom they might be personally indebted for his spiritual counsel and help, but also to the unknown sojourner who was dependent on them for love, care and hospitality. Remembering the times when they too were sojourners, the Israelites gave the best of their fruit to the homeless refugees and displaced persons who were travelling through their communities or were longing for a permanent home within their borders.

Those who rightly use the vehicle of worship to express their love

261

for God must not forget that he is adored as much by our giving as he is by our singing, by our serving as well as by our speaking.[14] When Paul wrote about Christians meeting together on 'the first day of the week' he was careful to mention that, on that day, believers were to look beyond their own ranks by making a collection for the needs of others less fortunate than themselves.[15] It was a first-century application of an Old Testament principle; those who adore God know that he is honoured by what we do for others as well as by what we say to him.

b.   The receptiveness of worship

It is far from being an exercise in which everything depends on us. Worship is an inspiring experience in which the Lord comes to the worshippers, forcefully reminding them of their unchanging status (*you are his people*), assured destiny (*he will set you in praise, fame and honour*), and eternal security (*holy to the LORD your God, as he promised*).

[14] 1 Jn. 3:16–18.   [15] 1 Cor. 16:1–2; 2 Cor. 8:1 – 9:15.

D. Confirming the covenant (27:1 – 30:20)

Deuteronomy 27:1 – 29:1
23. Carefully follow all his commands

We have now reached a new section in the book. The covenant regulations have been expounded both as general principles and also covering specific details. That main section of teaching closed with a passage which emphasized the necessity of unqualified obedience based on a unique relationship (26:16–19). This new section also reflects some characteristic features of the ancient Near Eastern treaty-structure. Once the terms of a treaty had been agreed, it was essential to prepare a written record of the agreement, ratify the covenant in a religious ceremony, and thereafter expect total commitment to its terms. In the next two chapters of the book we meet each of these features. Moses is told to write out the agreement (27:1–4, 8), and hold a special festival at which offerings are presented to the Lord of the covenant (27:5–7). He is to require Israel's people to make a decisive commitment either for or against the treaty (27:9–26), understanding their options, *blessing* or *curse* (28:1 – 29:1). We turn now to these covenant features. The pilgrims must display the law, build an altar, make a response and face the alternatives.

1. Displaying the law (27:1–4, 8)

Once the Israelites enter the land they are to *set up some large stones and coat them with plaster. Write on them all the words of this law.* This description of how the law was recorded for all to see makes special mention of four key aspects of biblical teaching concerning the written word of God. It is here presented as an imperishable, intelligible, reliable and obligatory word.

a. God's word is imperishable

This quality is emphasized in that it is to be written on stone. In such a context, the permanence of the word stands in deliberate

263

contrast to the transience of the preacher. God's servant was about to enter God's presence; soon, his stirring preaching would be a thing of the past. Long after the frail body of Moses had been laid in its unmarked grave, however, this imperishable word of God would endure for ever. Similarly, in times of change and upheaval, the early Christians were reminded of the indestructible, 'living and enduring' word of God.[1]

b. God's word must also be intelligible

And you shall write very clearly all the words of this law (8). Moses knows that he will not cross the Jordan with the Hebrew people and it is therefore essential that, when they could no longer hear the word vocally from him, they could see it visibly for themselves. From an educational viewpoint alone it was a highly perceptive command; we remember far more of what we see than what we hear. The word translated *very clearly* focuses on the necessary legibility of the law. It must be written 'very plainly' (RSV) 'clearly and well', 'engraving them with care' (NEB). Those who expound this unique word are likewise under a perpetual obligation to make its message unmistakably plain. To obscure, confuse or complicate this message is offensive to the God who gave it for everyone, not just for the intellectually curious.

c. God's word is reliable

What he had proclaimed for the future was confirmed by what he had fulfilled in the present: *Write on them all the words of this law when you have crossed over to enter the land the* LORD *. . . the God of your fathers, promised you.* Their very presence on Canaanite soil was an undeniable witness to the utterly dependable word of God. They would not be there if he had not spoken. On days when they could scarcely have believed it possible, God had told Abraham and Moses *very clearly* that they would take possession of the land. Therefore, if he promised in this law that obedience would be blessed, it would be. Likewise, if he had declared that disobedience would be cursed, then it would be. They must not trifle with his word.

d. God's word is obligatory

Their response to this permanent message is of crucial significance. The subsequent teaching of these chapters goes on to emphasize that the word must not simply be written and read; it must be done.

[1] 1 Pet. 1:23–25; Is. 40:6–9.

Obedience was their greatest priority. In telling them how to live (30:19), the Lord was not issuing an invitation; he was giving an order – *Obey . . .and follow his commands and decrees that I give you today . . . set up these stones . . . as I command you today* (10, 4).

2. Building an altar (27:5–7)

Once these ancient Near Eastern treaties had been set down in writing, the participants shared together in an act of worship at which they honoured each other's gods and, in their presence, solemnly agreed to the terms of the covenant. It was for this reason, among others, that the Hebrews were forbidden to enter in to political alliances with foreign nations. How could they share an agreement with such people when they had heard God's word, 'You shall have no other gods before me' (5:7)?

Their formal acceptance of this covenant, however, must also be marked by a special occasion for the worship of the one true God. In addition to engraving the word, the newly-arrived travellers must also *build an altar* so that they might begin their new life in the land on the note of exultant worship as well as exclusive obedience. They were to *offer burnt offerings on it to the* LORD . . . *Sacrifice fellowship offerings, eating them and rejoicing in the presence of the* LORD (6–7).

As they stood before that altar they gave expression to other inseparable themes, adoration and compassion, worship and works. In acknowledging the uniqueness of God they presented their burnt offerings,[2] those which were given entirely to God. In other words, God comes first and deserves the best. They were also, however, to offer their *fellowship offerings* or 'shared offerings' (NEB). These offerings were divided so that part was offered on the altar and the rest shared with the donor, the priest and needy people in the community. The Hebrew sacrificial system was designed from the beginning to teach the Israelites the inseparable nature of thanksgiving to God and love for others.

In later years, the Hebrew prophets pressed their message home by exposing the sins not only of disobedience but also of lovelessness. Vainly imagining that God would be enamoured by their ritual, they disobeyed his law by neglecting the needy. There was an abundance of sacrifices but a shortage of love. The eighth-century prophets condemned the rapacious practices of those who gave their sacrifices but robbed their neighbours. The Lord used people like Amos, Hosea, Micah, and Isaiah[3] to tell their contemporaries that the Lord desired covenant-love not elaborate animal sacrifices. If

[2] Lv. 1.   [3] Am. 5:21–24; Ho. 6:6; Mi. 6:6–8; Is. 1:11–17.

genuinely and gratefully presented, *burnt offerings* were a vehicle for their devotion to God, whilst *fellowship offerings* gave them the equal privilege of expressing love for their neighbours. The two were never meant to be competitive rivals. Dedication to God and compassion for others are as inseparable as worship and obedience.

3. Making a response (27:9–26)

Effective preaching demands a verdict. In the closing chapters of Deuteronomy the imperative nature of the choice is sharpened by presenting the stark alternatives in a vivid geographical setting. Two familiar mountains, Ebal and Gerizim, were designated for the purpose of eliciting a decision, one for blessing, the other for the curse. Travelling alongside or between these two mountains everyone was made to realize the necessity of commitment. The essential choice was also demanded by means of a vocal response from every passing Israelite. The liturgy demands that every individual must either assent to the covenant or not: *Then all the people shall say, 'Amen!'* (27:26). If subsequently any Hebrew became guilty of covenant-breaking, he had pronounced a curse upon himself.

Twelve curses are listed, suggesting specific examples of ways in which the terms of the treaty might be violated. Some explain how the Decalogue itself may be knowingly disobeyed, like making, carving or secretly worshipping an idol (27:15); or like slighting parents, where the word used (27:16) indicates a total and fierce rejection of parental authority such as that already mentioned earlier (21:18–21) in the insolent son reference ('Honour your father and mother'); or like moving (27:17) a neighbour's boundary stone ('You shall not steal').

Equally condemned as under the divine curse are serious breaches of social conduct like cruelly misdirecting a blind man in his journey (27:18) or taking advantage of *the alien, the fatherless or the widow* (27:19) in legal cases. Others are perverse moral offences, cases of appalling sexual deviancy which are offensive to a holy God. These latter sins (27:20–23) are particularly obnoxious to God because they describe patterns of immoral conduct associated with pagan religions such as Canaanite religious prostitution or Hittite bestiality. It was widely held that sexual intercourse with an animal effected spiritual union with the Hittite deity.

It is important to see from these curses that sins of *intent* (27:25) are viewed as seriously as those of action (27:24). A man who receives payment to murder someone is made to realize that such behaviour is a radical breach of the covenant whether he is successful in his sick enterprise or not. If he accepts the money for doing it, he has earned the curse of the covenant God.

4. Facing the alternatives (28:1 – 29:1)

Although the 'blessing and cursing' theme is continued in the passage which follows, it seems that, with the start of chapter 28, there is a deliberate change of scene. We are no longer listening to a description of the anticipated occasion across the Jordan at Shechem, between Mount Gerizim's blessings and Mount Ebal's cursings (27:12–13). We have moved from the future back to the present. Once again, we are with Moses in the plains of Moab listening to another pattern of blessings and cursings as we share in a covenant-renewal ceremony prior to entering the land. The conclusion to the present passage is probably in 29:1 (28:69 in the Hebrew text) which forms a summary of what has gone before: *These are the terms of the covenant the LORD commanded Moses to make with the Israelites in Moab.* The words *in addition to the covenant he had made with them at Horeb* probably describe a public renewal of the covenant that God made with his people when they came out of Egypt, an agreement whose 'presentness' needs to be reaffirmed by each generation of believers (5:2–3). Here, as God's people stand on the threshold of the promised land, they renew their commitment to the God of the covenant.

We recall that Israel was about to enter a 'fertility zone' where Baal-worship was the key factor in running the Canaanite economy. God's people would enter this 'zone', however, with a totally different doctrine of fertility and prosperity. Future productivity would be determined not by their participation in ritualistic religion but by their obedience to God's word.

God had taken the initiative. He had made his choice by setting his love upon the Hebrews as his covenant people but each individual Israelite was also compelled to make their decisive choice as well. That commitment would determine their future, either one in which they experienced God's promised blessing (28:1–14) or their self-determined curse (28:15–68).

The initial list of blessings and curses is deliberately presented as ten stark alternatives. The couplets aid the memory process but they also heighten the importance of choice: *You will be blessed in the city and blessed in the country . . . You will be cursed in the city and cursed in the country* (28:3, 16). Do the people want the abundant blessing of God upon their life, urban and rural, physical and material, herds and flocks, basket and kneading trough, returning home and going away – or do they deliberately wish to choose the reverse?

267

The Lord knew that, however attractive the 'blessings' might be, his people would, like ourselves, learn more through adversity than in prosperity. Dietrich Bonhoeffer proved that in a Nazi prison. In a letter to a friend he confesses to something which finds an echo in the experience of most of us: 'When all's said and done, it is true that it needs trouble to drive us to prayer, though every time I feel it is something to be ashamed of.'[4] Affliction is a persuasive teacher and its lessons are not easily forgotten. Instead of drawing us close to God, life's prosperous circumstances can lead to spiritual apathy and indifference. This book has already issued that warning: '. . . when you eat and are satisfied, be careful that you do not forget the LORD' (6:11–12).

For this reason, it is the curses which dominate the list. It is not that God is vindictive; the curses are merciful warnings. 'If you persist in doing that, then these consequences will inevitably follow.' The long list reads like a prolonged agonizing dirge but it is not simply a catalogue of grim catastrophe. As a good warning device it serves a distinctive educational purpose – 'Don't let this happen to you'. The solemn theme of divine judgment is presented with four facets.

a. The judgment is predicted

God's wrath will be manifested in the life of these potential offenders not primarily because of their offensive moral or social misdemeanours. Their cardinal sin is a spiritual one. It is not simply that they have disobeyed God's word; they have abandoned the covenant God. Grief will inevitably overtake them, *because of the evil you have done in forsaking him* (28:20).

The very fact that they have been warned in this way, however, is a token of God's generous mercy. He warns them because he loves them and does not want them to suffer. The land they are about to enter is populated with Baal-worshippers. Their god is capricious. He is capable of acting unpredictably and vindictively towards them. The Canaanites offer their sacrifices at the hilltop shrines in order to win Baal's favour or placate his wrath. Possibly he will act beneficently toward them, granting fertility to childless parents, abundant harvests to the anxious farmer, but only if they give to Baal those sacrifices which please him. A human sacrifice might be specially effective but, whatever the cost, it is important that Baal be coaxed and cajoled.

The picture of Israel's God in these chapters is totally different. He is neither capricious nor volatile. Even in a passage of extended

[4] Dietrich Bonhoeffer, *Letters and Papers from Prison* (Collins, Fontana, 1959), p. 67.

merciful warning he is portrayed as faithful (*as he promised you*, 9, 11), generous (*the LORD will grant you abundant prosperity*, 11) and sovereign (he alone, not Baal can *open the heavens, the storehouse of his bounty*, 12). Just as serious warnings were written into these ancient international treaties so, in graphic imagery, these potential Hebrew rebels are warned that deliberately turning their back on God will issue in dire consequences. They cannot deliberately flout the agreement made at Sinai and renewed in the plains of Moab, and then imagine that they can get away with it. Rebels will experience plague (20–22), drought (23), invasion (25–35), exile (36–52), famine (53–57), sickness (58–61) and desolation (62–68).

Therefore, should the people wilfully choose to disobey God's word, these judgments will surely not take them by surprise. They had been warned. On days when the ripening sun was replaced by the burning sirocco (24), the scorching desert wind which almost ignited their crops, then they would know that God was speaking to them. Their pain would be like the shrill, sharp blasts of a warning trumpet. The word they had ignored in their prosperity would become eloquent in their grief. A sovereign cannot be silenced. If we will not hear him in plenty, then poverty must be his messenger.

b. *The judgment is extensive*

God will treat all rebels alike. His undeserved favour can be enjoyed but it cannot be earned. The Israelites vainly imagined that, like Baal, God could be persuaded to change his mind simply by offering a few appropriate sacrifices. Human nature has changed little over the centuries. People are still like that. Men and women want a deity it is possible to manipulate and control, a god they can keep in their pockets and have on their terms, not his. They want a god who will punish evil-doers but will treat their case as an exception to the rule. Surely God will guarantee his favour if they show willing by occasional church attendance, uncostly living, social 'do-gooding', unsacrificial service? But the striking feature about these verses is that there are no exceptions. The judgment reaches everyone. All covenant breakers will be judged, every single one, whatever their religious achievements, moral conformity or social status. Like a determined hunter, the judgment of God will stalk the offender and find him, even when he sins in secret. All the sins listed in the grim cursing liturgy are secret transgressions (27:14–26) but God sees them all.

c. *The judgment is pervasive*

It is not only that it will find every offender but it will touch every possible area of life, private and public. Every aspect of human existence is bound to be affected; physical discomfort (28:20–22, 27–28, 35, 58–61), agricultural disaster (23–24, 38–40, 42), military defeat (25–26, 33–34, 48–57), economic collapse (29, 31), marital failure (30), domestic anguish (32, 41) and social ignominy (43–44).

These judgments need to be seen against the background of Baalism, Israel's chosen alternative in later decades. These curses are a form of arresting polemic. Baal was the god of plenty, the deity who guaranteed an abundant harvest. So, as in Elijah's time, only through drought (23) could disobedient Israelites be brought to the truth. Baal was the god of life, the fertility god who gave them their children. Only dire circumstances within family life (18) would convince rebels of the delusion of idolatry. Baal was the god of victory, the mighty warrior who gave his followers success in battle. Only by repeated military failure (25) would Israel come to understand that they had turned away from the Lord of incomparable might.

All the sad judgments described in these verses actually happened in Israel's fragile history. The warnings were certainly necessary. In the centuries which followed their settlement in the land, these sobering threats became a terrifying reality. A passage of this kind is saying, in highly persuasive Hebrew idiom that men and women cannot hope to live without God and experience life 'in all its fulness'.[5] We have been made for God and those who choose to ignore him thereby deny themselves essential spiritual resources.

Although this list of terrors faces the future, it graphically recalls the great moments of their history, as if to say, 'Remember what you were.' It is surely a touch of brilliant persuasiveness to use, even in a descriptive passage like this, phrases, images and ideas which remind them both of promise and fulfilment in the past. They were children of promise. *As numerous as the stars in the sky* (62) recalls the promise to Abraham. God's purpose was to form a new nation, a unique community which in its creation owed everything to a God of infinite strength. He could from one 'as good as dead'[6] bring to birth a mighty people. Moreover, a God of such incomparable power could multiply them again.

Alongside the solitary reference to Abraham, there are three which recall the experiences of Moses, even though it be the darker side of the exodus story. Egypt's diseases (27), plagues (59–60) and slavery (68) are specifically mentioned but in several other parts of the narrative there are deliberate echoes of the unspeakably painful experiences which preceded their redemption. The threatened onslaughts are similar to Egypt's judgment – boils (27, 34–35), locusts (38), smitten cattle (51), the afflicted fruit of the body (18,

[5] Jn. 10:10, NEB.   [6] Heb. 11:12.

41). The plagues seem to be recalled purposefully except that now they are upon Israel and not her enemies. God is no respecter of nations.

When they left Egypt under Moses' leadership the people were told that they would never again return. Those who chose to reject the God of Promise and Redemption, however, will again experience the pain of bondage. It did not suggest that the entire Hebrew people would return to Egypt though significant numbers of them did.[7] It is a vivid Old Testament way of saying, 'the final condition of that man is worse than the first'.[8] Mercifully, however, that is not the end of the story.

d. The judgment is avoidable

This unfortunate catalogue of woe is intended as a serious warning-device after the style of the threats which concluded every ancient Near Eastern treaty. There was nothing remotely inevitable about them. If the Israelite people kept the covenant they would be choosing life not death, blessing not curses.

A series of refrains are found within this extended passage which indicate why those judgments will take place. It will be entirely because of certain things the covenant people persistently did not do:

They did not heed God's word (45, 62): disobedience.
They did not appreciate God's mercies (46–47): ingratitude.
They did not honour God's name (58): irreverence.

If those treaty-breaking transgressions are avoided, these stern judgments need never be part of their future experience.

Throughout this long dirge there are words and phrases which read like the anticipation of wider humanity's greater plight. Here in this passage its pain and isolation is expressed in deeply sombre tones, like the mournful toll of a bell: *you will grope about like a blind man in the dark ... oppressed and robbed, with no-one to rescue you ... powerless to lift a hand ... in hunger and thirst, in nakedness and dire poverty ... an iron yoke on your neck ... no resting place for the sole of your foot ... never sure of your life* (28:29, 32, 48, 65–66).

It is the same grim, realistic imagery which is used centuries later by Jesus and the early Christian preachers. The anguish of universal sin is exposed in the New Testament as well as the Old. In biblical teaching, men and women without Christ are exactly like the people described in these verses – blind, lost, beggars, weak, sad victims of

[7] 2 Ki. 23:31–34; Je. 43 – 44.   [8] Mt. 12:45.

the ravages of sin, bereft prisoners and helpless refugees.

Taking our humanity upon himself, however, the perfect Son of God has invaded this dark world of powerless offenders. All that judgment he has freely borne and, through his unique sacrificial death, these doomed lives may be for ever changed. By God's grace the worst of things can always be different. Moses goes on to make that very point in the teaching which follows (30:1–10).

Deuteronomy 29:2 – 30:20
24. Choose life

The life and work of Moses is gradually drawing to its end. Four final things remain. He will give a closing address, commission his successor, teach the people a unique song and deliver a pastoral farewell. A brief historical narrative, describing the departure of Moses, will bring the book to a close.

An unbelieving generation who heard the covenant at Horeb had died in the desert, but their children and grandchildren are now about to cross the Jordan. For them the agreement must be renewed and in this closing address Moses reminds the people of the terms of the agreement[1] which God, the Eternal Suzerain makes with his uniquely chosen and greatly loved vassal people. Its teaching can be divided into four main sections: past blessings, present resources, future perils and timeless facts.

1. Past blessings (29:2–9)

As the Israelites face the future they are urged, once again, to recall the past. If we are to cope with tomorrow's problems we must remember yesterday's blessings. Those who want to march on must know how to look back.

When Moses addresses the people he speaks to them as a united community. When he says, *Your eyes have seen all that the Lord did in Egypt . . . With your own eyes you saw those great trials* (2–3), he knows only too well that the majority of those who stood before him had not seen those things personally. Most of those who saw them had died in the wilderness. Those disobedient Israelites had certainly lacked the perception to 'see' spiritually what the Lord had

[1] Like Deuteronomy as a whole, chapters 29 and 30 also follow the pattern of an ancient Near Eastern treaty. Moses' address seems to be constructed like the familiar covenant-agreement with its historical introduction (2–8), general stipulations (9–15), warnings if the covenant is broken by making an alliance with others (16–28), blessings and curses (30:16–18), and a concluding summons to witnesses (30:19).

shown them through the saving events of the exodus. Moses drove the point home by saying that although these *signs* and *great wonders* had been witnessed by the Hebrew pilgrims, the Lord had not given them *a mind that understands or eyes that see or ears that hear*. With its strong and healthy insistence on divine sovereignty, the Hebrew mind found it impossible to believe that their forefathers' spiritual blindness was something totally outside the Lord's will and control.

There were several things which ought to have been plainly evident to that generation. They had been miraculously delivered by a God of incomparable power: *all that the LORD did . . . to Pharaoh . . . and to all his land* (2). The people had been continually guided by a God of infinite patience: *the forty years that I led you through the desert* (5). Their unfailing resources were supplied by a God of compassionate provision: *your clothes did not wear out, nor did the sandals on your feet* (5). The Hebrews *ate no bread* because supernatural manna was always available. As pilgrims, they could not plant vineyards, *you . . . drank no wine or other fermented drink* (6), but the Lord quenched their thirst with water from the rock. Against all the odds, the people had gained strategic military victories. Their armies were led by a God of unique sovereignty: *Sihon . . . and Og . . . came out to fight against us, but we defeated them* (7). Some of them had the *eyes that see* (4) that such remarkable victories were entirely due to the fact that God had planned in advance that Israel's people should occupy those territories (2:26 – 3:11).

Before we accuse that generation of Israelites of being astonishingly obtuse, we need the honesty to ask ourselves whether there are things which 'we have seen with our own eyes' but from which we have had little to learn. Seeing, we have not seen. We did not see God's hand at work in that intense disappointment, or denial, or illness. It could have been such a helpful learning time but we did not have the *ears that hear*.

So, at the beginning of this address (as at the opening of Deuteronomy as a whole, 1:1 – 3:29), Moses reminded his contemporaries of the great lessons which were to be learned from their past. Those who can discern *all that the LORD did* (2) know that his mighty deeds are not irrelevant tales from distant history but eloquent encouragements to renewed confidence. For those who had *a mind that understands* (4), the conquests of Heshbon and Bashan were tokens that similar victories would be evident in Canaan. Men and women who would *carefully follow the terms of this covenant* (9) would be equally successful in their future battles.

2. Present resources (29:10–15)

Although Moses is rightly encouraged by the past, he is not an antiquarian escapist. The people are helped by his reminder of the deliverance from Egypt, but now they are confronting a different crisis. In these new and challenging circumstances the preacher assures them that the covenant is a *present* reality. It has immediate, widespread and lasting appeal.

a. The covenant has immediate appeal

'It is for you', Moses says, not just for their forefathers: *All of you are standing today in the presence of the LORD your God . . . in order to enter into a covenant . . . to confirm you this day as his people, that he may be your God as he promised you* (10, 12–13). In this short paragraph, the recurrent words *you . . . today* are a reminder that the covenant is not locked away in a remote past. The message does not merely address itself to the memory. It has present relevance and inspires renewed confidence in the God who will meet the immediate needs of those who will soon be on Canaanite soil.

b. The covenant has widespread appeal

'It is for all', Moses says, not just for a specially favoured, exclusive few. The blessings are for everyone; this agreement binds them all together, whatever their background, status or possessions. The God of the covenant demands the total submission of *all of you*, every man, woman and child in Israel, from their senior leaders (*elders and officials*, 10) to the socially insignificant aliens (*aliens living in your camps*, 11) engaged in the most menial household duties (*who chop your wood and carry your water*, 11).

c. The covenant has lasting appeal

'It is for ever', Moses says, not just for the immediate occupants of Canaan. It addresses the people of God in the centuries ahead: *I am making this covenant, with its oath, not only with you who are standing here with us today . . . but also with those who are not here today* (14–15). Generations yet unborn were to rejoice in the promised resources and guaranteed security of this enduring agreement. Bound closely to him in this dependable treaty, they are linked inseparably both to their forefathers (13) and successors (14–15). The contemporaneous God is sufficient for the needs of his covenant people in every generation.

3. Future perils (29:16–28)

Once this timeless covenant is made, however, what about the perverse individual, family or tribe which decides secretly to 'opt out'? Such people might display all the outward signs and evidences of belonging, go through all the ceremonial motions, but become secret idolaters. After all, any individual or group might listen to the outward terms of the covenant, outwardly agree not to make an alliance with other gods, but secretly decide to follow the gods of the nations they had left behind (like Egypt) or of the nations they had passed through in their journey.

The theme is not irrelevant for those who live in a different world. Secret transgression did not end with the death of Moses. Men and women of any generation who imagine that they can get away with 'secret' sinning have forgotten three crucial things. Secret sin deceives ourselves, affects others and grieves God.

Self-deception is a feature of secret sin (16–19a). In incredible folly the secret transgressor says to himself 'I can do this without fear. Nobody will ever know.' Stupidly ignorant of the true facts, the secret idolater says, *I will be safe , even though I persist in going my own way* (19). We persuade ourselves, 'All will be well with me' (NEB) when, in reality, all will be evil for us. That is one of the most frightening things about human sin – it dulls our perception and warps our judgment. It corrupts our thinking and distorts our values. Sin parades itself in a subtly attractive guise; we do not see it for the horror it truly is. It liberalizes our outlook, professing to release us from outdated traditions and mere social conventions. Instead of listening to what God says to us in his word, we listen to the changing, vacillating dictates of our own minds and the equally corrupt judgments of others.

Vainly, we imagine it is enough to be guided by our consciences, forgetting, or choosing to ignore, the biblical truth that even the most sensitive human conscience has not escaped the ravages of sin. That is why we all need the fixed and uncompromising standards of God's unchanging word so that we can have a clear objective test as to whether a thing is right or wrong. That is why we also need the further objective reality of Christ's exemplary life as a fixed, constant moral norm by which we may test our daily conduct: 'Would Jesus have said that?' 'Is that action truly Christlike?' 'Is it Scriptural?'

Secret sinning also affects others. *This will bring disaster on the watered land as well as the dry* (19b). People cannot live entirely to themselves. All our lives influence others in one way or another. 'Secret transgressors' fail to realize that by sinning they have automatically accommodated their lives to lower standards. They have sinned not only against their better selves but against those they meet once they emerge from their secrecy. They would have been far better people if they had not yielded to that sinister temptation. They would certainly have been a richer influence for good and for God had those 'hidden faults'[2] been faced, forgiven and conquered. Sin spreads like a *root . . . that produces . . . bitter poison* (18). Sin is not insular, isolated and self-contained, but a highly destructive, contagious force. That, in fact, is surely the most devastating thing about sin. It has the appalling potential and power to reproduce itself in the lives of other people.

Moses therefore warns the people that secret sinning 'will bring everlasting ruin' (NEB) to other people. The person who boasts *I will be safe* forgets that even if, for a time, it is safe for him or her, it will not be safe for others. The destructive effects of such conduct will not be remotely selective. It will create havoc everywhere, *on the watered land as well as on the dry.*

These verses are used in the letter to the Hebrews where the author quotes the Greek version of the Old Testament (the Septuagint) to support the argument that one corrupt life spreads like a 'bitter noxious weed' which can grow up to 'poison the whole' (NEB). A 'bitter root' can extend its tendrils under the ground to 'cause trouble' and defile many.[3]

Most serious of all, secret sinning grieves God (20–21). The 'poisonous root' of apostasy and idolatry is not merely 'a root from which springs gall and wormwood' (18, NEB), which spreads its toxic damage to other people. It is highly obnoxious to God. The Lord has clearly laid down the inflexible terms of the covenant. There can be no other gods; images are forbidden. There can be no compromising with that. The secret offender imagines that nobody knows about his spiritual disloyalty but God sees it all, reads his perverse thoughts, shines the bright searchlight of his holiness into the dark rooms of the iniquitous mind. God will *single him out* (21) so that everyone will know how foolish it is to imagine that, in a moral universe, sinners will not be judged.

The warning of these verses was certainly necessary. Across the centuries some of the Lord's best work has been marred by secret idolaters. They have worshipped at the shrine of success, materialism, power, popularity, unworthy ambition or some other personal gain. Everything became totally subservient to their greater loyalty. Achan adored possessions. Gideon and Samson idolized self. David worshipped sensuality. In each case the pain which followed their secret transgression was not confined to themselves alone, the suffering spread to others.

[2] Ps. 19:12.   [3] Heb. 12:15.

In New Testament times Paul illustrated this theme by describing an immoral situation in Corinth as 'a little yeast' which 'works through the whole batch of dough'. He urges the Corinthians to 'get rid of the old yeast that you may be a new batch without yeast – as you really are.'[4]

At times the Israelites did not have *a mind that understands* how God was at work in their history, but some of their pagan neighbours certainly had *eyes that see* unmistakable evidence of the divine displeasure. When the question was asked, *Why has the LORD done this to this land?* (24), even the ungodly acknowledged that it was because the Hebrew people *abandoned the covenant of the LORD, the God of their fathers* and *went off and worshipped other gods* (25–26). Even unbelievers could see how deeply they must have grieved their God.

4. Timeless facts (29:29 – 30:20)

Spiritually sensitive people in Israel and beyond it could discern God's hand at work in the world, even in judgment. In the light of these hard facts Moses goes on to remind the people of three truths about God which were part of the covenant's eternal message – his wisdom, mercy and word.

a. God's wisdom (29:29)

In his infinite wisdom, God has divided spiritual truth into two categories, secret and revealed things. The Hebrew is more striking; it contrasts the 'covered' and the 'uncovered'.

There are 'covered' things we are not meant to know. Because Israelites and pagans might be able to trace some of God's ways in the world (*e.g.* his judgment), that does not mean to say that they or we can fully understand everything. *The secret things* are not fully comprehensible in this life. It is not only those who do not have a mind to learn, eyes to see, or ears to hear who will from time to time be completely baffled by the Lord's dealings with them and others. The Lord plainly did not intend us to know everything. No matter how experienced we may be or however competent as Bible students, we cannot hope to understand all God's ways and

> take upon 's the mystery of things
> As if we were God's spies.[5]

Spiritual maturity does not guarantee an encyclopaedic knowledge of the divine will. There are times when, in his inscrutable

---

[4] 1 Cor. 5:6–7.   [5] Shakespeare, *King Lear*, V, iii.

wisdom, God intentionally keeps us in the dark. Those 'covered' things we desperately want to know *belong to the LORD our God*, not to us. Before the Lord Jesus left this earth his disciples asked him about Israel's political subjugation. Was the time approaching when their country might be liberated from the Roman oppressor? How long must they wait for freedom? Jesus told them that the answer to their painful questions belonged to God's 'covered' things: 'It is not for you to know . . .'.[6] When we cannot fully comprehend, it is best for us to trust and believe that God does not mean us to know that yet. One day I believe we may. Until then, as Paul says, there are times when 'we see but a poor reflection as in a mirror'. When we are 'face to face'[7] with him we shall surely realize that our temporary ignorance was all part of a superlatively wise plan.

The huge issues in life we cannot understand, however, are far outweighed by God's 'uncovered' facts. Moses says three things about this vast store, *the things revealed* in Scripture. They are ours to value, share and obey.

They are ours to value

These great biblical truths *belong to us*. When there are millions who do not have 'a mind that understands' (29:4), it is surely an immense privilege to have our spiritual eyes opened by the Holy Spirit[8] so that we can appreciate the Lord's word. We have been permitted to grasp these realities and we must not take them for granted.

They are ours to share

As well as belonging to us the truths also *belong . . . to our children for ever*. We have already seen that Deuteronomy has a great deal to say about the responsibility of parents to communicate God's truth to their families. Each new generation has a right to hear about God's word and God's Son. Ours is an increasingly pluralistic society and some children in our schools may well have a better understanding of Islam than of Christianity, especially when its leading tenets appear to be publicly disowned by seemingly embarrassed ecclesiastical leaders. Evangelical Christians have a responsibility to assume the role of Israel's parents so that they can share with unchurched children in their neighbourhood some of the life-changing *things revealed*.

They are ours to obey

The word has been *revealed . . . that we may follow* (literally 'do') *all the words of this law*. These treasured revelations are not simply

---

[6] Acts 1:6–7.   [7] 1 Cor. 13:12.   [8] 1 Cor. 2:10–16.

to be stored in the enquiring mind so that we merely amass an increasing store of biblical teaching, good as that may be. The truth is to be obeyed and that is possibly the most demanding aspect of 'uncovered truth'. Moreover, Moses makes it clear that we cannot be partial in our obedience. The Lord means us to do *all* that is taught in this unique and constantly relevant book.

b. God's mercy (30:1–10)

The Lord knew that his people would break the covenant and incur his threatened wrath (29:28), but in his generous love he made advance provision for their restoration. The Lord knows that his idolatrous and apostate people will be driven into exile but a further thing is equally certain – they will be forgiven. One of the 'revealed' things is that God loves us and, no matter how sinful we have been, we can be pardoned, cleansed and restored: 'he will fetch you home' (4, NEB). Moses tells the people that God's forgiveness is conditional, guaranteed and generous.

God's forgiveness is conditional (30:1–2)
There must be penitence: 'if you turn back to him' (NEB). The Hebrew word for *return* indicates an act of genuine repentance, a right about turn. It is the same word that was later on the lips of the Old Testament prophets as they begged their contemporaries to have done with their sins.[9] Those who have grieved God must be genuinely penitent or they will not be able to appropriate the forgiveness he longs to give. Moreover, the sorrow for sin must not merely be on the level of the emotions. Their conduct must be different for, in addition to their repentance over the past, God expects their obedience in the present: *and obey him . . . according to everything I command you today.*

God's forgiveness is guaranteed (30:3)
If they turn from their sin *then the LORD your God will restore your fortunes and have compassion on you.* No penitent individual Israelite or the entire nation of them need doubt for a moment that they will be forgiven and restored. Even though the enormity of their transgression had led to their banishment to the farthest corners of the world (literally 'to the end of the heavens', 4), still he will bring them home again if they repent and obey.

God's forgiveness is generous (30:4–10)
It is not simply that he will 'wipe the slate clean' and 'give us a fresh

---

[9] Is. 44:22; Je. 3:12, 22; Ho. 14:1; Zc. 1:3; Mal. 3:7.

start'. Our restored lives will be crowded with innumerable blessings. He not only welcomes us home like the waiting father in the famous parable;[10] he travels to the far country – *from there the LORD your God will gather you and bring you back.*

Despite their sins, the disobedient are reassured by the healing word: *He will make you more prosperous and numerous than your fathers* (5). They will be *most prosperous . . . the LORD will again delight in you and make you prosperous* (9). Baal was an agricultural and fertility deity, so his Canaanite worshippers maintained that it was he who could provide them with healthy children and abundant harvests. Moses makes it plain, however, that the Lord God is the only one who has the power to prosper the Israelite people in these ways, that is *in the fruit of your womb, the young of your livestock, and the crops of your land* (9).

c. God's word (30: 11–20)

Moses is about to call his fellow Israelites to total commitment to their covenant God. The challenge he has addressed to them in God's word is comprehensible and achievable. He is not confronting them with impracticable ideals. These imperishable truths are not totally impossible targets but God's superlative gifts, revealed to us and to our children (29:29). That unique word is then described.

God's word informs the mind (30:11–14)

It is not a message totally beyond our intellectual grasp. That does not mean that every single passage of Scripture is always easy to understand.[11] The Holy Spirit, however, is our teacher and, with his essential help, every Christian can be equipped for every aspect of Christian life, witness and service. God's truth in Scripture is intelligible: *Now what I am commanding you today is not too difficult for you.* The word is also relevant. It does not belong to a totally different world: neither is it *beyond your reach* or 'remote' (NEB). We are also assured that it is accessible: *It is not up in heaven . . . Nor is it beyond the sea.* Although Deuteronomy itself frequently anticipates and encourages the recording of the law in written form, it also emphasizes the necessary inwardness of God's word. It is best stored in the believing mind: *No, the word is very near you; it is in your mouth and in your heart so that you may obey it* (14). We are to see that his word has a secure place in our memories and is obeyed in our lives.

When the apostle Paul quotes these verses[12] he makes the point that God has fully revealed himself to us in the person of his Son.

---

[10] Lk. 15:20–24.   [11] 2 Pet. 3:15–16.   [12] Rom. 10:6–8.

The Lord Jesus is God's unique Word, immediately accessible to us all.[13]

God's word challenges the will (30:15–18)

In the concluding sentences of this address, Moses once again reminds his congregation of the necessity of commitment. As earlier (27:11–13; 28:1–2, 15) they are confronted with the stark alternatives, *life and prosperity, death and destruction ... keep his commands ... then you will live ... But if your heart turns away ... you will certainly be destroyed.* By his teaching, however, Moses is not encouraging cold and detached legalism; loving is the key to living. The Lord is not looking for merely dutiful obedience. He loves them. They must surely be convinced of that by now (4:37; 7:7–8, 13; 10:18; 23:5) and he looks for nothing less in return: *I command you today to love the LORD your God* (16).

God's word moves the heart (30:19–20)

Now choose life, so that you and your children may live and that you may love the LORD your God, listen to his voice, and hold fast to him (20). The language of love is frequently found in these ancient Near Eastern agreements we have mentioned. But we do not drift into loving; a choice has to be made. Jesus asked no less of Peter. Before the apostle could be told about the nature of his service Jesus had to be sure of the reality of his love.[14]

The treaties often concluded with a call for 'witnesses' (4:26; 31:28)[15] to confirm the terms of the covenant. That happens here as well: *I call heaven and earth as witnesses against you that I have set before you life and death, blessings and curses.* Normally, with these agreements, the witnesses were the distinctive gods of the parties concerned, but that is totally inappropriate for this covenant. There is only one God so the created order which he has made is summoned to testify to the reality of his offer and the reliability of his promise.

It is the note of tender appeal, however, which is dominant. The Lord longs for his people to *choose life.* Their ultimate decision is not a matter of indifference to him. In the language of compassionate entreaty, the Lord sets out before them the incalculable advantages which will be theirs if they commit themselves to him. Those who so decide, prove that he is the living God who imparts and sustains life to those who love him: *choose life, so that you and your children may live ... For the LORD is your life, and he will give you many years.* He is also a reliable God who remains true to his word, for he is even now about to bring them into *the land he swore to give to your fathers, Abraham, Isaac, and Jacob.*

---

[13] Jn. 1:1, 14–15.   [14] Jn. 21:15–17.   [15] See Mi. 6:2.

E. Sharing the covenant (31:1 – 34:12)

Deuteronomy 31:1–29
25. Israel's leaders and their message

In every society people must know how to deal with change. At a time of crucial transition in Hebrew history, this congregation is assured that they can cope with a radically different lifestyle if only they will value their resourceful leaders and their enduring message.

1. Israel's leaders

In these verses we are confronted with Israel's three leaders, the old, the new and the best.

a. The old leader

Moses is tired and does nothing to hide that fact from the waiting people. The old man has been a valiant warrior and his earthly work is almost at an end. He copes realistically with the problem of old age. He knows what he can do and also what is beyond him. *I am now a hundred and twenty years old and am no longer able to lead you* (2). Some elderly people find life impossibly frustrating and that is largely due to a sad inability to adapt to fresh circumstances. Wistful about the past, they do not always recognize that life's varied stages present us with different rather than diminishing opportunities.

Moses' reference to his *hundred and twenty years* invites reflection on his unique mission. The story of his life can be divided into three periods. In each of them he found himself in a totally different environment, but he did not waste time secretly sighing for the days that had gone. At each stage he was enabled by the Lord to benefit from the past and then respond creatively to life's new challenges.

Moses' first forty years were marked by luxury. Following his adoption by an Egyptian princess, his early years were set amid the extravagant opulence, limitless resources and social advantages of the royal court. In those years, everything he could possibly need

283

was at his finger tips. His luxurious life was in complete contrast to that of the deprived Hebrew slaves among whom he had been born. Yet, although he was physically removed from his own people, the Lord was quietly preparing him for his life's work among them. God knew precisely what Moses' future role would be and, during that highly impressionable period of his young life, provided him with insights and experience which were to be invaluable in his later ministry. Over those years he was given the best education open to any young man in the world. Skills in thinking, writing and communicating each formed part of his early training.[1] An acute awareness of the ancient Near Eastern world, its religions, economics, geography, politics, would all be used in equipping Moses for a task which in those days would have been beyond his wildest dreams and desires. In the economy of God, however, nothing is wasted. Every believer ought to make the most of life's present opportunities and not spend highly useful days constantly sighing for something else which is bigger and better. There are things to be learnt at this stage in life which are part of our essential preparation for the next chapter of our story.

For Moses, however, the next forty years were in marked and shattering contrast. It was when he was forty years old that he had that unexpected encounter with the Egyptian taskmaster which suddenly and radically changed his entire life.[2] Overnight, the wealthy courtier became a terrified refugee. Without warning, Moses passed from luxury to frugality; the distinguished prince became a country shepherd. There must have been times in those long years in Midian when his mind was tortured by the recollection of that act of manslaughter. Sensitive, kind and gentle character that he was, he must have gone over that unplanned event a thousand times. Dwelling regretfully on the past, however, is rarely helpful. When things appear to go wrong for us in life there are several things to learn.

We can learn that God is sovereign. Although Moses had lost his temper and killed a man, the Lord would not allow that uncontrolled action to go against him for ever. God is in control of all life and even our greatest mistakes can be overruled for the glory of God, the blessing of others, and our own ultimate good. Moses ought not to have slain the Egyptian taskmaster but there were things to be learnt in Midian's desert which could never be discerned in Egypt's palaces. If the Israelite people were to be taken to Canaan, God needed a sturdy, resourceful shepherd[3] more than a sophisticated prince.

The other lesson to be learnt in adverse times is that God is

[1] Acts 7:22.   [2] Ex. 2:11–15; Acts 7:23.   [3] Ps. 77:20; Is. 63:11.

merciful. He does not hold our sins and mistakes against us for ever, though there may well be times when, for our own good, we have to pass through the dark valley of remorse. In those days the Lord may seem to be far from us. There are things to learn, however, when we are weighed down with guilt which may be hidden from less burdened people. In our grief we may come to know something more about the enormity of sin, the seriousness of life, the generosity of providence, the support of love, the reality of forgiveness (human and divine), the optimism of grace – spiritual truths which may remain as mere theories to those who have not failed.

That sudden sin in Egypt and the long years in Midian taught Moses some lessons he could never forget, most of all that God is loving and can take even life's most bitter experiences and gradually transform them into something good and useful, even beautiful, for himself.

There is something else to be learnt from this second main period of Moses' life. It belongs to the experience of his earliest days in Midian. When life seems to deal a cruel blow, even though (as with Moses) part of the fault is certainly our own, we must take care that the bitter experience does not make us bitter. Although Moses was frightened,[4] grieved and stricken in conscience, he knew that he must not allow one damaging experience to harm him. Not long after that tragic mistake, God gave him the opportunity to show that he was a different man. One day by a desert-well he showed kindness to a group of young women who were being harassed by some Midianite shepherds.[5] In Egypt he had reacted aggressively to oppression. Now here was an opportunity to come to the aid of oppressed people without recourse to violence. Love dominated, not power. He got rid of the hostile shepherds but also obtained water from the well for these women and then went to the extra trouble of drawing further water for their flocks. He had nothing to gain personally from these acts of kindness but, in his providence, the Lord was to use them for Moses' benefit and blessing. They were to lead to the provision of a home for Moses as well as a wife and family. It might have been different if he had allowed the Egyptian experience to make him sour and bitter. Instead, he had learnt from his earlier mistakes and was enabled to live as a changed man.

The third period of his life was characterized by adversity. The forty desert years in Midian equipped him for another forty, infinitely more difficult, in the scorching wilderness, not now with a contented Midianite family but with a vast, frequently discontented multitude. At times the wearying months hung heavy with sadness

---

[4] Ex. 2:15.   [5] Ex. 2:17.

and sorrow. He must have looked back wistfully on the tranquility and security of the years in Midian. He had been prepared for this task, however, and he must face the new opportunity creatively and resourcefully. If the years which had passed had taught him anything they had certainly convinced him that God is good, and that he is sufficient for his people's needs, however dark the days may be. The assurance of the Lord's faithfulness saw Moses through some difficult years and, by the time the end had come, there may have been little sadness at the prospect of staying on that side of Jordan. During his long life he had often heard the Lord say 'You shall ...' and he had gone on to inherit immeasurable blessings. Now he could trust that same God when he said *You shall not ...* (2). Life's seeming disappointments often prove to be its greatest blessings.

In each different period of his eventful life Moses had proved the faithfulness of God. He was about to lay down his exacting responsibilities and hand them over to a younger man. Though he was soon to leave the scene, those *hundred and twenty years* had left a radiant example. Something of that remarkable commitment and persistent integrity which the people had seen in Moses was to stay with Israel for ever. They would march on, but his rich influence would never leave them.

b. The new leader

Israel's people were to enter Canaan with a fresh captain at their head. Two things happened before Joshua took up these new responsibilities – he was encouraged by Moses (7–8) and commissioned by the Lord (14–15, 23).

In the presence of the people he was about to lead, Moses reminded the younger man that the Lord had chosen him for the work: *Joshua ... will cross over ahead of you, as the LORD said* (3). If anyone wishes to serve the Lord, nothing is more important than a clear and compelling sense of call. Whether we are willing volunteers like Isaiah[6] or reluctant conscripts like Jeremiah,[7] we must know beyond doubt that the Lord wants us to do this particular work for him. Without that, we shall be easily deflected from the task and quickly give up when things are discouraging or difficult.

Having emphasized the importance of the 'call', however, we must note that the Lord has more than one way of revealing his will to us. That essential awareness of God's will for our lives does not come to everyone in precisely the same form. For Moses, it took

[6] Is. 6:8.　　[7] Je. 1:4–9.

place at a dramatic moment in time and in unforgettable circum-stances.[8] With Joshua it was different; the experience was more gradual. Initially, he worked unobtrusively merely as 'the servant' of Moses[9] but over the years he accepted new tasks and was entrusted with fresh assignments. Moreover, we do not all respond to God's call in the same way. In answering the call of God, Joshua does not seem to have had the reluctance of Moses.[10] The story of these two men reminds us that the Lord's dealings with us are not boringly predictable or monochrome. He deals with us differently but we must all be ready to do his will.

It was not enough for Joshua to hear these inspiring truths simply from the lips of Moses (7–8). Joshua needed a fresh encounter with God, and was commissioned by him. The Lord himself addressed him (23), reminding him of three things which everyone needs in God's work, the assurance of sufficiency for the future (*you will bring the Israelites into the land*), faithfulness in the past (*I promised to them on oath*) and companionship in the present (*I myself will be with you*).

c. The best leader

Moses was going home, Joshua was going on, but both men rejoiced in the truth that Israel's unchanging leader was the Lord himself. They were merely his privileged agents, appointed for a limited period to do his work. God's supreme leadership is forcefully emphasized (31:2–3) in the words to Moses: '*You shall not cross the Jordan.*' *The* LORD *your God himself will cross over ahead of you.* The passage conveys three great truths about the divine leadership; he is the Advance-Guard (3), Victor (4–5) and Companion (6) of his people. As he is about to leave them, Moses tells the congregation that the Lord will go before them, fight for them and be with them.

He is their Advance-Guard (31:3, 8)

The way ahead is unknown to them; strange terrain and alien inhabitants lie ahead. He is striding through Canaan's unfamiliar territory like a highly gifted military scout, carefully plotting the way ahead, ensuring that they find the best camp sites and are kept clear of particularly dangerous areas. The Lord fights some battles for them and routs their enemies even before the Israelites appear on the scene: *He will destroy these nations before you, and you will take possession of their land* (3). When the Hebrews left Egypt he was their rear-guard, skilfully cutting off the ruthless, pursuing Egyptians.[11] Now they are about to encounter a different enemy, he

---

[8] Ex. 3:10.   [9] *e.g.* Ex. 33:11.   [10] Ex. 4:10, 13.   [11] Ex. 14:19.

goes ahead of them, guiding their steps and preparing their way. He knows the right places for them to stay overnight and, once they are there, will surround them with his protective presence.

He is their Victor
When they encounter Canaan's armies they will discover that the Lord will fight for them. Yesterday's conquests guarantee tomorrow's success: *And the Lord will do to them as he did to Sihon and Og.* They must not dread the days ahead. The Lord who fought victoriously for them in the past will not fail them in the future. That promise of unfailing help is repeated in the passage as Moses spoke publicly to the people (6) and privately (8) to their new leader: *he will never forsake you.*

He is their Companion
The Lord guarantees his presence as well as his power: *for the Lord your God goes with you; he will never leave you* (6, 8). It is not only a reassuring testimony from the lips of Moses. An unfailing promise comes from the mouth of God: *I myself will be with you* (23).

2. Israel's message

One of the features of these ancient political treaties was that the terms of the agreement were to be set down carefully in writing and some regular opportunity found for their recitation in the presence of the people. Moses has preached about God's covenant to the Israelite congregation but the truth must now be preserved for generations who would never hear the preacher's voice. These paragraphs remind us of the written, visual and vocal word of God.

a. The written word

So Moses wrote down this law and gave it to the priests, the sons of Levi, who carried the ark of the covenant of the Lord (9). *This law* did not simply describe God's revelation in the past; it prescribed their lifestyle for the future. Deposited in the ark, the word of God was carried by the Levites in to the unexplored territory before them. Conveyed in this way by the priests, at the head of the marching people, it symbolized the sanctity, authority, priority, and relevance of God's word for his people. For us, as for them, it illustrates the truth that joyful submission to the Lord's will revealed in Scripture must come first in our lives. It is of the greatest importance that we allocate time in each day to read it carefully. As we respond obediently to its message, it will determine our moral, social and spiritual values and will shape our distinctive lifestyle as committed believers.

b. The visual word

But the covenant must not be locked away safely in an ornate box, the exclusive preserve of a select company of priests. The agreement was also handed over *to all the elders of Israel* (9) who were commissioned to arrange for its public reading *every seven years, in the year for cancelling debts, at the Feast of Tabernacles* (10). This special celebration was a highly fitting occasion for the reading of the covenant. God's plan was that the word be publicly recalled at a time of generous compassion (15:1–2) and at a festival of joyful thanksgiving (16:13–15). They were to read the law when the Hebrew people remembered with gratitude their indebtedness to God (*the Feast of Tabernacles* recalled their pilgrimage through the wilderness) and obligation to others (*the year of cancelling debts*).

These two features had been given special prominence in the covenant and it was right that at such a festival *this law* (which means 'teaching', 9, 11–13) should not only be heard by all the people but seen in action. Once they settled in the land, these special tents or booths, set up in their courtyards or on their rooftops, were visible reminders of the loving providence of God, and their 'release' laws were, if obeyed (15:4–5), another visual-aid, vividly illustrating in everyday life, the practical love of their caring God.

c. The vocal word

And the LORD said to Moses: '. . . these people will soon prostitute themselves to the foreign gods of the land . . . They will forsake me and break the covenant I made with them' (16). The Lord knows only too well that it will not always be festival time. He is the supreme realist. Sadly, their future life will be characterized by transgression as well as celebration. Moses is therefore told that he is to set down in writing the words of a song which can be taught to the people and carefully passed on from one generation to the next. Songs had played a relatively minor part in their spiritual life thus far[12] but, by means of the psalms, they were to figure more prominently once they established a central place of worship in the land.

This song was not, for the most part, a psalm of praise. It was a psalm of sad exposure, reminding generations to come of the awful degradation and grim consequences of human sin and disobedience. The song was a vehicle of education. Children would learn it from

[12] Ex. 15:1–18; Nu. 21:17–18, 27–30.

their parents and be warned in advance of the devastating perils of apostasy and idolatry. The sombre yet hopeful message of that song is found in the next chapter of the book.

Deuteronomy 32:1–47
26. Learning by singing

We come now to the truths expressed in Moses' famous Song. It is a hymn of bitter grief, expressing God's intense disappointment with his greatly loved people. Throughout the succeeding centuries it was to serve as an easily memorized teaching aid to educate the Israelite people about spiritual priorities and to communicate God's warning message to successive generations.

In biblical times God's people frequently used songs to give vocal expression to their faith. Songs of victory celebrated God's power,[1] songs of trust recalled God's faithfulness,[2] songs of distress appealed for God's help,[3] and songs of joy acknowledged God's deliverance.

We have already seen that the literary structure of Deuteronomy may well have been influenced by the form of ancient Near Eastern treaties. These political agreements, however, were not always honoured by both parties, and when a nation violated the terms of a covenant, a different kind of document was drawn up which exposed the disloyalty of the offending party. The literary pattern of this Song which Moses taught the people closely follows the structure of these 'declarations of guilt' which were drawn up when a vassal nation violated the agreement. Documents of this kind go back well before the days of Moses and, as a one-time Egyptian courtier, he is likely to have been familiar with these 'exposures of offence'. They usually began with a public exhortation. In the presence of witnesses, the offending party is commanded to pay special attention to the precise accusations which are being made. The nation concerned is then interrogated regarding their offences and reminded of the special privileges which they have jeopardized by their disobedience. The usual offence which transgressed the terms of these covenants was disloyalty by forming an alliance with

[1] Ex. 14; Jdg. 5.   [2] *e.g.* the Psalms.
[3] Lamentations, passages in Jeremiah and many psalms.

another nation. These documents go on to condemn such disaffection and describe the fierce punishment which will follow.

With this literary background we can see that the opening stanza of the Song (32:1–6) invites witnesses to attest the truth of the suzerain's accusations. As was common in such documents, heaven and earth are summoned to testify to the reality and seriousness of the transgression: *Listen, O heavens, and I will speak; hear, O earth, the words of my mouth* (1).

In the next section (32:7–14) the rebellious nation is reminded of the material benefits enjoyed under the covenant's terms, all of which have been spurned and disregarded by the disloyal people who have formed other alliances, in Israel's case with idols (15–18). The agreement has been broken, despite the reliability and generosity of Israel's unique Suzerain, God.

In the third section (32:19–42), the disloyal people are warned of the ultimate consequences of their persistent transgression.

So far Moses' Song closely follows this common literary structure but towards its close there is a striking difference. These documents normally conclude on a note of severe warning which often includes a vicious declaration of war against the offender. In contrast, Moses' Song ends on the note of exultant hope, with praise offered to a merciful Lord who has not simply exposed the offence but pardoned it by making atonement for his people's sins (43).

Moses was a highly sensitive realist. From his forty years of experience with these people in the wilderness he knew only too well how they were likely to behave once they settled in Canaan. After all, the newly released Israelite slaves were worshipping an idol within months of their release from Egypt.[4] For all his careful instructions, earnest appeal and repeated exhortations, they would continue to resist God's word and repeatedly go after other gods. So, anticipating such apostasy after their settlement in Canaan, this song was to be taught to the people and their children, then passed on from generation to generation. By the novel means of a popular song, Israel would always have access to a constantly renewed warning about the tragic effects of their recurrent spiritual disloyalty. The Song is in four parts. In it God's nature is described (1–14), his rivals condemned (15–18), his grief expressed (19–33) and his mercy promised (34–43).

1. God's nature described (32:1–14)

The Song does not begin with these sombre themes of disobedience and despair although, eventually, it moves to them. Like most of the

---

[4] Ex. 32:3–4.

great New Testament letters, the 'complaint' is postponed so that it may begin more positively on the twin notes of exhortation (*listen*, 1) and exaltation (*praise*, 3). At the start of the Song the rebels are encouraged to acknowledge the goodness of a God who speaks to them (1–2) and who is worthy of their praise (3). The believer's only appropriate response to the revelation of God in Scripture is attention and adoration.

God's first word to the world he has made is *Hear!* People who stubbornly resist his word cannot hope to please God, help others or fulfil themselves. The introduction to the song exalts the unique reviving power of God's word (2). Its arresting imagery would be highly meaningful in an agricultural community. The word of God in this Song would come to successive generations like refreshing rain. Just as God's gift of water is vital for the physical life of the people, so his creative word is an essential ingredient in their spiritual life. Once they settled in Canaan they would come to see that, for all their physical assets (6:10–12), true contentment depends on something more than material possessions. Lasting satisfaction is not by 'bread alone' but by the life-giving word of God (8:3). The Song begins with the appeal that the people will give themselves attentively and obediently to this vitalizing word, and that its teaching will *fall like rain* and *descend like dew*. If they will welcome this unique truth, it will be as productive in their lives as *showers on new grass*.

This word of God will sometimes come to them as the early morning dew, without great dramatic impact. Almost imperceptibly it would gently find its way into their receptive hearts. At other times, it would descend with powerful force, like *abundant* torrential rain, leaving them in no doubt that God had spoken to them with convincing power. This 'rain imagery' anticipated the prophetic utterance of Isaiah centuries later (55:10–11), words which applied with forceful relevance to a people who proved to be disloyal to the covenant and experienced for themselves the dryness and unfruitfulness of repeated disobedience.

Reverent attention to God's word will issue in grateful adoration. The fact that this song addresses the people with such transforming vitality will surely encourage them to *praise the greatness of our God* (3). Praise is a vital aspect of Christian as well as Hebrew spirituality. It is not that God needs it; we do. C. S. Lewis pointed out that believers praise God because there can be no proper enjoyment without the element of appreciation. Lovers praise their partners, readers extol the skill of their favourite writer, walkers magnify the beauty of the countryside.

The world rings with praise . . . praise of weather, wines, dishes, actors, motors, horses, colleges, countries, historical personages, children, flowers, mountains, rare stamps, rare beetles, even sometimes politicians and scholars ... I had not noticed how the humblest, and at the same time most balanced and capacious, minds praised most, while the cranks, misfits and malcontents praised least ... Except where intolerable adverse circumstances interfere, praise almost seems to be inner health made audible.[5]

This Song invites its hearers to join Moses in grateful adoration: *I will proclaim the name of the* Lord. *Oh, praise the greatness of our God!* (3).

This exhortation to praise is a recurrent element in psalmody: 'Glorify the Lord with me: let us exalt his name together.'[6] Commenting on this characteristic feature of repeatedly inviting other people to praise God, Lewis says

that just as men spontaneously praise what they value, so they spontaneously urge us to join them in praising it: 'Isn't she lovely? Wasn't it glorious? Don't you think that magnificent?' The Psalmists in telling everyone to praise God are doing what all men do when they speak of what they care about ... I think we delight to praise what we enjoy because the praise not merely expresses but completes the enjoyment; it is its appointed consummation. It is not out of compliment that lovers keep on telling one another how beautiful they are; the delight is incomplete until it is expressed.[7]

But there is an element of wistfulness in Moses' exhortation to *praise the greatness of our God*, for the song anticipates a time when the people ignore his greatness; their love, worship and admiration are directed elsewhere. With pastoral skill as well as literary artistry the song reminds the people that the God they have left has been their reliable Rock (4), caring Father (5–9) and protective Eagle (10–14).

a. A reliable Rock (32:4)

The highly appropriate imagery changes suddenly from the rain to the rock. The confession *He is the Rock* is the first of seven occasions when this imagery is used in the song. In Scripture the rock is a striking and familiar metaphor.[8] Rocks in the wilderness provided travellers with shelter in a desert storm, a shadow to protect them from the blazing sun.[9] In certain situations, they even became places

[5] C. S. Lewis, *Reflections on the Psalms* (Fontana, 1960), pp. 94–95.   [6] Ps. 34:3.
[7] C. S. Lewis, *Reflections on the Psalms*, pp. 94–95.
[8] 1 Sa. 2:2; 2 Sa. 22:2–3, 32, 47; 23:3.
[9] Pss. 18:2; 31:2; 61:2–3; 71:3; Is. 32:2.

where food might be found. This song later reminds the Israelite of times when God *nourished him with honey from the rock, and with oil from the flinty crag* (13). Yet, despite such provision, Israel *rejected the Rock his Saviour* (15); as a people they *deserted the Rock, who fathered* them (18). When they were routed by their enemies, did they not realize that their defeat was because, to teach them a lesson, *their Rock had sold them* and *had given them up* (30)? Whenever would they realize that substitute gods were useless? *For their rock is not like our Rock, as even our enemies concede* (31). God himself, as well as their enemies, comments on the utter futility of these alliances with idols: *He will say 'Now where are their gods, the rock they took refuge in . . .?'* (37). In these ways the Song skilfully develops the contrast between God the dependable Rock and the nations' idols, flimsy, unreliable rocks, which offer no firm foundation for their future.

From their experience in the wilderness these travellers knew the sharp contrast between the firm, secure rock and the constantly drifting sand. For forty years they had lived in the hazardous desert and now they yearned for something settled, permanent and reliable. The stability they longed for would never come about by a mere change of geographical territory; lasting security was to be found only in God himself. He, and he alone, is the strong, firm rock on whom every believer can rely. His total dependability, always keeping his covenant promises, is in marked contrast to the uncertain, perpetually shifting, sand-like experience of his unreliable children. They will frequently let him down, and disregard the agreement they have made with him. Like drifting sand they will love him one day and serve other gods the next. Though they disappoint him, however, God will never deal with them as they deserve. He is a *perfect . . . upright and just* God, not like the capricious nonentities which his disloyal subjects worship at idolatrous shrines.

In times of bewildering suffering they would find renewed comfort as well as distinct challenge in this exhortation to praise; *all his ways are just*, not just some of them. During periods of their history when they suffered as captives or exiles they could renew their confidence in a *faithful God who does no wrong*, who would use even their adversities, and transform them into the messengers of his unchanging and unfailing love.

b. A caring Father (32:5–9)

These literary 'accusations of guilt', familiar in the ancient Near East when a covenant's terms had been broken, described not only the qualities of the suzerain but also his deeds. In exposing the failure of the disloyal party the document exalted what had been done for the vassal nation. The Song goes on to portray God as a Father who creates, loves and supports his unique family.

The Father creates the family (32:5–7)

The word which describes God here as Creator indicates the activity of the Father who formed them into a believing community. The concept goes back to Abraham, the father of an innumerable multitude. It recalls the 'stars' imagery at the beginning of Deuteronomy (1:10). The exodus experience was used to sharpen that community consciousness of the Hebrew people. The exultant song of Moses at the Red Sea uses the same word as in 32:6 here when it refers to God's newly delivered children as 'the people you bought'.[10] The Song in Deuteronomy, however, anticipates times in their history when these rich privileges will be forgotten:

> *They have acted corruptly towards him;*
> *to their shame they are no longer his*
> *children,*
> *but a warped and crooked generation.*
> *Is this the way you repay the* Lord
> *. . . your Father, your Creator*
> *who made you and formed you?* (5–6)

The Song makes use of a clever word-play on divine and human fatherhood: *Is he not your Father? . . . Ask your father and he will tell you* (6–7). If you have forgotten God's fatherly care, ask your human fathers about *the days of old* and about *generations long past* and they will tell you of the Lord's generous love in creating, nurturing, protecting and sustaining his redeemed people.

The Father supports the family (32:8–9)

Although the Hebrew people are reassured in the Song that they are his chosen people, they must not imagine that God is not interested in other nations. In the beginning he *gave the nations their inheritance, when he . . . set up boundaries for the peoples.* The historical introduction to this book reminded its readers that when the pilgrims passed through countries like Edom, Ammon and Moab, they were not to stay there because those lands did not belong to the Israelites. God had determined that they should belong to others (2:5, 9, 19). This Song reminds the Hebrews that their God is totally committed to the world he has made, not simply to one exclusive group of people within it.

The saying that God originally allocated national boundaries

---

[10] 'created', Ex. 15:16, NIV margin.

according to the number of the sons of Israel is not easy to understand. It may be declaring that in his sovereign appointments for the nations *the sons of Israel* are the Lord's central and determinative consideration. He does everything with his people in mind. Moreover, they are 'numbered' people; every one is intimately known, specially valued and personally catered for as his treasured possession.

It is also possible to translate these words as *according to the number of the sons of God* (NIV margin), a reading supported by the Greek Old Testament (the Septuagint), by the unpointed Massoretic text and by a Hebrew fragment of this passage in the Dead Sea Scrolls. The picture is like that found in the prologue to the book of Job, that of angelic beings in the heavenly court. As in Daniel's vision (10:13, 20) specific angels are portrayed as having responsibility for particular nations on earth. When this allocation of nations takes place, however, the people of Israel are an exception; they are cared for not by a guardian angel but by the Lord himself: *For the Lord's portion is his people, Jacob his allotted inheritance.* And yet although they are so specially favoured, in eternity (God's unique protection, reflected in the 'heavenly court' allocation imagery), in history (*Your Father, your Creator, who made you and formed you*) and in experience (*Ask your father and he will tell you*), yet they become *a warped and crooked generation.* Their rebellion and disloyalty, however, does not diminish the Father's inextinguishable love for them.

The Father loves the family (32:10)

The truth of God's sovereignty, in choosing them, is superbly balanced here by the assurance of his compassion. He found the Israelite people when they were in the *barren and howling waste* of their Egyptian slavery. As their caring Father, however, God came to rescue them. He felt for them in their affliction, guarding them as *the apple of his eye.* The beautiful imagery here literally means that he was guarding them as everyone protects 'the little man' of his eye. The pupil of the eye is a most sensitive part of the human body and, if we are in physical danger, the defence-mechanism which shields the eye is immediately at work. The Lord guards his uniquely treasured people with that kind of instant help. He is there in a flash, as if he was shielding the 'little man' of his own eye.

c. A protective Eagle (32:11–14)

The imagery of a God who *shielded . . . cared* and *guarded* his people in their agonizing years of slavery probably suggests the next picture, drawn from the familiar world of nature – the strong eagle which the wilderness travellers had often seen encircling their desert encampments. The young must be encouraged to fly and venture into the wide world outside the comfortable nest. The mother must 'stir up' the nest or the young eagle will stay there longer than is good for it. The parent flutters its wings over the nest, compelling the young bird to move and then, in order to encourage its first flight, sweeps below with its wide wings ready to catch and support its young.

The Lord knows that some of the harsh and difficult experiences of life are a painful but necessary part of our spiritual training. They serve to build character. Paul knew that: 'suffering produces perseverance';[11] and so did Peter: 'make every effort to add ... to self-control, perseverance'.[12] Life's best lessons are learnt through hardship. Writing from his Aberdeen prison in 1636, Samuel Rutherford expressed the truth perfectly: 'grace grows best in winter'.[13] The important message of these verses is that the strong wings of the eagle are always beneath us. The Lord God is always there with that entirely sufficient, unfailing, supportive strength at the very moment we cannot possibly do without it. The next chapter presses the same message home with comforting reassurance: 'underneath are the everlasting arms' (33:27).

The note of grateful testimony is not missing from this opening stanza of the Song. *Generations long past* (7) as well as contemporary believers will confirm that God alone has been Rock, Father and Eagle to his people. No other power could possibly have achieved such conquests and deliverances: *The LORD alone led him; no foreign god was with him* (12). It was Israel's unique God, and Yahweh alone, who *made him ride on the heights of the land* (13), probably anticipating the future possession of the land and the destruction of the Canaanite hilltop sanctuaries, those immoral 'high places' of Baal-worship. It was Yahweh, not Baal, the agricultural deity of the Canaanite people, who *fed him with the fruit of the fields . . . and the finest grains of wheat* (13–14). In the fissures of Canaan's rocks, the bees were there to provide Israel with nourishing honey; the olive trees would flourish in unlikely places, even where other trees would find insufficient soil to root. The Lord would provide for them in the most unlikely circumstances and would anticipate all their needs – honey, oil, butter, milk, meat, wheat and wine. How could Israel possibly forsake such a generous God?

[11] Rom. 5:3.   [12] 2 Pet. 1:5–6.
[13] Samuel Rutherford, *Letters*, Edinburgh 1891 (Banner of Truth Reprint, 1984), Letter 74, to the Lady Culross.

2. God's rivals condemned (32:15–18)

Yet, despite this generous provision for their physical needs, ungrateful Israel became self-reliant and disloyal. A pair of tragic offences is exposed: their expulsive materialism and destructive idolatry.

a. Expulsive materialism

But *Jeshurun grew fat and kicked; filled with food, he became heavy and sleek. Jeshurun* means 'the upright one'. From time to time most people use pet-names or 'nick-names'. They are expressions of warm and secure affection, sometimes with hints of playfulness, even thinly veiled admiration. *Jeshurun* was God's lovename for his people Israel. He was proud of them as his upright people. They were meant to have this distinctive testimony of moral integrity and spiritual character, but the 'upright one' became 'warped and twisted to their shame' (5, NIV margin). The accusation made here by God (15) is pointed and tragic. Though it is not reflected in the NIV translation, the Hebrew text makes dramatic use of the second person singular; three times it reads '*you* grew fat and *you* kicked, filled with food *you* became heavy and sleek' – 'you actually did that when I gave you so much. You misused the provision I made for you, you worshipped the creature rather than the Creator,[14] you, of all people!' Israel *abandoned the God who made him and rejected the Rock his Saviour.*

The most tragic effect of their materialism was that, in their self-contented opulence, they no longer needed God. It was not simply that, in their secularist preoccupation with things, they absent-mindedly forgot God. They resolutely *abandoned* and *rejected* him. Literally it means that they 'scorned' a God of surpassingly generous kindness: Father, Creator, Rock and Saviour. Constantly increasing possessions reduced the value of life's greater priorities. Materialistic concerns expelled things of greater worth. Once they *grew fat* they ignored the God who had fed them. The fears expressed in the book's earlier chapters have come to pass: 'then when you eat and are satisfied, be careful that you do not forget the LORD' (6:11–12; 8:11–14). The self-satisfied life becomes so small and full that there is little room for God. It was Thomas Erskine of Linlathen who said that 'most men are so possessed of themselves that they have no vacuum in which God's deep water may arise'.[15] So many people are materialistically full

[14] Rom. 1:25.
[15] For this reference I am indebted to H. D. McDonald, *Forgiveness and Atonement* (Eerdmans, 1984), p. 29.

but spiritually empty. They possess nothing that lasts; all ends in dust.

b. Destructive idolatry

Everyone worships something or someone. Disowning God, they turned to the idolatrous shrines of their contemporaries. The hill-top Baal sanctuaries were the places where their pagan neighbours worshipped the fertility gods of the ancestors. These were the deities who provided their refreshing, life-giving rain. It was not simply that they forgot God. They ascribed to heathen deities the distinctive qualities, virtues and gifts which belonged exclusively to the Lord alone. The portraiture in the Song of the idolatrous Israelite is not that of self-satisfied ingratitude; it is of spiritually destructive disloyalty of the worst possible kind. The Song, however, is an important teaching-aid; clear reasons are given for the condemnation of idolatry. It is presented here as forbidden, detestable, demonic, novel and futile.

Idolatry is forbidden

The passage deliberately recalls the Decalogue's prohibition. *They made him jealous with their foreign gods* (16). There is an echo here, and later in the Song (21), of the second commandment's warning about the divine jealousy (5:9). Idolatry dishonours his person, ignores his word, and disregards his generosity. The practice is not confined to the pagan shrines of the ancient world. When John came to the conclusion of his first letter he urged his first-century readers to keep themselves from idols.[16] He is there addressing a committed Christian congregation and is hardly likely to be referring to ornate images and religious statues. He is surely referring to what Ezekiel exposed, centuries earlier, as idols in the heart.[17] Paul described all covetous people as idolaters. They have made the acquisition of things the prime reason for living.[18] That angers God for he knows that we are only likely to enjoy life fully if we put him first. Jesus taught that truth with unmistakable clarity.[19]

Idolatry is detestable

God has not only forbidden it, he hates it. He recognizes it for the evil that it is; knowing what havoc it creates within communities. The disobedient Israelites have *angered him with their detestable idols* (16). People in the ancient world spent huge sums of money on their idols, lavishly covering them with silver and gold[20] but, however attractive some of them may have been to the human eye, they

[16] 1 Jn. 5:21.   [17] Ezk. 14:4.   [18] Eph. 5:5.   [19] Mt. 6:24, 33.
[20] Is. 40:19; 41:6–7; Je. 10:3–4.

were utterly obnoxious in God's sight. Any kind of God-substitute in our lives is highly offensive and distasteful to the Lord.

Idolatry is demonic

Behind that heathen image or secret idol is the work of the devil himself. Those who presented their offerings at idol-shrines *sacrificed to demons, which are not God* (17). It is the enemy's device to deflect the religious mind from the unique and only God. It does not simply divert the worshipper to meaningless, non-existent, God-substitutes. It directs that worship to Satan himself who has used this subtle religious mechanism to deceive millions of sincere but totally misguided people the world over. Ignorant of his strategy, people who worship idols honour the devil and adore the one who has seriously misled them.

Idolatry is novel

These rebellious or misguided idolaters are engaged in a pathetic religious activity for they are acknowledging *gods they had not known, gods that recently appeared, gods your fathers did not fear* (17). These gods are physical representations or material projections of the corrupt and ignorant human imagination. Israel's one and only true God is pure and holy. Moreover, he is known to the Hebrew people, having manifested himself in nature (as their Creator), in redemption (the miraculous event of the exodus), through their community history and personal experience. In contrast to this, these so-called gods they are now worshipping are worthless nothings, achieving nothing. They have no record of saving deeds to authenticate themselves – only recently have they appeared on the scene! The nation's fathers did not recognize them so why have their *perverse* and *unfaithful* children suddenly become indebted to them?

Idolatry is futile

God says that they have angered him *with their worthless idols.* Their idols are useless and worthless. Such perverse practices will not get them anywhere. It will end in total spiritual bankruptcy. As Jeremiah was to say centuries later, those who pursue worthless things will themselves become worthless.[21] The day will come when they will realize the utter futility of their idolatrous worship (37).[22]

The special poignancy of Israel's sin is driven home by the deliberate use of both Father and Mother imagery in its accusation of human rebellion: *You deserted the Rock, who fathered you; you forgot the God who gave you birth* (18). They were fathered by a

[21] Je. 2:5.   [22] *cf.* Is. 45:20; Je. 2:27–28; 10:8.

God who made them in his own image and were carried by a uniquely compassionate Mother.[23]

3. God's grief expressed (32:19-33)

The LORD *. . . was angered by his sons and daughters* (19). The Song exposes three tragic aspects of human sinfulness; it laments that God's children have become loveless, disobedient and senseless.

a. God's children are loveless

They have forgotten all they owe to God. They have not listened to him (1-2). Consequently they have not praised (3), obeyed (5), honoured (6) and acknowledged (10-14) their generous God. In order to bring them to their senses, the Lord says *I will hide my face from them* (20). There are times when it is necessary for God to do that in order to correct and discipline his children. He does not totally abandon them (for all God's righteous anger, they are still his *sons and daughters*, 19) but he deliberately hides his face.

The Puritans often wrote about this experience of the divine withdrawal. William Bridge pointed out that so long as Christians find support and encouragement elsewhere, they will tend not to find their strength in the Lord.

> Many times with the children of God, the Lord sees that they grow secure, vain, frothy and wanton under their peace and comfort; then he withdraws himself and their peace fails.

He adds that because God has

> . . . a design of love upon his own children, he permits a damp and discouragement to pass upon all their comforts: their peace to be interrupted, their hearts disquieted and their souls discouraged, so that they may encourage themselves in God alone.[24]

In such times Thomas Manton, similarly, urged his seventeenth-century readers to 'Learn to trust in a withdrawing God and depend upon Him.'[25] Only as God lovingly hides his face will the Israelite people realize how impoverished they have become without him. God's loveless children must at least confess their poverty before their earlier love be rekindled.

---

[23] Is. 46:3-4; 49:15; 66:13.
[24] William Bridge, *A Lifting Up for the Downcast* (Banner of Truth reprint, 1961), pp. 32-34.
[25] Thomas Manton, *Works* (1870-73), Vol. VI, p. 81.

b. God's children are disobedient

They ... angered me with their worthless idols (21). In such sad situations, the Lord will use a variety of different circumstances to bring rebellious children back to himself. Internally, he creates an awareness of spiritual need by 'hiding his face' from us. Externally he may use a variety of adverse experiences to drive us penitently to himself. Notice the sovereign Lord's repetitive *I will*. God is determined, even by severe means, to bring his wayward children back to a pure and loyal faith: *I will hide my face ... I will make them envious ... I will make them angry ... I will heap calamities upon them ... I will send wasting famine ... I will send against them the fangs of wild beasts* (20–24). In extolling God's goodness we must not forget his severity. It certainly became necessary to chastise Israel for, without that discipline, their faith would have become tarnished beyond recognition. The distinctive revelation given through Abraham, later through Moses and the great prophets, would have almost disappeared, only occasionally recalled as a mere strand in the story of antiquated Near Eastern religion. The truth about God, his covenant, book, land, people and purpose had to be preserved faithfully until the coming of his unique Son. The nation's spiritual negligence could not be overlooked, if only because of the spiritual welfare of those who would follow. When the appointed time had fully come God sent his Son[26] but, until that time, there had to be a continuing witness to revealed truth. So to keep that unique faith pure, God rebukes his people by withdrawing his provision (famine, 22), protection (plague, 23–24) and peace (invasion, 25).

c. God's children are senseless

Totally obsessed with idolatrous religion the people of Israel were simply lacking in the basic covenant qualities of love and loyalty. They no longer even *think* about the most important issues in life: *They are a nation without sense, there is no discernment in them* (28). It is astonishing that when they have been vanquished by their less able foes, they have not sat down to think seriously about the precise reasons for their defeat. If they had been totally outnumbered by the enemy, their failure would have been understandable, but there were occasions when the reverse was true. At times Israel had far greater numbers, superior resources, advantageous positions, better strategy, yet they were beaten! After such humiliating military encounters, had they never reflected on the

[26] Gal. 4:4.

possibility that they had lost the battle solely because *their Rock had sold them* (30)? How could one pagan soldier chase a thousand Israelites unless God had deliberately withdrawn his support from his disloyal people? Had they never thought about that as a possibility? Could they not even learn something about God and themselves from their mistakes and failures? They had turned to another *rock* and relied on forbidden idols so, by withdrawing his invincible power, *the* LORD *had given them up* to their futile God-substitutes. There was no other way of bringing them to their senses.

The unthinking Israelites had been deceived by demonic powers into imagining that the Canaanite war deities could do something for them in battle, but they had not realized that Israel's worst enemy was within, internal not external. Their reliance on pagan gods was the secret foe, not their military invaders. Their useless gods had let them down because they had never thought seriously about their demonic origin (17), moral impotence (31), evil nature (32a), or destructive potential (32b–33).

The condemnatory reference to the *vine of Sodom* and *fields of Gomorrah* (32) sharply exposes the sexual profanities at the idolatrous Canaanite shrines (*cf.* 29:23). The apostate Israelite people vainly imagine that loyalty to these fertility gods will increase their grape harvest, but their vineyards will yield poisonous fruit. All forms of self-satisfaction which ignore God are not merely unsatisfying; they are ultimately poisonous, a wine which is *the venom of serpents, the deadly poison of cobras* (33). The devil's 'blessings' are disguised curses. These foolish people had exchanged *the red blood of the grape* (14) for *clusters with bitterness* (32). What folly, but how true to human experience. Yet, despite this appalling loveless, disobedient and senseless disloyalty, God has his own way of bringing *unfaithful* children (20) to the place of repentance, forgiveness and hope.

4. God's mercy promised (32:34–43)

His children are loveless, but God still loves them; he has *compassion on his servants* (36). They are disobedient, but he continues to be loyal to them, reaffirming his covenant name and nature as the great *I . . . am* (39).[27] They are senseless, but he acts sovereignly in perfect wisdom. Israel's foes are arrogantly strong but *in due time their foot will slip* (35). God knows precisely the right moment for his saving intervention. He assures Israel that there is a wise and providential purpose behind the seemingly disordered events of human life. His plans for Israel are *kept . . . in reserve and sealed . . .*

[27] *cf.* Ex. 3:14.

in my vaults (34). This sovereign mercy of God is revealed in four significant aspects of spiritual renewal. The Lord exposes our sin (34–38), promises our deliverance (39–42), inspires our praise and guarantees our forgiveness (43).

a. God exposes our sin (32: 34–38)

The transgression must be identified, condemned and confessed before it can ever be forgiven. God is angry about the sin, but is merciful towards the sinner. The offence is neither ignored or condoned but the offender can certainly be pardoned. Wrath and love are not alien but complementary characteristics of the divine nature: *The Lord will judge his people and have compassion on his servants* (36). Moreover, God not only exposes our iniquity but also our impotence, our total lack of human ability to put it right. It is *when he sees their strength is gone and no-one is left* to help them that he comes to their side not merely as Judge (36) but as Lover (36), Healer (39) and Victor (40–42). We sinners have to be brought completely to the end of our own resources, recognize our moral impotence, and then confess the gross error of our costly disloyalties, before we can be cleansed, pardoned, reconciled and equipped. Grace is not cheap. God invites us to look our idolatrous God-substitutes in the face to see how futile they are when we are in real need: *Now where are their gods . . .? Let them rise up to help you!*

b. God promises our deliverance (32:39–42)

See now that I myself am He! The choice of the 'I am' title for God is sensitive and deliberate. The name recalls the burning bush incident and the saving event of the exodus. It reminds the Israelites of the Lord's mercy to sinful individuals as well as enslaved communities. The 'I am' made himself known in compassion to guilty,[28] inadequate[29] and fearful[30] Moses. *There is no god besides me* reminds the people of the covenant affirmation in the Decalogue (5:7). God will release us from our sins but only on his terms; he must be acknowledged as our only deliverer, the one with unique power to kill and revive, wound and heal. God 'lifts his hand', as declaring an oath, that he will overcome our enemies and effect our salvation.

c. God inspires our praise (32:43a)

Appropriately for a popular song, it concludes on the note of praise and promise, inviting every individual Israelite to respond: *Rejoice,*

---

[28] Ex. 2:12–14.   [29] Ex. 3:11.   [30] Ex. 4:13.

O nations, with his people, for he will ... make atonement. The closing exhortation does not consist of *idle words ... – they are your life. By them you will live ...* (47). If we receive them genuinely (*Take to heart*) and obey them carefully (46), then we shall want to praise and rejoice in the mighty achievements of such an incomparable (39), dependable (40) and invincible (41) God.

d. God guarantees our forgiveness (32:43b)

He will *make atonement for his land and people*, literally, 'his land, his people'. The word *atonement* here belongs to the language of sacrifice. The idolatrous rebels had sacrificed at heathen shrines (37–38) but such forbidden offerings achieved nothing whatever. The *atonement* described here indicates that which is covered, cleared away, expiated. Though his disaffected people have broken the covenant-promises, causing him great sorrow, the Lord will not break his promise. His uplifted hand testifies to earth and heaven the reliability of his spoken oath: *As surely as I live for ever* (40) – their forgiveness is assured.

The concluding stanza of the Song is a paradigm of his dealings with us. He will cleanse our sins, every single one of them. He will cover them so completely that they need not haunt us on earth and will never be recalled in heaven. The Song uncovers human sin only that it may be divinely covered; exposure is an essential element in its atonement. All attempts to conceal or disguise our sins are ultimately useless. God sees everything now and will certainly do so in the future.[31] Our sins become almost vocal and cry out against us; only God can silence the accuser and assure us of an eternally effective covering. Across the changing centuries, the people who sang this Song were reminded of changeless truth – that the God who loved them (36) would not fail to restore them.

Inspired by God's Spirit, Moses is a master at the art of communication. One of the Song's most impressive aspects is the skill with which Moses uses a wide variety of literary forms to bring the people to repentance. We can trace his artistry here in using the device of

command: *Listen, Hear* (1)
exhortation: *Let my teaching fall* (2)
illustration: *rain, dew, showers, grass, plants* (2)
declaration: *He is the Rock* (4)
invitation: *Ask your father and he will tell you* (7)
description: the *desert land, howling waste,* hovering *eagle* (10)
exposure: *you grew fat ... You deserted the Rock* (15, 18)

[31] Heb. 4:13.

warning: *I will...?* (21–24)

interrogation: *Is this the way...? Is he not? How could one man chase a thousand unless...? Have I not kept...? Now where are their gods...?* (6, 30, 34, 37–38)

recollection: for example, the penetrating use of historical events to unmask contemporary sins (32).

The Song wants its last word to be not a description of human sin but of divine grace. The concluding lines exalt God's character as unique (39a), powerful (39b), compassionate (39c), reliable (40), alive (40), eternal (*for ever*, 40), sovereign (*he will*, 43) and merciful (43). With such a God the Israelite pilgrims can enter Canaan, even without Moses,[32] assured that the Lord who has made such promises is more than sufficient for their future needs.

With Joshua alongside him as the colleague who will soon take over his work, Moses publicly urges the people (44–47) to respond not only to the timeless warning of *this song* (44) but to the entire teaching of *this law* (46) of which the Song is a concluding part. The departing leader reminds them and us that *all* (44, 46) of God's word must be personally received (*Take to heart*), faithfully shared (*command your children*) and carefully obeyed (46). They are not the *idle words* of mere men, nor even the passionate words of a devoted leader but the life-imparting words of God himself. He knows that his people cannot possibly enjoy life (47) in the days ahead if they deliberately choose to ignore the word he has given to them in love.

---

[32] The passage in 32:48–52 will be treated with parallel material in the concluding chapter on 34:1–12.

Deuteronomy 33:1–29
27. Parting words

This chapter records the farewell blessing of Moses. He cannot travel with the people, and this is the last opportunity to open his heart to them. Final sayings are specially memorable. On two occasions during John Wesley's closing hours he testified afresh to the truth of Christian assurance: 'The best of all is, God is with us.' Before we turn to Moses' concluding message, it is important to recognize the patriarchal background, pastoral nature and poetic form of this passage.

First, we notice its patriarchal background. The fact that this farewell blessing is addressed to the individually named tribes deliberately recalls the occasion when Jacob pronounced distinctive blessings on his sons.[1] The people who listened to Moses were the natural successors of Jacob's children. Unique origins and subsequent history were extremely important to the Hebrew people. At a time when the natural preoccupation of the tribes was to look ahead to a threatening future, here is a deliberate act of 'looking back' to a treasured past. It is an account of another patriarch saying, in effect, 'Remember old Jacob; think of God's faithful generosity to him and his children, and to all our ancestors over the four or five hundred years since Jacob uttered those final blessings. The God who was true to them will not fail us: The best of all is, God is with us too.' They would cross the Jordan without Moses but they were not travelling without God. In this graphic way they are reminded that they belong to a long line of pilgrims, people whose lives are enriched by continuity and security. The God of their fathers would not disappoint them.

We must also consider its pastoral nature. In the earlier chapters of the book we have listened to Moses the Preacher and have often noticed that Deuteronomy is 'preached law'. But here Moses is the Pastor with a rare opportunity to address each of the tribes

---

[1] Gn. 49:1–27.

individually, remembering their distinctive characteristics and particular temptations. He has spent over forty years with these people and by now knows them extremely well. Through the long years he has moved among them hearing their problems, absorbing their complaints, sharing their trials, knowing their dreams, ideals, ambitions; he of all people knows what is best for them, and says all that is on his heart as he shares his final good-bye with them. It is rather like a parent speaking privately with a son or daughter about to leave home, the sort of thing that Shakespeare does with such artistry, and as a moment of light relief, in *Hamlet*. Laertes is about to go overseas but, first, he must listen, as patiently as possible, to his old father Polonius as he relates in precious minutes truths which should have been shared over years. He knows the young man best, however, and is disturbingly aware of the temptations and pressures of another country and a different lifestyle, and what new-found freedom might do to him once he is away from the natural restraints of life at home.[2]

Likewise, Moses had been more than a father to these people, and he knew the dangers of the land which lay ahead. This is his last opportunity to tell them about the things which matter most. The land on the other side of the Jordan had enormous material assets but there were also fearsome perils, spiritual dangers which far outweighed the physical, and the leader's children were specially vulnerable. Moreover, like any other family, these children were all different with distinctive characteristics; a necessary warning to one son or daughter would be almost improper if addressed to another. The parent knows the weaknesses as well as the strengths. It is no time for meaningless platitudes; the family needs clear pastoral guidance and encouragement. They need to be reminded of both certainties and priorities, and this is the last occasion when such a thing is possible.

Moses' final words in these concluding chapters are so superbly balanced. The Song in chapter 32 is intentionally severe as it emphasizes its stark truth with reiterated warnings. The message in chapter 33 is more personal, expounded with warmth and compassionate understanding. Both aspects are necessary; it is not always easy for God's messengers to maintain the necessary balance. If the preacher is always severe and demanding, the people are left breathless, despondent and broken. A gifted pastor, as well as compelling preacher, Luther knew just that. He reminded his students of Chrysostom's words, 'He who strikes a slow man makes him slower', and went on to say

Sinners should not be upbraided in such a way that they are only

[2] Shakespeare, *Hamlet*, I, iii.

wounded and driven to despair . . . Therefore sores should not be cut and left, but they should much rather be soothed with plasters.[3]

On the other hand, if the message is always tender and comforting, it has a soporific effect on the highly contented people. The congregation becomes permanently tranquilized, seriously lacking life's necessary dynamism, direction and challenge. The English Puritan, Thomas Gouge, knew the dangers: 'It is an ill sign to set down satisfied and rest content with a little.'[4] Or, as Bunyan put it, 'Departing from iniquity, is . . . a work that will last thee thy lifetime and *there* is the greatness and difficulty of it.'[5] It is worthy of everything we have got.

Further, we need to remember the poetic form of Moses' farewell blessing. Poetry is an extremely delicate, even vulnerable, vehicle for conveying truth. By its very nature it is open to a variety of different interpretations and that certainly applies to the Hebrew poetry in this fascinating passage. It is not fitting to be rigidly dogmatic about the precise meaning of a particular verse; other interpreters may offer equally helpful insights into its meaning. Graphic descriptive language like Zebulun's *treasures hidden in the sand* (19), or Dan's *lion's cub, springing out of Bashan* (22), or the prediction that Asher will *bathe his feet in oil* (24) may each be capable of variant interpretations. However, the main thrust of this parting message is unmistakably clear. Some of the themes overlap but it is possible to discern eight important truths which Moses wishes to leave with the Israelite pilgrims before they enter the unknown future. Here is an octave of divine encouragement. Its message is as relevant now as when it was first shared with these naturally apprehensive people.

1. The fact of love (33:2–5)

Like the Song in the previous chapter (32:1–2), the blessings begin by exalting the revelation of God in his word. Before addressing the tribes individually, Moses has something to say to them all. For the last time he reminds them of the nature, attributes and characteristics of the God who has brought them thus far. Once they cross the river, life may test them with a variety of unwelcome experiences. In times of bewilderment, temptation and adversity, they will need to recall the truth that God loves them. Here is a spiritual reality

[3] Martin Luther, *Lectures on Titus, Philemon and Hebrews*, Luther's Works, Vol. 29 (St Louis: Concordia, 1968), p. 184.
[4] Thomas Gouge, *The Young Man's Guide through the Wilderness of the World to the Heavenly Canaan*, 8. 5. 1.
[5] John Bunyan, *A Holy Life*, in *The Miscellaneous Works of John Bunyan*, Vol. 9, ed. Roger Sharrock (Clarendon Press, 1976), pp. 276–277.

beyond all possible doubt: *Surely it is you who love the people.* The emphasis, conveyed by the Hebrew participle *love* (not 'loved'), is on the timeless, unchanging love of God. It is one of Deuteronomy's central themes (4:37; 7:8; 10:15; 23:5) and Moses repeats it here for the benefit of all the tribes.

His opening words present a majestic word-picture of God coming to them, escorted by angels in triumphant procession to meet his gathered children. The tribes are about to journey to Canaan but Moses reminds them that, first, God has travelled to them. These verses illustrate our observation about the interpretation of Hebrew poetry. The precise meaning of the original text is not always easy to determine but the primary message is clear: their God is a totally faithful Lover who comes (2), protects (3), instructs (3–4) and rules (5).[6]

a. Their Lover meets those he loves

He takes the initiative. This initial portrait is a 'theophany', a poetic representation of God in strikingly human terms. God is moving towards them like a desert traveller, eager to meet with his people before they make their own momentous journey. He wants them to know that he is with them, not a God of the past, locked away in the experience of their ancestors or about to disappear with the departing Moses. He has travelled to the plains of Moab specially to meet with his assembled people. It is vivid, pictorial language similar to that found in passages elsewhere in the Old Testament like the Song of Deborah[7] and the psalm of Habakkuk.[8] This arresting introduction conveys the crucial message that in all our spiritual relationships the initiative is with God. We do not have to spend endless hours frantically searching for him; he comes to us. The truth is conveyed here at the beginning of the blessings and, as a final reminder, it appears again at the end. Here, the Lord journeys across the desert and over the mountains (2); later he comes crossing the heavens and riding on the clouds (26). The doctrine of the Incarnation is a rich theological description of the loving initiative of God. Jesus was called 'Immanuel' which means 'God with us'.[9] The Father loved so much that he gave his only Son. God was in Christ reconciling the world to himself.[10]

b. The Lover protects those he loves

All the holy ones are in your hand. Though in the Old Testament

---

[6] For the context and exegesis of 33:2–5, see Christopher J. H. Wright, *God's People in God's Land*, pp. 37–43.
[7] Jdg. 5:4–5. [8] Hab. 3:3. [9] Mt. 1:23. [10] Jn. 3:16; 2 Cor. 5:19.

holy ones is used both of angels and of the Lord's people, the context suggests that the latter is intended here. Those lives which have been consecrated to him are his special care. The Israelites could fear that they might fall into the hands of the Canaanites but, however difficult the way ahead, God has promised to keep them safe in his strong hand. Part of the agreement described in these covenants was that the vassal nation was always protected by the suzerain. The Lord had taken a pledge in his treaty with them that he would certainly not fail or forsake his covenant people.

c. The Lover instructs those he loves

It is from *Sinai* that the Lord comes, the place where he made his covenant with them. The picture of angelic communicators or witnesses at the original giving of the Law is a concept found in the New Testament as well as the Old; it figures both in the preaching of Stephen and the teaching of Paul.[11] God speaks his covenant word in the presence of *myriads of holy ones*, and this Lover who addresses his children through *the law that Moses gave* them anticipates their loving obedience: *At your feet they all bow down, and from you receive instruction* (3).

d. The Lover rules over those he loves

The portrait is of God as Israel's *king. Jeshurun*, the 'pet name' for Israel, is no longer self-satisfied and rebellious as in the previous chapter's condemnatory Song (15). Now she is true to her name, 'the upright one', responding in love to his regal commands and enjoying the protection of his sovereign power. This impressive theophany encourages God's people to praise his initiative, enjoy his protection, obey his teaching and trust his sovereignty.

2. The inevitability of conflict (33:6–7, 11, 20, 22)

Although God's people are in his hand they are not exempt from attack. The conflict-theme recurs in several of these tribal blessings. The believing soldier may feel dangerously outnumbered but Moses' prayer is that Reuben's tribe will *live and not die, nor his men be few*, and that as Judah *with his own hands . . . defends his cause*, the Lord will *be his help against his foes*. God is urged to *smite the loins of those who rise up against* Levi. The old leader pleads that the Lord might give to Gad the strength of *a lion, tearing at arm or head*, and that Dan will be like *a lion's cub, springing out*

---

[11] Acts 7:53; Gal. 3:19.

of Bashan. Before the people crossed the Jordan, two of these tribes, Reuben and Gad, had been allocated territory on the eastern side of the river. Together with half the tribe of Manasseh, they would be cut off from the main body of the Israelite people and might feel specially vulnerable. They needed the assurance that God would be their strong and invincible protector.

Every believer intent on living for God in a non-believing environment must be prepared for conflict and hardship. Writing to Joyce Hales in 1554, the imprisoned Reformer John Bradford told her that all genuine believers must be willing to suffer in one way or another. She had cared for him and his partners in dark times, and he told her bluntly that those who follow Christ cannot avoid the way of rejection:

> If you will embrace Christ in his robes, you must not think scorn of him in his rags ... Can the head Corner-stone be rejected and the other more base stones in God's building be in this world set by? ... Be content therefore to be hewn and snagged at ... You are one of Christ's lambs: look therefore to be fleeced, haled at, and even slain. If you were a market-sheep, you should go in more fat and grassy pasture. But because you are for God's own occupying, therefore you must pasture on the bare common, abiding the storms and tempest that will fall ... Suffer a little and be still ... for Christ is Emmanuel, that is, God with us.[12]

3. The priority of service (33:8–10)

Levi's tribe was devoted to the Lord's service. Their sons were to supply the Israelite priesthood and the blessing of Moses outlines their exemplary, pastoral, educative and liturgical responsibilities.

Their exemplary responsibility was to honour God's claim. The everyday lifestyle of this tribe was to embody the truth that God must be first in every human life. So that this truth was constantly demonstrated within the Israelite community, the Levites were required to put God's work even before the demands of their families. Levi said of his parents, *'I have no regard for them.' He did not recognize his brothers or acknowledge his own children* (9). The saying recalls the tragic golden-calf incident[13] when the Levite men were commanded to be the instruments of God's judgment on the idolatrous people, even if the offenders belonged to their own families. It is a stark reminder of an inflexible biblical

---

[12] *The Writings of John Bradford*, I (Parker Society ed. 1853), pp. 111–112.
[13] Ex. 32:26–29.

principle that obedience to God must take precedence over all other loyalties.[14]

Their pastoral responsibility was to discern God's will. The priest was the pastor in Israel, and individuals came to him in order to discern the mind of God when they had to make important decisions in life.[15] The *Urim and Thummim* were the flat stones which formed part of the High Priest's equipment.[16] Their respective names, inscribed on the stones, probably derive from words meaning 'curse' (Urim) and 'perfect' (Thummim). If, when they were thrown, both stones revealed the Urim side then the priest would confidently give a negative answer to the question posed by the person seeking his help; to ignore such advice might incur a curse. If one stone showed the Urim side and the other Thummim, then the priest would say that it was not possible to give a definite answer at that moment. In Old Testament times the people came to the Levitical priest to help them come to right decisions and in a primitive society outward evidence of this kind was objective and reassuring, just as later when lots were cast to discover the right person to replace Judas among the apostles.[17]

Now that the Holy Spirit indwells the life of every believer such outward means of obtaining guidance are neither necessary nor appropriate. Christian believers have a complete Bible, the perfect example of Jesus, immediate access into God's presence, the inward witness of the Holy Spirit, a sensitive conscience, the privilege of developing a mature Christian mind, and the prayerful advice of reliable friends. It is not fitting, therefore, for Christians to resort to a pious 'guess-work' mentality or one which is only convinced by unusual forms of spectacular confirmation. Gideon's demand for outward evidence (the miracle of the 'fleece') is hardly provided in Scripture as an example for trusting Christians to follow. In his gracious mercy, God met the weak man's request, but Gideon was seriously lacking in faith to keep asking for visible signs when the Lord had already spoken so clearly to him.[18]

The Levites' educative responsibility was to explain God's word. *He teaches your precepts to Jacob and your law to Israel.* The priest was the guardian of God's truth: *he watched over your word and guarded your covenant.* There was no point whatever in asking the priest to use the Urim and Thummim to discover whether it was right for an angry man to kill a noisy neighbour, or whether a poor man might rob a prosperous friend who could easily afford to part with some of his possessions. God had already spoken in the covenant about killing and stealing, and what he had said applied

---

[14] Mt. 6:33; 10:34–39.   [15] Mal. 2:6–7.   [16] Ex. 28:30; Lv. 8:8.
[17] Acts 1:23–26.   [18] Jdg. 6:14, 16, 36–40.

universally to everyone. No further word was necessary on such matters. However persuaded Christians might claim to be, they are seriously misguided if they claim that God has given them authority to do something which is forbidden in his word. He does not change his mind in order to make life a little more convenient to those who want to know what is right and best.

The Levites' liturgical responsibility was to exalt God's name. The *incense* of believing prayer and the *burnt offerings* of total sacrifice were expressions of the Levites' adoration, and their ministry as Israel's worship-leaders offers some fine insights to Christian believers. We also worship (acknowledge God's worth) when we prayerfully express our dependence and sacrificially surrender our bodies.

Ever since Reformation times the doctrine of 'the priesthood of all believers' has been an important Protestant concept. We need to remember that it means something far more than 'I'm as good as the Minister'; nobody doubts the possibility of that, least of all the Minister. Given the teaching of these verses the phrase ought to mean that, as believer-priests,[19] we too recognize the prior claim of God over every other allegiance, insist on pursuing his will whatever the cost, make it our determined aim to obey his word, and offer the worship of daily prayer and sacrificial living.

4. The assurance of support (33:12)

The tribe of Benjamin was never large[20] but they were *beloved of the Lord*. Despite their limited numbers and resources they could rely on his support in difficult times, for the Lord *shields* and protects those who feel weak, inadequate or outnumbered. The one whom *the Lord loves rests between his shoulders*. God carries his children.

a. God's carrying is compassionate

The book's great love-theme is here applied to a specific minority within Israel. It is a memorable picture, used earlier by Moses (1:31), of a loving and thoughtful father carrying his exhausted child home on his shoulders. It was a perfect message for people who faced a demanding journey.

b. God's carrying is pleasurable

They are *beloved of the Lord* and he is delighted to carry them. A father will gladly carry his young son or daughter in this way, not

---

[19] Rev. 1:6. [20] Ps. 68:27.

because it is either necessary or requested, but for the sheer pleasure it gives them to do so. The father is proud to carry and the child is pleased to be carried.

c. God's carrying is dependable

The believer can *rest secure in him*, knowing that *he shields him all day long*. Writing to his Northamptonshire congregation in the late seventeenth century, the imprisoned pastor, Thomas Browning, urged his persecuted people to be faithful to Christ. He reminds them that the Lord had promised to look after them; they too can *rest secure*. But if they want to be shielded they must stay near: 'My brethren do not flee. Keep your ground . . . There is no shadow like the shadow of God's wings, therefore keep close to God.'[21]

d. God's carrying is constant

They are shielded *all day long*. This father will never be too exhausted to lift them on to his strong shoulders; he will never let us down. At a particularly difficult period in his life, Luther found strength in the truth that he was being carried by Christ, the Strong Ferryman, who carries his people safely through life's greatest adversities: 'Christ alone is not only the Companion but . . . also the Helper, yes, the Ferryman . . . and He will cross over successfully.'[22]

5. The joy of fruitfulness (33:13–17)

Three features are immediately apparent in this message for the tribe of Joseph. It is the longest of these tribal blessings, the one which most closely recalls the blessing given originally to Joseph by his father Jacob.[23] It is also the message with the richest poetic imagery – the reviving dew, resourceful springs of water, *choicest gifts* from the mountains, abundantly fruitful fields, the security of the everlasting hills, and *the best gifts of the earth*. The members of this tribe treasured the story of their great ancestor. He had certainly lived a fruitful life[24] but it had been costly.[25] The names Joseph gave to his sons Ephraim and Manasseh (both mentioned in this Mosaic blessing) perfectly summarized his story of suffering and success: 'God has made me forget all my trouble . . . God has made me fruitful in the land of my suffering'.[26] The pilgrims about to enter a new land need this reminder that there is little blessing

[21] Matthias Maurice, *Monuments of Mercy* (1729), pp. 53–54.
[22] Martin Luther, *Lectures on Titus, Philemon and Hebrews*, Luther's Works, Vol. 29 (Saint Louis: Concordia), p. 226.
[23] Gn. 49:22–27.   [24] Gn. 49:22.   [25] Gn. 49:23.   [26] Gn. 41:51–52.

without suffering. Life in Canaan will not be without its adversities. Unavoidable pain is at the heart of spiritual fruitfulness. The Lord Jesus made that clear to his disciples; if the vineyard-owner is to enjoy a good harvest, his vines must be pruned carefully.[27] In his pastoral counsel to Joseph's tribe, Moses concentrates on the source, means and extent of fruitfulness.

The source of fruitfulness is the generous Lord himself. This tribe was about to enter territory where its people believed that Baal was the giver of abundant harvests. He must be honoured and placated if the land was to be fruitful. But this blessing begins with the strong corrective note of prayerful confidence: *May the LORD bless his land ... with the best the sun brings forth* (13–14). Everything is dependent on *the favour of him who dwelt in the burning bush* (16). The reference to *the burning bush* can hardly be accidental. Does this fascinating saying recall the personal experience of Moses himself, when God had promised to bring his people into this very land which now stretched before them? At the close of his ministry, is Moses now recalling that which gave him confidence at its beginning? At that time his confidence was in God alone, the dependable 'I am', the God of unchanging faithfulness,[28] the better future,[29] and of present security.[30] The *burning bush* was the place where the angel of the Lord first appeared to him and he was told to remove his sandals on such holy ground. When Moses' successor, Joshua, crossed the river he was also addressed by a messenger from God, and was likewise told to remove his sandals; that new ground was holy too.[31] The imaginative reference to the burning bush recalls the past and anticipates the future. The eternal 'I am' has promised to make his people fruitful.

The means of fruitfulness were the gifts of God himself. The people could not manufacture the morning dew; the deep springs that gushed from the earth were generously given by the Creator of life. The blessing reminds the tribe of their total dependence on God. The people could toil in their vineyards and fields but if they were to be fruitful, they relied on resources totally beyond themselves – dew and rain from heaven and precious water from underground springs (13), sun, moon, the orderly seasons of the agricultural year. Their pagan neighbours worshipped the sun and the moon, but the Hebrews knew that these magnificent aspects of creation were the creative handiwork of God himself[32] and to worship them was to dishonour and disobey the one who had made them. Moses' blessing to Joseph reminds the travellers of their indebtedness to God.

The extent of fruitfulness is vast and abundant. For decades

[27] Jn. 15:2.　[28] Ex. 3:6.　[29] Ex. 3:8.　[30] Ex. 3:12.　[31] Jos. 5:13–15.
[32] Pss. 8:3; 19:1; 89:11; 136:4–9.

God's people have journeyed through the barren desert, but he is about to give them *the best ... the finest ... the choicest ... the best gifts of the earth in its fulness* (13–16). Five times in these verses the Hebrew word *meged* is used to denote that which is of the highest quality. God is generous to his trusting people. It does not mean that we can have everything we want, but he will not deny us anything we need.[33]

The encouraging blessing to Joseph faces the future with realism. Agricultural prosperity will be useless unless it is accompanied by military strength. The tribe must have *the horns of a wild ox* if they are to protect and preserve their abundant crops. The harvest season was the very time the invaders came, robbing and plundering the rich fields. God would give them the power to resist their enemies as well as the strength to gather their crops.

6. The promise of security (33:18–19)

During the wilderness years, the people who belonged to the various tribes must often have wondered how life would work out for them. It was natural to feel apprehensive, uncertain, even fearful, but in these blessings they are assured that the Lord has their distinctive needs in mind. As Zebulun and Issachar[34] thought about their new life in a strange land, God promised them a happy, secure and enriching future.

a. Their happiness is anticipated

The opening greeting (*Rejoice, Zebulun ... and you Issachar*) invites the tribes to be grateful to God for the loving plans he has made for their future.[35] Their fear is a waste of emotional energy for God has good things in store for them.

b. Their security is described

They will be protected by God whether they are travelling away (*going out*) or staying at home (*in your tents*). Free from trouble and disturbance, they will be able to summon grateful worshippers to the local *mountain* so that they can *offer sacrifices of righteousness* ('right' offerings, not idolatrous worship) in peace and safety. The *mountain* may refer to Tabor, which lay between the two territories. Sadly, by the eighth century, it housed a sanctuary where Baal

[33] Pss. 34:10; 84:11.
[34] These tribes are also linked together in Jacob's blessing and Deborah's Song (Gn. 49:13–15; Jdg. 5:14–15).
[35] Je. 29:11.

sacrifices were offered.[36] It is a further example of biblical honesty and realism; there is often a tragic gap between what God intends and what we achieve.

c. Their enrichment is assured

Their days of limited resources are almost over. God has a new lifestyle in mind for them. Once settled in their allotted territories, they would *feast on the abundance of the seas, on the treasures hidden in the sand* (19). New forms of trade and commerce will be open to them; with convenient access to sea and lake they can engage in fishing, and develop skills in the manufacture of dyes (from shellfish) and glass-work (from sand).

7. The necessity of obedience (33:20–21)

The territory allocated to Gad was, like that of Reuben and half of Manasseh, on the east side of Jordan. These strong (*like a lion*) people came to inherit *the best land* for themselves but they would not be selfish in their enjoyment of God's gifts. In accordance with divine instructions they were to carry out *the Lord's righteous will* by crossing the river to fight alongside their fellow-Israelites. They left their wives, families and meagre possessions, and put their lives at risk, even though they were not to benefit directly and personally. They made those sacrifices so that their fellow-Israelites might be established in Canaan. God had demanded their participation, so it must be done. The two and a half tribes which eventually settled across the Jordan from the rest were specially commended by Joshua for their unselfish and total obedience.[37] The story of their unhesitating response to God's word is an example to us all.[38]

8. The guarantee of help (33:22–29)

Whatever their geographical location in the land every tribe needed the assurance that God was with them. They can confidently anticipate his strength (like a fearless, energetic young lion, 22), approval (*the favour of the LORD*, 23), and resources (abundant *oil*, 24). They are told that the Lord is near, around and beneath them.

a. God is near them (33:26)

The blessing closes with an arresting word-picture of Jeshurun's God coming speedily to their aid, riding *on the clouds in his majesty*.

---

[36] Ho. 5:1.   [37] Nu. 32:1–33; Jos. 22:1–3.   [38] Jn. 2:5.

At the beginning of the blessings he was portrayed in a majestic procession travelling across the desert sands; now he is hurrying to the side of his outnumbered yet dependent people. This portraiture of a God who travelled across the skies[39] was to become specially meaningful to them in the decades ahead. Here was the very symbolism with which Baal's warlike activities were described.[40] Before entering Canaan they were told that there *is no-one like the God of Jeshurun*; he is unique and he is near. He not only came in the past at Sinai (2) but will come in the future in Canaan. They are not to think of him as a detached and distant deity. He is a God who cares for his people and will not leave them alone.

b. God is around them (33:27)

After years in the wilderness, frequently striking their flimsy tents, they will soon encounter well-fortified cities with huge walls and strong gates. Their frail camps would shelter vulnerable, almost defenceless, communities. How would they fare? The Lord guaranteed his invincible spiritual fortifications. Their gate bolts would be as *iron and bronze*, physical strength would be miraculously renewed with every fresh sunrise, and they could count on the protecting bulwarks of God's own presence: *The eternal God is your refuge . . . He is your shield and helper* (27, 29).

c. God is beneath them (33:27)

The assignment ahead would be exceptionally demanding. There would be grim days when they would scarcely know where to find the strength to press on. But at such times they could recall these last words which Moses had shared with them: *underneath are the everlasting arms.*

In the closing moments of the blessing, God's people are reminded of their uniqueness: *Who is like you, a people saved by the LORD* (29)? No-one is like them because no-one is like him (26). Their settlement in the land was an eloquent witness to their pagan neighbours that nothing is impossible for Israel's God. Their opponents had superior soldiers but God made sure that they had inferior strength. Jeshurun's God would conquer their

---

[39] Pss. 68:4, 33; 104:3; Is. 19:1.

[40] J. Gray, *The Legacy of Canaan* (1957), p. 9, for the text from Ugarit (or Ras Shamra) where Baal is described as 'He who mounts the clouds'. The Ugaritic texts are a valuable primary source for Canaanite life and culture on the eve of the Israelite settlement.

enemies (27a) and renew their resources (28). To be reminded of that before embarking on a new and threatening assignment was to be assured, energized and equipped. *Blessed are you . . .* (29).

Deuteronomy 32:48–52; 34:1–12
28. None like him

This book's message is brought to its climax with a group of brief biographical vignettes, brilliantly drawn verbal pictures, which depict the priorities, pressures and achievements of an outstanding man of God. The first picture is of Moses looking out (32:48–52; 34:1–4) over the land he was not permitted to enter. Another is of the elderly man looking up (9), beseeching the Lord that his successor will be given sufficient strength for new responsibilities. In a final scene the portraiture looks back over the leader's life (10–12) as it surveys *all those miraculous signs and wonders the LORD sent him to do.* The Lord deliberately arranged the physical circumstances of Moses' death so that the Israelite people would never be able to visit his grave, but his inspiring epitaph is preserved in the closing sentences of this book. There were great believers before him (Enoch, Noah, Abraham, Joseph) and gifted personalities after him, but there was *none like him* (11, RSV). Moses is here portrayed as the servant God encouraged, equipped, disciplined and replaced.

1. God encouraged Moses

Across the long years Moses' attentiveness to God's word had taught him one lesson above all others – nothing is more important than being in the will of God. For the Israelite people, life was at its worst when they deliberately stepped out of God's revealed will. In earlier days Moses had prayed that every route would be firmly barred to him unless the Lord promised to walk that road with him: 'If your Presence does not go with us, do not send us up from here'.[1] God's servant wanted to enter Canaan and had said so (3:25) but throughout his days he had treasured a greater ambition which far surpassed any natural desire for self-satisfaction. That deeper yearning had been expressed in an earlier prayer[2] that he might *obey*

---

[1] Ex. 33:15.   [2] Ex. 33:13.

322

('teach me your ways'), *know* ('so that I may know you') and *please* ('continue to find favour with you') God. That threefold longing provided the essential motivation for Moses' entire life. Therefore, if a caring Father had said that he would not carry him (1:31; 33:12) across the Jordan, that was the end of it. Nothing mattered more to him than knowing, obeying and pleasing God. Moses knew that the things we wish for ourselves are not always best for us. There are times when only God knows the difference between what we merely want and what we genuinely need. Times when we feel ourselves to be seriously in 'want' are those which teach the best lessons. Moses gained far more by looking than would have been possible by travelling. Austin Farrer used to pray,

> O God, save me from myself, this self which throws the thick shadow of its own purposes and desires in every direction in which I try to look, so that I cannot see what it is that you, my Lord and God are showing to me. Teach me to stand out of my own light, and let your daylight shine.[3]

Although God said 'No' to his wish to enter Canaan, however, Moses was not left without help. In his natural disappointment and 'want' he was encouraged by what he saw and heard.

Moses saw the land. On several occasions in the narrative special mention is made of the fact that Moses could *view* (32:49) the territory even though he could not walk over it. Note how, time and again, the invitation about 'seeing' and the prohibition about 'entering' seem to be deliberately set alongside each other: 'Look at the land with your own eyes, since you are not going to cross this Jordan' (3:27), and *Therefore, you will see the land only from a distance; you will not enter* (32:52). *I have let you see it with your eyes, but you will not cross over into it* (34:4), and again, 'After you have seen it, you too will be gathered to your people'.[4] Why this repeated emphasis on seeing the land with his own eyes? Was there any point in viewing it when he was not allowed to go?

It is essential for us here to appreciate the principles of Hebrew law regarding land rights. It was not a matter of restricting him to a tantalizing peep at unfamiliar territory. In later Jewish times the practice of 'viewing' land had very significant legal implications among the Israelite people[5] but we see the same principle at work in the life of Abraham: 'Lift up your eyes ... and look ... All the land that you see I will give to you.'[6] We also see it at the

---

[3] Austin Farrer, *Sung and Said* (Faith Press, 1964), p. 174.   [4] Nu. 27:13.
[5] 'The legal transfer of land was secured by the purchaser's formal inspection' (Phillips); and see David Daube, *Studies in Biblical Law* (Cambridge, 1947), p. 34.
[6] Gn. 13:14–15.

temptation of Christ: 'The devil showed him all the kingdoms . . . "All this will I give you," he said.'[7]

We ought specially to bear this Jewish practice in mind when we read in a parable of Jesus what seems a discourteous excuse: 'I have just bought a field, and I must go and see it.'[8] We think it totally ridiculous that any purchaser should buy a field without first examining it, but what is being described here is the formal legal transfer of that man's newly acquired property. By looking out over the land Moses had been given the unique privilege of legally taking possession of that entire country on behalf of its new people. It is for this reason that he is told to look out as far as he can see in each direction (3:27) and discern the geographical features of its extensive territory: *the whole land . . . all the land of Judah as far as the western sea, the Negev and the whole region* (34:1–3). It was his, even though he was not personally allowed to take possession of it.

The story of Moses' viewing the land enshrines a vital spiritual principle; not everything which is 'given' to a believer is an immediately acquired possession. Some Christians seem to want everything this side of heaven. We are heirs to a rich inheritance, that is beyond doubt, but some of our assured possessions belong to a land we have yet to enter. It is a sad mistake when any believer insists that everything we inherit (totally sinless lives, constantly healthy bodies, perfectly harmonious relationships, assured unlimited prosperity) must be claimed *now*, when the Scripture makes it plain that much of what is promised is reserved for the future. There are better things to come. The 'inheritance that can never perish, spoil or fade' is not ours now; it is 'kept in heaven' for those who believe.[9] We can 'look' now but, for the moment, our feet must stay this side of the river.

Moses heard the promise. By seeing the land Moses knew that his people would have it as their immediate gift, but something more was necessary if he was to die in peace. True, it was (because he viewed it) their present right, but could he be sure that it would remain their lasting possession? When he looked out as far as his sharp eyes (34:7) could see, God spoke his final words to him, *This is the land I promised on oath to Abraham, Isaac, and Jacob when I said, 'I will give it to your descendants'* (34:4). By listening afresh to that repeated and dependable promise of God it was confirmed beyond doubt that the land was their permanent as well as immediate possession. He knew that all over that Canaanite territory there were serious threatening dangers and merely to view it might leave him with the fear that, although it was theirs now, it

---

[7] Mt. 4:8–10. [8] Lk. 14:18. [9] 1 Pet. 1:4.

might not remain theirs for long. His 'look' might permit their entrance but only what he heard could secure its retention. God's promise was that it was his continuing gift to them; it was *the land which I give to the people of Israel for a possession* (32:49, 52). That gift would be withdrawn only if they persistently abused its privileges (29:27-28) and, even then, it would be restored once they acknowledged their transgression (30:4-5).

What he saw (the land) and heard (the promise) brought Moses immense peace. He could not stride on with the marching people but would soon be 'gathered' with his 'arrived' people.[10]

2. God equipped Moses

The description of Moses as *the servant of the LORD* (34:5), is particularly relevant in the contemporary scene. The leadership theme is given repeated prominence in the modern world, and good training courses helpfully concentrate on necessary strategies, effective techniques and acquired skills. Nobody doubts that whatever we do for God ought to be done well, but there is a subtle danger that slick business methods can marginalize those prior qualities of personal spirituality and refined motivation. The essential servant-model, constantly emphasized by Jesus,[11] can be imperceptibly displaced by this world's model of the authoritative leader, effective manager, or successful director. Jesus deliberately dismissed such patterns of leadership: 'Not so with you'.[12] Every believer ought to be God's slave, which means that we are always preoccupied with his will rather than our rights, his pleasure rather than our position, his glory rather than our success.

These concluding sentences of Moses' Old Testament biography remind us that whenever God calls a man or woman to his service, he provides all the necessary physical, material and spiritual resources for the tasks in hand. The servants of God are never denied the blessings of God.

Moses received all the physical resources he needed. Although he was *a hundred and twenty years old when he died, yet his eyes were not weak nor his strength gone* (34:7). In his advanced years he was conscious of limitations (31:2) but as long as strength was necessary the Lord gave it to him. It is as though the biblical writers wanted to assure their readers that it was not physical difficulties which kept him in Moab. He could easily have crossed the Jordan and entered each of those Canaanite cities if that had been God's purpose for him. Throughout his entire life Moses had personal experience of the enabling promise he had recently shared

[10] Nu. 27:13.   [11] Mk. 10:42-45; Jn. 13:3-17.   [12] Mk. 10:43.

with the tribe of Asher: 'Your strength will equal your days' (33:25).

Moses received all the material resources he needed. Along with his fellow pilgrims he experienced the unique provision of God in all their persistent journeying – over those long years their clothing and footwear was never in need of repair (8:4; 29:5).[13] God always gave them the things they needed as well as the energy they wanted. It is a miracle of God's providence which is not confined to biblical times. The story of George Müller of Bristol is but one of a myriad testimonies to the continuing faithfulness of God in meeting the practical needs of his servants.[14]

Moses received all the spiritual resources he needed. The biblical narratives insist that Moses was uniquely privileged in the intimacy of his communion with God. A phrase in the epitaph shares the secret of his spiritual dynamic; he was someone *the LORD knew face to face* (34:10). The words are probably meant to recall his daily appointment with God in the tent of meeting when the Lord used to speak to him 'face to face, as a man speaks with his friend'.[15] That earlier narrative about Moses' discipline in prayer is set within the context of adversity and apostasy. At that time the Hebrew people were guilty of appalling disloyalty, idolatry and immorality.[16] It was one of the most difficult periods in the entire career of God's servant; the leadership demands were immense, but nothing kept him from the place of prayer. That daily 'face to face' communion with God enabled him to maintain his own spiritual integrity; it also ensured that he was given the necessary moral and spiritual perception both to detect and avoid the sins of his contemporaries.

3. God disciplined Moses

The life of Moses is a rich example to us all, but we do no credit to the teaching of Scripture, or to the great personalities of the Bible, if we only exalt their virtues. Moses was not faultless. The Bible is an honest book and does nothing to disguise the fact that its leading characters were sinners like ourselves. One alone was without transgression. They made mistakes, some of them exceptionally serious, but, in his righteousness, God exposed their sins and, in his mercy, washed them away. For all his unique achievements (34:10–12) Moses was far from perfect, and the failures of God's servant are

---

[13] Ne. 9:21.

[14] W. H. Harding, *The Life of George Müller* (1914), pp. 109–115, 138–151, *et passim*. See also a modern missionary story like Leslie Lyall, *God Reigns in China* (Hodder and Stoughton/O.M.F, 1985) for many illustrations of God's timely provision of material needs.

[15] Ex. 33:11.   [16] Ex. 32:1–10.

deliberately included in his biography. Without this honesty and realism, the stories of the great characters of the Bible would daunt us rather than inspire us. They would create an impression that all these great men and women lived impeccable lives, and that would put them completely out of our world. Instead, on reading the Bible, we are deliberately confronted by the enormity of their sins as well as the integrity of their faith.

The prohibition about Moses entering the land appears to be for two main reasons, the people's sins and his own. It was certainly because of the people's sins – note the repeated 'because of you' (1:37; 3:26). It was to teach them a lesson about corporate responsibility – when we sin, other people are affected as well as ourselves.

The prohibition, however, was also on account of Moses' own sin – to teach him a lesson about personal accountability. We need to look at the nature of that sin so that we can recognize its seriousness in our own lives. At this crucial point in the story there is a surprising ambiguity which is probably intentional. Possibly there was more than one reason why he was not permitted to enter the land with his fellow pilgrims. Perhaps we are meant to search our own hearts rather than presume to know his. The biblical story suggests that a number of factors may have been at work, each playing some part in his exclusion from Canaan.

Perhaps it was anger that kept him out of the land. The narrative certainly refers us back to the incident at Meribah Kadesh. The Lord tells Moses, *you did not uphold my holiness among the Israelites* (32:51). The occasion is described in Numbers 20 when the Hebrews found themselves without water in the wilderness of Zin. This was a hard time for Moses. He was emotionally stressed, suffering family bereavement, having just lost his sister Miriam.[17] Moreover, the people contended with Moses and Aaron because of their need for water. They grumbled that, under his initiative, they had been brought out of Egypt and now were about to die in the desert.

The Lord gives detailed instruction to Moses about what he is to do. He must gather the people together and, taking the rod of his God-given authority, 'Speak to that rock before their eyes and it will pour out its water'.[18] Moses was to *speak* to the rock but instead he struck the rock with his rod, possibly out of intense annoyance at the rebellious and insubordinate attitude of the people. Did that hasty temper of earlier days[19] quickly arise again in his heart and mind so that, suddenly and without warning, it overcame him? One thing is certain – we ought not to assume that the conquered sins of earlier days no longer have the power to bring

[17] Nu. 20:1.   [18] Nu. 20:8.   [19] Ex. 2:12.

us down again. Those who think they stand must be careful lest they fall.[20] We are utterly dependent on the Lord for strength right through to the closing moments of our dying day.

Perhaps impatience kept him out of the land. He did not only strike the rock; he struck it twice. Even if he had misunderstood the divine instruction about addressing the rock, there was little need to strike it twice. It is sad to think that the man who over the years had shown such astonishing patience and forbearance might have lacked it at such a crucial moment in Israelite history.

Perhaps it was disobedience that kept him out of the land. Possibly Moses knew what God had said about speaking to the rock but decided instead that he would do what he thought best rather than what God demanded. That is one way of interpreting the words in Numbers 27:14, 'when the community rebelled ... you disobeyed my command'. From his long years in Midian, Moses may even have known of an old Bedouin technique that under certain conditions the fierce striking of a brittle stratum of rock could suddenly release a hidden supply of refreshing water.[21] At this time Moses may well have been setting his own reason and experience above the divine revelation.

Perhaps arrogance kept him out of the land. When Moses addressed the discontented people, he cried out 'must we bring you water out of this rock?'[22] One psalm carefully preserves an old tradition that it was what Moses said which grieved God. It appears that at the waters of Meribah the people made the spirit of Moses bitter so that 'rash words came from his lips'.[23] The rash words may also have been proud words. How could a mere man say 'must *we* bring you water?' The humble man could only have said 'Shall *he*?'

Perhaps it was irreverence that kept him out of the land. The narratives in Numbers 20 and 27 record the fact that 'when the community rebelled', Moses lost the unique opportunity even in that hostile context to honour God 'as holy' in the presence of those rebellious pilgrims.[24] The event at that rock-face presented Moses with a unique occasion to show the people how much he revered God's name and honoured God's will, but he lost the opportunity and it became an event which displeased God, misled the people and grieved Moses.

[20] 1 Cor. 10:12.

[21] In his *Yesterday and Today in Sinai* (1936) Major C. S. Jarvis, Governor of the Sinai during the 1930s, recalls how on one occasion several men of the Sinai Camel Corps were 'digging about in the rough sand ... trying to get at the water which was slowly trickling out of the limestone rock'. An impatient colour sergeant hit the rock by mistake and 'out of its apertures shot a powerful stream of water! The Sudanese ... overwhelmed their sergeant with cries of: "Look at him! The prophet Moses!"' For this reference I am indebted to Ian Wilson, *The Exodus Enigma*, p. 149.

[22] Nu. 20:10.   [23] Ps. 106:32–33.   [24] Nu. 20:12; 27:14.

Although the people were contentious and discontented it was not God's purpose to deny them water. He is generous beyond all our deserving. The story is recorded for us in Scripture, however, as a further serious reminder of how easily we can do the right thing in the wrong way.

It would not be right to dogmatize about the precise reason for Moses' exclusion; possibly it cannot be tied down to one particular mistake. A number of things may well have come together to indicate that it was now time for the work of Moses to come to a quiet end. However, one thing is without doubt. The incident is persuasive in its message – we must not trifle with sin.

Before we leave this sombre aspect of the story, however, we must remember that God is merciful; the man who was excluded was only kept out for a time. The epitaph or obituary at the end of this book is not the final sentence in the story of Moses. A day came when he entered the land. Centuries after the invasion of Canaan, Jesus stood on the Mount of Transfiguration and Moses was there too, along with the prophet Elijah. That day, both Old Testament leaders, representative of Israel's law and prophets, had a greater privilege than inspecting a new land; they heard about a new life. They talked with Christ about the unique saving event he was about to accomplish at Jerusalem. Moses' longing to see the unfolding purposes of God was fulfilled far beyond his highest dreams. He actually spoke with God's Son, that unique 'prophet' whose coming he had predicted. As they communed together on the mount Moses hung on every word; he was more than ready to 'listen' to all that he said (18:18–19).

4. God replaced Moses

Moses knew that his life's mission was at an end. Although he could not travel with the pilgrims, he knew that they were in the capable hands of a man he had personally trained and with whom he had frequently prayed.[25] This book's closing testimony about Moses' successor provides the necessary transition to the next book in the Bible. Four things are said about Joshua: he was empowered, wise, teachable and dependent (34:9).

a. Joshua was empowered

The phrase *spirit of wisdom* may well be a reference to the work of the Holy Spirit (NIV margin). In Old Testament times the Spirit of God equipped certain people for precise tasks. He did not indwell every believer (as now) but came upon particular individuals for a limited

[25] Ex. 33:11–12.

329

period to give them the necessary qualities for their specialist ministries. No man could possibly take over Moses' responsibilities unless he possessed resources which far transcended his inevitably limited natural gifts. What Joshua was able to accomplish in Canaan was due entirely to the fact that he was a Spirit-filled man. Indeed, the Spirit's indwelling seems to have been fully evident in Joshua's personality at the time he was formally appointed as Moses' successor. The old man is instructed to 'Take Joshua ... a man in whom is the spirit, and lay your hand on him'.[26] It is as though the Lord is emphasizing that he was not Spirit-filled because of the prayer of Moses (34:9) but because of the gift of God.

b. Joshua was wise

The particular gift which God's Spirit imparted to Joshua was *the spirit of wisdom*. In Old Testament teaching, wisdom is something far more than intellectual prowess. It is the practical ability to discern the mind of God in any and every situation in life. This was certainly necessary for Joshua in the days ahead. If he was to take possession of Canaanite territory he would need the spiritual sensitivity which would enable him to discover God's plans for the people in varied situations – how to cross an overflowing river, how to conquer impregnable cities, how to find a secret and damaging offender, how to divide the land, how to inspire the people's worship, and so on. Only a spiritually wise man, with no other ambition than the glory of God, could possibly have succeeded in a constantly changing enterprise which demanded such a wide variety of different skills.

c. Joshua was teachable

It was Moses who *laid hands on him* (34:9), the man who had relied on him as a servant during Joshua's younger days.[27] The imposition of hands was an accompaniment to prayer, as if to mark someone out for the blessing of God, publicly identifying him as the one for whom special prayer was being offered. Moses, however, did not lay his praying hands on a stranger. This young man had been faithful, first of all, in less prominent service so now he could be trusted with more responsible demands.[28] Joshua must have learnt a great deal from Moses during those daily opportunities for conversation with God in the tent of meeting. How many times Moses must have unburdened his heavy heart to the dedicated young servant who accompanied him to the tent. Over the years Joshua

[26] Nu. 27:18. [27] Ex. 33:11. [28] Lk. 16:10.

received an immense amount from Moses. After all, when Moses left the tent, young Joshua was expected to stay there for a while, possibly meditating on what they had shared; now it was his turn to pass these things on to his contemporaries.

d. Joshua was dependent

Moses *laid his hands on him*. He longed that, in the unknown years ahead, the younger man would continue to be *filled with the spirit of wisdom*. Throughout this book we have seen Moses fulfilling the various assignments which were entrusted to him – pastor, teacher, administrator, counsellor, example, preacher. He was effective in these different and demanding ministries because, above all else, he was a man of prayer. He drew on resources beyond himself and he knew that everything which had been so generously given to him would not be denied to Joshua. It is fitting, therefore, that our final glimpse of this great man of God is as a compassionate intercessor, laying his hands in dependent prayer on his gifted but inexperienced successor.

Deuteronomy brings its message to a close by reminding those who are older in years that, like Moses, they have a responsibility to prepare the next generation for the work of God. It also reminds the elderly that they may yet fulfil their most significant role in life by serving as persistent, well-informed and sympathetic intercessors. Moreover, it tells everyone, whatever their age, that nothing we attempt for God is likely to succeed unless it is inspired, directed and maintained in submissive and reliant prayer. Men and women do not live 'by bread alone' but they must stretch out empty hands if they are to be fed.

The book closes, as it began, with a portrait of a leader, now a new leader, ready to take up God's work in a different land. It reminds us that in the Lord's service nobody is either indispensable or irreplaceable. It encourages us with the assurance that God's work is always bigger than the best of his workmen, and that whenever he appoints men and women to his service he has pledged to provide them with sufficient strength. Deuteronomy's closing words salute the past. Moses' ministry is described in terms of enviable excellence; there was 'none like him' (10, rsv). His life on earth was over, however, and his demanding responsibilities were now entrusted to another. In every generation, the lives of dedicated believers are constantly set on the threshold of fresh opportunities and unfailing resources.